LESSONS AND LEGACIES VIII

LESSONS AND LEGACIES VIII

From Generation to Generation

Edited and with an introduction
by Doris L. Bergen

NORTHWESTERN UNIVERSITY PRESS   EVANSTON, ILLINOIS

Northwestern University Press
www.nupress.northwestern.edu

Copyright © 2008 by Northwestern University Press. Published 2008. All rights reserved.

Printed in the United States of America

10   9   8   7   6   5   4   3   2   1

ISBN 978-0-8101-2533-9 (cloth)
ISBN 978-0-8101-2539-1 (paper)

Library of Congress Cataloging-in-Publication Data are available from the Library of Congress.

♾ The paper used in this publication meets the minimum requirements of the
American National Standard for Information Sciences—Permanence of Paper for
Printed Library Materials, ANSI Z39.48-1992.

Dedicated to the Memory of Sharon Abramson

Eshet Chayil, a woman of valor;

A woman more precious than rubies;

A woman of elegance and compassion;

A woman who, together with her husband Earl, infused her family with a love of Judaism and a thirst for knowledge;

A woman who, together with her husband Earl, was instrumental in the founding and in the continuous support of the Holocaust Educational Foundation;

A woman who forever will remain engraved in the hearts and minds of all those who loved and who were inspired by this extraordinary human being.

Contents

Theodore Zev Weiss

Foreword

THIS IS THE EIGHTH VOLUME OF SCHOLARLY PAPERS TO BE PUB-
lished as an outgrowth of the Lessons and Legacies Conferences that
the Holocaust Educational Foundation sponsors in partnership with
major centers of higher learning. Our partner for this publication of
Lessons and Legacies is Brown University. We gratefully acknowledge
the support of the administration and academic officers of Brown
University and are particularly grateful to the conference cochairs:
Professor Omer Bartov and Professor Dagmar Herzog. Their dedication and hard work made the conference extremely successful.

We are very gratified by the success of the Lessons and Legacies
Conferences and by the interest and support of professors from all
over the world who have participated in them. The success of Lessons
and Legacies is one area where the Holocaust Educational Foundation
has made rewarding strides in teaching the Holocaust in universities. The number of colleges and universities teaching Holocaust-
related courses continues to grow. To support the work of the professors, we are continuing the Institute for Holocaust and Jewish
Civilization at Northwestern University to educate current and future
college and university professors about the Holocaust and the faith
and culture of the Jewish people who were targeted by the Nazis for
extinction. All these efforts have brought us into evermore fulfilling
contact with a growing family of decent and dedicated academicians
who share our conviction that learning is the best antidote to humanity's inhumane impulses.

We also started a new program of awarding fellowships to graduate students who wish to pursue a doctorate in Holocaust studies.
This important step ensures the Holocaust will be taught to future

generations. I also want to express my deep appreciation and gratitude to our board members, who have contributed so generously to the foundation's work and who made all this possible.

My personal thanks and appreciation to Professors Omer Bartov and Dagmar Herzog and to all the scholars who participated and contributed so greatly to the success of the Lessons and Legacies Conference.

My personal gratitude to Professor Doris Bergen for her dedication and hard work in editing this volume.

Finally, my strongest sense of gratitude to my wife, Alice, and my children, Deborah, Gabi, Danny, and Jodi, who have encouraged the work of the foundation at every juncture and have replenished my energy at every step.

Editor's Acknowledgments

THIS BOOK INCLUDES THE WORK OF MANY PEOPLE AND REPRESENTS the efforts and support of many more. Thanks are due to the Holocaust Educational Foundation and its president, Theodore Zev Weiss; to Dagmar Herzog and Omer Bartov, who organized the eighth Lessons and Legacies Conference at Brown University; to all the presenters at that stimulating meeting; and to Peter Hayes and Ronald Smelser for encouragement and help.

Two wonderful editorial assistants worked with me on this project—Elizabeth Covington Strauss at the University of Notre Dame and Samantha Share at the University of Toronto—and I am grateful to them both for their dedication and insight. Thanks also to Notre Dame's Institute for Scholarship in the Liberal Arts, which funded a summer research assistantship for Liz Strauss, and to the Chancellor Rose and Ray Wolfe Chair in Holocaust Studies at the University of Toronto for covering other costs associated with this volume. Martina Cucchiara from the University of Notre Dame translated one of the essays included here and, as part of our writing group, provided valuable feedback on a draft of my introduction. I am grateful for comments from her and other participating members: Alexander Martin, Sheila Nowinski, Elizabeth Strauss, Lourdes Hurtado, Charles Strauss, and Tuan Hoang. Alan Steinweis and a second, anonymous reader for Northwestern University Press offered important advice that improved the manuscript considerably; Mairead Case did a fine job of moving the project along, even against unfavorable odds; and Jenny Gavacs and Jess Paumier joined the effort at a crucial moment. They deserve many thanks. Finally, I appreciate the opportunity to have worked with the remarkable group of people whose scholarship appears in this volume.

Doris L. Bergen

Introduction

You who live safe
In your warm houses,
You who find, returning in the evening,
Hot food and friendly faces:
    Consider if this is a man
    Who works in the mud
    Who does not know peace
    Who fights for a scrap of bread
    Who dies because of a yes or a no.
    Consider if this is a woman,
    Without hair and without name
    With no more strength to remember,
    Her eyes empty and her womb cold
    Like a frog in winter.
Meditate that this came about:
I commend these words to you.
Carve them in your hearts
At home, in the street,
Going to bed, rising;
Repeat them to your children,
    Or may your house fall apart,
    May illness impede you,
    May your children turn their faces from you.

                          —*Primo Levi*

PRIMO LEVI OPENED HIS MEMOIR *SURVIVAL IN AUSCHWITZ* WITH A call to remember, reflect upon, and teach about the Holocaust and its destruction of humanity. Levi's poem is at once an invocation and a curse: a challenge to repeat these things to our children and a warning that those who fail to do so deserve to be rejected by subsequent generations.

"From Generation to Generation" was the theme of the eighth Lessons and Legacies Conference on the Holocaust, held at Brown University in 2004. Like Levi's poem, the presentations at that meeting—fourteen of them now essays in this volume—reflect some of the many ways one can understand those words. The circular formulation—from generation to generation—points both backward and forward. Where do we locate the roots of the Holocaust, and how do its repercussions manifest themselves? These questions are addressed here from various disciplinary perspectives: history, cultural studies, psychiatry, literature, and sociology. But there is also a personal side to the associated issues of continuity and rupture. What has the generation of the Shoah tried to pass on to its descendants, in the forms of testimonies or taboos? What have subsequent generations—the children and grandchildren of the perpetrators, victims, witnesses, survivors, and accomplices—accepted, rejected, and adapted from those legacies? Contributions by people who survived the Holocaust, by children of survivors, and by scholars who engage living witnesses appear among the chapters that follow. They remind us that the Holocaust remains present—immediate, unsettling, and painful—more than sixty years after the end of World War II.

The chapters in this volume cohere around a general theme, but they also provide an impression of the state of Holocaust studies at least two generations after the inception of the field, an event often associated with the publication in 1961 of Raul Hilberg's monumental work: *The Destruction of the European Jews.*[1] Indeed, as Christopher Browning's essay here demonstrates, changes in the field can be tracked through the progressive editions of Hilberg's book. Study of the Holocaust has become an international endeavor: the contributors to this volume were trained and work in at least six different countries. Their range of vision extends beyond those geographic origins: these analyses spill over the borders of Germany, in its various configurations, to consider events and developments in Poland, Ukraine, Slovakia, Hungary, France, Israel, the United States, and elsewhere. The chronological reach of the field is remarkable, too: Christina von Braun's consideration of the symbol of the cross begins in the first century BCE, and Ruth Kluger identifies ghosts of the Holocaust in German popular culture of 2004.

Evident in this collection are significant tendencies to situate the Holocaust in its many contexts—as a component of the era of world wars; as part of the genocidal twentieth century; as linked to the concurrent totalitarian systems of National Socialism and Communism; and as a product of national struggles and conflicts about national power and identity. Such contextualization speaks to the maturity of the field. Gone are the days when scholars of the Holocaust struggled to have the importance of their subject recognized or sought to legitimate their efforts by making defensive claims of uniqueness. The result is an astonishingly dynamic field of inquiry that opens out in every direction.

Also apparent here is the (re)turn in the field since the early 1990s to local studies and personal accounts. This volume demonstrates the virtues of a micro-historical methodology that pays close attention to history in its local and singular contexts and seeks illumination through fidelity to discrete constellations of ideas, documents, experiences, and struggles. Martin Dean's historiographic survey captures this change with its emphasis on how regional studies have lent new force to our understanding of the Holocaust's complexity. In some cases, notably Omer Bartov's examination of the Holocaust in Buczacz in East Galicia, or Dori Laub's discussion of Holocaust survivors in psychiatric hospitals in Israel, both the trend toward broad contextualization and the seemingly opposed move toward micro-studies are at work.

In vital ways, this volume reflects the field's increased reliance on survivor testimony in its various forms: memoirs, published and unpublished; legal testimonies; and interviews. This short list conceals the remarkable and daunting range of materials involved, from accounts recorded under impossible conditions even before World War II had ended in Europe, to halting fragments of narratives told for the first time decades after the events, words written or spoken in all the languages of Europe and then some, words whispered in confidence or rehearsed, polished, and performed on film for the eyes of the world. Integrating such materials into the scholarship on the Holocaust poses massive challenges, as Saul Friedländer has described, but the result has been a methodological and even epistemological shift in the field that is both dramatic and irreversible.[2] This transformation is thematized here by Na'ama Shik and Elizabeth Baer, whose rigorous analyses of early survivor accounts allow them to revisit both familiar and long-taboo subjects regarding women's experiences of Auschwitz-Birkenau.

A glance at this book's table of contents reveals that attention to memory and its relations to history continues to generate valuable insights into the Holocaust and its repercussions. At the same time, studies of memory and the Holocaust—issues raised by Saul Friedländer and others over the past three decades—have sparked investigations of social memory in other historical settings, too.[3] Some of the essays here provide cases in point. Jürgen Zimmerer's empirical, nontheoretical approach to links between the German genocide of the Herero people in 1904–8 and the Holocaust shows that the memory of extreme violence can be mobilized to legitimate and even shape subsequent acts of destruction. Annette Becker's study of World War I takes a contrasting route—speculative and theoretical—to reach a related conclusion: practices of extreme violence in the Great War, suppressed, silenced, or appropriated in the two decades that followed, exploded with annihilatory force in World War II. Geneviève Zubrzycki addresses issues of memory in the ongoing aftermath of the Holocaust. Her close reading of the 1998–99 "war of the crosses" at Auschwitz reveals that, for Poles, this conflict called into question the very categories and divisions constitutive of a nation.

As the chapters by Kate Brown, Holly Case, and Ronald Smelser demonstrate, study of the Holocaust has also been taken up in more traditional areas such as political, diplomatic, and military history, to the benefit of everyone involved. It is no longer possible, as it once was, to write accounts of World War II that bracket out the destruction of Europe's Jews and related programs of mass killing. These matters have penetrated scholarly and public awareness in ways that shatter the barriers once erected by indifference, disinterest, or a desire to avert the eyes, on the one hand, and ahistorical claims of incomparability, on the other. The study of the Holocaust has developed to the point that it can accommodate contrasting and even conflicting approaches: the international and the local; the theoretical and concrete; the inclusive and exclusive. Indeed, such tensions energize the field and give it integrity by challenging easy pieties and keeping questions open.

The four chapters in the first section of this book examine some "Precedents and Antecedents" to the Holocaust. What led up to the Holocaust; who were its intellectual, military, cultural, and political progenitors? Christina von Braun's study of the cross focuses on the legacies of Christianity—including traditions of anti-Judaism—that facilitated murderous Nazi antisemitism. Jürgen Zimmerer points to colonial genocide in German South-West Africa as an example of mass killing that opened the door to subsequent horrors. Annette Becker analyzes how buried memories of atrocities from World War I returned, as the repressed so often does, reenacted and multiplied in the mass murders of World War II; and Kate Brown draws attention to ways that Soviet practices of ethnic identification laid the groundwork for Nazi German genocidal killing in Ukraine.

These four very different approaches highlight the complex mixture of forces that produced the Holocaust, from long-established habits of thought and behavior rooted in Christian teachings and rituals to short-term, practical factors like Soviet ethnographic maps. At the same time, these chapters reveal the challenges inherent in assessing the prehistory of the Holocaust. Indeed, the more ambitious the claims, the more difficult it is to clinch the case, so that von Braun's and Becker's provocative arguments about the roles of Christianity and World War I respectively in leading up to the annihilation of European Jewry must appeal to a kind of instinctive understanding on the part of readers. Cultural forces leave traces that skilled interpreters such as von Braun and Becker can uncover, but they rarely if ever produce smoking guns. Von Braun's implication that Christianity itself contributed to the Nazi murder of Jews and Becker's suggestion that practices of modern, total war in the twentieth century—including the impossibility of remembering "total" violence—anticipated and enabled the Holocaust, point to the necessity of studying history through the lens of the Holocaust but also reveal the problems inherent in this approach. How do we separate connections we see looking backward from the Shoah from causal links that operated in the opposite direction? Does our desire—and need—to learn from the past distort our understanding of it, or, as von Braun and Becker intimate, does this approach to the Holocaust offer a model for revisiting other historic events in morally informed ways?

In a sense, Zimmerer is more modest; there is no direct line, he asserts, from the German genocide of the Herero to the Holocaust, but there were connections. Military and bureaucratic institutions revealed a genocidal potential, and Germans in the colonies amassed a storehouse of cultural practices that served to rationalize and legitimize later acts of extreme violence. Zimmerer's approach picks up a line of thought first advanced by Raphael Lemkin and Hannah Arendt, who, in the mid-1940s and early 1950s respectively, drew attention to the linkage between European imperialism, Nazism, and the Holocaust.[4] Zimmerer's research into the genocide in German South-West Africa in 1904–8 allows him to trace in detail a relationship that Lemkin and Arendt could only suggest in general terms.

Kate Brown's argument is limited to a particular region—right-bank Ukraine, home to one of the largest concentrations of Jews in Europe—and as a result, she can show specific continuities between Soviet practices of ethnic identification and Nazi racial killing. Still, her piece too has broader implications for understanding how in large parts of Central and Eastern Europe, Nazism and Communism ended up reinforcing and exacerbating one another's brutal impacts. Brown's careful exposition highlights the mutually reinforcing devastation of Soviet and Nazi ethnic policies and practices without falling into the trap of relativizing or exonerating the crimes of one through comparison with the other. Her essay shows how much both Holocaust studies and scholarship on Eastern Europe have developed since the mid-1980s, when Ernst Nolte's assessment of Nazi atrocities as imitative of Stalinist crimes sparked what became known as the Historians' Debate in West Germany.[5]

The second set of contributions is grouped under the heading "Testimony, History, and Memory." These four chapters draw on individual testimonies of the Holocaust to uncover elements of the past and interrogate the processes by which it is remembered or forgotten. Omer Bartov combines historical and anthropological investigation with memory texts, on-site observations, and photographs to analyze the events of the Holocaust in his mother's home city of Buczacz in East Galicia. Na'ama Shik revisits early writings by Jewish women survivors of Auschwitz to reveal depths of despair and widespread sexual exploitation and abuse that later memoirs muted or denied. Elizabeth Baer's rereading of Liana Millu's Holocaust stories echoes Shik's findings in one particular case: Millu's book *Smoke Over Birkenau,* written in 1945, portrays sexual violence and bonding among women in ways that counter the common and comforting notions of the Holocaust as somehow a sexually "clean" genocide that prompted solidarity among its female victims. Dori Laub reports on a video-testimony study he conducted of chronically hospitalized Holocaust survivors in Israeli psychiatric institutions. Here, he indicates, was the "ultimate in the absence of narrative"—people who had never been asked about their experiences, some of whom did not speak at all.

These chapters respond to Primo Levi's plea to listen to the victims and attend to both the universal and the particular nature of their suffering. At the same time, they reveal the difficulties and dangers of such work. Bartov's study of Buczacz situates the destruction of the Jews there amidst a swirl of ethnic, religious, and political violence that involved local Ukrainians and Poles as well as Soviet and German occupiers. Layers of prejudice, recrimination, and self-protective denial contributed to the vulnerability of the Jews of Buczacz from 1941 to 1945, and those same forces obscure that history decades later. At most, Bartov concludes, we can achieve glimpses of understanding by immersing ourselves "in the complex fabric of testimonies and memoirs." As Shik's examination of Jewish women's early accounts of Auschwitz indicates, readers cannot expect such texts to provide meaning or solace. Instead, the more immediate the recounting, Shik argues, the less its author turned "Auschwitz into a story," and the more she provided unedited images of hopelessness, viciousness, and betrayal.

It is no coincidence that an effort to listen to the voices of victims leads to an investigation of Jewish women—people doubly marginalized by antisemitism and sexism.[6] As Levi's call for remembrance illustrates, Nazi destruction was gendered, both in its intent and in how its victims experienced it: to destroy someone as a human being requires annihilation of the person as a man or a woman.[7] Baer picks up this point with her insistence on breaking the taboo around the topic of sexual violence in the Holocaust. Facing the specific fact that Jewish women were raped and accepting the complexity of Millu's narrative in general are, for Baer, important antidotes to redemptive interpretations of the Shoah.

Laub's essay points in a different direction: to the healing possibilities of giving and taking testimony. He compares interviewing survivors who were long-term psychiatric patients to "the work of dislodging something from stone." Yet the results, as he shows, were astonishing: dramatic reduction of trauma-induced symptoms in the interview subjects and emergence of a healing spirit of cooperation—a kind of "testimonial community"—that included the treatment staff as well as their patients. Laub's findings make explicit a point suggested in the preceding essays by Bartov, Shik, and Baer (and addressed in the chapters that follow by Martin Dean and Ruth Kluger). Rather than diminishing the value of scholarship, personal involvement—including direct and passionate engagement with the subject(s) of one's research—can enhance and even generate insight.

Essays in the third group analyze and embody "Approaches to Historical Study of the Holocaust." Christopher Browning's discussion of the three editions of Hilberg's *Destruction of the European Jews* (1961, 1985, and 2003) demonstrates how that influential work both set the agenda for generations of researchers and reflected changes in the field over more than forty years. Martin Dean asks how the collapse of Communism affected study of the Holocaust and concludes that the impact was enormous: access to sources long sealed behind the Iron Curtain sparked the production of local and regional studies that shed light on who perpetrated the crimes of the Holocaust, how, and why. Holly Case's examination of territorial conflicts between Hungary and Slovakia during World War II exemplifies many of the processes Dean describes. As Case shows, for Hungarian and Slovakian diplomats and policymakers, the top priority was achieving maximum territorial gain. The fate of Jews was at most of secondary importance, although as leaders of both states discovered, participation in anti-Jewish initiatives was an effective way to curry favor with the Germans.

Taken together, the contributions by Browning, Dean, and Case show that old debates focusing on German perpetrators—the so-called intentionalist-functionalist debate; the controversy surrounding Daniel Goldhagen's claims about a "uniquely German, eliminationist antisemitism"; and the discussion regarding the timing of Hitler's decision for the "Final Solution"—have been expanded to a Europe-wide frame and transformed in the process.[8] New questions and disagreements have emerged, many of them voiced by Jan Gross in his work on the murder of the Jews of Jedwabne, and by Gross's critics.[9] What roles did non-Germans play in the Holocaust? What forms did collaboration, opportunism, and resistance take, and how were divisions between these and other categories of involvement (like the familiar "perpetrators, victims, and bystanders") blurred? How did different groups of people targeted by Nazi Germany interact? How did local conditions affect the situation of Jews? What were the impacts of the war itself?

After the emotional intensity of the contributions by Bartov, Shik, Baer, and Laub, the chapters by Browning, Dean, and Case may seem detached, even cold. And yet here too, a sense of the horrific suffering in the Holocaust and the profound sadness of the human condition are apparent, coded but not concealed by familiar scholarly conventions. Browning links changes in Hilberg's editions to debates about the Nazi decision-making process and the perpetrators' motivations, but it is not those historiographic revelations that stop the reader short. What takes your breath away, about three-quarters into the essay, is Browning's claim that, in the third edition, Hilberg admitted the Holocaust had lost its singularity. With the 1994 genocide of the Tutsi in Rwanda, Hilberg concluded, "History has repeated itself." This terse statement does not imply that the Holocaust has somehow been displaced from its position of centrality or downgraded in its significance. To the contrary, Hilberg's remark, and Browning's tacit acceptance of its veracity, locates the Holocaust firmly in a long and violent history of the building and destroying of empires and the creation and explosion/implosion of nation-states.

There is a comparable, shattering moment in Dean's chapter. The end of the Cold War opened sources, Dean emphasizes, and events associated with it—especially the bloody wars that accompanied the breakup of Yugoslavia in the 1990s—drew scholars' attention to issues of ethnicity and violence that had previously been neglected. But 1989 also introduced another change: it enabled scholars from the West to travel to the sites of events they studied. Experiencing a place brings certain insights (as evident in Bartov's study of Buczacz and reproduced here for readers through the inclusion of photographs), and it also cuts the distance between researchers and their subjects. Notice Dean's reaction to a photograph he found in the archives showing Belorussian orphans dressed as angels and the Central or Eastern European equivalent of leprechauns, called in Polish *krasnoludki*. By September 1942 those children were dead, shot by German police. Dean's description of that picture and allusion to his emotional response to it reveal that even someone like him, who has spent decades immersed in the records of the Holocaust, at times encounters the reality of destruction and loss in ways that are overwhelming, even unbearable. For Dean's generation of historians, born after World War II, such experiences, not personal memories of the Holocaust, fuel the engagement that is essential to productive scholarship.

Holly Case models another principle of good history, to which Gerhard Weinberg has frequently pointed: the most useful analyses recognize the complex and often unbalanced relations between cause and effect.[10] Case, like Weinberg, shows that the tools of diplomatic history can be particularly useful in uncovering chains of decisions and actions taken with little or no regard to Jews that nevertheless had enormous repercussions on Jewish lives and deaths.

The final set of essays delves into long-term echoes of the Holocaust with three perspectives on its "Postwar Legacies." These chapters remind us of the enormous difficulty—perhaps impossibility—of (re)building viable societies on the ruins left by total war and genocidal destruction. Efforts by perpetrators to escape punishment, the moral devastation of witnessing and collaborating in violence against neighbors, the emotional appeal of myths of heroism and resistance, even survivors' need to start new lives as best they can—all work against a full and open confrontation with the horrors of the past. Ronald Smelser, a historian, demonstrates how U.S. military men, in the service of American and Cold War interests, played a central role in developing an image of the Wehrmacht as somehow unsullied by the crimes of the Third Reich. Ruth Kluger, a scholar of literature and survivor of Theresienstadt, Auschwitz, Gross-Rosen, and a number of other camps, offers personal reflections on some "German works of the imagination" since World War II. Her discussion reveals how Germans remain haunted by Jews, resentful of the past and what Jews represent about it, yet obsessed with the memory of the Holocaust. The sociologist Geneviève Zubrzycki analyzes the "war of the crosses" that erupted in 1998 just outside Auschwitz, near the Polish town of Oświęcim. As Zubrzycki demonstrates, the controversy over what to do about the hundreds of crosses erected by a group of Polish Catholics highlighted tensions between Poles and Jews. At the same time, she shows, it opened debates among all Poles regarding the relationship between Catholicism and Polish national identity.

Together these three essays make a compelling case for the international scope and the far-reaching repercussions of the Holocaust. Destruction on such a scale cannot be contained by physical or temporal borders, and denial, dishonesty, and cowardice have a way of returning—as Levi predicted—in the reactions of subsequent generations. Building on the work of Joseph Bendersky, Smelser shows that highly placed Americans identified with their German counterparts and shared some of their prejudices, including, in many cases, anti-semitism.[11] Small wonder that they, like many ordinary Americans, preferred an interpretation of events that separated good Germans from evil Nazis. Implied, though not stated, in Smelser's discussion is another factor: for many Americans (and others), then and now, the magnitude of Nazi destruction and the depth of suffering it created were too awful to contemplate. It was easier to turn away or take refuge in counter-narratives of heroism and triumph over tribulation.

Kluger's essay draws attention to a topic broached in the contributions by von Braun, Bartov, and Shik, but all too rarely thematized in analyses of the Holocaust: the matter of guilt and its close cousin, shame. In the 1950s, Kluger points out, even the words *Jew* and *Jewish* made Germans uncomfortable. Readers ashamed of the recent past could drown their discomfort with the "double gin-and-tonic of contempt and pity" offered by books like Hans Scholz's *On the Green Banks of the Spree*. Kluger recounts a scene from Scholz's best-selling novel that showed Jewish adults, in 1939 Poland, beating a Jewish girl so that she ran to a German soldier for help. The extreme improbability of that invented incident reveals a process of moral inversion at work. Transforming the Germans from murderers of Jews not only into innocent bystanders but into saviors necessitates a concurrent reversal of the Jewish role: from the victims to the perpetrators of violence. Psychologists consider shame one of the earliest and most persistent of human emotions. An event as shattering as the Holocaust produced massive quantities of shame among everyone involved: perpetrators, victims, witnesses, even rescuers. Kluger's analysis helps us recognize the many forms shame can take and the force it can exert, long after the fact, against truth.

This volume begins and ends with analyses of the cross. Zubrzycki's account of late-1990s Poland constitutes another step in the "secularization of a metaphor" that von Braun outlines in the first chapter. As Zubrzycki shows, the symbol of the cross as a metaphor for suffering became a central motif in a Polish national narrative of victimization, a story that leaves little or no room for recognition of the Jewish catastrophe at the heart of World War II. But Zubrzycki's contribution, like Kluger's, also points to some remarkable ways in which, over the past decades, the fact of the Shoah has been integrated into official discourse and popular awareness in some of the societies that masterminded, perpetrated, collaborated in, and witnessed the murder of the Jews. German and, more recently, Polish confrontations with the past have been—and remain—imperfect, incomplete, and vehemently contested, but they are more than has occurred in many other places in the wake of extreme violence and genocide.

Like the essay by von Braun that opens this volume, Zubrzycki's contribution reminds us that the study of the Holocaust is inseparable from the histories of both Judaism and Christianity. Indeed, the Holocaust and its legacies bind these already profoundly linked religions together in new and complicated ways. As the range of scholars and topics represented in this book indicates, the Holocaust also connects Europe with the rest of the world and traditions from the past with actions in the present and prospects for the future. Together these contributions suggest the burdens of continuity but also the hope of change that is passed down from generation to generation.

NOTES

The poem "You who live safe . . ." is from *If This Is a Man* (*Survival in Auschwitz*) by Primo Levi, translated by Stuart Woolf, copyright © 1959 by Orion Press, Inc., © 1958 by Giulio Einaudi editore S.P.A. Used by permission of Viking Penguin, a division of Penguin Group (USA) Inc.

1. Raul Hilberg, *The Destruction of the European Jews,* 1st ed. (Chicago: Quadrangle Books, 1961).

2. Saul Friedländer's efforts to create what he calls an "integrated history" of the Holocaust are best understood by reading his masterful study, *Nazi Germany and the Jews,* vol. 1, *The Years of Persecution, 1933–1939* (New York: Harper Perennial, 1998), and vol. 2, *The Years of Execution, 1939–1945* (New York: HarperCollins, 2007).

3. Key to this process has been the journal *History and Memory,* founded in 1989 by Saul Friedländer and now published by Indiana University Press.

4. Raphael Lemkin, *Axis Rule in Occupied Europe: Laws of Occupation, Analysis of Government, Proposals for Redress* (Clark, N.J.: Lawbook Exchange, 2005), 79–95; and Hannah Arendt, *The Origins of Totalitarianism* (Danvers, Mass.: Schocken, 2004), 123–25. Further exploration of the linkages between military practices, colonial warfare, and World War II is provided in Isabel Hull, *Absolute Destruction: Military Culture and the Practices of War in Imperial Germany* (Ithaca, N.Y.: Cornell University Press, 2006). For a study that connects state-building, terror, and "ethnic cleansing" in colonial regions with developments in Eastern Europe, see Peter Holquist, "Violent Russia, Deadly Marxism? Russia in the Epoch of Violence, 1905–21," *Kritika* 4, no. 3 (Summer 2003): 627–52.

5. For an account and analysis of the Historians' Debate, see Charles S. Maier, *The Unmasterable Past: History, Holocaust, and German National Identity* (Cambridge, Mass.: Harvard University Press, 2003); and also

Dominick LaCapra, "Reflections on the Historians' Debate," in *Representing the Holocaust: History, Theory, Trauma* (Ithaca, N.Y.: Cornell University Press, 1996).

6. This notion of double marginalization or victimization is captured in the titles of two important works: Judith Tydor Baumel, *Double Jeopardy: Gender and the Holocaust* (Portland, Ore.: Mitchell Valentine, 1999); and Elizabeth Heineman, "Sexuality and Nazism: The Doubly Unspeakable?" *Journal of the History of Sexuality* 11, nos. 1/2 (January–April 2002): 22–66.

7. See especially Marianne Hirsch, "Marked by Memory: Feminist Reflections on Trauma and Transmission," in *Extremities: Trauma, Testimony, Community*, ed. Nancy K. Miller and Jason Tougaw (Urbana: University of Illinois Press, 2002).

8. Daniel Jonah Goldhagen, *Hitler's Willing Executioners* (London: Abacus, 1997); Robert R. Shandley, ed., *Unwilling Germans? The Goldhagen Debate* (Minneapolis: University of Minnesota Press, 1998).

9. Jan T. Gross, *Neighbors: The Destruction of the Jewish Community in Jedwabne, Poland* (Princeton, N.J.: Princeton University Press, 1988); Antony Polonsky and Joanna B. Michlic, eds., *The Neighbors Respond: The Controversy over the Jedwabne Massacre in Poland* (Princeton, N.J.: Princeton University Press, 2003).

10. See in particular Gerhard L. Weinberg, "The 'Final Solution' and the War in 1943," in *Germany, Hitler, and World War II: Essays in Modern German and World History* (Cambridge, Eng.: Cambridge University Press, 1996), 217–45.

11. Joseph W. Bendersky, *The "Jewish Threat": Anti-Semitic Politics of the U.S. Army* (New York: Basic Books, 2000).

LESSONS AND LEGACIES VIII

I. P·R·E·C·E·D·E·N·T·S
A·N·D
A·N·T·E·C·E·D·E·N·T·S

Christina von Braun

The Symbol of the Cross: Secularization of a Metaphor from the Early Church to National Socialism

THE CROSS IS THE CENTRAL SYMBOL OF THE CHRISTIAN STORY OF the life and sufferings of Christ, and it also appears as a symbol—albeit in an altered form—in National Socialism. This recurrence is not surprising. The cross is marked by paradoxes: it signifies both death and resurrection, the body and renunciation of the flesh, agony and victory. To Christians, the cross is a promise of salvation that links earthly existence with eternal life. For Jews its associations are very different: it speaks of Christian triumphalism and the accompanying violence and threat of erasure. These paradoxes and conflicting meanings emerged and developed over centuries, but they achieved a specific expression in National Socialism and its annihilatory assault on Judaism and Jews. For this reason, study of the cross exposes some deep roots of the Holocaust in the rituals, beliefs, and practices of Christian Europe, including especially Christian antisemitism. At the same time, investigation of the historical evolution of the symbol of the cross suggests ways in which Nazi iconography continued a process that appropriated and secularized Christianity and its powerful, central metaphor. This essay explores these two interrelated strands of analysis.

The cross had particular uses in National Socialism and constitutes one of the many elements of a "political religion," a term that Eric Voegelin coined in the 1930s.[1] But Nazism's usurpation of Christianity, which Voegelin depicted as a fatal step in a process of secularization rooted in the Enlightenment, coexisted with and depended upon the continued vitality of traditional Christianity within Germany. Indeed,

elements within Nazism that sought to replace Christianity and pro-
ponents of the Christian churches in familiar forms found common
ground in claims of German spiritual superiority, in hostility toward
Jews, and in the conviction that redemption and atonement came
through suffering and the shedding of blood. It is only when one looks
back at the long history of the symbol of the cross that one can fully
comprehend the basis of the swastika, its attraction, and the historical
traditions on which it could build. (See figure 1.)

I begin this discussion with a citation from the conversations with
Hitler that were recorded by Hermann Rauschning. There are many
such quotations in the archives of National Socialism. Then I move
far back in time in order to give a detailed account of the history of
the symbolism of the cross and the paradoxes it embodies. Rauschning
remembers Hitler saying:

> Easter is no longer the resurrection, but rather the eternal renewal
> of our People. Christmas is the birth of our Savior: the spirit of
> heroism and freedom of our People. They will replace the cross
> with our swastika. Instead of the blood of their former Redeemer,
> they will celebrate the pure blood of our People. They will receive
> the German fruit of the field as a holy offering and eat it as the
> symbol of the eternal community of the Nation as they have until
> now savored the Body of their God. And then, when this has come
> to pass, the churches will become full again. If we so desire, so it
> shall be; if it is our faith that is observed there.[2]

In all the ceremonies of the Nazi faith, one can sense Christianity's
legacy, for instance, in the cult of the martyr. In front of the Feld-
herrnhalle in Munich, those who died in the Hitler Putsch (or Beer
Hall Putsch) of 1923 were honored every year on November 9. The
funeral cult stands at the center of this religion, just as the cross stands
at the center of the Christian faith. The rituals allowed the dead who
have sacrificed their lives for this "religion" to rise again. Equally, the
blood that was shed is holy. Hitler kissed the *Blutfahne* (blood banner) just as the devout Christian kisses the bleeding wounds of the
Savior. Not only implicitly but explicitly, the reliance on Christian
images excluded Jews from the community of the "Aryan" faithful.
The Jew, said Hitler, differentiated himself from the Christian in that
the Jew was not capable of self-sacrifice. Reference to the cross and
its connotations of sacrifice lent legitimacy to attacks on Jews who,

Figure 1. Antisemitic poster from Germany, 1935: cross, swastika, erotics, and anxiety intertwined. From Theodor Pugel and Robert Koerber, *Antisemitismus: Der Welt und Bild* (1935); courtesy of United States Holocaust Memorial Museum; copyright unknown.

accused in Christian tradition of deicide, were cast as enemies of the cross and the crucified one.

In Christianity, devotion to the cross contributes to the realization of the Passion. The Passion story must be repeated within every single believer so that he or she may share in Christ's life and suffering. Paul stated quite clearly that the believer is "put to death with Christ on his cross. . . . Since he has died with Christ, he believes that he will also live with him. For he knows that Christ has been raised from death and will never die again."[3] But the cross signifies not only the death of the crucified but also resurrection and victory over death. This double meaning, which has sometimes been paraphrased as the "paradox of the cross," has a long history. On the one hand, it refers to the pre-Christian meaning of the cross that was assimilated by Christianity; on the other hand, it also implies a codification of the body. Its influence extends far beyond the main periods of Christianity and emerges again in National Socialism. At the same time, a dimension of gender is inherent in this history that is expressed in the martyr and resurrection rituals of National Socialism to which Rauschning referred and that were solely a matter for men.

SYMBOLISM OF THE CROSS

The cross can be found in almost all cultures, regardless if they are formed by oral traditions or written culture. In societies with an oral tradition, the cross mainly symbolizes the encounter between heaven and earth.[4] This mediatory function of the cross is also preserved in many written cultures; however, it additionally took on the meaning of a mediation between the sign and the material world, between symbol and symptom. In ancient Egypt, the *crux ansata* (ankh) was the hieroglyph for *life*. The Copts adopted the sign and gave it a new meaning of *eternal life*, as in the Christian sense.[5] In the swastika, which, with the exception of Australia, was common worldwide, a gendered symbolism is additionally manifested. In Hinduism, whereas the clockwise swastika stood as the principle of masculinity of the god Ganesh, the counterclockwise swastika symbolized the principle of femininity of the goddess Kali. The counterclockwise swastika in Buddhism often appears on the breast, the palms of the hands, or the soles of the feet of Buddha figures—all points on the body that, as stigmata, also hold great meaning for the Christian system of metaphors of the crucifixion.[6] The two forms of the swastika make it clear that the gender ascription deals less with the derivation of biological fact than with the attempt to confer the appearance of physiological "reality" via the gendered codification to an abstract classification. This means that the category *gender,* or rather the gender system, contributes to the "charging" of abstract elements or symbols with seemingly physiological efficacy. In the Christian story of the cross—and this is what I attempt to illustrate—the function of the gendered images becomes especially apparent.

A major exception to the gendered-physiological charge of the cross is represented by the symbolism of the cross in the Hebrew sign system. Whether as a vertical or horizontal cross, it simply means—in accordance with the Hebrew phonetic symbol *taw*—"sign" or letter. Contrary to the Christian cross, it does not signify anything but itself. All the same, the fact that a sign merely symbolizes "the sign" in a religion in which God reveals himself solely via the letters of the written language also has a thoroughly transcendental meaning. This reference to the transcendental meaning is again expressed in the symbolic gender system. The symbolic gender system of the Jewish religion— something I cannot address in detail here—allows itself to be read as a ritual ascription of difference into the male and the female body. On the one hand, this difference reflects the insurmountable difference between God's eternity and human mortality; on the other hand, it reflects the strict differentiation between sign and the material world.[7] It is precisely the continued cultural practice of this difference that is the basis for the Jewish ban on images (iconoclasm).[8] Contrary to this difference in the Jewish religion, *sema* and *soma* merge in Christianity. Just as Christ is the "word become flesh," the cross simultaneously means sign and corporeality: it is symbol as well as symptom. This union is already expressed in the paradox that the cross symbolizes death as well as resurrection; that it tells of both an execution and of a victory over death. This paradox of the cross, which also allows itself to be rewritten as the incarnation of the decarnification, remains in that the cross has both historical and symbolic meaning in Christianity.

THE HISTORICAL CROSS

In contrast to the Persians and the Romans, the Jewish penal code of ancient Palestine was not familiar with execution by crucifixion.

However, judging by the reports of Herodotus, the practice was already widespread elsewhere in the fifth century BCE. It must have been the most painful and demeaning form of execution, designed to inflict a long, slow, and extremely painful death. It was primarily reserved for rebellious slaves, and it is precisely for this reason that it was often carried out in Palestine. From the beginning of Roman rule in Palestine (63 BCE) until shortly before the outbreak of the Jewish War (66 CE), all known reports of crucifixions in Palestine refer to rebels and their sympathizers crucified by Romans. The Latin word for *cross* (*crux*) actually means *wood of the martyr* or *stake*.

Because it was considered especially disgraceful to die on the cross, it took a long time before Christians were willing to accept the cross as the symbol of their faith. The concept first began to be observed in the fourth century, after Constantine the Great repealed the sentence of crucifixion and then, around 320 CE, had Christianity installed as an official religion. The supposed discovery of the true cross by his mother Helena, which was later dated to the year 328, contributed to the symbolism's new transvaluation. That Constantine also provided for repeal of the Christian ban on images is one indication among others that Christianity developed itself away from a God who only revealed himself in signs and was turning toward a God who was to be understood as a symptom that had become a sign.

Thanks to the paradox of the cross, Christianity developed the most multilayered and lasting symbolism of the cross. For the Gnostics (in the first centuries CE, the boundary between gnosis and Christianity was by no means clear), the historical death on the cross was important, and the resurrection was interpreted according to Gnostic thought. According to Marcion, who lived around 139 CE, the mortal body of Jesus was merely an illusionary body, which, after its death, was rejoined with the true body of the self in the realm of light. The Gnostics' promise of salvation was based precisely on overcoming bodily existence. According to Irenaeus, whoever observed the corporeality of the crucified was already subject to the power of the archons.[9] However, with the gradual establishment of the Christian church, the idea increasingly developed that Christ's suffering, the Passion, and the crucifixion were to be understood as a real, bodily, earthly suffering, endured by a God who had become a human being and who was therefore capable of suffering. The martyrs' and the flagellants' movements that originated in the monasteries from around 1000 CE and that spread through all of Christian Europe were kept alive by the concept of the material, real suffering that should be administered—and in this manner, "realized"—on one's own body. Before I return to the flagellants, I will sketch the further development of the symbolism of the cross from the time of the early church.

Early Church

For the early church, the cross became the dominant theological theme. As Gregory of Nyssa maintained, it proclaimed "the truth": the fulfillment of the promise of a God become incarnate.[10] For the early church, Christ and the cross became nearly interchangeable: the crucified Christ was the word of God.[11] But the crucifixion itself was not depicted.[12] This changed with a gradual shift of the cross's significance, from suffered death to sign of victory. With this shift, the motif of the "victorious cross" also developed on a secular level, such as when Constantine the Great ascribed his victory over Maxentius (312 CE) to a vision of the cross. "The invincible sign of the cross" became a well-established expression,[13] and Christians increasingly came to understand the cross as a guarantee for ascent into heaven.[14] This victory symbolism of the cross has been preserved until today. The first construction to be erected on New York's "Ground Zero" after September 11, 2001, was a cross built from the debris of the collapsed buildings.

Sometimes the cross was also associated with the "tree of life" that is cited in Genesis 2, an anticipation of the later topos of the cross's "fertility."[15] Unlike in the Jewish Bible, in the Christian context the "tree of life" was meant to imply "fertility via the spirit." In the early church, the cross in the house of worship was gradually superseded by representations of the crucifixion: above all it was the iconographic intention to portray the death with the resurrection, but then also to stress the theme of suffering itself. The linking of death and resurrection was primarily expressed in depictions in which the cross was embellished with motifs of plants and blossoms—thereby referring to the "tree of life"—or it was adorned with gemstones.

From the fifth century on, depictions of Christ carrying the cross or being nailed to the cross began to appear.[16] The first representations of the crucifixion originated in Syria and in a sense already anticipated the iconoclasm. The issue was whether representations of the Passion of Christ and the martyrs dealt with a symbolic testimonial, or whether they should assist the believer to "share" in the death and suffering; in other words, whether they represented a "true" experience. This was a point of controversy that would later be revived in the debates surrounding the doctrine of transubstantiation in connection with the interpretation of the bread and the wine at communion. By the end of the seventh and the beginning of the eighth centuries, the struggle had been decided in favor of iconophilia. From this point on, representations of the events on the cross—that is, representations of the Passion—predominated.

The early Middle Ages dealt hesitantly with such representations; however, already in the High Middle Ages, images of the Passion moved to the center of iconographic interest.[17] Even in the churches themselves—as cross-shaped constructions—the cross was represented. With this architecture, one has to bear in mind that the church congregation was perceived as the body of Christ. The church's construction gave this idea a visible, petrified form. Christian teaching bound together the beginning of the world (Adam) with the completion of the world (Christ).[18] The crucifixion's intense scenes of suffering became the occasion for a "com-passion" that was reflected both in numerous visions and in the self-flagellation movements. Already in the early church, monastic life was construed as an existence on the cross: hermitage and asceticism counted as preliminary forms of the cross.[19] Caesarius von Heisterbach noted, "Twice is the crucifixion of the monks: one of the inner being through compassion for others, and one of the external being through the mortification of one's own flesh."[20]

Gradually, the flesh was not only "silenced" but also aroused through blood and suffering, first in the cloisters and then on the streets. Believers branded the sign of the cross on their bodies with red-hot brass crosses; they carried a cross set with sharp nails; or they nailed themselves to the cross.[21] It was as if a sign were to be inscribed on the body, comparable to circumcision in the Jewish religion that seals the union between God and Israel. Here, however, it dealt with a union between Christ and his community of believers that was constantly renewed via an active realization of the cross in the suffering body of the believer. Such an equation of Christian self-castigation with Jewish circumcision can be supported by the fact—among others—that numerous church fathers and dogmatists from the second century up to Thomas Aquinas in the thirteenth century attempted to reinterpret the circumcision of Christ in a Christian sense, in that they explained the circumcision as the first station of the cross.[22]

Among the influential mystics, Bernard of Clairvaux and Francis of Assisi most clearly identified with Christ's suffering.[23] In the monastic communities that emerged around them, numerous depictions portray the founders as "Those Pardoned by the Cross." This was especially often the case for a vision of Bernard of Clairvaux, in which Christ descends from the cross in order to embrace the praying devotee.[24] Alternately, they themselves were venerated as the crucified—especially in depictions of Francis of Assisi.[25] If early Christianity had shown a reserved distance toward the cross, the High Middle Ages sought closeness to and intimacy with the cross. This intimacy also had erotic connotations for men as well as for women, in which the desire for suffering was preserved. An intensely experienced Christianity produced a high bodily valorization of pain and suffering.

Especially in Germany and in Italy, the "type" of a sensually laden *crucifixus dolorosus* took hold.[26] (See figure 2.) Such images increased in the thirteenth century.[27] Through them, the cross linked itself on the one hand with the Jewish symbolism of blood as the allegory for "life." But on the other hand, the term *life* was vested with a new meaning—a meaning that would be directly reflected in the implementation of the doctrine of transubstantiation. According to this doctrine, the wine and the bread of the Eucharist were no longer to be understood as symbols of the Lord's body but rather were transformed into his body and blood; they made the Lord's body "present."

The doctrine of transubstantiation could be called the beginning of a secularization of the Christian message—and it revealed itself especially clearly in the metaphors of the blood, the cross, and pain. The secularization of the Christian message implied that the boundary between the Lord's body and the mortal body became increasingly blurred. This development was accompanied by a paradox: on the one hand, the Lord became man; bread and wine became body and blood. On the other hand, the body of the believer developed increasingly spiritualized dimensions. This spiritualization, however, did not correspond to the hereafter as did the "transfigured body" of Christ. Rather, it consisted in a concept of the domination of the body and its mortality via self-discipline. The movement of the flagellants clearly shows that it did not have to do with a passively endured suffering,

Figure 2. The vision of Saint Bernard of Clairvaux seeing Christ descend to greet him during prayers (a sensually laden *crucifixus dolorosus* from the fourteenth century). "Vision des Heiligen Bernhard," fourteenth century; Repro: Rheinisches Bildarchiv Köln, © Rheinisches Bildarchiv, Cologne.

but rather with the fantasy of a victory over the body, comparable to the representation of the cross as a sign of resurrection. This increase of power through suffering explains the "desire" for self-castigation that characterized the flagellant movements of the Middle Ages.

The Flagellant Movements

Beginning in the second Christian millennium, self-flagellation with whip, staff, or rod became an important component of the practice of the Christian faith in many monasteries.[28] The act of self-flagellation had less to do with penance or a punishment for sins committed than with the "representation" (in every sense of the word) of the Passion. The believer's body became a site of presentation and of the "active realization" of the Passion story. Via self-flagellation, the believer simultaneously made himself torturer and tortured; it presented him with the possibility to bring time to a standstill, to unite past, present, and future. If asceticism and celibacy were means for the early Christians to resist the inexorable flow of time, the never-ending cycle of death and rebirth, then the dominating paradigm of the transcendence of corporality and decay via spiritual control of the body stood behind the practice of monastic self-flagellation.[29]

But why did the practice of self-flagellation increase from about 1000 CE on? One of the answers can be found in the fact that, in this time, the Christian West switched over from a culture of oral tradition to a written culture, that is, to textuality and abstract symbolism.[30] The rise of written culture reveals itself in a new understanding of legislation and jurisdiction, just as in the increasingly influential role of money (currency being the system of sign par excellence), and last but not least in the discovery of the mechanical clock's train of gears, which would gradually contribute to the synchronization of wide geographical and cultural spheres.[31] The culture of writing implied exactly that which the great ascetics practiced—domination of the body and the material world by the spirit. Self-flagellation therefore presented the "inscription" of the spirit or of the law of the script onto the body.

The whip and the rod not only became instruments of an "inscribing" of the body; they were also the tools of a theater of the eyes. If the suffering body of the Savior or of the martyrs formed the basis and the justification of Christian iconolatry, then the flayed and bleeding body of the ascetic became a *tableau vivant* of iconophilia. Self-flagellation and asceticism are hardly to be separated from the debate surrounding the veneration of the image or from the subsequent doctrine of transubstantiation. It was also not merely chance that self-flagellation and asceticism gained in meaning within Christian thought when iconoclasm was finally overridden in favor of iconolatry. From this correlation in which the cross is most clearly expressed, the peculiar concurrence between the German terms *Mal* (a wound or a marker on the body, as well as the "instance," and "time") and *malen* (to paint), as well as *Zeichen* (sign, revelation) and *zeichnen* (to design, to sketch), may be explained.[32]

The Christian mysticism of the Middle Ages was deeply influenced by the idea of a union with God through immersion in a picture of the crucified or of a martyr. As Meister Eckhart put it, the soul is nothing but an "image of God" and cannot be separated from God:

> I have often said this: no one can separate an image as image from that which is represented in the image. If the soul lives in that, by which it is the image of God, it will give birth; here is true union, this union could not be torn asunder by all the creatures together. In defiance of God himself, defying the angels, defying the souls and all creatures, I say, they cannot separate the soul, when it is the image of God, from God. That is true union, and therein lies true blessedness. Some teachers search for blessedness in reason. But I say: blessedness lies neither in reason, nor in the will, but above both: it is there where blessedness resides, there lies blessedness as blessedness and not as reason, and God as God and the soul as God's image.[33]

The "image" through which the union took place was, however—as with the host and the wine—understood less and less as a symbol and more and more as an earthly, visual reality.

The self-flagellants "staged" and celebrated exactly this transformation on their own bodies. Their processions, which could include up to several thousand people, grew to become mass movements that toured Europe to give "performances" from town to town. In groups of as many as a few hundred people, with heads hidden under hoods and exposed backs bleeding and injured by self-inflicted blows, the penitents undertook journeys that lasted several weeks. During this time they simultaneously withdrew and offered themselves to "the world." For a short time, they lived in the "pure present." Wherever they arrived, they drew new initiates. In a few areas, especially in Italy and France, territories that would later remain true to Rome, priests and monks made themselves leaders of the flagellants' pilgrimages.

By contrast, in many northern areas of Europe, the penitence movements appointed their own leaders, a development that made the clergy and Rome uneasy and led the church to criticize the self-flagellation groups. In fact, at times this movement had brought about a new, self-defined Christian belief in which, for instance, the bleeding wounds were proclaimed to be the true "baptism." A few leaders of the flagellant groups, whose appearance foreshadowed the Reformation and the fall of Rome, were sentenced as heretics and executed. The Reformation would end flagellation—together with iconolatry—as Christian practice. By the time the self-flagellation movement dissolved, the paradigm of a domination and spiritualization of the body through pain had long since become self-evident and crossed over from the sphere of faith into that of secular power.

Victory over the Body

The victory over the body that the Middle Ages celebrated through the staging of suffering had both political and gendered dimensions. Political developments brought about a signification of the cross that implied worldly power. The cross became the emblem of the emperor upon his entering the city.[34] Crosses decorated the crowns of rulers, the insignia of kings and princes, and the scepter of the emperor. In general, recourse to the Christian body of thought and its metaphors was made in order to legitimize the ruler.[35] The "ability to rule and to conquer is based on the power of the cross," as it was often said—a concept that on the one hand declared the ruler to be God's "chosen one," but on the other hand granted him the power to rule over death and danger.[36] Therefore, the cross was also transferred to armor—most especially to that of the crusaders. Later it became the standard of the missionaries, or rather, the sign of the conquest of an area: wherever the conquistadors arrived, they erected a cross.[37]

The gender symbolism of the cross also signified domination and "potency" in another manner. I will present this aspect briefly, based on the dispute between the medievalist Caroline Walker Bynum and the art historian Leo Steinberg, who have each interpreted the representations of the cross in differing ways. In both cases, it has to do with the gendered codification of the cross, or rather, with the question: is pain a masculine or a feminine privilege?

Taking a series of representations from the Middle Ages, Bynum illustrates that the body of the crucified was armed with all of the insignia of femininity: his sacrificed blood was shown as the feminine nourishing breast. (See figure 3.) Such representations were in keeping with the statements of mystics such as Saint Catherine of Siena, who wrote:

> We must do as a little child does who wants milk. It takes the breast of its mother, applies its mouth, and by means of the flesh it draws milk. We must do the same if we would be nourished. We must attach ourselves to that breast of Christ crucified, which is the source of charity, and by means of that flesh we draw milk. The means is Christ's humanity which suffered pain, and we cannot without pain get that milk that comes from charity.[38]

In many representations, the Lord's wounds also took the form of a bleeding vulva, and the analogy of crucifixion and motherliness made it possible for the crucifixion itself to appear as the moment of birth and delivery. Marguerite d'Oingt, a highly spiritual, French mystic nun of the thirteenth century, prioress of the Carthusian monastery of Poleteins near Lyon, explained:

> My sweet Lord ... are you not my mother and more than my mother ... For when the hour of your delivery came you were placed on the hard bed of the cross ... And your nerves and all your veins were broken. And truly it is no surprise that your veins burst when in one day you gave birth to the whole world.[39]

In contrast to Bynum, the art historian Steinberg makes reference to numerous depictions that stress the masculinity of the Redeemer. Not only does the Holy Mother point to the member of the newly born Savior, but also—and most importantly—representations of the crucifixion emphasized the genitals. The more the story of the Passion progressed, the more the representation of masculine potency developed, which leads Steinberg to make the connection between "erection" and "resurrection."[40] He concludes that the meaning of the phallus from antiquity was carried over to the Christian religion.

Figure 3. Quirizio da Murano, "The Savior," c. 1475. Here, as in other representations, the wounds of the crucified Jesus take forms linked to femaleness and reproduction. "Il Redentore," Quirizio da Murano, c. 1475: Venice, Gallerie dell'Accademia, with permission from the Ministry for Cultural Assets and Affairs ("Su concessione del Ministero per i beni e le Attività Culturali").

In antiquity, the phallus stood for both power and fertility, and it therefore could be seen at many grave sites.[41] In the Christian context, the conquest of death lies in the conquest of bodilyness itself. For, as Steinberg continues, God became Man in order to overcome mortality in just this way.

Jesus's genitalia played an increasingly important role in representations from the late Middle Ages and the Renaissance, because God took on a gender when he became Man. Steinberg states, "It was this flesh which Christ assumed in becoming man, and to declare him free of its burden, to relieve him of its temptations, is to decarnify the incarnation itself."[42] This concept differs from that of antiquity, where the idealized male body refers to the power of the intellect. In contrast, these medieval depictions deal with the conquest of gender and of sexuality itself. Therefore, Jesus's genitals do not need to be hidden from the observer's view—quite the contrary: "We may say that Michelangelo's naked Christs—on the cross, dead or risen—are, like the naked Christ child, not shameful, but literally and profoundly 'shame-less.'"[43] (See figure 4.)

One could also interpret the development in another manner: the image of sexual potency contributes to a procreative power of the spirit, and power is codified as both secular and masculine. This means that if the representation of the crucifixion implied "victory of the spirit" over the body, then it connected this promise of salvation less and less with a message for the hereafter and increasingly with a message for this world. In other words, the cross symbolized earthly potency, an "erection tool" that could disarm nature and the other, symbolized by the female body.

The Reformation clearly articulated this new masculine codification. Luther said, "Regardless if I want to or not: whenever I hear of Christianity, an image of a man hanging on a cross projects itself in my heart."[44] The body of the Lord and his power of resurrection had become identical with the male body. And therefore Jakob Böhme, a sixteenth-century theological autodidact whose mystical teaching as a "philosophus teutonicus" was deeply influential in Protestant Germany and many other European regions, declared death on the cross to be a male privilege: "The blood of the woman would not have appeased God's anger. This must only be done by the blood of the man, because the woman belongs in the man and will become a male virgin in the heavenly kingdom, just as Adam was—not a woman."[45]

Figure 4. Maarten van Heemskerck, "Christ as the Man of Sorrows," c. 1550 (Museum voor Schone Kunsten, Ghent). Like many artists depicting the crucifixion, van Heemskerck stressed the masculinity of Jesus. Another painting, by the same artist in the same series, emphasizes the genitals much more directly, illustrating Steinberg's connection between "erection" and "resurrection." That particular painting and the rights to it are held by Bob Jones University in South Carolina. According to a representative of the art museum there, permission to reproduce it is never granted. "Christus als de man van smarten," Maarten van Heemskerck, c. 1550; MSK Ghent © Reproductiefonds-Lukas.

The history of the cross recounts the history of what one could call a "culture of empowerment" through pain—which reveals itself among other things via a gradual gendered reinterpretation of the symbolism of blood. Thus, the varying interpretations of images by Bynum, who refers to representations of the High Middle Ages, and Steinberg, whose examples stem from the late Middle Ages and from the beginning of modern times, do not necessarily present a contradiction. In pre-Christian traditions, which were preserved until well into the Middle Ages, female blood symbolized fertility and procreative power (in keeping with blood as a symbol of "life" in the Jewish religion). This symbolism explains on the one hand the fascination of the Middle Ages for blood and suffering; on the other hand, it also accounts for representations of the wounds as a "nourishing breast." This fertility symbolism of the blood was taken on in the staging of suffering and replaced with a new meaning that now corresponded to the male body. The pain and the exuberantly flowing blood took on the meaning of "intellectual fertility," and this was coded as masculine. The gradual shift of the symbolism of the blood (which implies "life," "salvation," and "suffering") becomes clear when observing a few of the images to which both Bynum and Steinberg refer. In some representations, the blood of the Savior flows from the wound into the abdomen and genitals: this representation allows both for the association of the wound with menstrual blood (which traditionally has symbolized fertility), a female codification of events at the cross, and also for a bringing together of the Passion with circumcision, a masculine codification of suffering.

The shift in gender significance that blood symbolism underwent in the Middle Ages was reflected in a demonization of menstrual blood,[46] which sometimes was even equated with "poison."[47] This development is not comparable to the ritual representation of the woman's blood in the Jewish religion, where the strict "segregation" of the male and the female body is symbolically portrayed, celebrated, and consistently recognized.[48] In Christianity, however, a process of exchange took place in which the blood of the man was invested with the traditional connotations of the blood of the woman, and for just this reason, the blood of the woman experienced a devaluation that can still be seen today, for example, in images of "impure" menstrual blood.[49]

The Desire for Self-Castigation in the Secularization Process

The cross and pain both became metaphors for empowerment and also accompanied the development of feelings of power—including sexually coded feelings of power. Thus, in the process of secularization, the practice of self-flagellation increasingly became a factor not only of sexual arousal and lust but also an integral component of every form of pornography—a form of "sexuality" in which the satisfaction of desire goes hand in hand with the domination of the "other body." Paradoxically, this development first came about as a criticism of the church. The Enlightenment "unmasked" the practice of self-flagellation as a method of the church to arouse women and make them submissive to priests.[50] From 1800 on, the number of texts increased in which priests were accused of having attempted to guide young women "to faith" and "to purity" by whip and by rod in order to satisfy their own sadosexual needs. Such accusations were partially based on court records; however, for the most part they corresponded with wishes and fantasies in which the secularization process, and not only a secularization of the promise of salvation, can be detected.

Sadistic and masochistic fantasies became the major component of erotic and pornographic literature in the late eighteenth and the entire nineteenth centuries, whereby a good portion of the events were transferred to the monasteries. Although such stories were largely heterosexual in nature, flagellation and self-flagellation were soon to become a dominating motif of the erotic fantasy in the homosexual literature and fashioning of images. This explains the fact that the saints more or less disappeared from the body of visual imagery of the nineteenth century, but the flayed and pierced body of Saint Sebastian experienced a revival in the visual representations of homosexual magazines such as *Der Eigene* (*The Personalist*).[51] Certainly this motif stemmed from the conception that a true artist has to suffer in order to be creative and bring about "great works." Pain and suffering became prerequisites for artistic potency and fertility, and this suffering was again connected with the erotically charged motif of the suffering body.

The image of the cross loomed over these developments. Its presence was especially evident in the literature of the *décadence,* where the cross and the desire for violent acts (directed at a foreign or one's own body) surfaced as a possibility to escape the horrors of ennui. The cross still played an important role, but now it was erotically charged. The English poet Algernon Charles Swinburne, who, while receiving Communion at the age of twelve experienced an "ecstasy of worship," prayed to "Our Lady of Sensual Pain":[52]

> I have passed from the outermost portal
> To the shrine where a sin is a prayer;
> What care though the service be mortal?
> O our Lady of torture, what care?
> All thine the last wine that I pour is,
> The last in the chalice we drain,
> O fierce and luxurious Dolores,
> Our Lady of pain.[53]

It was not by chance that many authors of the *décadence* were drawn to Catholicism, which, with respect to blood, was less ascetic than Protestantism. Oscar Wilde professed Franciscan Catholicism in *De Profundis,* and in the same manner, French writers like Jean-Marie Villiers de l'Isle Adam, Jules Barbey d'Aurevilly, and Joris-Carl Huysmans—all of them deeply influential in fin-de-siècle literature and aesthetics—displayed deep piety, which, in the case of Huysmans, ultimately led to the monastic life.[54] Sadism, as Huysmans himself wrote, is a "bastard of Catholicism."[55]

In short, by the beginning of the twentieth century the symbolism of the cross had made itself independent; it had become a factor in a worldly culture of self-empowerment through pain, and it corresponded to a new secular practice and set of metaphors. This development cannot be conceived without the preceding Christian charging of the cross that continued over many centuries. The cross was ascribed with the meaning of suffering and death on the one hand; on the other hand, it was charged with resurrection. Salvation, atonement, and eternal life, it proclaimed, required bloodshed and pain.

NAZISM AS CULMINATION OF THE SECULARIZATION AND APPROPRIATION OF THE CROSS

Of all the "holy wars" that have their roots in Christian traditions, the National Socialist attack on Jews and on Judaism was the most terrible and the most violent. And in a manner both conscious and unconscious, it encompassed all the stations that the symbol of the cross had passed through: the cult of death, the cult of suffering and martyrdom, and the cult of empowerment with its pretension to superior spirituality. Indeed, claims to "purity" of the blood and race derived from the notion of spiritual superiority. The idea of "degeneration" (*Entartung*), the concept of a "sacrificial love for Germany"—all these imaginings that characterized the pseudo-religious side of National Socialism had an origin in teachings and metaphors created by Christian theology and spread by popular religious thought over the course of centuries.

With Nazism, the Christian idea of the "purity" of the blood of the Savior (linked to Jesus being born of an "immaculate" mother and without sexual intercourse) was transferred to the idea of the "purity" of the blood of the Aryan race. This "biological" definition of purity was accompanied by a "sexualization" of the very concept of purity. As early as 1887, Theodor Fritsch published an *Antisemiten-Katechismus* (*Antisemitic Catechism*) in which he named among the first of the "Ten German Commandments": "Thou shalt keep thy blood pure. . . . Consider it a crime to corrupt the noble nature of your people with the Jewish nature. For thou must know that the Jewish blood is indestructible and will form body and soul for generations to come."[56] The Nazis would disseminate Fritsch's book widely under the title *Handbuch der Judenfrage* (*Manual of the Jewish Question*).

The new concept of "purity" led to a complete reversal of the meaning of *Blutschande* (literally "blood shame") which took place over the course of a century. Whereas the term originally meant to "sin against one's own blood," that is, to commit incest, it now referred to relationships with those of the "other blood," those to whom one was not related. When the term *Blutschande* occurred, it referred exclusively to Jews and sexual relations with Jews.[57] At the same time, an idealization of incest can be observed in many German literary texts: in Robert Musil (*Der Mann ohne Eigenschaften; The Man Without Qualities*), Thomas Mann (*Der Sünder; The Holy Sinner* and *Wälsungen Blut; The Blood of the Walsungs*), Frank Thiess (*Die Verdammten; The Damned*), Leonard Frank (*Bruder und Schwester; Brother and Sister*), and the poems of Georg Trakl, to name only the best known.

The links between sexual images and the image of the Jew also become evident in the case of Otto Weininger, a young Jewish

philosopher who had converted to Protestantism. His fantasies of
the body of the "Jew" illustrate a "symptom of conversion" in every
sense of the word:

> Some reflection [on both the woman and the Jew] will lead to the
> surprising result that Judaism is saturated with femininity, with
> precisely those qualities the essence of which I have shown to be in
> the strongest opposition to the male nature. It would not be diffi-
> cult to make a case for the view that the Jew is more saturated with
> femininity than the Aryan, to such an extent that the most manly
> Jew is more feminine than the least manly Aryan.[58]

Weininger was twenty-three years old when his book *Geschlecht
und Charakter* (*Sex and Character*) appeared in 1903, causing a sensa-
tion—especially following Weininger's suicide a few months later in
Beethoven's house in Vienna. Weininger's suicide was acknowledged
by Hitler with the remark that he was the "only respectable Jew." One
of the reasons for the success of Weininger's book, which appeared in
numerous editions and was translated into many languages, was not
only the close link he created between "femininity" and "Jewishness,"
but also his insistence on the Christian concept of self-empowerment
through suffering. He wrote that humanity (which he equated with
Christianity) would find "salvation" only after having overcome all
female—and Jewish—elements within the self, Judaism being "the
abyss over which Christianity is erected."[59] Nazi propaganda and antisemitic papers like *Der Stürmer* drew heavily upon such images.

There are many examples of how, at the level of ideology, but
also in concrete, tangible ways, National Socialism drew energy from
Christianity and manifested the paradoxes of the cross. Already in the
1930s, Nazi propaganda depicted "the Jew" as a danger that was simultaneously spiritual, material, and sexual, and assaults on German Jews
included all three components. In the Kristallnacht pogrom of November 1938, for example, Nazis torched synagogues and desecrated
objects of ritual significance, but they also destroyed Jewish businesses,
violated Jewish homes, and abused and humiliated Jewish women
and men.[60] Throughout the Nazi period, Himmler presented the attack on homosexuals as a purifying act, in keeping with conventional
Christian morality.[61] At the same time, Nazi spokesmen promised
sexual pleasure to "pure" Germans.[62] German leaders declared the
war of annihilation against the Soviet Union that began in 1941 to be

a crusade against so-called Jewish Bolshevism. Meanwhile, Bavarian Catholics insisted that crucifixes remain on display in schools and other public places, and in the interest of national unity in wartime, party officials conceded.

Even if it did not replace it, the swastika absorbed and appropriated many meanings of the cross, as became especially evident in allegations of ritual murder. These had been important in the late Middle Ages, and from the middle of the nineteenth century onward they again swept through Europe like an epidemic. But whereas the ritual murder allegations of the Middle Ages referred to murdered infants (chaste and innocent children who reflected the purity of Christ), those of the nineteenth century mostly implied the "sacrifice" of young women. This transfer was due to a secularized concept of redemption. In both "religions"—the Christian as well as the Aryan—sacrifice was the prerequisite of "redemption," and it was the Jew who was charged with the act of sacrifice.

In the German language, the double meaning of the word *Opfer* (both "sacrifice" and "victim") makes this transposition possible and points to another "paradox of the cross." On the one hand, Christians claim that God has "sacrificed" his Son for the redemption of mankind; on the other hand, Christ is considered the victim of a "Jewish crime." It is always the latter to which allegations of ritual murder refer, and yet the religious sacrifice is meant at the same time.

Why the transfer from infant murder to the murder of young women? To put it briefly: in racial antisemitism, the "sexual crime" or *Rassenschande* (racial defilement) replaced crucifixion. This substitution is the key to the meaning of sexual images in secular antisemitism. The *Volkskörper* (Aryan body politic) emerged from the *corpus dei*, and its signifier was not an allegorical female body (*Ecclesia*), not even the national allegory (*Germania*), but rather the biological body of the individual "Aryan" woman. (See figure 5.) As in the New Testament and the Passion of Christ, it became the role of the Jew to incur the "sacrifice" of the *Rassenschande* to this "sacralized" body; to provide for a "crucifixion" in sexual terms and on a secular level.

The historical origins of the symbol of the cross at least partly explain the impact that images of blood and "passion" had on secular Germany in the 1930s and 1940s, among both intellectuals and nonintellectuals. The fact that these images were at the same time erotically charged enhanced their power. Eroticism is not a political

Der Nürnberger Jude Otto Mayer

pflegte seine Opfer zu kreuzigen. In völlig nacktem Zustande band
er sie an ein eigens dazu angefertigtes Holzkreuz und schändete
sie, sobald aus den Wundmalen das Blut floß.

Figure 5. "Der Nürnberger Jude Otto Mayer" (an "Aryan" female nailed to the
cross by "the Jew"). Originally published in *Der Stürmer,* this image came with
the following caption: "The Jew from Nuremberg, Otto Mayer, had the habit
of crucifying his victims. He bound them, completely naked, to a wooden cross
made for this purpose and defiled them until blood flowed from their wounds."

From *Der Stürmer,* public domain. This image is not in the collections of the *Stürmer* Archive at the
Stadtarchiv in Nuremberg.

power as such, but it helps to wipe out the faculties of judgment and critical thought. Like religious ideas, erotically charged images—be they yet so "calculated"—will always pretend to address directly the unconscious (or the "unknown," the "unspeakable," the "mysterious"), and it is from this claim that they draw their fatal influence.

NOTES

Thanks to David James Prickett for translating the body of this text from the original German into English.

1. Eric Voegelin, *Die politischen Religionen* (Vienna: Fink, 1938).

2. Hermann Rauschning, *Gespräche mit Hitler* (New York: Europa Verlag, 1940), 51. Rauschning's notes are not word-for-word renderings of the conversations with Hitler. They have been taken from memory. Nevertheless, historians cite these because to an astounding degree they match both Hitler's characteristic speech and many of his statements. In particular, the statements about religion match word for word the table talk that was written down by Heinrich Heim and Henry Picker at the request of Martin Bormann.

3. Romans 6:5–10 (Revised Standard Version). See also Colossians 3.

4. Maya Deren, *Divine Horsemen: The Living Gods of Haiti* (London: Thames and Hudson, 1953).

5. Maria Cramer, *Das altägyptische Lebenszeichen im christlichen (koptischen) Ägypten* (Wiesbaden: O. Harrassowitz, 1955).

6. See *Theologische Realenzyklopädie,* vol. 19 (Berlin: de Gruyter, 1990), 712 (hereafter referred to as *TRE*). See also Jörg Lechler, *Das Hakenkreuz: Die Geschichte eines Symbols* (Leipzig: C. Kabitzsch, 1921); and Thomas Wilson, *The Swastika: The Earliest Known Symbol and Its Migrations* (Washington, D.C.: Government Printing Office, 1896).

7. See Christina von Braun, "Ist die Sexualwissenschaft eine 'jüdische Wissenschaft'? Vortrag zum 50. Jahrestag der Deutschen Gesellschaft für Sexualforschung," *Zeitschrift für Sexualforschung* 1 (2001).

8. See Christina von Braun, "Das ein-gebildete Geschlecht: Bilderverbot, Bilderverehrung und Geschlechterbilder," in *Der Zweite Blick: Bildgeschichte und Bildreflexion,* ed. Hans Belting and Dietmar Kamper (Munich: Fink, 2000).

9. See *TRE,* 723.

10. Gerhardt B. Ladner, "St. Gregory of Nyssa and St. Augustine on Cross Symbolism," in *Late Classical and Mediaeval Studies in Honor of Albert Mathias Friend, Jr.,* ed. Kurt Weitzmann (Princeton, N.J.: Princeton University Press, 1955), 88–95.

11. See Aloys Grillmeier, *Der Logos am Kreuz* (Munich: M. Hueber, 1956).

12. *TRE,* 726; see also Erich Dinkler, *Signum Crucis* (Tübingen: Mohr, 1967).

13. As in Gregory of Nazianizus, Or. 45, 21.

14. *TRE,* 726.

15. Ibid., 727.

16. Ibid., 730. See also Joseph Wilpert, *Die römischen Mosaiken und Malereien der kirchlichen Bauten vom 4. bis 12. Jahrhundert* (Freiburg: Herder, 1916).

17. Hans Belting, *Das Bild und sein Publikum im Mittelalter: Form und Funktion früher Bildtafeln der Passion* (Berlin: Mann, 1981); Karl Young, *The Drama of the Medieval Church,* 2 vols. (Oxford: Clarendon, 1933).

18. See Bruno Reudenbach, "Die Gemeinschaft als Körper und Ge-bäude: Francesco di Giorg Stadttheorie und die Visualisierung von Sozial-metaphern im Mittelalter," in *Gepeinigt, begehrt, vergessen: Symbolik und Sozialbezug des Körpers im späten Mittelalter und in der frühen Neuzeit,* ed. Klaus Schreiner and Norbert Schnitzler (Munich: Fink, 1992), 171–98; see also Günter Bandmann, *Mittelalterliche Architektur als Bedeutungsträger* (Berlin: Gebrüder Mann, 1951).

19. As Paul states in Galatians 5:24 (RSV): "Those who belong to Christ Jesus have put to death their human nature with its passions and desires."

20. Caesarius von Heisterbach, *Dialogus miraculorum,* ed. Joseph Strange (Cologne: H. Lempertz, 1851), distinctio 8, chap. 19.

21. *TRE,* 748.

22. See Leo Steinberg, *The Sexuality of Christ in Renaissance Art and in Modern Oblivion,* 2nd ed. (New York: Pantheon Books, 1983; Chicago: University of Chicago Press, 1996), 53.

23. *TRE,* 754. See also Kurt Bauch, "Christus am Kreuz und der Heilige Franziskus," in *Eine Gabe der Freunde für Carl Georg Heise zum 28.6.1950,* ed. Erich Meyer (Berlin: Gebrüder Mann, 1950), 103–12; and Daniel Russo, "Saint François, les Franciscains et les représentations du Christ sur la croix en Ombrie au XIIIe siècle," *Mélanges de l'Ecole française de Rome, Moyen Age* 96 (1984): 647–717.

24. Alberich Altermatt, "Christus pro nobis: Die Christologie Bern-hards von Clairvaux in den 'Sermones per annum,'" *Analecta Cisterciensia* 33 (1977): 3–176.

25. Oktavian Schmukki (von Rieden), "Das Leiden Christi im Leben des Heiligen Franziskus von Assisi," *Collectanea Franciscana* 30 (1960): 5–30; Optatus van Asseldonk, "François d'Assise, imitateur du Christ cru-cifié, Dieu-Homme, dans la tradition françiscaine et capucine," *Collectanea Franciscana* 52 (1982): 117–43.

26. "The head, contorted from pain, is deeply sunken; the body is turned into itself and has wasted away so much that the ribs strongly protrude. In addition to this, it is marked by drops of blood and other traces of the Passion, and from the wounds—most especially from the wound in his side—blood springs forth" (*TRE,* 757).

27. Ibid., 755.

28. For a history of Christian self-flagellation, see the illuminating book by Niklaus Largier, *Lob der Peitsche: Eine Kulturgeschichte der Erregung* (Munich: C. H. Beck, 2001).

29. See Peter Brown's excellent portrayal, *The Body and Society: Men, Women, and Sexual Renunciation in Early Christianity* (New York: Columbia University Press, 1988).

30. See Brian Stock, *The Implications of Literacy: Written Language and Models of Interpretation in the Eleventh and Twelfth Centuries* (Princeton, N.J.: Princeton University Press, 1983).

31. See David S. Landes, *Revolution in Time: Clocks and the Making of the Modern World* (Cambridge, Mass.: Belknap, 1983).

32. The connection between the German *Mal* (mark, instance, time) and *Malerei* (painting) was a preoccupation of Walter Benjamin. See Walter Benjamin, "Fragmente, Ausgewählte Schriften, Ästhetische Fragmente" (1917), in *Gesammelte Schriften,* ed. Rolf Tiedemann and Herrmann Schweppenhäuser (Frankfurt am Main: Suhrkamp, 1982), 613ff. *Mal,* which denotes both "mark" and a period of time (of eating: German, *das Mahl* [the meal]), is in fact etymologically related to *malen* (to paint), which actually means "to apply a mark." In addition to this, Christianity establishes a sensual relation between *Wundmal* (stigmata) and the *Mahl* (meal), or *Heiligen Abendmahl* (Eucharist).

33. Meister Eckehart, *Deutsche Predigten und Traktate,* ed. and trans. Josef Quint (Zurich: Diogenes, 1979), 399.

34. See Joseph Deér, "Das Kaiserbild im Kreuz: Ein Beitrag zur politischen Theologie des frühen Mittelalters," *Schweizer Beiträge zur allgemeinen Geschichte* 13 (1955): 48–110.

35. See the excellent study by Ernst H. Kantorowicz, *The King's Two Bodies: A Study in Medieval Political Theology* (Princeton, N.J.: Princeton University Press, 1957).

36. Otto Treitinger, *Die oströmische Kaiser- und Reichsidee nach ihrer Gestaltung im höfischen Zeremoniell* (Jena: W. Biedermann, 1938). See also *TRE,* 740.

37. *TRE,* 751.

38. Quoted in Caroline Walker Bynum, *Fragmentation and Redemption: Essays on Gender and the Human Body in Medieval Religion* (New York: Zone Books, 1991), 96. The chapter in Bynum's book that refers to Steinberg's

thesis, "The Body of Christ in the Later Middle Ages: A Reply to Leo Steinberg," is not included in the German edition of Bynum's book: *Fragmentierung und Erlösung* (Frankfurt am Main: Suhrkamp, 1995).

39. Quoted in Bynum, *Fragmentation and Redemption*, 97.

40. Steinberg, *Sexuality of Christ*, 83.

41. Ibid., 46.

42. Ibid., 18.

43. Ibid., 24.

44. Martin Luther, *Martin Luthers Werke: Kritische Gesammtausgabe*, vol. 18, chap. 83, pp. 9–10.

45. Jakob Böhme, *Von der Menschwerdung Gottes*, in *Sämtliche Werke*, ed. K.W. Schiebler (Leipzig: Johann Ambrosius Barth, 1843), 105.

46. See Esther Fischer-Homberger, "Krankheit Frau: Aus der Geschichte der Menstruation in ihrem Aspekt als Zeichen eines Fehlers," in *Krankheit Frau* (Darmstadt: Luchterhand, 1984), 34ff.

47. As in the words of Paracelsus, *Opus Paramirum*, in *Volumen Paramirum und Opum Paramirum*, ed. Franz Strunz (Jena: Diedrichs, 1904), 155. See also Hanns Bächtold-Stäubli, ed., *Handwörterbuch des deutschen Aberglaubens*, vol. 2 (Berlin: de Gruyter, 1929–30), col. 1756.

48. See Christina von Braun, "Die kulturelle Codierung des männlichen und des weiblichen Körpers," in special issue, ed. Regina Amnicht Quinn and Elsa Tamez, *Concilium* 38, no. 2 (2002): 133–43.

49. In Greece, menstrual blood was designated as the "supernatural red wine" that mother Hera—as Hebe (the Greek goddess of youth)—gave to the gods. See Robert Graves, *The Greek Myths* (Baltimore, Md.: Penguin, 1955), 188.

50. See Largier, *Lob der Peitsche*.

51. George Mosse translates *Der Eigene* as *The Personalist*. See George Mosse, *The Image of Man: The Creation of Modern Masculinity* (New York: Howard Fertig, 1985), 42.

52. See Mario Praz, *The Romantic Agony* (New York: Oxford University Press, 1951); in translation as *Liebe, Tod und Teufel* (Munich: C. Hanser, 1963), 194.

53. Quoted in Praz, *Romantic Agony*, 211.

54. See Edouard Roditi, *Oscar Wilde: Dichter und Dandy* (Munich: Herbert Kluger, 1947), 143.

55. See Joris-Karl Huysmans, *Gegen den Strich [A Rebours]*, trans. Franz Jacob (Zurich: Diogenes, 1985).

56. Theodor Fritsch, *Antisemiten-Katechismus: Eine Zusammenstellung des wichtigsten Materials zum Verständnis der Judenfrage* (Leipzig, 1887), 313.

57. See Christina von Braun, "Blutschande: From the Incest Taboo to the Nuremberg Racial Laws," in *Encountering the Other(s): Studies in Litera-*

ture, History and Culture, ed. Gisela Brinker-Gabler (Buffalo: State University of New York Press, 1995).

58. Otto Weininger, *Geschlecht und Charakter,* 16th ed. (Vienna and Leipzig: Wilhelm Braumüller, 1917), 415–16. All English translations of Weininger's book have been taken from Weininger, *Sex and Character,* authorized translation from the 6th German edition (London: William Heinemann/New York: G. P. Putnam's Sons, 1906); this quote is from p. 187.

59. Weininger, *Geschlecht und Charakter,* 449–50; *Sex and Character,* 200.

60. See Martin Gilbert, *Kristallnacht: Prelude to Destruction* (New York: HarperCollins, 2006).

61. See Geoffrey J. Giles, "The Institutionalization of Homosexual Panic in the Third Reich," in *Social Outsiders in Nazi Germany,* ed. Robert Gellately and Nathan Stoltzfus (Princeton, N.J.: Princeton University Press, 2001), 233–55.

62. See Dagmar Herzog, *Sex After Fascism: Memory and Morality in Twentieth-Century Germany* (Princeton, N.J.: Princeton University Press, 2005).

Jürgen Zimmerer

The First Genocide of the Twentieth Century: The German War of Destruction in South-West Africa (1904–1908) and the Global History of Genocide

[I] FOLLOWED THEIR TRACKS AND CAME UPON SEVERAL WELLS, where I beheld a terrible sight. Dead cattle lay in heaps around them. Having reached the wells with their last strength, they had no longer been able to drink. The Herero continued to flee ahead of us into the Sandveld. Over and over, the terrible spectacle repeated itself. In feverish haste, the men had worked on digging wells, but water became increasingly sparse and watering holes more rare. They fled from one to another and lost almost all of their cattle and a great many of their people. Slowly falling into our hands, their numbers shrank to a meager remnant; some escaped then and later through the Sandveld into English territory. It was an equally absurd as well as gruesome policy to destroy these people in this way. If we had spared them and welcomed them back, many of them, along with their wealth of cattle, could have still been saved; they had certainly been sufficiently punished. I suggested this to General von Trotha, but he wanted their complete destruction.[1]

This eyewitness account of Major Ludwig von Estorff documents firsthand the German policy of destruction in South-West Africa. Major von Estorff was the commander of one of the cavalry units that pursued the Herero people after the "battle" of Hamakari (Waterberg) in August 1904 into the Sandveld of the Omaheke Desert. Although the career officer von Estorff had most certainly seen his share of violence and cruelty, he was noticeably disturbed by what he had experienced. He used a code when he spoke about the cattle

that had succumbed to thirst. What he meant were dying human beings, men and women, children and the old. As we know from other
sources, thousands of Herero died in the cruelest manner imaginable
in the desert. They cut the arteries of their cattle to quench their thirst
with the blood and tried to squeeze the last drops of liquid from the
contents of their livestock's stomachs.[2]

Von Estorff's account is a remarkable testimony to one of the darkest chapters in German history, a chapter that has largely disappeared
from Germany's public consciousness, pushed aside by the memory of
both world wars with their millions of victims and, above all, by the
incomprehensible crimes of the Holocaust. It could easily be ignored,
since many Germans wish to extirpate the Nazi past by presenting
a more positive, immaculate picture of German history before those
fateful twelve years. Yet the occurrences in German South-West Africa,
today's Namibia, during the years 1904–8 reveal a number of things
about the destructive and misanthropic potential that was an integral
part of the military and bureaucratic institutions of imperial Germany,
long before the Nazis came to power.

In the minds of many people, connections between colonial and
Nazi practices of murder cannot be allowed to exist, because the thesis
of unprecedented Nazi crimes saves German national history prior to
1933. Indeed, for a long time German colonial history—if it was not
forgotten that such a thing had existed in the first place—has been
held up as exemplary, as humanely focused on the cultural "education"
of the "natives." How and why this view, which was shaped by the
popular response during the Weimar Republic to the "colonial guilt
lie" in the Treaty of Versailles, was upheld for so long in the Federal
Republic, is an interesting phenomenon in itself.

Does examining the German genocide in Africa contribute to
understanding the Holocaust? Whoever looks for simple answers to
this question will be disappointed. There are no monocausal explanations for Nazi crimes, nor is there a linear progression from German
colonialism to the murder of the European Jews. Auschwitz was neither
the logical consequence of the events in South-West Africa nor was
it, as seen from Windhoek, inevitable. Auschwitz, to use this image,
happened because the Nazis were in power in Germany and because
the majority of Germans apparently shared the antisemitic and racial
views of their leadership or found it neither necessary nor worth their
while to oppose those views. And still, there is a connection between

the colonial adventures of the Wilhelmine empire and Nazi crimes, the Holocaust, and the war of annihilation in the East. The colonial example illustrates the genocidal potential already present in parts of the bureaucratic and military institutions of Germany.

In addition, colonialism produced a reservoir of cultural practices that Nazi thugs could appropriate for themselves. Even when they did not draw directly from this cultural reservoir, Nazi perpetrators could, to a certain degree, legitimize their actions by pointing to similarities with colonial times. Elsewhere I have analyzed three trajectories of colonial knowledge: personal experience, institutional memory, and collective imagination.[3] Intellectual familiarity with genocidal policy, racial thinking, and social Darwinian population management was key to enabling a relatively large number of Germans, without much hesitation, to participate both in the Nazi occupation and in the war of destruction. In particular, the positive connotations associated with European colonial rule until well beyond the middle of the twentieth century may have helped contemporaries veil the criminal character of German rule. Familiarity with the expulsion and destruction of entire peoples, with resettlement and slavery that benefited the German "masters," familiarity with the most brutal "struggle against partisans" and annihilation through neglect, allowed perpetrators to contextualize events "in the East" during World War II as a historically normal, colonial process. Whoever so desired could therefore legitimize what he was experiencing.

That in reality German colonial rule had been much more complex, not monolithic, does not change the findings. Most important was how colonialism was imagined during the Third Reich and also that German colonial rule, especially in German South-West Africa, was marked by terrible brutality. This brutality was common knowledge in Germany. The most conspicuous characteristic of the genocide of the Herero was undoubtedly the fact that no one sought to conceal it. On the contrary, the events were popularized through countless memoirs, official reports, and novels. It was, for example, openly presented in the official German military chronicle:

> This bold undertaking shows the merciless energy of the German leadership during the pursuit of the defeated enemy in a glorious light. No effort, no deprivation was too great to rob the enemy of their last will to resist; like game that had been nearly chased

to death, the enemy was pursued from watering hole to watering hole, until he finally became, no longer possessing a will of his own, the victim of the nature of his own land. The waterless Omaheke brought to an end what the German weapons had begun: the extermination of the Herero nation.[4]

No words of pity, no words of regret. "Mission accomplished," the reader was probably supposed to think. But the report is not entirely accurate. Though German actions were indeed extremely brutal in nature, the campaign was not quite as victorious as the official historiography suggested.[5] The Herero had been successful in their resistance, and several thousand of them survived the horror of the Omaheke. They managed to sustain the Herero nation and were able either to resurrect or build anew their destroyed political and cultural structures. The projected image of a German military machinery that proceeded with absolute precision and power is therefore misleading.[6]

In addition, not everyone believed that the policy of destruction was successful and sensible. Major von Estorff, for example, was not of the opinion that the strategy to "destroy" the Herero had been successful, let alone sensible. Von Estorff stood out from among his fellow officers because he was an "old Africa hand," a soldier who had already been stationed in the German South-West African colony prior to the war. The first governor, Theodor Leutwein, was also such an officer, and he too criticized the strategy of his successor, General von Trotha. Leutwein, however, could not assert himself. Within a few months of the outbreak of the war, he was more or less forcibly demoted. He was seen as too lenient toward the African population. Full of bitterness, Leutwein commented that, with the help of several hundred million Reichsmarks and the engagement of several thousand soldiers, of the three pillars of the German colonial economy—mines, cattle, and the African workforce—the second had been completely and the latter two-thirds destroyed. Why had it come to this catastrophe?

CAUSES OF THE WAR

Germany entered the history of formal colonial rule very late, because prior to 1871 it had lacked the national framework to do so. After the founding of the empire in 1871, however, an enthusiastic public demanded that Germany too must have its share in the partitioning of the globe. These voices eventually became so loud that Chancellor Otto von Bismarck agreed in 1884 to the formal acquisition of colonies.[7] Until then he had always rejected the idea. In the course of a few years, the areas roughly of today's African states Togo, Cameroon, Tanzania, and Namibia, as well as a few smaller holdings in the South Seas, were declared German protectorates.[8] Due to the climate, only German South-West Africa was suitable for permanent settlement by Germans. This circumstance fueled the fantasies of a generation of Germans and would prove decisive in the shaping of Namibia's history.[9]

In 1885, Reichskommissar Heinrich Göring and two of his colleagues took formal possession of the colony. However, this was little more than a symbolic act. It must have been clear to those responsible within the empire that with the help of only three bureaucrats they could not establish a functional bureaucracy within this huge territory, a territory where toward the end of the nineteenth century approximately ninety thousand to one hundred thousand Ovambi, seventy thousand to eighty thousand Herero, fifteen thousand to twenty thousand Nama, thirty thousand to forty thousand Bergdamera and San, and three thousand to four thousand Basters lived. Not until the first governor, Theodor Leutwein, took office in 1893 did the systematic establishment of German rule and the methodical building of a German bureaucracy commence. The increasing sophistication of the bureaucratic structures amply illustrates this process. In 1894 the protectorate was divided into three regions, Keetmanshoop, Windhoek, and Otjimbingwee. By 1903 this number had already doubled, and in 1914 sixteen regions, along with independent districts that oversaw police stations, existed.[10]

Leutwein and his young administrators also began implementing a utopian vision for colonial rule, with the ultimate goal of building a model colonial state based on racial ideology. Through a variety of treaties with African rulers like Samuel Maharero and Hendrick Witbooi, to name only the two most important, the colonizers superficially secured the territory for the short term, in an effort to convert the African societies into a "black working class." Though not to be left completely without rights, Africans would nonetheless face severe discrimination. This aim was directly tied to the continuous expansion of the German bureaucracy. Accompanying the entire process was the concept of a "master class" made up of the increasingly numerous German settlers entering the country. Fraud, murder, and rape of Africans, as well as the continued land disenfranchisement of the Herero, ultimately led to war.[11]

COURSE OF THE WAR

Current research still disputes who fired the first shot in 1904.[12] Much evidence, however, points to the fact that the provocations of Lieutenant Zürn, district chief of Okahandja, contributed to the escalation. It is certain that the attack by the Herero on January 12 was unexpectedly successful, partly because the German colonial army was engaged in another conflict in the south of the country. Within only a few days, the Herero occupied the whole of central South-West Africa, with the exception of military establishments, and had plundered settlements and farms. Rumors of the murder and maiming of hundreds of men, women, and children spread like wildfire and contributed in no small way to the radicalization of the war. As became evident later on, during these initial raids, a total of 123 Germans lost their lives. However, the Herero, following the orders of their leaders, had in fact spared women and children as well as missionaries and even led some of them to German settlements.

The Herero did not use their early successes to force a quick victory on the barricaded Germans. Instead, the latter were able to gather their strength and increase their numbers with additional soldiers from the empire. Because of these quickly deployed troops, impending defeat was averted. A series of small skirmishes followed without a decisive victory on either side. Newly arrived reserve troops and incensed settlers engaged in acts of retaliation and committed massacres that drove the remaining neutral Herero into the war. Everywhere there was talk of "cleaning up, hanging, battering down to the last man, of showing no mercy."[13] However, these were uncoordinated, individual attacks, not a systematic strategy.

Nevertheless, a certain rhetoric anticipating genocide was already developing. It was clearly reminiscent of Emperor Wilhelm II's infamous *Hunnenrede,* in which he admonished troops on their way to China to crush the Boxer Rebellion to be particularly brutal. In the first few months of the war, this kind of agitation became so strong that Leutwein had to step in to defuse the situation. Even though he shared the demand for the unconditional capitulation of the Herero, he warned about the "rash voices . . . who want the Herero's complete destruction." In his opinion, not only philanthropic reasons stood in the way of this course of action. Aside from the fact that a nation of sixty thousand to seventy thousand people "would not let itself be so easily exterminated," Leutwein believed that the Germans still needed the Herero as "small cattle breeders and especially as laborers." That they were to be "politically silenced," their social structures destroyed, and their people forced into "barely adequate" reservations, he saw, on the other hand, as a legitimate aim of the war.[14] Individual "guilt" was not a decisive factor in this "punishment." Expressly, uninvolved Africans should also submit to their disarmament and to their "incarceration within the reservations." Although Leutwein did not demand mass murder, even in his view, a politically and socially independent future for the Herero no longer existed as early as February 23, 1904, a mere forty days after battles had commenced. Though they had not (yet) physically been slain, in the German plan, the Herero were already politically dead.

It is necessary to point out a few misunderstandings regarding the interpretation of the history of the war and the postwar period. Political and military aims do not instantly become reality, and orders and commands must not be mistaken for their actual execution, let alone for their effectiveness. During the first days of the war, German settlers, soldiers, and bureaucrats did not become passive victims of their African adversaries but developed defense strategies instead. Once the colonial army gained the upper hand, the Herero also reacted flexibly to developments. Just like the Germans, the Herero—as well as the Nama—were at no time passive victims. Nonetheless, the German army displayed such brutality in South-West Africa that it reduced the Hereros' ability to act autonomously to a minimum. Though the Herero continued to react in a skillful and to an extent even successful manner to increasing German pressure, thus securing the survival of their nation, the extremely repressive nature of German policy must not be minimized in the effort to highlight this autonomy.

Colonial rule was marked, as postcolonial authors rightfully stress, by a multitude of possible interactions, and hence relations between master and servant were negotiable. A genocidal war of destruction like the one Germany waged in South-West Africa, however, was aimed at the elimination of the colonial other. It represents one of the most extreme forms of unequal master-servant relations throughout history. It is important, not least to preserve a dignified memory of the victims, to name this genocidal situation openly, rather than cloaking it with an emphasis on flexible interactions and on a few individual, successful survival strategies. The war meant certain death for tens of thousands. There was nothing to negotiate.

THE DECISION TO COMMIT GENOCIDE

The decision of the leadership in Berlin not to allow Governor Theodor Leutwein and the local colonial army to lead the campaign proved decisive in escalating the war to the first genocide in German history. Instead, this task was given to General Lothar von Trotha, a protégé of the influential chief of the general staff, Count Alfred von Schlieffen. During the colonial wars in German East Africa (1894–97) and in China (1900–1901), von Trotha had already acquired a reputation as a particularly ruthless officer. In 1907 he would add to his record in China. Although he knew neither the land nor the people of South-West Africa, he nonetheless had very firm ideas about a future "racial war." Africans, he believed, would only "yield to force." He was willing to apply this force "with blatant terrorism and even with cruelty." "The rebellious tribes" should be "finished off with streams of blood."[15] Hence, when von Trotha set foot on South-West African soil, he may not have known exactly how he would conduct the war, but he did already know how it would end: with the destruction of the Herero. Factors such as the radicalization in response to military developments like the "battle" of Hamakari or unfavorable natural conditions that wore on German troops were merely secondary considerations.[16]

While still in transit, von Trotha declared martial law in South-West Africa and empowered his officers immediately to shoot all armed "rebels." In his words:

> a. Every commanding officer is authorized to have the following colored inhabitants shot without prior trial and in accordance with the existing German manual for war: those who are caught committing a treasonous act against German troops; for example, all armed rebels with war-like intentions.
>
> b. All other colored inhabitants arrested by German military personnel and who are suspected of having committed criminal acts will be tried by a special field court.

    c. The troops are to be educated that the autonomous dispensing of penalties against colored inhabitants will be severely punished in accordance with the laws on inflicting bodily harm, manslaughter, and murder. The use of weapons outside of combat is only permitted for the purposes of self-defense and to prevent attempted flights.[17]

The intention of this order was twofold. First, von Trotha attempted to shift the spontaneous, illegal actions that had been occurring since the beginning of the war and that had led to literal massacres of Herero at the hands of incensed settlers and soldiers toward a more orderly pattern. He further sought to gain control over the executions his soldiers carried out. Second, although von Trotha's order did put a stop to the arbitrary actions of individuals, he nevertheless made massacres and terror an instrument of German warfare. Whoever resisted the Germans was to be shot. Without a doubt, this measure represents an important radicalization. It was not necessary to protect or treat fairly a prisoner who was seen merely as a rebel acting illegally rather than as an equal opponent. During colonial wars this was a typical conviction, behavior, and course of action.

    When von Trotha arrived in Windhoek, Leutwein tried to dissuade him from his policy of destruction. He attempted to convince him instead to enter into peace negotiations with the Herero. Leutwein cited economic reasons for this course of action and pointed out that the Herero's labor was needed. Von Trotha replied that South-West Africa was allegedly a colony of white settlers and therefore the whites should do the work themselves. The two men's opposing visions for colonial rule—Leutwein's colonial-economic vision and von Trotha's military-genocidal vision—could not be more pointedly illustrated. Von Trotha prevailed. It is revealing that this discussion took place even before the Battle of Hamakari: genocide was already a realistic aim for von Trotha. Military developments were not the cause of his genocidal visions, but merely enabled him to make them a reality.

    The desired battle finally occurred on August 11, 1904, at the Waterberg, where a majority of the Herero nation had gathered with women, children, and herds of cattle. Apparently they anticipated an offer of peace in the spirit of Leutwein's policy. Militarily, the battle ended in favor of the colonial army. However, the greater part of the Herero escaped the trap and fled into the largely waterless Sandveld of the Omaheke semidesert, located in the east of the protectorate. At that point the war had been decided militarily, and the actual genocidal phase commenced, because German troops now began chasing the Herero in a pincer movement ahead of them in the direction of the Omaheke. Already at this juncture, terrible scenes must have unfolded: "Masses of sick and helpless men, women, and children, who had collapsed in exhaustion, lay, tormented by thirst . . . in the bush. No longer possessing a will of their own, they awaited their destiny."[18] Thus reads the official history of the campaign. As Captain Bayer wrote, wherever the pursuing German units came upon Herero, summary executions occurred: "Now and then, whenever our patrols came upon stragglers, a shot was fired to the right and left into the bush."[19]

VON TROTHA'S "GENOCIDE ORDER"

To the German military leadership, it now seemed possible that the Omaheke could bring to a conclusion "what German weapons had begun: the annihilation of the Herero nation," as it was written in the above-cited passage of the official war chronicles. German soldiers therefore systematically occupied all known watering holes along the edges of the desert, and at the beginning of October von Trotha, in his infamous proclamation, ordered that all returning Herero be shot:

> The Herero are no longer German subjects. They have murdered and stolen, they have cut noses and ears and other body parts from wounded soldiers. And now out of cowardice they no longer want to fight. I say to the people: Whoever brings one of their captains as a prisoner to one of my stations will receive one thousand Marks. Whoever turns in Samuel Maharero receives five thousand Marks. The nation of the Herero, however, must leave the country. If they will not go, I will force them with the Groot Rohr [i.e., cannon]. Within the German border every Herero, with or without a rifle, with or without cattle, will be shot. I will no longer grant sanctuary to women and children. Chase them back to their people or let them be shot.[20]

Von Trotha further clarified that, in order to preserve the good reputation of German soldiers, the order "to shoot women and children" was to be understood as "shooting above their heads to force them to run." He "was certain that this decree would lead to no more male prisoners and would also not degenerate into cruelty toward women and children." The latter would certainly "run if shot twice above their heads."[21] But their only retreat was the Omaheke where, as a consequence of this decree, thousands died of thirst.

Considering the military situation along with the geographic location where this proclamation was issued, it becomes apparent that genocide had indeed been the objective. Though the talk is of "expulsion," the only possible escape was to the waterless area. This fact alone would already be considered a particularly brutal course of action during a colonial war, although not yet genocide. However, the passage in question serves merely as camouflage. Reading the "genocide order" along with a letter von Trotha composed two days later to the General Staff in Berlin illuminates the intentions of the former:

> The only question I am posing to myself now is how to end the war with the Herero. The opinions of the governor and some of the "old Africa hands" on this subject differ greatly from mine. For quite some time, there has been a desire on the part of the former to enter into peace negotiations, and they are calling the Herero nation a necessary labor force for the future. I am of a completely different opinion. I believe that the nation as it currently exists must be destroyed, or, if that proves tactically not possible, they must be expelled from the country via further operations and individual actions. Through the successful occupation of watering holes from Grootfontein to Gobabis and through the active movement of the columns, it might be possible to find those groups of their people who have begun flowing back toward the west and finish them off.[22]

Researchers of genocide have established that in order to commence a war of destruction, and in particular a genocide, certain processes of exclusion are necessary that prevent a possible identification between perpetrator and victim. The potential victims must be dehumanized. They must be robbed of their human dignity and must be placed outside the sphere of moral responsibility. They must be banned from the circle of those "whom we are committed to protecting and whom we have a duty to take seriously and toward whom we have a responsibility."[23] Racism, the inherent crutch of colonialism, had already set the stage for this process. It was further strengthened by negative propaganda that spread at the outbreak of the war. Hence, immediately after January 12, 1904, it was said that the Herero had "slaughtered" women and children and maimed their victims.

In his proclamation, von Trotha specifically made reference to this accusation in order to justify his policy of murder and expulsion. Applying this logic, the Herero themselves were made responsible for what was happening to them, due to the allegedly inhumane way they had conducted the war. They were the "barbarians" and "savages" standing opposite the "civilized" and "disciplined" German army. It should be noted, however, that nearly without exception the Herero spared women and children, whereas many German soldiers deliberately waged war against them.

Von Trotha's proclamation did not mark the beginning of the genocide, which was already in progress at that point. But it helped to legitimize it, and it proves that genocide was the intention of the German army. Von Trotha was serious about the annihilation of the Herero. It was not just a matter of breaking their armed resistance. This was a matter of the mass murder of men, women, and children, warriors and non-warriors, old and young; mass murder that the responsible military leaders in Berlin looked upon as normal—as explained in an official war chronicle—and that no one attempted to cover up. It was the deliberate inclusion of women and children in this war, the intentional physical destruction of an entire people, that made what happened in the colony into the first genocide in German history.

After World War II, the United Nations legally defined the term *genocide* as follows:

> any of the following acts committed with the intent to destroy, in whole or in part, a national, ethnic, racial or religious group, such as:
>
> a. Killing members of the group;
>
> b. Causing serious bodily harm or mental harm to members of the group;
>
> c. Deliberately inflicting on the group conditions of life calculated to bring about its physical destruction in whole or in part;
>
> d. Imposing measures intended to prevent births within the group;
>
> e. Forcibly transferring children of the group to another group.[24]

Using this definition as the basis of a historical analysis, the actions of von Trotha and the German army must be classified as genocide.

Even the fact that Emperor Wilhelm II reversed von Trotha's "genocide order" after a few weeks does not change this finding. By that time, the crime had already been committed.[25]

It was not due to humanitarian concerns that von Trotha's order was overturned in December 1904. Rather, Berlin was afraid other countries could use it against the German Empire for propaganda purposes. But above all, military requirements demanded a change in strategy. The existing strategy ultimately foundered on the vastness of the land and on the typhus and malaria epidemics plaguing the colonial army troops. It made the constant patrol of the entire edge of the desert impossible and, as a consequence, small groups of Herero regularly penetrated German lines in secret and returned to the protectorate. Only their voluntary submission along with their internment until the end of the war could ward off the danger they posed.

THE WAR OF DESTRUCTION AGAINST THE NAMA

While the battle against scattered pockets of Herero and "the misguided actions against the entire unfortunate nation" detained "a great military force in this thankless task," as von Estorff wrote, German troops were soon needed elsewhere.[26] In the south of the country the Nama had in the meantime also taken up the struggle against the Germans. Bound by "defensive alliances," parts of the Nama nation had continued to provide military aid to the Germans until the Battle of Hamakari, after which they turned against the Germans.[27] Because of this new development, even Chief of the General Staff von Schlieffen ultimately pleaded for the reversal of the genocide order. He did so without distancing himself from von Trotha's strategy, as he wrote to the chancellor:

> I can agree with his [von Trotha's] quest either to destroy the entire nation or to drive them from the country. . . . The burning racial struggle can only end with the destruction or complete enslavement of the one party. Under the present circumstances, the latter course of action is, however, not sustainable for the duration. General v. Trotha's intentions can therefore be condoned. He merely lacks the power to implement them.[28]

Von Trotha also lacked this power because the Nama waged an extremely successful guerrilla war. They had recognized the difficulties associated with the colonial army's pursuit of the fleeing Herero. Consequently, they avoided an open battle and began a guerrilla war. Because they knew the land better than the Germans did and because they possessed greater mobility, they were able to compensate for the advantages held by the more numerous and better equipped colonial troops. They were able to drag the war on and keep many of the colonial forces engaged, eventually wearing them down and destroying them.

The Germans reacted to the Nama with a strategy of extermination, and they systematically occupied watering holes, so that their opponents—as in the Omaheke—would succumb to thirst. The deliberate destruction of the livelihoods of those who supported the guerrillas was a tactic that had been tested during von Trotha's tenure in German East Africa. Already during the punitive expeditions against the local Wahehe people in the 1890s, burning villages and crops and "eating up the land of the Mkwawa [Leader of the Wahehe]," as Governor Eduard von Liebert wrote, was seen as a promising tactic.[29] Likewise in the war against the Maji-Maji in German East Africa, taking place almost at the same time as the war against the Herero and the Nama, it was part of the colonial army's tactics "to appropriate the opponent's possessions (cattle, reserves) and to devastate his villages and crops," as could be read in a military memorandum. The goal was the erosion of the crucial popular support of guerrilla fighters through the destruction of people's livelihoods and their infrastructure.[30]

As in the war against the Herero, the Germans tactically employed the hostile living conditions found in parts of the country against the Nama. Once again the campaign turned into a war against women and children, whose deaths were accepted, if not desired, as part of the strategy of extermination.

The Concentration Camps

At the same time, the Germans banked on the "cleansing" of the country through mass internments. Hence von Trotha called on the Nama to surrender, because otherwise they might meet the same fate as the Herero:

> To the rebelling Nama.
> The powerful and great German Emperor would like to show mercy to the nation of the Nama, so that those who surrender

on their own accord will be granted their lives. Only those who at the beginning of the rebellion murdered whites or gave orders that they should be murdered have, according to the law, forfeited their lives. This I tell you, and I further say to you that those few who will not submit will face what the nation of the Herero has faced. In their delusion they believed they could wage a successful war against the powerful German Emperor and the great German people. I ask you, where is the Herero nation today, where are their chiefs today? Samuel Maharero, who once called thousands of cattle his own, ran, chased like a wild animal, across the English border. He has become as poor as the poorest of the Field-Herero and no longer owns anything. The other nobles, most of whom have lost their lives, and the entire Herero nation have fared the same. Some died of hunger and thirst in the Sandveld, some were killed by German cavalry, some were slain by the Ovambos. If it does not surrender and give up its weapons, the nation of the Nama will not fare any differently. You shall come to us with your weapons and with a white cloth on a stick and nothing shall happen to you. You shall receive work and food until, after the end of the war, the great German Emperor orders the territory anew. Whoever hereafter believes that this offer of mercy does not apply to him shall emigrate, because wherever he is spotted within the German territory, he will be shot at until all have been annihilated. For the handing over of those guilty of murder, dead or alive, I set the following reward: For Hendrik Witbooi five thousand Marks, Stürmann three thousand Marks, for all other guilty leaders one thousand Marks. Signed Trotha.[31]

This call to capitulate only appears to abandon the policy of genocide. It is the fate that awaited the Nama in captivity that is the decisive factor in judging the military leadership's intention. Therefore it can, with complete justification, be called a continuation of the murderous policy, because the camps to which the Nama were deported represented another instrument of the war of extermination. These were a part of the camp system established across the country immediately following the reversal of the genocide order. This system included "collection camps," operated by the mission and used to bring scattered and hidden Hereros under control, and concentration camps, established and operated by the military administration. Along with the actual "concentration" of the Herero and Nama to prevent them from supporting fighters, the latter also served as labor camps, providing urgently needed labor to state institutions. At the same time, it was hoped that by "educating" prisoners in the camps "to work," they could be disciplined and prepared for their new "role" as laborers in the postwar period, as Governor von Lindquist wrote in 1906:

> Utilizing the Herero as laborers during their captivity has proven very salutary for the same, yes, indeed it is their good fortune that they learn to work before they are given back their full freedom. Otherwise, they would most likely continue to mill about in the country shirking work and, since they have lost all their cattle, they would lead a wretched life.[32]

This conviction was joined by the thought of revenge. In response to the conditions prevailing in the concentration camp Swakopmund—by no means uncommon—Deputy Governor Tecklenburg stated the following in 1905:

> The more the Herero nation physically experiences the consequences of the rebellion, the less likely they will, for generations, lust for a repetition of the revolt. Our actual military successes have made less of an impression. I believe the period of suffering they are currently living through promises a more enduring result, though without, by expressing this opinion, wanting to break the lance for General Lieutenant v. Trotha's Proclamation from October 2 last year. Economically speaking, however, the death of so many people represents a loss.[33]

The Camp on Shark Island and "Annihilation Through Neglect"

Worse conditions prevailed on Shark Island near Lüderitzbucht, the largest of the prisoner camps. Herero as well as Nama were interned there and left to their fate, and once more the threshold to genocide was crossed. Eyewitness Missionary Laaf from Lüderitzbucht described the conditions:

> At the time about two thousand Herero prisoners of war were interned at the farthest end of Shark Island. . . . As long as people were in good health, they worked for the troops and for other whites. For this purpose they were allowed to leave Shark Island, but returned every evening. . . . Due to the great exertions and deprivations the prisoners had endured in the field, they were very weak and much misery and illness reigned among them. To make

matters worse, the wet and harsh sea climate did not suit them initially, and they had also been forcibly removed from their familiar surroundings. It was mostly scurvy and intestinal ailments that forced people onto the sick bed and a certain percentage died at the time. . . . On September 7, 1906, yet another large transport of prisoners of war arrived in Lüderitzbucht from the North. That time they were Nama from various tribes, primarily Witboois and Bethanier. Under the leadership of Captain Samuel Isaak, they had surrendered to the Germans at Gibeon. Including women and children, their numbers totaled 1,700 persons. Regrettably, with their transfer to Lüderitzbucht a great injustice was done to these people. After surrendering their weapons, both sides had mutually agreed that these prisoners should be settled in the Gibeon district. No wonder that they, with Samuel Isaak first among them, harbored a great wrath against the German government in their hearts. A period of suffering and misery had now begun for these people. They were settled on the furthest tip of Shark Island. . . .

Above all they did not receive the nourishment that the conditions demanded. The refined German flour they received was unsuitable for baking bread, and unrefined flour from the Cape was not brought in. Though they received plenty of legumes, they could not cook them. Fresh meat was an extreme rarity. When Samuel Isaak complained to Missionary Laaf that they received so little meat and the latter advised him to look for the very popular mussels on the beach, he replied: "We have collected all of them, there are none left."

Even worse than these miserable conditions was the isolation in the furthest corner of Shark Island that contributed to the obliteration of the people's will to live. They eventually became indifferent to their suffering. By three tall, barbed-wire fences they were separated from the world. . . .

The number of sick increased daily. To profitably employ the people, the tribes had initially started work on a sizable blasting operation. The aim was to create a quay facing Roberts Harbor. At the outset, about five hundred men had been employed for this blasting operation. Within a short period of time, however, their numbers shrank so drastically that work had to be halted. There was hardly a hut left in which one or more sick could not be found. A few large rooms, also built from sacks, were turned into an infirmary. The care, however, was by no means attuned to the needs of the sick. Food was placed in front of those suffering from scurvy and then the saying was: "Eat bird or die." If there was no rela-

tive who took pity and who helped the sick, he could starve to
death. . . . At the time mortality rates were shockingly high. On
some days up to twenty-seven deaths occurred. The dead were
taken to the cemetery by the cartloads.[34]

Not even the need for laborers could move those responsible to
provide better conditions for the prisoners. They accepted instead the
cessation of construction work. That behind all of this also lurked a
murderous intent is confirmed by a statement attributed to the regional
commander Berthold von Deimling and recorded by Missionary Laaf.
Von Deimling cynically replied to the charges that conditions on Shark
Island were unbearable and that the camp should be transferred to the
mainland, where better climatic conditions could be found, "that for
as long as he [Deimling] had a say, no Nama must leave Shark Island
alive."[35] Although the "genocide order" had been reversed and von
Trotha had been recalled to Germany in November 1905, a segment
of the officers apparently clung to his policy of extermination.

The conditions on Shark Island finally improved when Ludwig
von Estorff was named commander of the colonial army. Even prior
to this command, he had been one of von Trotha's critics. He felt
that his honor as an officer had been wounded and he therefore no
longer wanted to take responsibility for these "executioner duties,"
particularly since there were among the prisoners those who had been
promised different treatment upon their surrender.[36] In April 1907
he therefore ordered the camp to be moved to the mainland. Consequently, the mortality rate immediately and sharply declined due to
the better climatic conditions.

In the camp on Shark Island murder was deliberately committed
through neglect. The selection of victims was based solely on their
actual or assumed ethnicity; individually committed "crimes" or acts
of resistance played no role in the motive for internment. The intent was to destroy entire "tribes" or, in the eyes of Germans, "racial
units." Therefore, this policy can be judged according to point c of
the United Nations Genocide Convention ("deliberately inflicting
on the group conditions of life calculated to bring about its physical
destruction in whole or in part")—to say nothing of the killing of
individual members of the group (point a) or of the "causing of serious bodily or mental harm to members of the group" (point b) that
also marked the survivors. These homicides already show signs of a

bureaucratization of the process because the inmates were counted and guarded. The bureaucracy is also visible in the administration of death, such as in the form of preprinted death certificates reading "death through exhaustion."

Even though conditions in the concentration camp on Shark Island were particularly horrific, elsewhere prisoners also died in massive numbers. According to an account of the colonial army, between October 1904 and March 1907, a total of 7,682 inmates died. This number corresponds to between 30 and 50 percent of the total inmate population. Even though the end of the war had already been declared on March 31, 1907, the captivity of prisoners of war was not formally ended until January 27, 1908, on the *Kaisers Geburtstag* (the birthday of Emperor Wilhelm II), when the last of the Herero and Nama were released.

COLONIALISM, RACISM, AND GENOCIDE

The study of the genocide of the Herero and the Nama is not an end in itself. It is also more than merely a contribution to Namibian history. It holds meaning both for German history and for the general history of genocide.[37] When von Trotha spoke of a racial war that had to end with victory for one side and with the destruction of the other, he moved within a certain discourse and vision that had been deeply influenced by colonial tradition, a vision that was no stranger to genocide.

It is difficult to summarize the five-hundred-year history of European colonization in just a few lines. In particular, research conducted under the auspices of postcolonialism in recent years has placed an increased importance on regional and epochal differences and emphasized the meaning of the situational context in the formation of relations between the colonizers and the colonized. Nonetheless, the history of colonialism is also a violent history of crimes committed on a grand scale.

As differently as individual European colonial structures evolved over time, the concept of the binary coding of the world was fundamental to all. Even though the justification for expansion and European rule over the indigenous population in the newly "discovered" and conquered territories changed, whether missionary work to the "pagans," "the white man's burden," or a "manifest destiny" was advanced as legitimization, the emphasis on one's own righteousness, or on the conviction to have been chosen, always played an important role in the ideological preparation to rule.[38] True equality between Europeans and the respective native population hardly ever existed. The dichotomy of colonizers and the colonized, Christians and pagans, "blacks" and "whites," humans and nonhumans that forms the basis of the concept of the binary opposite also homogenized the inherently disparate groups of rulers and the ruled. For the colonial—that is, asymmetrical—exercising of colonial power, it further created the necessary distance between the groups.

Increasingly influential in the late nineteenth century, social Darwinism directly emphasized the hierarchy among nations and their competition with each other—both in reference to the relationship of the colonizers and the colonized and in reference to the relations of the colonial powers among themselves. Within this mind-set, the vision of a racial war à la Schlieffen, von Trotha, and other members of the German colonial army could be justified. With the gravest of consequences, this dichotomy manifested itself in the settler colonies. There, the newly arrived Europeans were of the opinion—if they did not imagine the land completely devoid of human inhabitants in the first place—that they could embark on organizing the land as they saw fit to bring "order" to the "chaos," without regard for indigenous settlements and economic spheres. In this endeavor, the native peoples who already lived there (contrary to popular European imagination) were only in the way. If their labor could not be exploited, they were either expelled or murdered. Within the racial worldview, this was the "normal" course of world history. The existence of "higher" races was deemed a fact and, with that, already in their formative discourse, the existence of "lower" races was the logical consequence. Way at the bottom of the racial hierarchy, the peoples condemned to perish according to the laws of history could be found. Helping this process along merely accelerated the inevitable.

Genocide on the Frontier and Colonial Conquests and Wars of Destruction

Before indigenous people became victims, they were dehumanized, robbed of their human dignity. The Australian example of "shooting practice" illustrates how this dehumanization of the natives manifested itself in individual perpetrators. An eyewitness reported the following in 1889: "There are instances when the young men of station have employed the Sunday in hunting the blacks, not only for some definite purpose, but also for the sake of the sport."[39] This was possible because the Aborigines were viewed as no longer belonging to human society, as the defense of this practice printed in the newspaper *The Queenslander* confirms:

> And being a useless race, what does it matter what they suffer any more than the distinguished philanthropist . . . cares for the wounded half dead pigeon he tortures at his shooting matches. "I don't see the necessity," was the reply of a distinguished wit to an applicant for an office who remarked that "he must live," and virtually and practically say the same about the blacks.[40]

From this attitude it was but a small step to the murder of women and children. Comparing Aborigines to animals that could be "shot down" for sport was the plainest evidence of dehumanization. In other cases, a pronounced negative propaganda fulfilled this function. Africans, Indians, and Aborigines were accused of raping women and (sexually) maiming men. Thus, the indigenous nations themselves were blamed for their fate because they had emerged as "animals" that could be slaughtered. The war with the Herero and von Trotha's proclamation are classic examples of this way of thinking.

Mass murder found even broader acceptance when individuals claimed to be protecting their private property. Hence in 1889 it was said of an Australian squatter: "He shot all the men he discovered on his run, because they were cattle killers; the women, because they gave birth to cattle killers; and the children, because they would in time become cattle killers."[41] Applying this logic, the murder could only end with the complete annihilation of the Aborigines. Similar arguments seeking to justify genocide are also known from North America. Hence, H. L. Hall, an infamous murderer of Indians, rationalized the murder of small children with the saying, well known since King Philip's War (1675–77), that "a nit would make a louse."[42]

Whereas the aforementioned squatter still committed murder by himself, others went hunting together. Hence in 1867, readers of *The Queenslander* learned about an act of reprisal carried out by several settlers in retribution for real as well as imagined Aborigine attacks:

There is not much more in the present system by which blacks are shot down most ruthlessly for weeks and months after a case of murder or theft has been reported, and when many innocent are either killed in order that the guilty party may be included in the number or so hunted about that the spirit of revenge is aroused in them.[43]

Numerous examples of the slaughter of men, women, and children at the hands of settlers or local militia can be found in North America as well as in Australia. The perpetrators justified such acts by pointing to real or imagined attacks by the "savages."[44] Especially on the actual frontier, private actions predominated on the local level. One of the frontier's defining characteristics was that of a mixed zone, where the newly arrived settlers came into contact with the indigenous population. In the beginning, however, whites were not yet in the majority, and official structures were lacking. Over time, specially assembled troops, such as the Native Police of Queensland, were deployed that functioned as death squads and cleansed the frontier of Aborigines.

The genocidal wars of conquest and "pacification" represented a further escalation of these homicidal raids. They were larger military actions that required a corresponding organization. The war the imperial army waged against the Herero and Nama in German South-West Africa serves as an important example. The fact that the Germans already constructed camps on a large scale at this juncture underscores the organized degree of this genocide. Though it is not clear if Kaiser Wilhelm had ordered the genocide—von Trotha merely indicated that the kaiser had given him the task to crush the "rebellion" at all costs—von Trotha nonetheless unambiguously acted in the name of the emperor. He was the emperor's deputy, and therefore the crimes committed at that time can be viewed as having occurred officially in the name of Germany. Von Trotha represented the German state, and this fact makes the war of destruction into a criminal act perpetrated by the state, one of the generally acknowledged identifying characteristics of genocide. Not least for this reason, the destruction of the Herero and Nama constitutes an important degree of radicalization, chronologically situated in between the genocides committed by settlers within the colonial context and the crimes of Nazism.

World War II as a Colonial War

When compared to the gigantic battles and the millions of victims of World War II, the colonial war in South-West Africa seems but a minor prelude to the barbarisms of the twentieth century. Nonetheless, the colonial war's numerous structural similarities to the Nazi "war of annihilation in the East" reveals that it too is an important part of German history. Looking back to World War II, much that appeared like an unimaginable breach of taboo had already been common practice in German South-West Africa.[45] Exposing the structure of the "war in the East"—in other words, the tactics behind the modern weapons, the armadas of tanks and aircraft—the "war of annihilation" then reveals elements clearly reminiscent of the colonial war. Already during colonial times, official reports described the battles waged by the German colonial army in German East Africa as "war[s] of destruction," influenced by the "campaign[s] of annihilation."[46]

Although formally the war against the Soviet Union was labeled a regular war between European powers, from the beginning, the Germans did not conduct it as such. Instead, deliberately abandoning international rules of war, the German aggressors launched a war of exploitation that more closely resembled a colonial war than a "typical" war within Europe. One component was to deny the adversary the status of a legitimate, equal opponent, who also in defeat and captivity was entitled to minimal rights. There further prevailed a racially driven willingness to let prisoners of war perish or to murder them outright.

Heinrich Himmler's order of the day from August 1, 1941, almost reads like a quotation from von Trotha's proclamation. In it, Himmler ordered the massacre near the Pripet Marshes: "All Jews must be shot, Jewish women to be driven into the swamps."[47] Very much like the Herero women and children who perished in the Omaheke, the Jewish women too would die, and no German soldier even had to lift his weapon. The binary coding of the world had also paved the way for this crime. There were only "Aryans" and "Jews," "Germans" and "Slavs," "humans" and "subhumans." This dichotomous segregation, functionally equivalent to the colonial differentiation between the "savage" and the "civilized," ultimately made it possible, as then happened, to treat humans in this cruel and misanthropic way.

The Holocaust and Colonialism

It would also be incorrect, however, to view Nazi crimes, and particularly those of the Holocaust, as mere copies of colonial events, as postcolonial authors and activists have asserted. Here the debate started to resemble a competition in victimhood. It was emphasized that in the process of colonizing the Americas, multiple holocausts had occurred. An estimated one hundred million dead was many times worse than six million dead, it has been claimed.[48] This emotional and politicized approach has damaged research into the connection between colonialism and the Holocaust. Such a comparison is overly simplified, and the differences between events in the colonies and those in Central and Eastern Europe in the 1940s must also be clarified.

An important difference, for example, is the fact that the Jewish victims came from the midst of German and European society, whereas the colonial victims had been viewed by their killers as subordinate from the onset. The Jews had first to be transformed into the "absolute other," something the colonized already appeared to be, due to the color of their skin. The process of "othering," of binary coding, was similar. The designation of those who became victims, however, was, in the case of the Jews, completely different: antisemitism going back centuries was combined with the racist extermination that originated in the colonies.

A further difference lies in the bureaucratization of murder and hence in the role the state played in genocide in the colonial context and in the Third Reich. It is especially this systematic, almost industrialized murder that is meant by "Auschwitz"—symbolized by barbed wire, heaps of eyeglasses, and mountains of bodies—and which became the universally recognized symbol for absolute evil. In the colonial state, which was far less centralized and bureaucratized, murder could not take such forms.

Nonetheless, bureaucratized and state-orchestrated homicide is less a question of a fundamental structural difference than it is a difference in degree, directly linked to the historical level of the state's development. Hence, the massacres that American settlers and militias carried out were in sync with the less mature state of the new frontier. As states established themselves, instruments of genocide expanded along with them, such as in Queensland. In the United States, violence evolved into mass murder committed by the state itself through the army or local police. In the modern, bureaucratized state, the beginnings of which can be found in the colonial army's campaign in South-West Africa, camps appeared as a place of destruction. Even if active "industrial killing" did not yet exist, murder through neglect can already be found there.

Nazi crimes cannot monocausally be ascribed to the tradition of European colonialism. National Socialism was too complex and too eclectic in its ideology as well as in its policies. Nonetheless, in the sense of an archaeology of Darwinian population management and genocide, colonialism served as an important source of ideas. Even the murder of the Jews, which—as mentioned—stands out in many ways from other genocides, would perhaps not have been possible if the ultimate breach of taboo—to think and then to act on the belief that groups of people could simply be destroyed—had not already happened before. And it had occurred, during colonial times.

Within the tradition of genocidal thinking, colonialism also occupies such a prominent place because the "discovery," conquest, and development and settlement of the world had and still has positive connotations; indeed, it has served as a model. At the same time, the similarity to colonialism helps us understand why the expulsion and resettlement of Jews and Slavs and, as a final consequence, their murder, was perhaps not even recognized as a breach of taboo. At the very least, colonial history offered the perpetrators an opportunity to exonerate themselves and to blind themselves to their own horrific acts.

Auschwitz marked the perverse culmination of state violence against domestic and alien populations. The war against the Herero and Nama was an important step in this development and a warning at the beginning of the twentieth century of what was yet to come. The genocide in German South-West Africa is therefore neither simply a local event in the histories of Namibia or Germany nor an isolated incident in colonial history. Rather, it stands out in the global history of violence that would reach its zenith in two world wars. It has often been asked whether a path existed from Windhoek to Auschwitz. I think there were many paths. Seen from Windhoek, the Third Reich was by no means a necessary consequence. But to stay on point: of the numerous routes that fed the criminal policies of National Socialism, one originated in the colonies, and that particular path was neither minor nor obscure.

NOTES

The text of this chapter was translated into English from the original German by Martina Cucchiara.

1. Ludwig von Estorff, *Wanderungen und Kämpfe in Südwestafrika, Ostafrika und Südafrika 1894–1910,* ed. Christoph-Friedrich Kutscher (Windhoek: J. Meinert, 1979), 177.

2. For an introduction to various aspects of the wars against the Herero and Nama, see Jürgen Zimmerer and Joachim Zeller, eds., *Völkermord in Deutsch Südwestafrika: Der Kolonialkrieg (1904–1908) in Namibia und seine Folgen* (Berlin: Links, 2003); English translation, *Genocide in German South-West Africa: The Colonial War of 1904–1908 and Its Aftermath,* ed. Jürgen Zimmerer and Joachim Zeller, trans. E. J. Neather (London: Merlin, 2008). See also Jan-Bart Gewald, "Imperial Germany and the Herero in Southern Africa: Genocide and the Quest for Recompense," in *Genocide, War Crimes and the West: History and Complicity,* ed. Adam Jones (London: Zed Books, 2004), 59–77; Dominik J. Schaller, "'Ich glaube, dass die Nation als solche vernichtet werden muss': Kolonialkrieg und Völkermord in Deutsch Südwestafrika 1904–1907," *Journal of Genocide Research* 6 (March 2004): 395–430; Dominik J. Schaller, "Kolonialkrieg, Völkermord und Zwangsarbeit in Deutsch Südwestafrika," in *Enteignet—Vertrieben—Ermordet: Beiträge zur Genozidforschung,* ed. Dominik J. Schaller et al. (Zurich: Chronos, 2004), 147–232; Reinhart Kössler and Henning Melber, "Völkermord und Gedenken: Der Genozid an den Herero und Nama in Deutsch-Südwestafrika 1904–1908," in *Jahrbuch 2004 zur Geschichte und Wirkung des Holocaust,* ed. Irmtrud Wojak and Susanne Meinl (New York: Campus, 1996), 37–75.

3. Jürgen Zimmerer, "The Birth of the 'Ostland' out of the Spirit of Colonialism: A Postcolonial Perspective on the Nazi Policy of Conquest and Extermination," *Patterns of Prejudice* 39 (February 2005): 197–219.

4. *Kriegsgeschichtliche Abteilung I des Großen Generalstabs: Die Kämpfe der deutschen Truppen in Südwestafrika,* vol. 1 (Berlin: Ernst Siegfried Mittler, 1906–7), 211.

5. Isabel Hull has shown in great detail the many problems that the German army faced in South-West Africa. She provides empirical data to support the hypothesis of the "weak" German army first put forward by Brigitte Lau. See Isabel V. Hull, *Absolute Destruction: Military Culture and the Practices of War in Imperial Germany* (Ithaca, N.Y.: Cornell University Press,

2005); and Brigitte Lau, "Uncertain Certainties: The Herero-German War of 1904," in *History and Historiography—Four Essays in Reprint,* ed. Brigitte Lau and Annemarie Heywood (Windhoek: Michael Scott Oral Records Project, 1995). Although there can be no doubt that the image of the all-powerful German military machine is misleading and itself a product of colonial myth-building, I disagree with this argument in two respects: the question of ideology and the genocidal intent. Hull's argument neglects the ideology that especially influenced von Trotha's decisions. And she ignores new archival evidence that shows the genocidal policy was launched independently of military developments and logistical problems. See Jürgen Zimmerer, "Das Deutsche Reich und der Genozid: Überlegungen zum historischen Ort des Völkermordes an den Herero und Nama," in *Namibia—Deutschland: Eine geteilte Geschichte; Widerstand, Gewalt, Erinnerung,* ed. Larissa Förster, Dag Henrichsen, and Michael Bollig (Cologne: Rautenstrauch-Joest Museum, 2004), 106–21. For a summary of the debate between Hull and myself, see *Bulletin of the German Historical Institute,* Washington, D.C., no. 37 (Fall 2005).

6. When Brigitte Lau argued against this misinterpretation, she threw the baby out with the bathwater. Completely misunderstanding the concept of genocide, she denied one had occurred in South-West Africa, because she equated genocide with absolute power. Because of this, she regrettably became the principal witness for the causes of revisionists and right-wing extremists, who eagerly accepted her denial of genocide. Without a doubt, German troops committed genocide in South-West Africa, but without simultaneously exercising complete power. See Lau, "Uncertain Certainties."

7. For various interpretations of Bismarck's decision to establish a formal colonial empire, see Horst Gründer, *Geschichte der deutschen Kolonien,* 3rd ed. (Paderborn: Schöningh, 1995), 51–62.

8. For the initial phase of the history of the various colonies, see Gründer, *Geschichte der deutschen Kolonien.* Later, Kiaochou, located in China, was also added.

9. Regarding the fantasies connected with the "South West," see, for example, Birthe Kundrus, *Moderne Imperialisten: Das Kaiserreich im Spiegel seiner Kolonien* (Cologne: Böhlau, 2003).

10. About this gradual saturation, see Jürgen Zimmerer, *Deutsche Herrschaft über Afrikaner: Staatlicher Machtanspruch und Wirklichkeit im kolonialen Namibia,* 3rd ed. (Hamburg: LIT, 2004), 13–31, 112–18. About the history of the bureaucracy, see Udo Kaulich, *Die Geschichte der ehemaligen Kolonie Deutsch Südwestafrika (1884–1914): Eine Gesamtdarstellung* (Frankfurt am Main: Peter Lang, 2001). For a comparison of the history of colonial power structures from an African perspective, see Jan-Bart Gewald, *Towards Redemption: A Socio-Political History of the Herero of Namibia Be-*

tween 1890 and 1923 (Leiden: Research School CNWS, 1996); and Gesine Krüger, *Kriegsbewältigung und Geschichtsbewußtsein: Realität, Deutung and Verarbeitung des deutschen Kolonialkriegs in Namibia 1904 bis 1907* (Göttingen: Vandenhoeck und Ruprecht, 1999).

11. I have already, on multiple occasions, analyzed this vision of colonial rule and its consequences in detail. See Zimmerer, *Deutsche Herrschaft;* Zimmerer, "Der total Überwachungsstaat? Recht und Verwaltung in Deutsch-Südwestafrika," in *Das deutsche Kolonialrecht als Vorstufe einer globalen "Kolonialisierung" von Recht und Verwaltung (Schriften zur Rechtspolitologie),* ed. Rüdiger Voigt (Baden-Baden: Nomos, 2001), 175–98; and Zimmerer, "Der Wahn der Planarbeit. Vertreibung, unfreie Arbeit und Völkermord als Elemente der Bevölkerungsökonomie in Deutsch Südwestafrika," in *Menschenhandel und unfreie Arbeit,* ed. Michael Mann (Leipzig: Leipzig University Press, 2003), 96–113.

12. For a summary of the course of the war, see Jürgen Zimmerer, "Krieg, KZ und Völkermord in Südwestafrika: Der erste deutsche Genozid," in *Völkermord,* ed. Zimmerer and Zeller, 45–63.

13. Missionary Elger to the Rhenish Mission, February 10, 1904. Quoted in Horst Drechsler, *Südwestafrika unter deutscher Kolonialherrschaft: Der Kampf der Herero und Nama gegen den deutschen Imperialismus 1884–1915,* 2nd ed. (Berlin: Dietz, 1984), 146ff.

14. Gouvernement Windhoek to Kolonialabteilung Berlin, February 23, 1904. Quoted in Drechsler, *Südwestafrika,* 149ff.

15. Von Trotha to Leutwein, November 5, 1904. Quoted in Drechsler, *Südwestafrika,* 156.

16. This seems to be the decisive difference between my interpretation and that of Isabel Hull, who ignores ideology and intention in order to stress the situational dimension, combined with structural characteristics of the German army's organization. See Hull, *Absolute Destruction.*

17. Proclamation made by von Trotha on board the steamship *Eleonore Woermann,* June 1904. Namibian National Archives, Windhoek, Zentralbureau des Gouvernements: *Geheimakten* (9.A., vol.1, p.1b).

18. *Die Kämpfe der deutschen Truppen,* 1:203.

19. Maximilian Bayer, *Mit dem Hauptquartier in Südwestafrika* (Berlin: W. Weicher, 1909), 162.

20. Proclamation of von Trotha, Osombo-Windhoek, October 2, 1904. Bundesarchiv Berlin-Lichterfelde, Reichskolonialamt, R 1001/2089, p. 7af.

21. Ibid.

22. Von Trotha to chief of the General Staff, October 4, 1904. Quoted in Drechsler, *Südwestafrika,* 163.

23. Helen Fein, "Definition and Discontent: Labelling, Detecting, and

Explaining Genocide in the Twentieth Century," in *Genozid in der modernen Geschichte,* ed. Stig Förster and Gerhard Hirschfeld (Münster: LIT, 1997), 11–21, 20.

24. Article 2, United Nations "Convention on the Prevention and Punishment of the Crime of Genocide," December 9, 1948, printed in Frank Chalk and Kurt Jonassohn, *The History and Sociology of Genocide: Analyses and Case Studies* (New Haven, Conn.: Yale University Press, 1990), 44–49.

25. For an in-depth debate on the occurrence of the genocide, see Zimmerer, "Das Deutsche Reich und der Genozid"; and Jürgen Zimmerer, "Kolonialer Genozid? Vom Nutzen und Nachteil einer historischen Kategorie für eine Globalgeschichte des Völkermordes," in *Enteignet—Vertrieben—Ermordet,* ed. Schaller et al., 109–28.

26. Estorff, *Wanderungen,* 117.

27. On the history of the Nama war, see also Andreas Heinrich Bühler, *Der Namaaufstand gegen die deutsche Kolonialherrschaft in Namibia von 1904–1913* (Frankfurt am Main: IKO-Verlag für Interkulturelle Kommunikation, 2003).

28. Schlieffen to Bülow, November 23, 1904. Quoted in Drechsler, *Südwestafrika,* 166.

29. Edward von Liebert, *Neunzig Tage im Zelt—Meine Reise nach Uhehe Juni bis September 1897* (Berlin, 1898), 33. Quoted in Martin Baer and Olaf Schröter, *Eine Kopfjagd: Deutsche in Ostafrika* (Berlin: Links, 2001), 57.

30. *Militärpolitische Denkschrift über die Auswirkungen des Aufstandes,* Dar-es-Salaam, June 1, 1907. Quoted in Detlef Bald, "Afrikanischer Kampf gegen koloniale Herrschaft. Der Maji-Maji-Aufstand in Ostafrika," *Militärgeschichtliche Mitteilungen* 19 (January 1976): 23–50, 40. Regarding the Maji-Maji, see also Felicitas Becker and Jigal Beez, eds., *Der Maji-Maji-Krieg in Deutsch Ostafrika, 1905–1907* (Berlin: Links, 2005).

31. Von Trotha, Proclamation to the Nama, April 22, 1905. Printed in *Die Kämpfe der deutschen Truppen,* 2:186.

32. Gouvernement Windhoek to Kolonialabteilung Berlin, April 17, 1906, Bundesarchiv Berlin-Lichterfelde, Reichskolonialamt, R 1001/2119, pp. 42a–43b.

33. Gouvernement Windhoek to Kolonialabteilung Berlin, July 3, 1905, Bundesarchiv Berlin-Lichterfelde, Reichskolonialamt, R 1001/2118, pp. 154a–155a.

34. "Chronik der Gemeinde Lüderitzbucht" (report by Missionary Laaf regarding the time from the establishment of the Protestant mission until 1920), Archives of the Evangelical Church in the Republic of Namibia, vol. 16, pp. 1–31, here pp. 21–26.

35. "Chronik der Gemeinde Lüderitzbucht," pp. 26ff.

36. Estorff to the colonial army in South-West Africa, April 10, 1907, Bundesarchiv Berlin-Lichterfelde, Reichskolonialamt, R 1001/2140, p. 88a ff.

37. Unfortunately, this issue can only be discussed in a cursory manner. For a more detailed discussion and a more critical look at the current research, see arguments presented elsewhere: Jürgen Zimmerer, "Colonialism and the Holocaust: Towards an Archeology of Genocide," in *Genocide and Settler Society: Frontier Violence and Stolen Indigenous Children in Australian History*, ed. A. Dirk Moses (New York: Berghahn Books, 2004); and Zimmerer, "Birth of the 'Ostland.'" See also Jürgen Zimmerer, *Von Windhuk nach Auschwitz: Beiträge zum Verhältnis von Kolonialismus und Holocaust* (Münster: LIT, 2007).

38. Expressions such as *Europeans* and *colonial lords* should not be misconstrued as describing a homogenous group with the same goals. See the instructive essay of Anna Laura Stoler, "Rethinking Colonial Categories: European Communities and the Boundaries of Rule," *Comparative Studies of Society and History* 31 (1989): 134–61.

39. Quoted in Alison Palmer, *Colonial Genocide* (Adelaide: Crawford House, 2000), 44.

40. Quoted ibid., 45.

41. Quoted ibid., 43.

42. Ward Churchill, *A Little Matter of Genocide: Holocaust and Denial in the Americas, 1492 to the Present* (San Francisco: City Lights Books, 1997), 229.

43. Quoted in Palmer, *Colonial Genocide*, 43.

44. Most of the few studies that exist on this topic seek fervently to enlighten readers about the suffering of a particular group and then lobby for the recognition of that suffering. See Churchill, *A Little Matter of Genocide*, and David E. Stannard, *American Holocaust: The Conquest of the New World* (New York: Oxford University Press, 1992). Dirk Moses demonstrates what an objective, scientific debate can accomplish. See Moses, *Genocide and Settler Society*, especially his introduction to the problem of an activist vs. a scientific perspective, and the problem of the singularity of certain victims' experiences and the connected problems for scientific treatment. See also Dirk Moses, "Conceptual Blockages and Definitional Dilemmas in the 'Racial Century': Genocides of Indigenous Peoples and the Holocaust," *Patterns of Prejudice* 36 (April 2002): 7–36; and Zimmerer, "Kolonialer Genozid?"

45. I have treated the structural similarities between colonialism and the German policy of occupation and extermination in the "East" during World War II in depth in Zimmerer, "Birth of the 'Ostland'"; Jürgen Zimmerer, "Im Dienste des Imperiums: Die Geographen der Berliner Universtät zwischen Kolonialwissenschaften und Ostforschung," *Jahrbuch für Universitäts-*

geschichte (July 2004): 73–100; Jürgen Zimmerer, "Von Windhuk nach Warschau: Die rassische Privilegiengesellschaft in Deutsch-Südwestafrika—ein Modell mit Zukunft?" in *Rassenmischehen—Mischlinge—Rassentrennung: Zur Politik der Rasse im deutschen Kaiserreich,* ed. Frank Becker (Stuttgart: F. Steiner, 2004), 97–123. A connection between colonial rule in German South-West Africa and the Third Reich had already been alluded to in Helmut Bley, *Kolonialherrschaft und Sozialstruktur in Deutsch-Südwestafrika 1894–1914* (Hamburg: Leibniz, 1968); Drechsler, *Südwestafrika;* and Henning Melber, "Kontinuitäten totaler Herrschaft: Völkermord und Apartheid in Deutsch-Südwestafrika," *Jahrbuch für Antisemitismusforschung* (January 1992): 91–116.

46. Liebert, *Neunzig Tage im Zelt,* 33. Quoted in Thomas Morlang, "'Die Kerls haben ja nicht einmal Gewehre': Der Untergang der Zelewski-Expedition in Deutsch-Ostafrika im August 1891," *Militärgeschichte* 11 (February 2001): 22–28, 27.

47. Quoted in Christian Gerlach, "Deutsche Wirtschaftsinteressen, Besatzungspolitik und der Mord an den Juden in Weißrußland 1941–1943," in *Nationalsozialistische Vernichtungspolitik 1939–1945: Neue Forschung und Kontroversen,* ed. Ulrich Herbert (Frankfurt am Main: Fischer, 1998), 236–91, 278.

48. For an extreme example, see Churchill, *A Little Matter of Genocide;* and Rosa Amelia Plumelle-Uribe, *Weisse Barbarei: Vom Kolonialrassismus zur Rassenpolitik der Nazis* (Zurich: Rotpunktverlag, 2004).

Annette Becker

Suppressed Memory of Atrocity in World War I and Its Impact on World War II

IN AN INTERVIEW, THE JEWISH PHILOSOPHER EMMANUEL LEVINAS, who lived in Lithuania in 1914, recalled those times:

> Trouble began at the end of August 1914, trouble which never ended, as if order had been disrupted, forever. . . . Very few memories. Things come back to mind in total disorder. . . . The family leaving Lithuania, which had become a frontier zone; migrating all over Russia, waiting and hoping for the war to end . . . the images get all mixed up in the changes of setting, and memories run the risk of being "known" [i.e., from being repeatedly related] rather than truly remembered. In 1916, Kharkov in the Ukraine, where refugees were crowding . . . the 1914 war felt like it would never end; the [Russian] Revolution, the post-revolution chaos, civil war . . . all those things fuse in the mind and become part of the 1914 war.[1]

It is this "trouble," the "disruption" Levinas describes, that I would like to analyze. More accurately, I reflect upon the atrocity of World War I—I use the singular in order to include all its atrocities, real and mythical—from its suppressed or distorted memory to its impossible recollection. Levinas tells us that, on what had been Germany's eastern front, it never stopped being wartime. I agree and argue that that was not the only place where war never stopped after 1914, although the experience of war, especially that of civilians, tended to disappear into oblivion. It is very important that we recognize and think about such gaps in memory in order to conceptualize the impossible exit from violent and tragic confrontation. Put another way: the atrocities of

World War II were not without precedent in the recent past, but the public and even private forgetting of the brutalization of the Great War made knowledge of that war's crimes inaccessible just decades later. Amnesia and denial, in turn, facilitated disbelief and indifference to reports of massive destruction, particularly that of the Jews. Thus, one root of the political and human failure we associate with the Holocaust and responses to it was an epistemological block, an unwillingness or inability to acknowledge and integrate the atrocity of the previous world war.

Between 1914 and 1918, the energies of the world were fully engaged in what by 1915 was already known as the Great War. From the men in the trenches to the women and children on the home front, no one escaped the war. The suffering of soldiers and civilians was at the heart of the totalization of the conflict; it was part of the combatant nations' great struggle for civilization, dating from the actual war period through the 1930s, "from death to memory."[2]

In essence, mental suffering was the same for civilians as for the mobilized men, and for many of them the war meant terrible deprivation; but it was the prisoners, both military and civilian, along with the inhabitants of the invaded and occupied regions—the people of northern and northeastern France, Belgium, Serbia, East Prussia, and western Russia—who paid the highest price, plus the Armenians, victims of the extermination plan of the Ottomans. The invasions and retreats that so strongly marked the beginning (1914 and 1915) and the end (1917 and 1918) of the war raised the problem of relations between armies, occupation governments, and enemy civilians. How were civilians in occupied territories to be fed when the totality of economic resources became a target for the enemy? This was the question that the British naval blockade posed for the German authorities. How were civilians in occupied regions to be treated when they could still be considered linked to the enemy? What position was to be adopted as to the goods or even the citizenry of enemy countries marooned in the hands of opposing powers?

The thorny problem of internal minorities was at the heart of the political and cultural mobilization for a war that was now conceived in terms of the totality of national resources and culture. In different cases, such minorities could either be included in the mobilization or else suspected of sympathy, if not worse, with the enemy. Hence mobilization might occur in a negative fashion, by exclusion. This scapegoating mechanism was clearly at work in Russia—especially, as Levinas recalls, for the Jews—and above all in Ottoman Turkey in 1915–16 and in 1917–18, after the Russian Revolution added more chaos in the Transcaucasian arena. What would much later be dubbed the Armenian "genocide"—after Raphael Lemkin coined the term in 1943 to speak at the time about the Jewish Holocaust—had, of course, deep historical roots. But then, that was true of all the forms of extreme violence of which the war became the great accelerator. It nonetheless remains true that the Armenian genocide occurred during a war of which it constituted a major episode.

Although many historians reserve the epithet of *total* for World War II and speak instead of aspects of totalization in the first world-wide conflict, it is undoubtedly true that the conditions for many people between 1914 and 1918 turned this period into a laboratory of extreme violence, and thus a base from which to try and understand a century of political murder. And yet the terrible warnings of the Great War years were almost completely forgotten. As I show here, forgetting and mythification developed together, and the peoples of Europe, who would undergo far worse twenty years later, were unable to make use of past experience. Accordingly, my chronological scope is 1914–1942/1945, from Germany's western front to Treblinka and the end of the war of annihilation.

The sociologist Michael Pollack has shown how the concentration camp experience of World War II, precisely because it was so extreme, contained the potential for intellectual catharsis: "Any extreme experience reveals the elements and conditions of 'normal' experience, whose very familiarity often blocks analysis."[3] Using Pollack's insight as my starting point, I show here that the various traumas suffered by the civilian populations between 1914 and 1918, and especially at the end of the war, expose the complexity of the Great War—a complexity that is often forgotten in a denial of memory for this part of the population, people who were sorely tried but whose war experience differed from the only one seen as important: that of the soldiers. My discussion continues in two parts: first, the trauma of invasion, occupation, internment, and annihilation during the Great War; and second: forgetting, suppression, and denial in the years from 1918 to 1945.

THE TRAUMA OF INVASION, OCCUPATION, INTERNMENT, AND ANNIHILATION IN THE GREAT WAR

During the advance of enemy armies on every front, troops committed many atrocities against civilians: they burned villages, raped women, and shot hostages. The soldiers suspected all civilians and were not inclined to show mercy. How could those who fled before the rapidly advancing troops not have circulated increasingly horrifying tales? The armies did not respect the 1907 Hague Conventions—surely therefore they must all be criminals! The war created and fostered violence and fear. Those who were advancing into enemy territory could only be barbarians. Their war was not, as was that of their adversaries, a just war. It is not surprising that Raphael Lemkin, in the famous book in which he invented the word *genocide* in 1943–44, chose to include in an appendix the Hague Conventions, and especially article 44 which Germany, although it had added some qualifications, was among the first to sign: "A belligerent is forbidden to force the inhabitants of territory occupied by it to furnish information about the army of the other belligerent or about its means of defense."[4]

It is as part of this atmosphere, at once phantasmagorical and genuinely terrifying, that the different occupations must be imagined. In Belgium and northern France, for example, the local population, bewildered by defeat, had to take in and feed in their own homes men whom they could see only as barbarians. In addition to their continually deteriorating living conditions, the civilians were forced to undergo experiences that they described as "atrocities," frequently the result of the enemies' difficulty in obtaining their requisitioning demands. Many situations that have become commonplace throughout the world in the last hundred years were created: hostage-taking, rape, forced labor, deportation, concentration camps, repression, resistance, then fresh repression: the vicious cycle of all wars against civilians.[5] World War I saw many thresholds of violence overstepped and, as part of the process, prisoners—civilian and military, transformed into pawns in the various stages of warfare—bore the full brunt of the drama as the conflict became universal; as, for example, when one nation carried out reprisals against another. One of the darkest features was undoubtedly the use of prisoners as human shields at the rear of the enemy lines, where they were hit by shells from their own armies.

Forced to work for the enemy war effort, prisoners bore a crushing sense of guilt: did not working for the enemy mean working against one's own nation? All of this was particularly traumatizing.

How to Overcome Trauma: Accuse the Enemy. A Handy Concept: Race

The term *race* was then used everywhere, displaying a concept of the entire war as a struggle between intrinsically opposed "races." Scientists in particular went much further than the declarations of many intellectuals on both sides, namely that this was a war to preserve civilization. It was in biological terms that the contrast between the French, Germans, or Russians began to be expressed. German prisoner-of-war camps became laboratories for racial experimentation. Since they did not deploy colonial troops on either the eastern or western fronts, the Germans showed, through their colonial prisoners, that the entire world was against them, including the "underworld"—the African and Asian soldiers who belonged to the French and British armies, along with their "barbaric" allies, the Russians. Furthermore, to prove that the accusations of "German atrocities" were totally false, they explained that only colonial troops, barbarous and atrocious "by nature," committed atrocities, thus turning all French arguments on the War of Rights and the Right War inside out.

This inversion was made as early as 1914 in the "Manifesto to the Civilized World," signed by ninety-three well-known German intellectuals—artists, poets, and physicians. The fifth point of the manifesto reads: "It is not true that we disregard the precepts of international law in our methods of warfare, in which there is no unbridled cruelty." The passage continues: "In the East, the ground is soaked with the blood of women and children slain by the Russian hordes, and in the West the breasts of our soldiers are lacerated with dumdum bullets. No one has less right to pretend to be defending European civilization than those who are the allies of Russians and Serbians, and are not ashamed to incite Mongolians and negroes [*sic,* uncapitalized] to fight against white men."[6]

During the entire war and especially at the end, the Germans accused of atrocities on the battlefields answered with incredible rancor, accusing the French of much worse, for example in their treatment of prisoners. Typical was the following denunciation of the French:

A chamber of torture, where the screams of the tormented enter the ears of the people of the XXth century. . . . A nation which takes pride in calling itself the civilized nation par excellence . . . falls into the abyss of the worst barbarity. Only savages thus torture the enemies they have taken alive. France is transforming its war zones into slaughterhouses and its treatment of prisoners into torture chambers.[7]

In the German argument, all the devastation they themselves committed was done for military reasons and for protection of their soldiers, who were following the rules of war, unlike the Russians, the French, or the British, who acted from savage impulses. In the words of one report: "Why is the entire so-called civilized world acting with such barbarity?"[8] The worst accusation for the Germans was that of having used a factory to process human bodies, or *Kadaververwertung,* in order to dispose of corpses. The Germans asserted that in German, "*Kadaver* [the word] is only used for animals. The diabolical fantasies of our enemies found in this word *Kadaver* the pretext to confuse the world and make everybody believe that the word was not used for dead animals, but for fallen soldiers. It is totally wrong; the Germans are taking care of the dead with the greatest piety, be they Germans or enemies."[9]

In their postwar struggle, the people of northern France sought recognition of the distinctive nature of the disasters they had undergone in their region, particularly in order to win reparations and war damages. In October 1918, even before the war ended, two Socialists set the tone in an exchange in the Chamber of Deputies. The tone of hatred is all the more significant because it came from Socialists, whom some might have suspected of peace-loving, or even pacifist, ideas: "M. Delory: I have never favored territorial conquest; I shall continue to oppose it. But not to claim a just peace would be a crime against France, a crime against humanity! M. Brunet: . . . Monsieur le Président, I demand publication of my colleague's speech, evidence of Germany's crimes against humanity."[10] French prime minister Georges Clemenceau himself would often use the phrase "crime against humanity" during the negotiations of the peace conference in 1919, linking war guilt and reparations. "The conduct of Germany is almost unprecedented in human history. . . . Justice, therefore, is the only possible basis for the settlement of the accounts of this terrible war."[11]

"Crime against humanity." The expression had been used in 1915 by the British, French, and Russian allies when denouncing the massacre of the Armenians in the Ottoman Empire: "these new crimes of Turkey against humanity and civilization."[12] The expression was to have a full life ahead of it in the twentieth century. At the time, however, this crime was only a retaliatory formula and not yet a legal injunction, which it became only at the Nuremberg Trials after World War II. The massacre of the Armenians is a paradigmatic case of war violence transformed into violence inside the war, the passage from war crime to "crime against humanity" and then to "genocide," before international law had even dealt with such terms.

FORGETTING, SUPPRESSION, AND DENIAL IN THE YEARS 1918 TO 1945

In such a huge conflict between nations, all forms of suffering are claimed by one camp or another; every life, every wound, and every death is added to the tally. At the end of the war, in contrast, the heroism of the troops is enough for ordinary people who passionately want to return to normality. Why memorialize prisoners, military or civilian, who were mainly seen—sometimes even by themselves—as guilty of treason? Why remember the Armenians? Crimes against Armenians had been used as a tool of propaganda when these crimes could furnish a reason to go on with the war, but then were as quickly forgotten when the war was over: from the "banality of evil" to the "banality of indifference."[13]

And how should a war be commemorated when it had neither the name nor the glamour of a war? Even when soldiers were seen as victims of the butchery of war, it was a heroic victimhood. But how should banal, everyday victims be commemorated, as opposed to soldiers, heroes of the trenches? How to commemorate the incommemorable—hunger, cold, forced labor, concentration camps, rape, hostages, requisitioning, fines, tuberculosis, and more? Michael Pollack puts it very well: "Cyclical silences are not simply the result of prohibitions from on high; they may be the consequence of an interiorization of feelings of inferiority, shame, or anticipated discrimination."[14]

There was no question of recalling a period of distress that did not appear sufficiently heroic, nor did it make sense to remember efforts to provide help. The humanitarian challenges and those who had attempted to remedy them had to be expunged, suppressed from memory. Many war victims had lived through total war: the memory of their painful experience could not be "total."[15]

For the Armenians in particular, secrecy, denial, and the impossibility of judging the guilty were at the heart of the process of annihilation. Here we see the internal dynamics of impunity at work: denial stands in for truth, and amnesia wins when, the war being over, the cause of the atrocities and extermination is not useful anymore. The demonizing of the enemy's war had been all-important at Versailles; afterward it lost that utility.

As a result, the total war on unarmed populations vanished from memory. Once the goal was attained, it was possible to disregard the pretext for the punishment meted out to the Germans at Versailles. The paradox is striking: accusatory and guilt-inducing arguments over Germany's treatment of defenseless enemies were used in order to achieve a more effective punishment—then they were quickly forgotten. The treaty of 1919 aimed to delegitimize the enemy by assigning sole responsibility for this particular war—that is, to delegitimize the war undertaken by the enemy. But the result was instead the relegitimization of the war in the eyes of a defeated enemy who felt fully justified in taking it up again. And it is this warmongering that finally won the day, in another war where violence and cruelty were to reach the extremes that we know too well. The blindness expressed at Versailles was extended throughout the interwar generations, who failed to perceive the infection of the world by the culture of violence derived from the Great War. This failure to perceive how far its brutalization had irretrievably linked them together demonstrates how deeply the atrocity was now inscribed in the heart of Western societies.

From Myth to Propaganda and Denial: Approaching World War II and the Holocaust

Between 1914 and 1918, the peoples of Europe had discovered that war now meant more than conflict between the armies and the patriotic cultures of wholly mobilized nations. But even as they learned this terrible lesson, they forgot too much. The Armenian massacres are a paradigmatic example: in 1918, persecution returned when the Turks took advantage of the chaos brought on by the Russian Revolution in order to occupy territories in Transcaucasia where thousands of Armenians had taken refuge. In this case, even the Germans, like

General Erich Ludendorff and Field Marshal Paul von Hindenburg himself, did not hide the atrocities. Nevertheless, in apocalyptic terms, the Turkish press again accused the Armenians of being responsible for the atrocities: "The Armenian organizations have a systematic plan to annihilate the Turkish race. . . . But the Turkish race is so strong that it is guaranteed by nature and God from extermination. . . . Since the Armenians have been condemned by God to live in the middle of this world, wherever they are will become hell for them."[16]

It was in Germany, in part because of the wartime alliance with the Ottoman Empire, that more questions were asked: missionaries, starting with Johannes Lepsius, told judges what they had witnessed, in particular at the trial of Soghomon Tehlirian, who had killed ex-Grand Vizier Talaat Pasha in Berlin in 1921.[17] At the time, the young Lvov student of linguistics Raphael Lemkin did make use of the lesson: he asked one of his teachers why the Germans had not arrested Talaat, knowing he was in Berlin, whereas his killer was being judged: "It is a crime for Tehlirian to kill a man, but it is not a crime for his oppressor to kill more than a million men? This is most inconsistent."[18]

This inconsistency was not going to escape a clever, defeated soldier of World War I: Adolf Hitler. As early as 1931, the bitter war veteran linked his desire for revenge to the issue of deportation: "Everywhere, people are awaiting a New World Order. We intend to introduce a great resettlement policy. . . . Think of the biblical deportations and the massacres of the Middle Ages . . . and remember the extermination of the Armenians."[19] And yet in 1939 the führer was able to jeer at the failure of Europeans to remember the massacre of Armenians in 1915: "After all, who still speaks today of the elimination of the Armenians?"[20]

Implied in Hitler's dismissive remark was a psychological, diplomatic, and moral calculation. Because no one "remembered" or acknowledged the murder of the Armenians in a public way, Hitler reasoned, their killers had got away with the crime. The Germans too, he implied, could do as they liked against the Jews, without fear of outside intervention. Thus, erasure of one group of victims' suffering facilitated targeting another group of people with impunity.

Of other aspects of the totalization of war even Hitler's cynicism retained no memory, and he was not alone. In 1915 and 1916, everybody had known. A caricature showing German soldiers in Lille said it very well: "They are complaining! What would they do if they were in Armenia?" But apart from the victims, who cared? Everyone had forgotten. Beyond the confidence of murderers in their impunity and their belief that the battle of death and memory had been settled once and for all, the denial of specific recollections of the sufferings of the civilians in invaded and occupied territories also contributed to the obliteration of memory. The cynical suppression of memories belonged to totalitarianism, but democracies knew about it and let it go. The atrocity reports, however, contained some irrefutable eyewitness accounts; they also included narratives that were recognized sooner or later as a form of myth, like those about the corpse factory and the cutting off of children's hands. The Allied nations' propaganda, particularly that of the British, faithfully circulated accounts of every crime, whether real or fabricated; so faithfully that, from after the war until publication of the work of historians in the 1990s and the first decade of the twenty-first century, these "atrocities" were often thought of as invention, pure and simple.[21]

The baby was thrown out with the bathwater, at both ends of the political spectrum. Former combatants turned pacifists, especially the militant pacifists, thought of war itself as an atrocity, and it was therefore not necessary to put forward any account of exaction that might be neither more nor less than propaganda. In pacifist eyes, such accounts only served to deflect popular attention from the true struggle to be undertaken: the fight against war itself. Atrocity propaganda therefore became the pacifists' scapegoat, the all-too-obvious explanation for the willingness of nations to fight each other, their consent to this tragedy that left ten million dead: they had been misled, and it would not happen again. This approach did not prevent the future perpetrators from playing with such inverted memories. In *Mein Kampf*, Hitler claimed that the superiority of English propaganda, particularly when it came to "inventing" atrocities, would not be forgotten in future conflicts.[22]

In 1939–40, the people of Europe saw the drama of invasion and occupation revived. But this time the atrocities took on a different dimension, as can be seen in the May and June massacres in France perpetrated by members of the SS Totenkopf (Death's Head) Division at different sites along their path. In France, they deliberately chose to terrorize the population by killing civilians, especially refugees who had nowhere to hide, and colonial troops, for racist reasons. These horrors happened everywhere in occupied Europe, but during the entire war, a tendency persisted to see the atrocity reports as at least partly exaggerated, and this weakened any impact that their disclosure might have had.

Worse, there was a total confusion between Nazi atrocities in general (Lidice or Oradour, for example) and the specific destruction of the Jews.[23] This selectivity constitutes what Raul Hilberg called "functional blindness." Levinas, again, as early as 1934, had foreseen what was at stake, in his illuminating article, "Some Thoughts on the Philosophy of Hitlerism": "Perhaps we have succeeded in showing that racism is not opposed only to this or that particular point of Christian or liberal culture. It is not one or another tenet of democracy, of parliamentary government, of dictatorial regimes, or of religious polities that is at stake. It is the very humanity of man."[24] But Levinas remained alone in this position for a long time.

Deborah Lipstadt has shown that for the American press—and this can certainly be applied even to many of our contemporaries—doubts arose from the absence of eyewitnesses.[25] I call this doubt the Saint Thomas syndrome—the easily understood mistrust of information that came from the Soviet Union, and the universalization of suffering during the war, which itself was perceived as the ultimate atrocity, a direct heritage of World War I.[26]

It is important to emphasize the precedent of World War I atrocity stories, as the *Christian Century* admitted in May 1945: "We have found it hard to believe that the reports from the Nazi concentration camps could be true. Almost desperately we have tried to think they must be widely exaggerated. Perhaps they were products of the fevered brains of prisoners who were out for revenge. Or perhaps they were just more atrocity-mongering, like the cadaver factory story of the last war. But such puny barricades cannot stand up against the terrible facts."[27]

How could the murder of the Jews in Europe even be hinted at to those who believed that the worst tales of the Great War had all been lies and propaganda? This skepticism provoked a special message broadcast by Cardinal Hinsley, the archbishop of Westminster, on July 9, 1942: "Some people there are who reject offhand anything and everything that does not directly touch their own noses. . . . There are still other people who dismiss even the clearest evidence with the sneer, 'Oh! British Propaganda.' But mighty is the truth; murder will out. Here and now I am going to tell some items of the truth about the murderous work of the Nazis in Poland."[28]

Raphael Lemkin himself linked his invention of the word *genocide* to 1918; this connection is made clear in various parts of his Axis book of 1944.[29] There, in particular, he examined forced labor for deportees from Belgium and France during World War I and quoted writers who addressed these practices.[30] He also stated that, as early as 1933, he had presented a report to the Madrid International Conference for the Unification of Penal Law, "to the effect that actions aiming at the destruction and oppression of populations (i.e., what would amount to the current concept of genocide) should be penalized."[31]

In his 1945 article "Genocide, a Modern Crime," Lemkin summarized his thoughts. First he quoted Field Marshal Gerd von Rundstedt "aping the führer" in 1943: "One of the great mistakes of 1918 was to spare the civil life of the enemy countries, for it is necessary for us Germans to be always at least double the numbers of the peoples of the contiguous countries. We are therefore obliged to destroy at least a third of their inhabitants. The only means is organized underfeeding, which in this case is better than machine guns." Then Lemkin continued with his own commentary: "Hitler was right. The crime of the Reich in wantonly and deliberately wiping out whole peoples is not utterly new in the civilized world. It is only new in the civilized world as we have come to think of it. It is so new in the traditions of civilized man that he has no name for it. It is for this reason that I took the liberty of inventing the word 'genocide.'"[32]

The manipulation of opinion based on false reports of atrocities in 1914–18 or ignorance of real atrocities is found at the center of the Holocaust. In 1942 the French philosopher Jacques Maritain, who, along with his Jewish wife, was a refugee in Princeton during the war, said: "People don't like being told of atrocities. They don't like agonizing problems. They don't like problems which might perchance result in some self-examination. They would prefer to ignore the problem of anti-Semitism, yet Nazi ferocity obliges them to confront it. Indeed anti-Semitism is at the very core of the outburst of barbarity which is today making the world bloody."[33]

But it is the actors and victims themselves who are able to give us more revealing clues. In 1942 the Jewish publicist Victor Gollancz published a book in England, *"Let My People Go,"* to warn the British public of what was happening in Poland. It opens with two pages in which he had to distinguish between what was truly happening in 1942 and the invention of atrocities in the past.[34] The same year, the Polish Jew Calel Perechodnik wrote his devastating account of the deportation of his family to Treblinka, *Am I a Murderer? Testament of a Jewish Ghetto Policeman,* although it would be years before the book appeared, first in Polish and subsequently translated into English.[35] What is particularly strange in Perechodnik's book is the general absence of the Germans. They were the promoters of a fiendish drama in which the actors were principally Polish, particularly Catholics, and Jews, including Perechodnik himself, because as a member of the Jewish ghetto police, he had been forced to shut his wife, his little girl, and his friends into cattle trucks departing for the death camp of Treblinka.[36]

What is striking, initially as a secondary consideration, and then like a missing link that suddenly falls into its proper place, is the fact that a victim of the Holocaust himself sends us back to the Great War, and in particular to one of its most mythologized, distorted, forgotten, and denied aspects: the "German atrocities." Perechodnik addressed his lost friends and loved ones: "You ran away from Treblinka in order to tell the world untrue things about Greater Germany! You will be preaching *Greuelpropaganda* [atrocity propaganda]? No, Germans, don't worry about escapees. They will come with a transport of Jews from another town."[37]

In his memoirs, Gerhart Riegner, the secretary of the World Jewish Congress who, in 1942, sent the first telegram from Geneva warning the world about the "Final Solution," tried to explain how it was totally impossible to convey what had been going on in Eastern Europe since 1939. In his chapter titled "Why We Failed," Riegner gave a first reason, "a persecution whose scale was with no imaginable precedent," and then he came to the "legendary atrocities of the First World War." "A second factor, little known but devastating, was the number of reports on the German atrocities of World War I, reports that, after the war, had been proven false. This was very damaging to us. People were telling us: 'All this is invented, exactly as during the First World War.' We had to make an enormous effort to try to convince them of the truth of our reports about the Shoah."[38] Thus the inability and the lack of desire to distinguish between truth and lies—most amazingly, even among the victims themselves—can be linked to the worst horror of the twentieth century. Already in 1940, as in 1942 or 1945, it was too late to invent myths about atrocities.

NOTES

All my thanks to the Fondation pour la Mémoire de la Shoah, whose funding allowed me to speak at the Lessons and Legacies Conference; and to Dolores Burdick, who not only transformed my French-English into English, but gave a soul to this text.

1. Interview from 1986 with François Poirié, in *Emmanuel Lévinas: Qui êtes-vous?* ed. François Poirié (Lyon: Editions La Manufacture, 1987), 63–65. All translations in this chapter are by the author and Dolores Burdick unless otherwise noted.

2. Annette Becker, *War and Faith: The Religious Imagination in France, 1914–1930* (Oxford: Berg, 1998).

3. Michael Pollack, "'Le témoignage' et 'La gestion de l'indicible,'" *Actes de la Recherche en Sciences Sociales* 62–63 (June 1986): 3–53.

4. Raphael Lemkin, appendix, "Hague Convention, article 44," quoted in *Axis Rule in Occupied Europe* (Washington, D.C.: Carnegie Endowment for International Peace, 1944).

5. In World War I, concentration camps were used against civilians for the fourth time at least. The Spanish general Valeriano Weyler invented this punishment in Cuba in 1896–97. He called it "reconcentration," which meant interning civilians in addition to burning lands and homes. The British continued the system during the Boer War, and the Germans did so in South-West Africa during the extermination of the Herero. For a detailed study of the occupation of northern France, see Annette Becker, *Oubliés de la Grande Guerre: Humanitaire et culture de guerre, 1914–1918: Populations occupées, déportés civils, prisonniers de guerre* (Paris: Noêsis, 1998); Annette Becker, "La genesi dei campi di concentramento: da Cuba alla Grande Guerra" ["The Genesis of Concentration Camps: Cuba, Boer War, First World War"], in *Storia della Shoah: La crisi dell'Europa, lo sterminio degli ebrei e la memoria del XX secolo*, vol. 1, *La crisi dell' Europa: le origini e il contesto*, ed. Marina Cattaruzza and others (Turin: UTET Garzanti, 2005).

6. Text in English quoted in G. F. Nicolai, *The Biology of War* (New York: Century, 1918), xii.

7. Vatican Archives, box 302, "Nonciature de Munich," a file of 63 pages, item 1:

"I Tedeschi prigionari di guerra nelle mani dell'esercito francese." Violazione del diritto internazionale e barbarie come nel fronte francese (ed inglese) e in zona di guerra. (par le ministère de la guerre prussien) "Una stanza di tortura e la grida dei tormentati che se essa risuonano, penetrano negli orecchi dell'umanità del secolo 20 con tanto più terribile effetto in quanto che al senso di raccapricio si coniunge purtropo una delusione immensa. Una nazione che fa parte della famiglia dei popoli civili; che anzi si compiace di chiamarsi la nazione civile per excellenza, rinega il progresso copiuto dall'umanità dall epoca dei martiri . . . se precipite nell abysso della più spietata barbarie . . . Solo i popoli selvaggi tormentano i nemici caduti vivi nelle loro mani . . . La Francia transforma in ammazzato le sue zone di guerra e in stanze di tortura i suoi accompamenti di priggioneri."

8. Ibid.

9. Vatican Archives, box 302. Report of May 16, 1917, regarding various accusations against the Germans at the Somme and including a May 1917 interview with General Hermann von Stein, Prussian minister of war, by an Argentine journalist for *La Nación*. During the Leipzig trial in 1921, this accusation (of a factory for processing human corpses) would be brought before the tribunal, but to this day, no proof has been found. See Becker, *Oubliés de la Grande Guerre*, 371–74. Twelve Germans accused of war crimes were tried at Leipzig. The Allies insisted on trials in the postwar settlement at Versailles, but the German government undertook the prosecution and German judges presided. Six of the men were convicted. The maximum sentence received was four years.

10. Session of the Chamber of Deputies (October 22, 1918).

11. Clemenceau quoted in Philip Mason Burnett, *Reparation at the Paris Peace Conference from the Standpoint of the American Delegation* (New York: Octagon Books, 1965), 143.

12. Affirmation of the United States Record on the Armenian Genocide Resolution, 106th Congress, 2nd Session, House of Representatives, May 24, 1915.

13. Yair Auron, *The Banality of Indifference: Zionism and the Armenian Genocide* (New Brunswick, N.J., and London: Transaction, 2000).

14. Pollack, "'Le témoignage' et 'La gestion de l'indicible,'" 22.

15. On memory and forgetfulness, see Annette Becker, *Maurice Halbwachs: Un intellectuel en guerres mondiales, 1914–1945* (Paris: Agnès Viénot, 2003).

16. *Hilal,* March 14, 1918. Vatican Archives, "Guerra 14–18," box 244; folder 112. 1918:

On frémit devant les tableaux des atrocités commises pas eux . . . On ne raisonne pas avec des illuminés et des insensés . . . 850 corps mutiles et défigurés . . . des enfants de 2 mois, des vieillards de 90 ans, des femmes enceintes, des jeunes filles violées, etc. . . . Dans cette vaste étendue ils ont tué tous ceux qu'ils ont rencontré, ils ont brûlé les villages, abattu les animaux. . . . Aussi parmi les Turcs de Transcaucasie . . . C'est ainsi que les organisations arméniennes appliquent systématiquement leur plan d'anéantissement de la race turque . . . L'histoire se prononcera certainement un jour sur le compte de ces criminels civilisés. Quant au présent, ces insensés doivent savoir que leurs crimes leur coûteront cher. Ce n'est pas à une poignée d'Arméniens conduits par des officiers anglais et français, qu'il est donné d'exterminer la race turque; celle-ci est si forte qu'elle est garantie par la nature et Dieu même contre l'anéantissement. Tout au plus ces crimes et ces atrocités provoqueront-ils une indignation inoubliable dans le vaste monde qui va jusqu'aux confins de la Chine et comme les Arméniens sont par Dieu même condamnés à vivre justement au milieu de ce monde, quelles que soient les mains dans lesquelles ils se trouvent, il deviendra un enfer pour eux. Voilà le seul résultat auquel peut aboutir tant de crimes!

17. *Justicier du génocide arménien: Le procès de Tehlirian* (Bayeux: Imprimerie Bayeusaine, 1981).

18. Samantha Power, *A Problem from Hell: America and the Age of Genocide* (New York: Basic Books, 2002), 17.

19. Quoted in Vahakn Dadrian, *The History of the Armenian Genocide* (Oxford: Berghahn Books, 1995), 408.

20. Ibid., 406.

21. John Horne and Allan Kramer, *German Atrocities 1914: A History of Denial* (Cambridge, Eng.: Cambridge University Press, 2000); Stéphane Audoin-Rouzeau, *Le fils de l'Allemand* (Paris: Aubier, 1996); Annette Becker, "Life in an Occupied Zone: Lille-Roubaix-Tourcoing, 1914–1918," in *Facing Armageddon: The First World War Experienced,* ed. Hugh Cecil and Peter Liddle (London: Cooper, 1996); Stéphane Audoin-Rouzeau and Annette Becker, *14–18: Understanding the Great War,* trans. Catherine Temerson (New York: Hill and Wang, 2002); Leonard Smith, Stéphane Audoin-Rouzeau, and Annette Becker, *France and the Great War, 1914–1918* (Cambridge, Eng.: Cambridge University Press, 2003).

22. Adolf Hitler, *Mein Kampf* (Munich: F. Eher, 1925).

23. Or "Holocaust": the term was used for the Armenians as early as the massacres of 1895.

24. Emmanuel Levinas, *Quelques réflexions sur la philosophie de l'Hitlérisme* (Paris: Rivages, 1997), 120.

25. Deborah Lipstadt, *Beyond Belief: The American Press and the Coming of the Holocaust, 1933–1945* (New York: Free Press, 1986).

26. For the specificity of the Russian, then Soviet, violence, see, among other works, the illuminating article by Nicolas Werth, "Les déportations des 'populations suspectes' dans les espaces russes et soviétiques, 1914–1953,"

Communisme 78/79 (2004): 11–43. Werth shows the difference between the violence against civilians in 1914–17 during total war, like expulsions and forced displacements to "help" the war effort, where the Jewish population was particularly chosen because it was living in the area of the front line; and the later deportations of Stalinist times, which were seen as "social engineering." At least five hundred thousand to six hundred thousand Russian Jews were deported during World War I. See S. Ansky, *The Enemy at His Pleasure: A Journey Through the Jewish Pale of Settlement During World War I,* ed. and trans. Joachim Neugroschel (New York: Metropolitan Books, 2002).

27. *Christian Century,* May 9, 1945: quoted in Lipstadt, *Beyond Belief,* 575.

28. Quoted in David Wyman, *America and the Holocaust,* vol. 1, *Confirming the News of Extermination* (New York: Garland, 1990), 29.

29. Lemkin, *Axis Rule in Occupied Europe.*

30. "The enormous scale on which the policy of deportation was carried out and the harsh and indiscriminate, not to say cruel, way in which it was executed, makes it comparable to the slave raids on the Gold Coast of Africa in the seventeenth century. It appears to be without precedent in modern wars. . . . Not since the beginning of the modern age—not even during the Thirty Years' War—has any invader seized and virtually enslaved a large part of the civil population in order to carry on his own industries at home and release his own able bodied men for military service." James W. Gardner, *International Law and the World War* (New York, 1920), 183: quoted in Lemkin, *Axis Rule in Occupied Europe,* 72.

31. Lemkin, *Axis Rule in Occupied Europe,* 91.

32. Raphael Lemkin, "Genocide, a Modern Crime," *Free World* 4 (April 1945): 39–43. For more on Lemkin, see Anson Rabinbach, "The Challenge of the Unprecedented: Raphael Lemkin and the Concept of Genocide," in *Simon Dubnov Institute Yearbook,* vol. 4 (Göttingen: Vandenhoeck and Ruprecht, 2005), 397–420.

33. Jacques Maritain, "Anti-Semitism as a Problem for the Jew," *Commonwealth* (September 25, 1942), in Maritain, *Oeuvres complètes,* vol. 8, *1944–1946* (Fribourg: Editions Universitaires, 1982), 734.

34. Victor Gollancz, *"Let My People Go": Some Practical Proposals for Dealing with Hitler's Massacre of the Jews and an Appeal to the British Public* (London: V. Gollancz, 1942).

35. Calel Perechodnik, *Am I a Murderer? Testament of a Jewish Ghetto Policeman* (Boulder, Colo.: Westview, 1996), xxxi, 255.

36. The fascinating account of the pogrom in Jedwabne (July 10, 1941) told by Jan Gross in *Neighbors: The Destruction of the Jewish Community in Jedwabne, Poland* (Princeton, N.J.: Princeton University Press, 2001) can

be put in relation with Perechodnik's book. (Of course, Gross also factors in the Soviet occupation of eastern Poland from 1939 to 1941).

37. Perechodnik, *Am I a Murderer?* 51.

38. Gerhart M. Riegner, *Ne jamais désespérer: Soixante ans au service du peuple juif et des droits de l'homme* (Paris: Éditions du Cerf, 1998), 87. Texts of the exchanges between U.S. authorities and the president of the American Jewish Congress are published in Wyman, *America and the Holocaust,* 1:185–210.

Kate Brown

The Final Solution Turns East:
How Soviet Internationalism Aided
and Abetted Nazi Racial Genocide

UNTIL RECENTLY, HISTORIANS OF THE HOLOCAUST HAVE PAID little attention to the genesis of the Final Solution in occupied Ukraine and Belorussia.[1] Yet this eastern chapter of the history of the Final Solution is essential to understand it. For once the German army crossed into Soviet territory in the summer of 1941, there was a marked shift in Nazi racial policies. In right-bank Ukraine—i.e., that part of Ukraine lying west of the Dnieper River, in the former tsarist Pale of Settlement, a region containing one of the highest concentrations of Jews in Europe—SS killing squads began for the first time to kill not only Jewish men, but women and children en masse.

As opposed to Western Europe or Poland, in the territories of the former Soviet Union, Nazi officials did not trouble with the expense of shipping Jews to remote death camps for extermination. Nor did Nazi officials in Ukraine bother with long-term ghettos set up to impoverish and isolate Jews before killing them.[2] Instead, SS units killed Jews in Ukraine without a vast bureaucracy, sophisticated technology, and the years in ghettos, which elsewhere in Europe served to weaken communities of Jews emotionally and physically. Throughout the summer and fall of 1941 and again in the summer and fall of 1942, Jews of right-bank Ukraine were simply marched to the outskirts of towns and cities and shot into mass graves. The process was uncomplicated, expedient, and brutal. The only major factor that hindered the killing of Jews in Ukraine was the cold and snow of the winter of 1941–42. Why was the killing of Jews less complicated in Ukraine than elsewhere in Europe? Why did the first mass murders of entire Jewish communities begin in occupied Ukraine and Belorussia?

B. F. Sabrin is representative of a group of historians who argue that the murder of Jews in Ukraine was facilitated by an age-old Ukrainian antisemitism. Ukrainians in every village, town, and city, he argues, were all too willing to aid Germans on their killing path.[3] Indeed, at the start of the war, Nazi propagandists produced newsreels showing angry Ukrainians attacking Jews in retribution for the crimes of Soviet Communism. These scenes, however, derive largely from the former Polish territory annexed by the Soviet Union in 1939.[4] Nazis found it easier to target Jews as the scapegoats for Communism in the former Polish lands, where the two-year Soviet rule had been brutal, was popularly associated with Jewish Communists, and had been preceded by years of official government and popular antisemitism in interwar Poland.

In contrast, however, in the pre-1939 regions of the Soviet Union, SS squads had great difficulty inciting locals in pogroms against Jews. In 1941, reporters assigned to SS killing units in right-bank Ukraine frequently grumbled that "carefully planned attempts to incite pogroms against Jews have unfortunately not shown the results hoped for."[5] Especially in Soviet Ukraine, German officials complained that locals showed "a greater accommodation to associate with Jews," a habit, they said, which had developed over centuries of cohabitation. "Almost nowhere," an official wrote, "could the population be induced to take active steps against the Jews."[6]

Less than indigenous antisemitism, the relative ease in killing Jews in Soviet Ukraine had more to do with the strongly racial nature of the war in the East, the failure to that date to find a "solution" for Jews gathered in ghettos in Poland, and, as I will show, the Soviet organization of space and populations. For once in occupied Ukraine, SS killing units had very little trouble identifying, isolating, and killing Jews. The hard work of combing through populations and sorting people by blood had been done before the German Wehrmacht arrived in Ukraine. German officials in the Soviet Union did not need ghettos and concentration camps to identify and isolate Jews because the Soviet administration had already sorted the population by nationality.[7] Nationality, in fact, was so thoroughly inscribed onto the bureaucratic and physical landscape that German officials had only to consult published Soviet demographic maps to find Jews. In the

Reich, Soviet nationality maps of Ukraine had been available for years. They were published by Wolodymyr Kubijowytsch, who generally translated Soviet demographic maps into Ukrainian and German and published them under his own name.[8]

Once they arrived in a town or city, German officials sent messages anxiously asking if the advance troops had seized the Soviet records.[9] They desperately wanted Soviet records because they knew their value. For example, in the archives of the U.S. Holocaust Memorial Museum in Washington, D.C., I came across a handwritten document in Ukrainian buried among administrative tax records. It was a Soviet census record that German officials had seized from the Vinnytsia city archives.[10] The document lists names of city residents in rows down the page, while columns record date of birth, registration, and nationality. Next to every person identified as Jewish someone had placed a check mark in pencil, a mundane yet deadly identifying marker. In this way, Soviet records provided a map for Nazi genocide.

To put it another way, progressive Soviet internationalism paved the way for Nazi racial genocide. Thanks to decades of careful ethnic accounting of space and bodies by Soviet reformers, Nazi occupiers found a pre-sorted racial terrain. They could look at maps and pinpoint populations of Jews, Poles, Ukrainians, and ethnic Germans. They could enter a town, a factory, or a collective farm, seize the records, and determine the nationality of everyone there. Yet more than just ease, the Soviet creation of ethno-territorial space made the enactment of racial hierarchies seem natural, almost inevitable, because once populations had been demarcated and categorized, the next step involved putting the puzzling mosaic of nationalities in order, "ethnographic order," as Adolf Hitler called it.[11]

Comparisons of Nazi and Stalinist totalitarianism notwithstanding, Soviet state-builders of the late 1920s and 1930s and Nazi German occupiers can hardly be conceived as natural allies. Throughout the 1930s, Soviet Communists were openly committed to internationalism and, more than any other power in Europe, they focused on contesting Nazi racism and national fascism. Moreover, the job of categorizing and labeling the Soviet Ukrainian population by race had been a long and costly process. Why would Soviet officials work so hard to designate not only every individual but all space with ethnicity, a category they saw as only a passing phase?

The irony is that Soviet nationality policy was directed at the eventual disappearance of national differences. Soviet nationality theorists hoped to trump the tsarist legacy of official Russian nationalism and forced assimilation by elevating all national languages and cultures to official status. In so doing, they hoped to deliver the socialist message in nationalist form to create a truly internationalist landscape. In Ukraine, more than any other Soviet republic, officials took this policy very seriously, pouring money and energy into national-minority programs. By 1926 there were eleven officially chartered national minority regions in Ukraine and nearly three hundred national-autonomous villages. To support these minority regions, socialist reformers created an entire infrastructure of publishing houses, newspapers, courts, schools, libraries, cultural centers, radio programs, clubs, and theaters for each ethnic group in each minority language. No minority, no matter how humble and inconsequential, could be overlooked. In Dnipropetrovs'k, for example, city leaders set up a newspaper in Hungarian for all of the thirty-six Hungarians who lived there.[12]

To carry out this policy, Soviet officials first had to take a count. The census and demographic map became a vitally important instrument for Soviet reformers to figure out what kinds of programs to fund and where. Counting, however, was not easy, especially in right-bank Ukraine, along the western border with Poland. Investigators found that people supposedly belonging to different nationalities were indiscernible. As one census-taker noted: "Ukrainians and Poles hardly differ from one another in their material existence beyond their conversational language—however, language too is problematic, because the local Polish sounds very much like the local Ukrainian."[13] When asked to state their nationality, many peasants replied simply "Catholic." Other peasants said they spoke "in the peasant way" (*po-chlopski*), or "in the simple way" (*po-prostomu*), or "the language of here" (*tutai'ishi*).[14] Investigators went from location to location reporting that no two villages were alike; each place contained a different blend of language, ethnicity, and social composition.

After the revolution when the native elite fled, the majority of the population consisted of villagers and peasants, most of whom in 1925 were illiterate. Literacy promotes the standardization of language and identity. In the absence of literacy, people spoke in fluid dialects that differed from year to year, village to village, and even speaker to speaker. As one frustrated census-taker in right-bank Ukraine noted,

"There is no one picture of the border region. There are many; the picture is diffuse."[15] In the 1920s, the boundaries that standardized languages generally establish between peoples were still blurry. Yiddish mixed with German and Polish, while Polish wrapped around languages eventually identified as Ukrainian and Belorussian.

This situation should come as no surprise, because there were few aspects of the local economic and political structure to promote unifying ethnic identities. The region was known for its small farms, poor, sandy soil, and general poverty, all exacerbated by classic tsarist undergovernance. After the devastation of World War I, the revolution, the civil war, and the Polish-Soviet War, most people had retreated to subsistence economies, gathering in the forests for fuel and calories, heating with pine splinters instead of kerosene, trading in local markets with cumbersome bags of rye.[16] After the Treaty of Riga in 1921 established the Polish-Soviet border through right-bank Ukraine, this territory, once on the route to the Polish territories of the Russian Empire, became a forgotten borderland where highways and trade ended in border guard posts. Because of the many swamps and lack of good bridges and roads, some communities were cut off entirely for the rainy spring and fall months. In short, there were few common currencies, commodities, and means of communication to universalize local cultures and languages.

Religion too functioned in a decentralized way. Jews in the region inclined toward Hasidism, each community following its own zaddik, each dynasty named after the local community. Christian communities showed a similar trend. Instead of following the centralized Orthodox or Catholic churches, an estimated 75 percent of Christians participated in local evangelical sects led by a member of the community.[17] Anyone could start a new religious community; all they needed was to have been inhabited by the spirit of Christ or the Virgin Mary. Jewish Hasidim and Christian evangelicals alike stressed divine, received knowledge over that of religious texts and religious ecstasy and feeling over doctrine. As a consequence, religion too was hardly a centralizing force in Ukraine before World War II. In fact, the community-centered nature of local religions fostered regional syncretism over nationalizing trends.

Contemporary voices noted these haphazard meeting points of mostly poor, village Jews and Christians. The ethnographer P. P. Chubinskii marveled in the 1870s: "Among Jews there are many mythological stories of the same kind that circulate among the local [non-Jewish] population."[18] Peasants went to the *banya*. Jews went to the *mikvah*. In both places, unclean forces floated in the steamy mists. The braided bread called *challah* by Jews and *kalach* by Christians possessed sacred qualities in both cultures. For Jews and Christians, homes were haunted by spirits and demons; so too were the forests, swamps, and crossroads. As the Yiddish writer Der Nister put it, "Jews conjured away the disease of the peasants in [their] own language, Yiddish, while peasants conjured away Jewish illnesses in their Polish tongue."[19] Perhaps because knowledge and belief were local, passed down orally, and derived from personal divine sources, there was no great impetus to acquire literacy and thus the standardized and standardizing forms of knowledge that came with it. Outsiders to the region, who noted this trait and the large numbers of illiterates, called it "backward." But there are uses to backwardness. One of them is a cultural self-sufficiency that translates into local power.

Precisely because of the puzzling borderland nature of right-bank Ukraine that made it so difficult to rule, Soviet officials worked all the harder to define ethnicity in this territory. Soviet officials spent more money and effort on national minority programs in right-bank Ukraine than in any other region of the country.[20] And with a head count, they could construct an important tool of modern governance—a demographic map. With a map they could draw borders and make what was illusionary plain for all to see: concrete ethnic territories encircling tangible ethnic bodies.[21] For this reason, Soviet officials embarked on a painstaking search for the national. The subdivision of territory went on endlessly, splitting not only villages but families down the middle, even dividing sister from brother.[22] Each new territorial subdivision meant that the numbers of national villages and schools continued to grow, the charts showing a majestic march upward. By 1930, the last national minority territories were formed, and the map was wholly filled in with nationalized space. It was a proud moment: the socialist state magnanimously gave to all that which the tsarist regime had once taken—language, self-determination, and local autonomy.

The only problem was that the census and map were gross simplifications of reality. As Benedict Anderson states, "The fiction of the census is that everyone is in it, and that everyone has one—and only one—extremely clear place. No fractions."[23] The borderlands, however, by their very nature consisted of fractions. National identity was a characteristic that could change depending on marriage, education, and fate. "Nationality was not a race, but a choice," the Polish memoirist Jerzy Stempowski notes. "A Pole could become a German," or "if a Pole married a Russian, their children would usually become Ukrainian or Lithuanian."[24]

As a consequence, it took many years of hard work by Soviet officials to try to get people to make primary numbers of their divided identities. Soviet officials found that once they issued ethnic identities, people resisted them. Jews did not want to send their children to Yiddish schools. Germans did not know enough German to write and edit a German news sheet. Ukrainians preferred to learn Polish because it was the language of the *Pan* (the master), and Poles continually slipped into Ukrainian in the Polish village council meetings.[25]

Eventually because of this lack of interest, by the mid-1930s these "affirmative action" programs had faded away.[26] What remained of the ambitious national minority program was only the data: charts, statistics, and maps that sorted populations by language and ethnicity in almost every conceivable administrative situation so that ethnicity was thoroughly inscribed on the Soviet landscape. By the mid-1930s, this data began to take on an agency of its own. Soviet security officials worried about the failure of socialist programs in general and, specifically, about a mass peasant uprising in right-bank Ukraine in 1930, which had stopped collectivization in its tracks.[27] They turned to their charts to figure out what was wrong. They found, strangely enough, that people labeled Polish and German joined the Communist Party and collective farms at lower rates than people labeled Ukrainian and Jewish. From this information, they logically reasoned that Poles and Germans were in league with fascist Poles and Germans in Poland and Germany. Soviet leaders "logically" postulated that "the low level of collectivization in German villages is a sign that the villages support fascist Germany."[28]

This assumption made sense in the simplifying narrative of national affiliation: people who had no connection with one another were linked on a page, digit added to digit, so that the failure of socialist programs in right-bank Ukraine looked very much like a nationalist plot to undermine the Soviet Union by people united statistically as Poles and Germans acting as a fifth column on behalf of Nazi Germany and fascist Poland, both sworn enemies of the Communist U.S.S.R.

With this evidence in hand, Soviet security officials took action. In 1936 they deported Poles and Germans from Ukraine to remote Kazakhstan. During the Great Purges, from 1937 to 1939, security officials established national "lines," networks of insiders and experts (Polish, German, Jewish), to hunt for traitors.[29] With the deportations and arrests, the ambiguities of identities turned into discrete, precise national categories. These categories took on a new agency. People learned that ethnic identity could determine, in a terrible way, the course of one's life.

This is the terrain that the Wehrmacht occupied in the summer of 1941. It was a place where ethnic identity had acquired very concrete meanings—inscribed by cartographic and statistical replication and then repression. Yet, even so, the hybrid qualities of identity still existed beneath the seemingly clear-cut, national designations. In other words, although Soviet census data was extremely thorough and ubiquitous, the numbers and maps they produced lied.

German officials in occupied Ukraine realized just how wrong the data was once they started trying to apply it to enact their racial hierarchies. SS killing squads found that in pre-1939 Soviet territory they could not incite the local population in pogroms against Jews. Nazis were amazed to find that despite the clarity of the numbers that distinguished Jews from non-Jews, in reality people did not live these categories in their daily lives. In 1941, reporters assigned to SS killing units in right-bank Ukraine grumbled about the failure to incite locals in pogroms against Jews.[30] Occupying Germans saw what had confounded tsarist and Soviet ethnographers: a pattern of "cohabitation" between Jews and Christians in communities of which Jews were seen as an essential part.

For Nazi planners, the Final Solution was a means to a larger goal: the transformation of Soviet Ukraine into German colonial space. Sonderkommando units arrived in occupied Ukraine not only to kill Jews, but to locate and save ethnic Germans. Theoretically, the *Volksdeutschen* would be easy to locate because, as briefing bulletins promised, one would be able to distinguish the 1.4 million ethnic Germans in the Soviet Union "from their foreign neighbors by their better economic well-being and cleanliness."[31] Karl Stumpp, who led Sonderkommando Stumpp, expected to find self-contained German villages where ethnic Germans had preserved their German character and spoke only German.

To their great disappointment, Stumpp and other German officials found that the *Volksdeutsch* of Ukraine hardly lived up to their racial heritage. As one official noted, "They [ethnic Germans] are poor and raggedly dressed and look disorderly, and one does not take them for Germans. Also, the homes and villages look wrecked, wild, and derelict, no longer like clean, well-kept German villages."[32] Officials complained that ethnic Germans were lazy, undisciplined, poorly suited for work, and easily susceptible to a "welfare mentality."[33] One German administrator wrote to Stumpp, "You know, we are not wholly enraptured with your *Volksdeutsch*."[34] Another occupying German official in Vinnytsia commented, "From a racial point of view the ethnic Germans are on a low level. Also in terms of character they do not make a good impression. In the countryside, we have only two families that are of pure German stock and can speak German."[35] A member of Stumpp's unit explained this scorn for *Volksdeutsch* as a result of their hybrid quality: "Over 50 percent of ethnic Germans have married Ukrainians and have taken on many Ukrainian customs and traditions. This has caused [German] civil administrators to form an unfavorable opinion of ethnic Germans."[36]

German occupiers were not the only ones who failed to recognize their co-nationals in the borderland terrain of right-bank Ukraine. Ukrainian nationalists in the Organization of Ukrainian Nationalists (OUN) from western Ukraine filtered into villages with the German army. The OUN propagandists called meetings where they told villagers that the Ukrainian people had united with Germans to fight Bolshevism, and that Stepan Bandera was the new leader of the Ukrainian people.[37] They asked people to join the OUN, but few accepted their offer. Many villagers scoffed at the idea of an independent Ukraine, saying they had no use for it.[38] The nationalists were surprised and disappointed over this "lack of national feeling among the population," and they found it "difficult to get the youth to collaborate for the good of Ukraine." They were disturbed when borderland Ukrainians did not express hatred of Russians and Poles, but considered them "our own" (*svoi*), and they expressed frustration when people they considered Poles called themselves "Catholics" instead.[39] Like Soviet and German officials, Ukrainian nationalists were confounded by locals' refusal to accept standardized national categories as defining parameters for their lives.

The war was long and had a profound impact on the borderland ure of identity in right-bank Ukraine. Soviet rule in Ukraine had begun the process of imposing nationality through repression. German rule finished this process by violently forcing people to live within racial designations. Education, food, employment, child care, housing, medicine, and punishment—nearly all aspects of life in Nazi-occupied Ukraine—were dictated by identities pegged to the racial hierarchy. Ethnic Germans at the top of the hierarchy were to be the initial stock to repopulate the territory as German nation-space. As a consequence, *Volksdeutsch* were given homes, clothing, and territory taken from Jews and Slavs. Ukrainians were next on the racial ladder. They were recruited for positions of leadership and security in occupied Ukraine. Poles and Russians followed, slated for eventual removal east or annihilation. Jews, of course, were killed without delay.

Soviet educators first categorized and quantified communities and individuals. In so doing, they taught people, especially those with a formal education, to think in terms of ethnic categories. German officials rounded off this education by instructing indigenous populations to hate based on racial categories.[40] Frequent repetition of expressions of hatred, combined with the visible starvation, humiliation, and destruction of Jews, Communists, and Russian prisoners of war, gave Nazi propaganda new meaning.[41] It was easy to recognize the *Untermensch* in the straggling, tattered, and starved columns of Jews. To make the point clearer, German officials staged shows in which Jews were dragged through the streets, poked, and beaten, holding them up as scapegoats for all the problems that afflicted Ukraine.[42]

With policies in place to punish and reward based on race, the Nazi vision of a racially segregated society became a reality in right-bank Ukraine. During the war, society began to polarize in a new way around racial designations. Antisemitic and racist assertions began to find wider appeal among both insurgent and loyal, unoccupied Soviet populations. Even prominent members of Soviet society began to appropriate the antisemitism of the Nazi foe. Before the war, expressions of antisemitism were severely reprimanded in official Soviet society. In 1943, however, members of the Ukrainian Union of Soviet Writers objected to the fact that the president of the union was a Jew, Natan Ribak. At the union meeting, held well behind Soviet lines, the celebrated film director Alexander Dovzhenko made a speech in which he stated, "Jews have poisoned Ukrainian culture. They have hated us, they hate us now and will always hate us. They try to crawl

in everywhere and take over everything."[43] Dovzhenko was not reprimanded by his colleagues, and his speech was followed by a discussion
of whether to dismiss Ribak.

The notion of demographically commanding racial space also
became more compelling during the war. In 1943, Ukrainian nationalists in the Ukrainian Insurgent Army began a campaign to erase all
traces of Poles from "Ukrainian" territory. Poles retaliated in what became a violent fratricidal war that simmered beneath the larger war of
the big powers. After the war, both trends continued. Antisemitism
flourished in postwar Soviet society, and the mutual wars to cleanse
territory became institutionalized in the Polish-Soviet population
transfers.

In sum, during the war, identities were not simply "imagined,"
but were bestowed, dispensed, and forged through violence. Soviet
officials had created maps to understand a complicated terrain. The
maps, however, were a fiction, and officials had trouble compelling
people to live within them. German occupiers borrowed the maps
and gave the imagined national terrain etched on them terrifying new
meaning. In other words, as people were ranked and made to live in
National Socialist racial categories, the categories—dreamt up both
by internationalist socialists and nationalist racial theorists—became
real and took on an alarming power in people's lives. This marriage
of Soviet national minority policy with Nazi racial hierarchies was
violently potent. As a result, not just one but several "final solutions"—
expulsions, expropriations, and genocides—occurred in occupied
Soviet territory.

After the war, it became impossible to be a self-consciously ethnic
German in Ukraine. Ethnic Germans either left with the retreating
Wehrmacht or were arrested as collaborators, hanged immediately, or
sent to the gulag. After the war, Soviet leaders also decided that Jews
had no rightful place in Soviet society. In the midst of the Doctors Plot,
there were rumors that Stalin had issued orders to remove all Soviet
Jews to the Far East. Stalin died and these plans were never carried out,
but the emigration of Soviet Jews to Israel was encouraged instead.
After the war, Ukrainians and Poles too decided that after centuries of
cohabitation, coexistence was no longer feasible, and both Polish and
Soviet leaders violently purged territories and histories of the other in
the postwar population transfers. Indeed, by the end of the century, the
once-colorful demographic map of right-bank Ukraine had become

simple and monochrome. The former multiethnic borderlands now exist as an unambiguously Ukrainian heartland.

NOTES

1. Among those who have focused on the East as the genesis of genocide, see Omer Bartov, *The Eastern Front, 1941–45: German Troops and the Barbarisation of Warfare* (London: Macmillan, 1985); Götz Aly, *"Final Solution": Nazi Population Policy and the Murder of the European Jews* (London: Oxford University Press, 1999); Kate Brown, *A Biography of No Place: From Multiethnic Borderland to Soviet Heartland* (Cambridge, Mass.: Harvard University Press, 2004); Karel Berkoff, *Harvest of Despair* (Cambridge, Mass.: Harvard University Press, 2004); and Wendy Lower, *Nazi Empire-Building and the Holocaust in Ukraine* (Chapel Hill: University of North Carolina Press, 2005).

2. One can see this escalation in cities in Ukraine with large Jewish populations. During the course of the summer of 1941, SS killing squads evolved from first killing only Jewish men to shooting all categories of the Jewish population by August and September. In the Zhytomyr Region, ghettos were used mostly as a pretext to gather Jews before execution and then as a residence for the few Jews working temporarily for the German civil administration. Most of these Jews were killed in the second wave of killing in the summer and fall of 1942. After September 1941, commanders in the Zhytomyr Region found ghettos "not useful." See Wendy Lower, "Nazi Colonial Dreams: German Policies and Ukrainian Society in Zhytomyr, 1941–1944" (Ph.D. diss., American University, Washington, D.C., 1999), 146–48.

3. Sabrin makes no distinction between Ukrainian territory held since 1921 by the Soviet Union and that which had been annexed from Poland in 1939, where the Organization of Ukrainian Nationalists, the OUN, allied initially with Germany, had a stronger presence. See B. F. Sabrin, *Alliance for Murder: The Nazi-Ukrainian Nationalist Partnership in Genocide* (New York: Sarpedon, 1991).

4. See Raul Hilberg, *The Destruction of the European Jews* (New York: Holmes and Meier, 1985); and Jan T. Gross, *Neighbors: The Destruction of the Jewish Community in Jedwabne, Poland* (Princeton, N.J.: Princeton University Press, 2001).

5. In general, pogroms broke out in pre-1939 Soviet Ukrainian territory only after the arrival of the German army and the SS. See Yitzhak Arad, Shmuel Krakowski, and Shmuel Spector, eds., *Einsatzgruppen Reports: Selections from the Dispatches of the Nazi Death Squads' Campaign Against*

the Jews in Occupied Territories of the Soviet Union, July 1941–January 1943 (New York: Holocaust Library, 1989), 79, 131.

6. Ibid.

7. For the larger story of the progressive labeling of space and populations by nationality and the slide of that program into punitive ethnic cleansing, see Brown, *A Biography of No Place;* Terry Martin, *The Affirmative Action Empire: Nations and Nationalism in the Soviet Union, 1923–1939* (Ithaca, N.Y.: Cornell University Press, 2001).

8. See "Ethnografichna mapa Ukrain'ska sotsiialistichnoi radians'koi respubliki," published by the Commission of National Minorities Affairs in Kharkiv in 1925. (The copy in the Library of Congress has the stamp of the German army.) The German-language map published by Wolodymyr Kubijowytsch also relies heavily on the Soviet census and maps. For comparison, see the 1925 map cited above, the "Nationality Map of Ukraine" (Lemberg, 1938), and the "Etnographische Karte der Ukraine" (Reichsamt für Landesaufnahme, 1942).

9. Arad, Krakowski, and Spector, *Einsatzgruppen Reports,* 133–35.

10. "Vinnitsaia gorodskaia uprava, pasportnii otdel," Archives of the United States Holocaust Memorial Museum (hereafter referred to as USHMM), RG 31.01M, reel 1.

11. See a translated copy of "NO 3075: Decree by Führer and Reich Chancellor for the Consolidation of German Folkdom," in Robert Koehl, *RKFDV: German Resettlement and Population Policy, 1939–1945* (Cambridge, Mass.: Harvard University Press, 1957), 247–49.

12. By 1930 there were twenty-five national autonomous regions and 1,087 national village councils (including 254 German, 156 Jewish, 151 Polish, 45 Bulgarian, 30 Greek, 14 Moldavian, 12 Czech, 4 Belorussian, and 3 Albanian). See Gosudarstvenni Arkhiv Rossiskoi Federatsii (hereafter referred to as GARF), 3316/48/73, p. 6 (1927); and Bohdan Chyrko, *Natsional'nye men'shinstva na Ukraine* (Kiev: Chetverta Khvylia, 1990), 7.

13. Tsentral'nyi Derzhavnyi Arkhiv Vykonnykh Orhaniv Ukrainy (Kiev; hereafter referred to as TsDAVO Ukrainy), 413/1/13, p. 60.

14. Tsentral'nyi Derzhavnyi Arkhiv Hromads'kykh Ob'iednan' Ukrainy (Kiev; hereafter referred to as TsDAHO Ukrainy), 1/20/3801, pp. 54–56 (1925).

15. GARF, 374/27/594, p. 118 (1925).

16. V. G. Bogoraz, *Evreiskoe mestechko v revoliutsii* (Moscow, 1926), 6.

17. Sergei Zhuk, "Russia's Lost Reformation: Peasants and Radical Religious Sects in Southern Russia and Ukraine, 1830–1905" (Ph.D. diss., Johns Hopkins University, Baltimore, 2002), 6.

18. P. P. Chubinskii, *Trudy etnografichesko-statisticheskoi ekspeditsii v zapadno-russkii krai,* vol. 7 (St. Petersburg, 1872), 50. For a similar view

on the similarities of Christian and Jewish culture in right-bank Ukraine in 1929, see Iosyp Pul'ner, "Obriady i povir'ia spolucheni z vahitnoiu porodileiu i narozhdentsem u zhydiv," *Etnografichnyi visnyk* 9 (1929): 101.

19. Der Nister, *The Family Mashber,* trans. Leonard Wolf (New York: Summit Books, 1987), 144.

20. By 1927, no republic in the Soviet Union had surpassed Ukraine in the statistical rendering of nationalities. While in other republics officials had trouble reporting the national composition of their populations, the Bureau of National Minorities in Kharkiv sent charts to Moscow indicating precisely where national minorities lived, and in what number and density. Ukraine's charts won praise in Moscow: "The most eloquent figures come from Ukraine" (GARF, 3316/48/73, pp. 5–23 [1927]).

21. See Thongchai Winichakul, *Siam Mapped: A History of the Geo-Body of a Nation* (Honolulu: University of Hawaii Press, 1994).

22. For a complaint by villagers that the division of the village of Novo-Ushitsia into Polish and Ukrainian sections did in fact divide families, see TsDAVO Ukrainy, 413/1/99, p. 26 (1925).

23. Benedict Anderson, "Census, Map, Museum," in *Becoming National: A Reader,* ed. Geoff Eley and Ronald Grigor Suny (New York: Oxford University Press, 1996), 244–45.

24. Jerzy Stempowski, *W dolinie Dniestru: Listy o Ukrainie* (Warsaw: LBN, 1993), 11.

25. GARF, 374/27/594, p. 96 (1925).

26. Terry Martin first associated this term with Soviet nationalities policy in *The Affirmative Action Empire.*

27. The uprising was massive, and many government documents were generated in response. For examples, see TsDAHO Ukrainy, 1/20/3184, pp. 48–53 (1930); TsDAHO Ukrainy, 1/20/3184, pp. 17–22 (1930); TsDAHO Ukrainy, 1/20/3154, pp. 12–13 (1930). For a document collection about the uprising, see Valerii Vasil'ev and Lynne Viola, eds., *Kollektivizatsiia i krest'ianskoe soprotivlenie na Ukraine* (Vinnytsia: Lohos, 1997).

28. GARF, 3316/28/775, p. 27 (1935). See, as well, TsDAHO Ukrainy, 1/16/12, p. 278 (1935).

29. Of the 1.3 million people who were sentenced in the Great Purges, one-third were arrested in the "national operations," nearly half of these in the "Polish line." See N. V. Petrov and A. Roginskii, "'Pol'skaia operatsiia' NKVD 1937–1938 gg.," in *Repressii protiv poliakov,* ed. A. E. Gur'ianov (Moscow: Zven'ia, 1997), 28.

30. Arad, Krakowski, and Spector, *Einsatzgruppen Reports,* 79, 131.

31. "Völker und Volksgruppen der Sowjetunion," Der RMfdbO, Haupteilung II (Politik), USHMM, ZA 21/31, p. 38 (20/IX/41); and Karl Stumpp, "In the Wake of the German Army on the Eastern Front, August 1941 to

May 1942," part 1, trans. Adam Giesinger, *American Historical Society of Germans from Russia* 7, no. 1 (Spring 1984): 12. See also Karl Stumpp, "In the Wake of the German Army on the Eastern Front, August 1941 to May 1942," part 2, trans. Adam Giesinger, *American Historical Society of Germans from Russia* 7, no. 2 (Summer 1984).

32. "Abschrift, Kommando Dr. Stumpp," 31/X/42, USHMM, RG 31.002M, KAOR reel 11/4, 138.

33. Ibid. For reference to ethnic Germans as the least fit for work, see "Teilbericht Politik, 13/VIII–3/IX/42," USHMM, RG 31.002M, reel 11, Rosenberg AOR 3602-2-26. See also Doris L. Bergen, "The Nazi Concept of 'Volksdeutsche' and the Exacerbation of Antisemitism in Eastern Europe, 1939–45," *Journal of Contemporary History* 29, no. 4 (October 1993): 569–82.

34. "Stimmungsbericht, no. 12, 27/IV/42," USHMM, RG 31.002M. On local German officials holding back aid, see as well "Stimmungsbericht, no. 34, 17/IX/42," USHMM, RG 31.002M, reel 6, KAOR reel 11/69, p. 58, and KAOR reel 11/16 (16/III/42), on a six-week inspection visit through Zhytomyr Region.

35. "Bericht," USHMM, RG 31.002M, reel 13, AOR 3602–26 (10/IX/42).

36. Alfred Erdmann, "Sonderkommando Stumpp to RmfdbO, 30/IV/43," USHMM, RG 31.002M, reel 11,165.

37. USHMM, ZA, R-1151/1/16, pp. 53–67, and ZA 1/2, 82.

38. FK 675 (25/VIII/41), USHMM RG 11.001 M3, reel 92. In his memoirs, M. Omeliusik describes the difficulty of "stirring peaceful people to the [Ukrainian] underground." See M. Omeliusik, "UPA na Volyni v 1943 rotsi," in *Litopys Ukrains'koi povstans'ko armii*, ed. E. Shtendera (Toronto: Litopys UPA, 1953), 22.

39. Mykhailo Seleshko, *Vinnytsia: Spomyny perekladacha komissi doslidiv zlochyniv NKVD v 1937–1938* (New York: Fundatsiia im. O. Ol'zhycha, 1991), pp. 150–52, 132. Soviet espionage units noticed the same lack of enthusiasm for the national cause. See TsDAHO Ukrainy, 1/20/930, pp. 11–22 (10/II/44).

40. Nazi functionaries translated antisemitic texts for training sessions with indigenous militia units in Ukraine. See Martin Dean, "The German Gendarmerie, the Ukrainian Schutzmannschaft, and the 'Second Wave' of Jewish Killings in Occupied Ukraine," *German History* 14, no. 2 (1996): 179. See, as well, Stumpp's report of his education of a captured Soviet pilot, in Adam Giesinger, "Dr. Karl Stumpp (1896–1982): A Life of Service to His People," *Journal of the American Historical Society of Germans from Russia* 5, no. 1 (1982): 11. For the latest scholarship, see Eric J. Schmaltz and Samuel D. Sinner, "The Nazi Ethnographic Research of Georg Leibbrandt

and Karl Stumpp in Ukraine and Its North American Legacy," in *German Scholars and Ethnic Cleansing, 1919–1945*, ed. Ingo Haar and Michael Fahlbush (Oxford and New York: Oxford University Press, 2005), 51–86.

41. Mordechai Altshuler describes how the wartime years of German antisemitic propaganda "indirectly penetrated a broad strata of the population." See "Antisemitism in Ukraine Toward the End of World War II," in *Bitter Legacy: Confronting the Holocaust in the USSR*, ed. Zvi Gitelman (Bloomington: Indiana University Press, 1997), 83.

42. An Einsatzgruppe reporter stated: "In order to . . . break the spell which adheres to the Jews as carriers of political power in the eyes of many Ukrainians, Einsatzkommando 6 in several instances marched the Jews through the town under guard prior to execution." See Arad, Krakowski, and Spector, *Einsatzgruppen Reports*, 131.

43. TsDAHO Ukrainy, 1/20/685, pp. 82 (29/I/43).

II. T·E·S·T·I·M·O·N·Y, H·I·S·T·O·R·Y, A·N·D M·E·M·O·R·Y

Omer Bartov

Interethnic Relations in the Holocaust as Seen Through Postwar Testimonies: Buczacz, East Galicia, 1941–1944

BORN IN 1910 TO A POOR POLISH FAMILY, JULIJA MYKHAILIVNA Trembach married a Ukrainian man in the town of Buczacz in 1940, where she has lived ever since. Located in East Galicia, between Stanisławów (now Ivano-Frankivsk) and Tarnopol (now Ternopil'), Buczacz on the eve of World War I numbered about twenty thousand inhabitants, of whom about half were Jews while the rest were Poles and Ukrainians. (See figure 6.) Trembach's daughter was born in June 1941, three days before Germany attacked the Soviet Union on June 22. Recalling these events in 2003, Trembach remarked that before the war "our city was populated mostly by Jews. They were cultured, wealthy, enterprising, and intelligent people. All the stone houses in the center of town belonged to them. [They] constituted the local intelligentsia."

Then the Germans came and ruined this harmonious community:

> I remember well how the Hitlerites committed crimes against the Jews, how they buried them alive on Fedir Hill, and how those people dug their own graves. From the street where I live (which is situated opposite that hill) I could see how the ground was moving over the people who were still not dead. I will never forget the moans and cries of those people. And they committed no crime. The Germans forbade us to help the Jews and to give them shelter. It was prohibited even to bury dead bodies. Anyone who broke the prohibition would be killed. But our people—Ukrainians and Poles alike—tried to help them however they could. They made dugouts in the ground, and the Jews hid there. Secretly people would bring food to those dugouts. And God only knows how much food I myself brought.

Figure 6. General view of the town of Buczacz. Postcard from the 1920s; photographer unknown; from the private collection of Omer Bartov.

One day a young woman with a baby came running to Trembach: "[She] was crying and exhausted. She whispered: 'Save us, hide us.' At my own risk I hid them in the loft of the cowshed. . . . I fed that little girl with my own breast, because I had a baby myself . . . and I shared my own food with that woman." Later the woman and baby left with some other Jews. But, according to Trembach,

> that was not the only case. I tried to help [the Jews] however I could, and my husband never objected. We pitied those people, for they were beaten, always scared for their lives and never knowing what would happen to them next. [The Germans] had no mercy for anyone, not even for women and little children. Everyone was scared at that time, but the Jewish people suffered for all. Even now they still have that fear, when they come here as tourists.

One such "tourist" was Willy Anderman, who was saved by one of Trembach's relatives and later immigrated to Israel. Half a century later he visited Buczacz for the first time since the war. And yet, as Trembach recounted, Anderman told her that before leaving Israel, "his wife Batia warned him: 'Don't fall behind your group, those bandits will kill you.' He told us about it himself. But he saw that it was not true. Our people try to remember something, to help those who came to their fatherland after long years. When Willy Anderman came to Buczacz we met him. He couldn't help crying and said: 'I've been looking for the people who saved my life for a long time, but finally I have found you after all those years.'"

Despite the horrors she experienced as a young woman and the hardship of the postwar years, Julija Trembach draws a positive conclusion from her life: "I was good to people and tried to save them from death, so God gave me good health. Now I'm ninety-three, but I still have a good memory and a clear mind. . . . As for the Jewish people, we respect them for their ability to appreciate and remember."[1]

Visitors to Buczacz are unlikely to agree with Trembach's claim. There are no visible signs of the town's past Jewish existence. Nothing indicates where the great synagogue, inaugurated in 1728, or the Talmudic school (*beit hamidrash*) adjacent to it, had stood. (See figure 7.) Contrary to contemporary local assertions, the Talmudic school was still standing in 2000. (See figure 8.) It was finally torn down only the following year. (See figure 9.) Over its foundations a new commercial center was built. The site of the great synagogue serves now as a marketplace. Nor has any sign been put up to indicate where the Jewish hospital, the most modern of its kind in the region before 1914 and between the wars, had once stood. The site is now an empty lot. Nothing indicates where the Jews had lived, where they were buried, and where they were murdered. The only prominent memorial on Fedir Hill commemorates Ukrainian nationalist victims of the Soviets.

All these sites are within walking distance and view of each other. From the Jewish cemetery one can easily see Fedir Hill, separated by the town in the valley below.[2] The only public reference to the town's Jewish past has been the renaming of the street where its most illustrious son, writer Shmuel Yosef Agnon, was born. But the commemorative plaque mentions neither his Jewish identity nor that he is the only Nobel Prize laureate for Hebrew-language literature. (See figure 10.) Tourists from Israel have recently donated copies of his books to the local museum. Other famous sons of the city, such as Emanuel Ringelblum and Simon Wiesenthal, are unknown in Buczacz. Only David Ashkenazi, who survived the Holocaust as a boy in Buczacz and subsequently became a general in the Red Army, has recently been featured as a local hero in the town's newspaper.

On Fedir Hill, where thousands were shot, a small edifice commemorating a single mass grave of some four hundred victims was

Figure 7. Great synagogue and Talmudic school (*beit hamidrash*) in Buczacz, front view, 1921. Beth Hatefutsoth, Photo Archive, Tel Aviv.

Figure 8. Talmudic school in Buczacz a few years before its destruction in 2001.
Photograph by Ruchama Elbag; from Omer Bartov's private collection.

Figure 9. Destruction of the
Talmudic school, 2001. Photograph by Ruchama Elbag; from Omer
Bartov's private collection.

Figure 10. New sign by house of the author and Nobel laureate Shmuel Yosef Agnon. Photograph by Omer Bartov.

restored in the early 1990s after lying broken on the ground for several decades. (See figure 11.) But only a local guide can locate it in the forest.

On Bashty Hill, site of the Jewish cemetery, the remaining tombstones include that of Shalom Mordechai Czaczkes, Agnon's father. The stones have recently been cleaned up by Tom Weiss, a retired professor from the Massachusetts Institute of Technology, and his sons, who trace some of their family to Buczacz. The overgrown slope of Bashty Hill is inhabited by hens. Descending steeply to the Strypa River, this is the site where thousands of Jews were executed. A memorial put up just after the liberation by the few survivors has meanwhile vanished.[3]

Maria Mykhailivna Khvostenko was born in Buczacz in 1929 to a Ukrainian family and worked there as a schoolteacher until her retirement. In 2003, shortly before she died, Khvostenko wrote a brief memoir. She recalled that before the war Ukrainian, Polish, and

Figure 11. Fedir Hill memorial for victims of the "registration *akcja*." Photograph by Omer Bartov.

Jewish schoolchildren "respected each other" and that there was no interethnic or interdenominational conflict, nor any antisemitism. Once the Soviets arrived in 1939, many Ukrainians and Poles were deported. And soon after the Germans came in 1941, they perpetrated "*akcjas* [roundups and killing operations] against the Jews and seized Ukrainian youths for forced labor in Germany." Khvostenko, however, attended the gymnasium, the academic high school:

> One day . . . something drew us to a window [in the gymnasium] that faced the town center, the ratusz [municipal hall]. . . . In the middle of the main street a crowd was going around the ratusz toward the bridge over the Strypa [River]. Gendarmes with dogs, Gestapo, and militia with hexagonal stars surrounded the crowd, hurrying it toward Fedir Hill. What a horrible sight it was! There were women, men, old people and young—our schoolmates and friends. . . . They were our neighbors and strangers, but they were people![4]

Alicia Appleman-Jurman had a very different vantage point. Before fleeing to hide in the villages, this eleven-year-old girl hankered
to return to the normality represented by the gymnasium. In the fall
of 1941, she writes in her memoir,

> I climbed up a tree outside the window of my classroom and
> watched my former classmates sitting at their desks. One of these
> was my friend Slavka . . . a Gentile, but then, so were many of
> my friends. . . . When Slavka turned to look, our eyes met. . . .
> Our exchange was bittersweet—my misery at not being allowed
> in the school, her sympathy mingled with helplessness to correct
> the situation. In a moment she looked away and didn't turn around
> again.[5]

The roundups and killings were not happening at some far-off
site. Maria Khvostenko recalls:

> From about the fall of 1942 to the end of 1943 they [the Germans]
> would hold *akcja*-shootings, always on Fridays. . . . On Tuesday
> evening the Jewish militia would collect jewels and other valuable
> things. . . . On Thursday evening the [Germans] would come. . . .
> They would "act" or "work" all night, and the next morning as
> we were running to school we could see the results of their work:
> corpses of women, men, and children lying on the road. As for
> infants, they would throw them from balconies onto the paved
> road. . . . It was not hard to guess what was happening on Fedir
> Hill: we could hear machine-gun fire.

Khvostenko consistently neglects to mention the all-important Ukrainian militias, speaking only of the Jewish police and the Gestapo.
But her account demonstrates that the evidence of constant massacres
was there for all to see. Some who tried to help paid a heavy price.
Her Polish neighbors were denounced and shot for hiding Jews. Their
daughter, who survived, went mad with grief. Many others, however,
profited from the liquidation of the Jews, gaining property, businesses,
money, and loot. Khvostenko remembers that her mother used to
send her to bring milk and vegetables to the family of Mina Pohorille
(later Rosner). "My parents were friendly to all their neighbors," she
writes, "they respected other people and people paid them back by
treating them well."[6]

Rosner, who lost her entire family, including her toddler son, felt
differently when she visited Buczacz in the 1980s: "As we walked on

I saw a group of elderly women tending a field, and I couldn't help wondering, was it one of those women who handed my family over to the Nazis? . . . Were some of the collaborators . . . still walking the streets of Buczacz?"[7] Yet Rosner was saved by the Polish peasant Mieczysław Wicherek and his family. Even after Wicherek's wife and daughter were killed by an artillery shell, this courageous man and his remaining daughter protected the Jews they were hiding.

This is the conundrum in reconstructing the event from such testimonies: on the one hand, almost all the Jews who survived in Buczacz—and I have the records of some 170 men and women who were there at some point—were helped by Poles or Ukrainians. On the other hand, they are the most direct witnesses to the denunciations, betrayals, and collaboration that played such a prominent role in the destruction of the community. No wonder that the mere thought of returning to this site often fills them with terror.

I too recently visited my mother's hometown. My maternal great-grandfather had managed estates for the noble Polish Potocki family, moving from nearby Potok Złoty to Buczacz shortly after my mother was born in 1924. She retained fond memories of her childhood there and had vivid recollections of picking mushrooms in the forests with her Ukrainian friends. (See figure 12.) But my grandfather sought independence from his authoritarian father, and there were few opportunities, especially for Jews, in 1930s Galicia.[8] His application for immigration to Palestine was approved in March 1935. The family disembarked at the port of Haifa in December of that year. My mother was still wearing a stylish beret that soon came off as too indicative of her foreign origin. My grandfather became a blue-collar worker. My grandmother, who had never worked in Buczacz, packed oranges twelve hours a day and cleaned the neighbors' house on Saturdays. Apart from one uncle who went to Uruguay, the rest of the family stayed in Buczacz and vanished without a trace a few years later.

Buczacz was established in the mid-fourteenth century by the noble Polish Buczacki family as one of a series of fortified border towns intended to halt invasions from the east. It became a center of commerce between the Polish-Lithuanian Commonwealth and the Ottoman Empire in the sixteenth century, and passed into the hands of the Potocki family in the early seventeenth century.[9] Jews had resided in Buczacz since at least 1500, and by the late seventeenth century

Figure 12. The author's mother as a child in Buczacz, late 1920s. From Omer Bartov's private collection.

they made up a substantial portion of the population. They also took part in the fighting against Tatars, Cossacks, and Turks. A spring in the city is said to have been used by Jan Sobieski, who liberated Buczacz from Turkish rule. In 1772 East Galicia came under Austrian Habsburg rule, and initial restrictions on the Jews were lifted after 1848. The first elected municipal council of 1874 included twelve Jews, nine Poles, and nine Ukrainians. Indeed, between 1879 and 1921 the city had a Jewish mayor, who also served as representative in the Austrian Parliament. By 1880 Jews constituted over 60 percent of a population of just under 10,000.[10] A 1914 Polish travel guide noted a population of 3,500 Poles, 2,000 Ruthenes, and 7,500 Jews. It gave this "picturesque city" a star because "especially on Friday evenings (*Szabbes*) hundreds of candlelights flicker in the windows."[11]

Buczacz was devastated in World War I and the Polish-Soviet War. About 60 percent of the houses were destroyed and the population was halved. (See figure 13.) Coming under Polish rule in 1921, the town gradually revived. The Polish census of 1931 quoted a total

Figure 13. Destroyed houses in Buczacz in World War I. Österreichisches Staatsarchiv, Kriegsarchiv, Vienna.

population of close to 24,000 people: 12,000 Roman Catholics, 5,000 Greek Catholics, and 7,000 Jews.[12] But these figures seem to have been manipulated to demonstrate Polish preponderance in a region where Poles had traditionally been a minority.

Jewish sources estimated dramatically different figures for September 1939, citing 10,000 Jews, 5,000 Ukrainians, and 2,000 Poles.[13] But these are also unreliable figures, because with the outbreak of World War II and the partition of Poland agreed upon in the Nazi-Soviet Pact, thousands of Jewish refugees were streaming in from German-occupied areas of Poland; numerous Jews, Poles, and Ukrainians were deported by the Soviets who ruled the region in 1939–41; and many other young men were conscripted into the Red Army.

The Germans entered Buczacz in July 1941. Following an early mass killing that summer, so-called *akcjas* (or *Aktionen* in German) began in October 1942 and lasted until the city was declared *Judenfrei* (Jew-free) in May 1943. About half of the ten thousand victims were deported by train to the Belzec extermination camp and gassed there. The rest were shot in or near Buczacz. The Germans were assisted by the Jewish council (*Judenrat*), the Jewish police (*Ordnungsdienst*), and especially by the Ukrainian militia. The few instances of armed

Jewish resistance were largely ineffectual. In March 1944 the Red Army liberated Buczacz. But most of the eight hundred surviving Jews who came out of hiding were murdered when the Germans recaptured the city in April. By the time the Soviets returned in July, fewer than one hundred Jews were still alive in the area.[14]

With the subsequent expulsion of the Polish population, this multiethnic community ceased to exist. Buczacz was never an idyllic pluralistic society, but neither was it a site of constant conflict. Mutual fear and ignorance went together with constant interaction in schools, the marketplace, and some public events and cultural institutions. People lived and prayed separately and often had traditionally distinct occupations. Jews and Christians rarely intermarried, though Poles and Ukrainians did. Life had gone on this way for generations. But the advent of nationalism in the late nineteenth century grafted the notion of a distinct ethnic community onto traditional religious allegiances. People began to think of their town as a place that belonged more to some than to others and to distinguish between alleged outsiders and the indigenous population. Economic impoverishment, divisive governmental policies, strident political ideologies, wars, and foreign occupation transformed a community of coexistence into a community of genocide.

Contemporary East Galicia is littered with ruined synagogues and cemeteries used as marketplaces and shows a striking dearth of any public remembrance of Jewish life and culture. (See figure 14.) One often hears it said: "The Jews are rich; if they wish to restore their sites, they should pay for it." Maria Khvostenko disagrees: "It is time for our city . . . to pay attention to the place where the Fascists murdered many Jews and to honor their memory by putting up a decent monument or sculpture. For they were honest citizens . . . who loved our land and our city, worked for it, and suffered guiltlessly."[15]

This is not a common view. The regional newspaper *Nova Doba* asserted in December 2000 that while in Buczacz "many things have changed, . . . people's memories have been left unchanged."[16] In fact, the city has changed very little, but the memory of the Jews and the Holocaust has been all but erased. The few who do remember treat the past with much ambivalence.[17] Ivan Synen'kyi witnessed several *akcjas* as a sixteen-year-old boy. To his mind, "the Jews . . . behaved in a strange way. Rarely if ever did they try to escape. There was no fear in their eyes. Some of them explained their behavior by

Figure 14. The synagogue in Brzeżany-Berezhany. Photograph by Omer Bartov.

old prophecies that came true, others would turn to local people and say: 'We are the first, but you will be the next.'"

In Synen'kyi's view, the Jews were dying either because of their ancient guilt or as a warning to the Ukrainians. If the first explanation derives from traditional antisemitism, the second is a coded condemnation of Ukrainian complicity. Synen'kyi concedes that "the local people were very careful about associating with the Jews. . . . Most were scared for their lives; others did help, but very cautiously." Such conditions were dangerous, but could also be profitable: "There was also a shop in the city where the clothes of the murdered were sold cheaply." This lasted into the postwar period. When the only surviving son of Liumcio Rosenbach, who lost his father, mother, and twelve sisters, "wanted to get his house back . . . the price fixed by the new owners was too high." He thus "had to abandon his dream" and move to Israel.[18]

Even rescue could cause long-term public embarrassment. Stefania, a woman from Buczacz who was six years old during the war, recalled her mother saying that "she was hiding a strange woman called

Hanka in the cellar. . . . Neither her father nor the other five members of the family knew about it." Astonishingly, "Stefania and her mother kept their secret for half a century. Only on her deathbed did the old woman relate this event to the whole family."[19]

This reluctance to admit acts of rescue is a crucial factor in interethnic relations. Was the mother afraid of the social stigma attached to such altruism? In his influential study *Neighbors,* Jan Gross mentions the Wyrzykowski family, who had to leave Jedwabne after the war because they had sheltered Jews during the occupation.[20] In Buczacz, Poles were more likely to help than Ukrainians, no doubt because they too were threatened. But those Ukrainians who did help normally wanted to conceal their actions from their own neighbors. Joe Perl, born in nearby Monasterzyska in 1931, was hidden with his mother by a local leader of the Ukrainian "Banderivtsy" (militia) who was involved in hunting down and killing Jews. When the Soviets arrived, the man said to Joe and his mother: "Don't walk out of my house [in the daytime] because I don't want anyone to see that I had been helping Jews."[21]

There were good reasons to beware of one's neighbors. Rescuers had more to fear from their neighbors than from the Germans, who often could not distinguish between Jews and gentiles in these foreign environs. On March 8, 1944, two weeks before Buczacz was liberated, Etunia Bauer's entire surviving family—father and three siblings—was murdered by Ukrainian militiamen acting on a tip from neighbors who had known the Bauers for many years. Etunia was saved by two Polish boys who were protecting their own village from attacks by Ukrainian bands.[22]

Etunia's eldest brother had already been murdered in the first mass shooting on August 27, 1941, which claimed the lives of up to six hundred men, including Alicia Appleman's father. In January 1944 Alicia was finally told how he died by a Jew she met hiding in a barn, the sole survivor of that massacre: "The German [officer], seeing [Alicia's father's] medal for bravery from the Austrian Emperor Franz Joseph, was impressed enough to let him escape . . . but a Ukrainian policeman shot him in the back."[23] We also know about the man Alicia met in the barn from a postwar account by his son, Yisrael Munczer. Unlike Alicia's father, Yisrael's father was saved from the 1941 massacre by a Ukrainian acquaintance. But shortly after meeting Alicia, Munczer was denounced and shot.[24]

Some time earlier, while still living in Buczacz, Alicia was arrested and brought to the local jail. She found herself face-to-face with her childhood friend's father, now a police officer: "I still remembered when he told his daughter [before the war] . . . how glad he was that we were friends." Recognizing the twelve-year-old Alicia, the man instructed her to "get down on [her] knees and beg for [her] life" when the Germans arrived. When she refused, he struck her powerfully on both cheeks, after which she was taken to Gestapo headquarters in nearby Czortków, where she barely escaped death.[25]

Having lost her three brothers, Alicia was hidden with her mother by an eccentric peasant, who later turned out to be a Polish aristocrat who had decided to withdraw from society and found himself sheltering Jews in his isolated cottage. Returning to Buczacz after its first liberation in March 1944, Alicia and her mother were denounced by their neighbors as soon as the Germans recaptured the city. Alicia's mother was shot in front of her eyes, and she somehow escaped yet another mass shooting but was left completely alone in the world. Like so many others, her survival is a story of rescue and betrayal, altruism and denunciation.

Rosa Brecher, nine years old when the war broke out, hid between May 1943 and March 1944 with the peasant woman Antosia Sztankowska in the village of Myszkowce. Like virtually all the hiding places of the Jews of Buczacz, the village was within a couple of hours' walk of the city. But Rosa never felt safe. The greatest threat to her safety was not the Germans but Antosia's brother-in-law Hryń, a Ukrainian peasant who collaborated with the Germans, was frequently drunk, beat up both his wife and Antosia, and seems to have molested the young Jewish girl, whom he constantly threatened to denounce. Rosa's testimony reveals extreme physical and psychological terror from this man, but it is also full of compassion for Antosia and for some of the other peasant women who confided in this terrified yet better educated girl, telling her about their hard-drinking and abusive husbands, fathers, and in-laws.[26]

The close link between providing shelter and denouncing is ever present in survivors' testimonies. It is of course true that virtually all of the survivors were rescued by their gentile neighbors. It is also true, however, that the vast majority of the handful of survivors experienced denunciation by other neighbors, as well as on occasion by their own temporary rescuers. Joe Perl relates that his mother was offered shelter in their town of Monasterzyska but refused to go. Others who went there were robbed by those who had promised to hide them and were then reported to the authorities and killed.[27] Mina Rosner's family hid in a bunker in the center of Buczacz, built under the house of a Polish woman named Janka. Some weeks later Mina heard that Janka had called in the Gestapo. Mina was the only member of her family to survive.[28]

Simcha Tischler, who was born in Buczacz in 1921, was sheltered for much of the time by Jozef and Troika Luczow, a Ukrainian family living in a village near the city. In a 1997 videotaped testimony he commented about his rescuer: "You can say that a brother would not have done more [for me] than he did." He ate the same food and drank the same vodka with his hosts. Tischler had contempt for the Jewish police and respect for his Ukrainian friends. But he and his father were also denounced and ended up spending eleven months in a pit underground with hardly any food or water.[29] Manko Swierszczak, the undertaker of the Polish cemetery in Buczacz, hid the Rozen brothers and their mother in a grave, and during the winter of 1944 built a bunker for them under his house. His heroism was all the greater because he was suspected by the Ukrainian militia of harboring Jews, was arrested and given a severe beating, yet he never betrayed the Rozens.[30] (See figure 15.)

Arie Klonicki (Klonymus) was born in Kowel in 1906. He studied mathematics and physics at the University of Wilno (Vilnius) and then worked as a teacher at the Hebrew high school in Pinsk. There he met Malwina Herzman, who was born in Buczacz in 1912 and was working as a Polish language teacher at the gymnasium and the Hebrew "Tarbut" school. They married in 1937. The couple was visiting Malwina's family in Buczacz when Germany attacked the Soviet Union in June 1941. Unable to return home, they remained in the city, where their son Adam was born in 1942. They did all they could to save the baby, but few people were willing to take a circumcised Jewish boy. Shortly before the city was declared *Judenfrei,* they handed Adam to the Basilian Monastery and then agreed with a local woman who had previously hidden them to leave her all their property (inherited from Malwina's murdered parents) as payment for hiding at her mother's house in a nearby village. Upon reaching the village, however, they were robbed by a Ukrainian acting on behalf of their Polish "rescuer." They now had neither property nor shelter.

Figure 15. Manko Swierszczak beside the tomb in Buczacz where he hid four Jews for close to two years. Yad Vashem Archive.

Hiding in the fields, they could hear the peasants working a few feet away from them discussing the advisability of denouncing Jews and sharing stories about mass executions.

It was during these few weeks in July 1943 that Klonicki decided to write an account of these events. The diary was written in Hebrew and signed with his previous name Klonymus, as a gesture of defiance against his Christian compatriots.[31] Meanwhile, Adam was ejected from the monastery and delivered to the forced-labor camp in Buczacz, from which his parents barely managed to save him. Adam was now cared for by the Polish peasants Franka and Stanisław Węszyk, in whose field his parents were hiding. But news about denunciations and more mass shootings made the Poles reluctant to keep the baby or allow the parents to remain in the field. Most feared of all was a Pole called Nahajowski, a former dogcatcher who had transformed himself, as conditions demanded, into an expert at finding Jewish hiding places, for which he was apparently rewarded by the Germans. Nahajowski was eventually shot by an armed Jew, but the denunciations persisted.

A second attack on another professional Jew-catcher called

Kowalski also had little long-term effect. Eliasz Chalfen, who was born in Buczacz in 1930 and described these events in an account he wrote in 1947, noted the following dynamic:

> The [Jews] who were hiding with peasants paid high sums of money for their shelters, and the simple-minded peasants went to town and bought large amounts of whatever they wanted. . . . This made the work of the Ukrainian murderers all the easier. They followed those peasants . . . and found Jews in attics, cellars, and so forth . . . [and] shot them on the spot. . . . Then . . . the peasants themselves started killing the Jews or expelling them, because [of] . . . rumors that [those] . . . sheltering a Jew would be executed. . . . The Jewish fighters could do nothing . . . because at the time all kinds of gangs were established . . . especially the German-Ukrainian police, which did all it could to destroy [them].[32]

It was in this growing chaos and violence that the Klonickis tried to survive. The odds were against them. Arie wrote in his diary: "In the forests rules the law of the jungle. The strongest is victor. There are several bands of youngsters there. . . . They have pistols. If they hear that anyone has entered the forest, they attack him and rob him of everything."[33]

On July 18, 1943, the Klonickis were robbed of the rest of their money by a local peasant and expected to be denounced. Arie wrote: "The hatred of an enemy such as Hitler is not enough, added to it is the hatred of the immediate surroundings, which knows no boundaries. Millions of Jews have been slaughtered and it is not yet satiated!"[34] The last entry in the diary was made on July 22, 1943.

Four years later, Arie's eldest brother Jacob, then living in the United States, received a letter from the Węszyks informing him that Arie and Malwina were killed on January 18, 1944, but that their son was alive. Jacob eventually retrieved the diary that Arie had left with the Polish couple, but all attempts to find Adam ended in failure. The Węszyks, who expected considerable compensation for their troubles, claimed the boy was baptized, given the name Taras, and put in an orphanage in Buczacz, while they were deported to Poland. But he could not be located there. In 1962 a last communication arrived: "As I wrote you, he lives in the Lwów area, but does not want to know about his origin, because he sees himself as Ukrainian and is ashamed of having an uncle who lives in Israel."[35]

Apologetics and recriminations concerning the role of interethnic relations in the Holocaust have relied both on personal experience and anecdotal evidence, and on wide-ranging generalizations. While everyone agrees that the Germans were the real culprits, Jewish accusations of gentile collaboration—especially in Eastern Europe—have been met by allegations of Jewish economic dominance, collaboration with the Soviets, lack of patriotism, unwillingness to fight, and eternal guilt for the murder of Christ.

Conversely, both the survivors of the Holocaust in Eastern Europe and their neighbors carried a heavy burden of guilt through the following decades. Whether acknowledged or suppressed, this sense of guilt was a response to what had been done and what had not been done at a time of almost indescribable horror. Nor was life after the war easy for any of the protagonists. The Poles were expelled and had to rebuild their lives in what became western Poland in areas from which the Germans had in turn been driven out.[36] The Ukrainians came under a particularly harsh Soviet regime after a fruitless struggle against their new occupiers that lasted until the late 1940s. (See figure 16.) Not a few Jewish survivors reproached themselves many years later for not having expressed sufficient gratitude to their rescuers. At times, decades after the end of the war, they sought them out and proposed their names to Yad Vashem as righteous gentiles.

This belated step was not merely the result of first having to rebuild one's life and to struggle with the memories of loss and atrocity. It also had to do with the ambivalence felt by the survivors. For everyone who survived was rescued; but everyone who was rescued was a living testimony of betrayal, denunciation, greed, and indifference. Yet when the recognition of the rescuers came, it did more than provide a moment of glory to the aging, often wretchedly poor "righteous gentiles." It also provided a new sense of self-respect and dignity to the survivors, for it allowed them to acknowledge that even in the darkest, most desperate hour of their lives, there were those who saw them first and foremost as human beings. And this recognition, in turn, gave the rescuers an added glory: not simply as brave and kind, but also as beacons of humanness at a time when the lives of men, women, and children became less important than a few stale potatoes.

All this can be glimpsed only by immersing oneself in the complex fabric of testimonies and memoirs. Generalizations are ultimately

Figure 16. Funeral procession with the Ukrainian nationalist flag and the flag of the Ukrainian Insurgent Army of the 1940s passing under the statue of Taras Shevchenko. Photograph by Omer Bartov.

inescapable if one wishes to draw some conclusions from the evidence. But here nuance rules. A few anecdotal testimonies mean very little, for each experience was unique. A mass of testimonies from a wide variety of locations is just as meaningless, for it robs the evidence of its context. Ultimately, we must learn to know the place and the circumstances through the voices of the protagonists who lived there and experienced the event. This chapter is merely a first step in this direction. But it may provide some indication of where I am heading.

NOTES

A version of this chapter has appeared in French. See Omer Bartov, "Les relations interethniques à Buczacz (Galicie orientale) durant la Shoah selon les témoignages d'après guerre," in *Cultures d'Europe Centrale,* vol. 5, *La destruction des confines,* ed. Delphine Bechtel and Xavier Galmiche (Paris: Centre Interdisciplinaire de Recherches Center-Européennes, Université de Paris-Sorbonne, 2005), 47–67. I am grateful to Tom Weiss, who brought the photograph of destroyed houses in Buczacz in World War I (figure 13) to my attention.

1. Julija Mykhailivna Trembach, written on her behalf by Roma Nestorivna Kryvenchuk, collected by Mykola Kozak, translated from Ukrainian by Sofia Grachova.

2. "Fedir" Hill is the Ukrainian name for the location of the memorial site. It was known as "Fedor" Hill in Polish. "Fedir" Hill will be used throughout this chapter.

3. The Soviet version of events had its own logic. In Igor Duda, *Buczacz* (Lviv: Kameniar, 1985), a guide to the city, we read the following lines, translated from Ukrainian by Sofia Grachova: "On July 7, 1941, the Hitlerites occupied Buczacz. During the time of the occupation they exterminated about 7,500 civilians from the city and the district villages; 1,839 young men and women were driven to forced labor in Germany. 137 buildings were destroyed, as well as a number of industrial enterprises and schools. Nevertheless the population did not submit to the fascists." Neither in this section nor in any other part of the peculiarly Communist-nationalist Ukrainian narrative history of the city is the word *Jew* mentioned even once. Fedir Hill, on which some five thousand Jews were slaughtered, is mentioned twice: first, for the discovery there by archaeologists excavating in 1924 of tools from the late Stone Age; and second, as part of the very detailed tour of the city—which excludes any Jewish site and the name of any of the well-known former Jewish inhabitants—as the location of a common grave for the Soviet soldiers who fell while liberating Buczacz. The guide also provides an apocryphal interpretation of the name "Fedir." The tour ends on the top of Bashty Hill, from which one may have an especially charming view of the city. This also happens to be where the Jewish cemetery is located, but no mention of it is made, nor of the fact that thousands of Jewish inhabitants were massacred there in 1942–43.

4. Maria Mykhailivna Khvostenko (née Dovhanchuk), collected by Mykola Kozak, translated from Ukrainian by Sofia Grachova.

5. Alicia Appleman-Jurman, *Alicia: My Story* (New York: Bantam Books, 1988), 21–22.

6. Khvostenko, collected by Kozak, trans. Grachova.

7. Mina Rosner, *I Am a Witness* (Winnipeg, Man.: Hyperion, 1990), 8.

8. S. Ansky, *The Enemy at His Pleasure: A Journey Through the Jewish Pale of Settlement During World War I,* ed. and trans. Joachim Neugroschel (New York: Metropolitan Books, 2002).

9. Adam Zamoyski, *The Polish Way: A Thousand-Year History of the Poles and Their Culture* (New York: Hippocrene Books, 1994), 185–87.

10. *Pinkas hakehillot Polin: entsiklopedyah shel ha-yishuvim ha-Yehudiyim le-min hivasdam ve-'ad le-ahar Sho'at Milhemet ha-'olam ha-sheniyah 2, Galicia*

Hamizrahit [*Pinkas Hakehillot: Encyclopedia of Jewish Communities: Poland,* vol. 2, *Eastern Galicia*], ed. Danuta Dąbrowska, Abraham Wein, and Aharon Weiss (Jerusalem: Yad Vashem, 1980), 83–85.

11. Mieczysław Orłowicz and Karol Kwieciński, *Ilustrowany Przewodnik po Galicyi: Bukowinie, Spiżu, Orawie i Śląsku Cieszyńskim* (Lwów: Unia, 1914), 141.

12. Office Central de Statistique de la République Polonaise, Statistique de la Pologne, series C, fascicle 78: "Deuxième recensement général de la population du 9 Décembre 1931: Logements et ménages; Population; Professions: Voïévodie de Tarnopol" (Warsaw, 1938), 30, 33.

13. Ivan Bobyk, "Spivzhyttya Buchatchkich mishhan iz zhidisvkim naselennyam" ["Coexistence of the Citizens of Buczacz of Jewish Nationality"], in *Buchach i Buchachchyna: istorychno-memuarnyi zbirnyk* [*The City of Butchach and Its Region: A Historical and Memoiristical Collection*], ed. Mykhailo Ostroverkha and others (London and New York: Shevchenko Scientific Society, 1972), 475. According to Bobyk, a census hurriedly taken by the Soviets just before they retreated showed a population of 8,000 Jews, 3,600 Ukrainians, and 3,500 Poles. Thanks to Sofia Grachova for translations.

14. *Pinkas Hakehillot,* 2:86–89; Yisrael Kohen, ed., *The Book of Buczacz: In Memory of a Martyred Community (Ukraine)* (Tel Aviv: ʾAm ʿOved, 1956), 39–74, 233–302.

15. Khvostenko, collected by Kozak, trans. Grachova.

16. Tetiana Pavlyshyn article on the Holocaust in Buczacz, in *Nova Doba* 48 (December 2000), collected by Mykola Kozak, translated from Ukrainian by Sofia Grachova.

17. See Bobyk, "Spivzhyttya Buchatchkich mishhan iz zhidisvkim naselennyam," in *Buchach i Buchachchyna,* 475–77, for a typical tone. According to Bobyk, a Ukrainian postwar exile, the pre-Habsburg Jews "had immunity from the city authorities; they were exempted from taxes, but profited from fairs and markets. . . . All this resulted in the impoverishment of our citizens, who were forced to move to the outskirts of town." Nevertheless, Bobyk continues, "Buczacz citizens were well-disposed toward the Jews and lived together in peace." The Jews "did not like to serve in the [Austrian] army." During the Soviet occupation of 1939–41, while the "Jewish merchants, intelligentsia and craftsmen were not delighted with Bolshevik rule . . . everybody knew that the leadership of the Communist Party in Buczacz was mainly Jewish." During the German occupation,

> the Ukrainian population sympathized with the grim fate of the Jews and tried to help them whenever they had an opportunity, exposing

themselves to the worst consequences. . . . However, it is very strange that almost all Jewish publications on World War II accuse the Ukrainian population of having helped the Germans to exterminate the Jews. It is true that in some cases the local Ukrainian police took part in police actions as escorts. But in some other Galician cities there were Jewish police as well. Besides, Ukrainian policemen never took part in executions. There were also some individual cases when local policemen persecuted the Jews, but this is no reason to accuse the entire Ukrainian population, just as we cannot accuse all the Jewish population on the grounds that some of them collaborated with the NKVD and helped to arrest and exile to Siberia the most prominent citizens of Buczacz.

It should be noted that Ivan Bobyk was the mayor of Buczacz during the German occupation. Bobyk cites a long letter sent him in 1969 by Isidor Gelbart, a Jewish friend who survived in hiding along with his family (Bobyk, "Spivzhyttya Buchatchkich mishhan iz zhidisvkim naselennyam," in *Buchach i Buchachchyna*, 477–79). Gelbart's letter, and his postwar testimony, confirm Bobyk's own decent behavior but indicate the collaboration of Ukrainian policemen in the killings (Yad Vashem Archive [hereafter referred to as YVA], 033/640).

18. Ivan Synen'kyi's account, collected by Mykola Kozak and translated from the Ukrainian by Sofia Grachova.

19. Pavlyshyn, in *Nova Doba* 48.

20. Jan Gross, *Neighbors: The Destruction of the Jewish Community in Jedwabne, Poland* (Princeton, N.J.: Princeton University Press), 129–30.

21. Joe Perl, Shoah Foundation, video interview, October 14, 1996.

22. Etunia Bauer Katz, *Our Tomorrows Never Came* (New York: Fordham University Press, 2000), 96–99.

23. Appleman-Jurman, *Alicia*, 163.

24. Yisrael Munczer, *A Holocaust Survivor from Buczacz* (Jerusalem: Gefen, 1990), 15, 33. Munczer writes that on the day of the massacre "the Ukrainian and German policemen, thirsty for Jewish blood, treated them like wild beasts" (ibid., 14).

25. Appleman-Jurman, *Alicia*, 69–71.

26. There are two testimonies by Rosa Brecher. The first is a relatively short text, taken down in German on May 20, 1945, at a refugee home in Bucharest: Jewish Historical Institute, Warsaw, 301/4911. The second, written in Polish with a fair amount of Ukrainian influence, is longer, more confused, but also richer in details and emotionally more revealing, and was probably taken down a few months earlier in Czernowitz: YVA, 033/765 (originally from the Jewish Historical Institute).

27. Perl, video interview.

28. Rosner, *I Am a Witness,* 70–71, 76.

29. Simcha Tischler, transcript of videotaped testimony, June 26, 1997, YVA, 03/10229, cassette VT-1585.

30. Zev Anderman, interview with the author, Tel Aviv, December 3, 2002.

31. Arie Klonicki-Klonymus, *The Diary of Adam's Father* (Jerusalem: Jerusalem Post, 1969).

32. Eliasz Chalfen (Elijahu Chalfon), YVA, M1/E 1559 (in Polish; trans. Eva Lutkiewicz), and YVA, 03/8553 (in Hebrew), October 21, 1947; and Kohen, *Book of Buczacz,* 269–70. One member of the Jewish partisans was Yitzhak Bauer, who was born in Buczacz in 1923. In an interview I conducted with him on November 6, 2003, in Tel Aviv, he rejected the notion of "Jewish partisans." In his words, "We posed no threat to the Wehrmacht. All we wanted was to survive." But he acknowledged that assassinating some of the more notorious "Jew-catchers" had a certain impact. He also provided a very detailed account of the botched attacks on Kowalski's home and his father's funeral.

33. Klonicki-Klonymus, *Diary of Adam's Father,* 40.

34. Ibid., 47.

35. Ibid., 71.

36. Since writing this chapter, I have collected numerous testimonies of Poles who were deported from Buczacz by the Soviets, as well as other personal accounts provided by former Polish residents of the town. It has not been possible to integrate this material into the present chapter, but my future work on Buczacz will make extensive use of Polish materials.

Na'ama Shik

Infinite Loneliness: Some Aspects of the Lives of Jewish Women in the Auschwitz Camps According to Testimonies and Autobiographies Written Between 1945 and 1948

"ONE CAN BEAR ANYTHING, WITHSTAND ANYTHING, IF ONLY YOU turn it into a story," said Isak Dinesen. Usually the way of overcoming horror is to become familiar with it, to become reconciled with it in some way.[1] But as Primo Levi understood, "human memory is a marvelous but fallacious instrument," and turning the past into a story is itself among the variables that influence and distort memory: "A memory that is evoked too often, and expressed in the form of a story, tends to become fixed in a stereotype, in a form tested by experience, crystallized, perfected, adorned, installing itself in the place of the raw memory and growing at its expense."[2]

Can we refine our understanding of the Auschwitz experience? Can we reach some essence of "truth" in the story of the camp? When we examine the corpus of survivors' early testimonies and memoirs about the camp, do we obtain a picture different from that in the prevailing research? In this essay I try to answer these questions. It is almost superfluous to say that obtaining some pure truth is not possible. No Holocaust researcher can ignore Primo Levi's penetrating words: "At a distance of years one can today definitely affirm that the history of the Lagers has been written almost exclusively by those who, like myself, never fathomed them to the bottom. Those who did so did not return, or their capacity for observation was paralyzed by suffering and incomprehension."[3] The deeper we delve into the world of the camp, the more we encounter barriers, archaeological mounds of evasive questions that reach into psychology, sociology, and history.

Nevertheless, with the help of a body of writing that so far has not been properly examined, I will attempt to shed light on a number of questions central to Auschwitz research in general and gender research in particular, that is, on questions regarding the uniqueness of the female experience in Auschwitz and women's ways of surviving.

I focus on Auschwitz for several reasons. First, the network of Nazi camps included two major camps for women: Ravensbrück and Auschwitz-Birkenau. The other women's camps were attached to sites essentially designated for men (for example, Buchenwald). Of the two, only Auschwitz combined death, concentration, and work camps, and unlike Ravensbrück, most of its prisoners were Jews. Second, only a few hundred people survived the other death camps—Chelmno, Belzec, Sobibor, and Treblinka—but some tens of thousands of prisoners, Jews and non-Jews, survived Auschwitz. As a result, the corpus of testimonies, memoirs, and autobiographies from Auschwitz is far more extensive than from the other death camps. Third, the historiography of Auschwitz demonstrates a surprising dearth of research on the experiences of female prisoners, especially Jewish women.

To the question of whether there was a difference between the experiences of men and women in the camp, a positive answer has already been given.[4] Still, despite recognition of the importance of such differences, no systematic research has yet been undertaken on the corpus of testimonies and autobiographies pertaining to Auschwitz-Birkenau. Most work on women in the Holocaust is eclectic rather than systematic or comparative, and it tends to lump together death camps, concentration and work camps, and ghettos. As "corrective" history, it has usually avoided comparing men's and women's experiences and writings. In contrast, I deliberately compare the experience of female Jewish prisoners with that of their male counterparts. I do not discuss the experiences of non-Jews, whose situation in the camp was different, often completely different, from that of the Jews, except to add the perspective of people who observed male and female Jewish prisoners at close quarters.

SOURCES

The body of material on which this article is based was written or verbally transmitted between 1945 and 1948, mainly by Jewish survivors from Eastern Europe. The choice of this period is intentional.

I wished to examine descriptions of the camp experience that were as detached as possible from postwar life. In addition to the freshness of the memories, I wished to examine survivors' recollections before their return to "regular" life: before they emigrated from Europe; before they set up new families and homes; before they were influenced by reading the memories of others, or reading historical, psychological, and sociological research; before they became members of a community whose views about the survivors' opinions would have to be taken into consideration; before they gave birth to children of whom they also had to be "considerate"; before they were exposed to a variety of conceptions about Holocaust survivors; before memory was "shaped"; and in many respects before knowing "how it would all end."

What then is this corpus? As Shmuel Krakowski has pointed out, hundreds of survivors who returned from the camps, from places of hiding and the forests, immediately began writing down their memories.[5] In the initial years following the war, many Jewish remembrance projects were also set up. The main ones were established in the first three years after liberation. Here we need to differentiate between testimonies and autobiographical literature. In this essay I focus on testimonies from three remembrance projects: the collection of the Jewish Historical Institute (JHI) in Poland, the Historical Commission in Munich, and the Boder Collection.

The Jewish Historical Institute was established in August 1944 in liberated Lublin, in accordance with a decision of the Central Committee of Polish Jews. During its first months of existence, it expanded its activities and became the Central Committee, with branches in other cities. The committee's director was Philip Friedman. In March 1945 the Central Committee moved to Łódź. At the end of 1947 it relocated to Warsaw, where the enterprise continued operating under the name Jewish Historical Institute. Among the institute's prominent employees were Yeshaya Trunk, Yosef Carmish, Nahman Blumental, and Rachel Auerbach, who had worked in the Ringelblum Archive (Oneg Shabbat).

In the first two years of its operation, the institute's workers collected about four thousand testimonies of Holocaust survivors. Within a few years they had gathered seven thousand testimonies. In addition, parts of the Ringelblum Archive, found in the ruins of the Warsaw ghetto, were transferred to the institute, as well as certificates and important documents from other ghettos, and the Rumkowski Archive from Łódź. Already by 1946, the institute had become involved in research and in publishing compilations of documents, memoirs, and research findings. These materials are preserved in the Jewish Historical Institute in Warsaw, and copies of the collection of testimonies are now kept in the Yad Vashem Archive in Jerusalem. Thanks to the translating work undertaken by Yosef Cremin from Kibbutz Magen together with a handful of volunteers, the material is now accessible in Hebrew.[6]

The Central Historical Commission of the Central Committee of Liberated Jews was established in Munich in December 1945. The commission set up about fifty branches in various displaced persons camps in Germany. Among the commission's founders were its director Yosef Feigenbaum, Israel Kaplan, and S. Gluber. The Historical Commission collected about 2,550 testimonies on the fate of Jews in twelve countries during the Holocaust, as well as photographs and items of folklore. Original documentation was collected regarding administration of the Dachau camp, treatment of Jews in the municipality of Munich, and the lives of Jews in displaced persons camps (a vast collection). The Historical Commission in Munich also published a periodical. After three years of activity, the Historical Commission ended its work and transferred the material to the Yad Vashem Archive, where it is now available in Yiddish, Polish, and Hebrew.

The Boder Collection includes about one hundred testimonies compiled in 1946. That year David Boder, a psychologist from the University of Illinois, undertook the task of collecting testimonies in displaced persons camps in Germany and parts of France where survivors had congregated. Boder recorded his interviewees in their mother tongue. The testimonies themselves were later translated into English, and all are available in the Yad Vashem Archive and at the United States Holocaust Memorial Museum in Washington, D.C.

Like the testimonies, the memoirs I examined were written between 1945 and 1948. The vast majority of Jewish survivors of Auschwitz did not write during their imprisonment. When could they have written? How? Of those few who did manage to write in the camp, most did not survive. Nevertheless, accounts and books about life in the camp began to appear right after the war. Some were published in the writer's mother tongue: Polish, Yiddish, Italian, French, or German; some came out in English or Hebrew translations. Over the years the lion's share of this corpus was translated into

English and Hebrew. There are dozens of such books. Contrary to the widespread view, and in contrast to the almost complete absence of women from subsequent historiography of the Holocaust, a not inconsiderable number of these early testimonies and memoirs were by women.

Women's and men's testimonies and writings from the immediate postwar period constitute a historical source of great importance. In them the horrors, the difficulties, and the various abuses appear in a far more blatant and less "literary" manner than in later writings. Their descriptions are laconic, emotionally "flat," lacking what could be called "philosophical musings." Almost completely absent are interpretations of the significance of evil, the banality, and other psychological issues. The stories were told "as they are." In some cases, especially in testimonies from the Boder Collection, when the interviewer drew attention to pauses, it can be seen that the interviewees or the writers stopped for a moment, overwhelmed by an emotionally laden, almost intolerable burden, but then regained their composure and continued. They were not directly asked to deal with painful feelings, among them guilt.

Batia Druckmancher was transported from the Łódź ghetto to Auschwitz on October 20, 1944, together with her infant daughter:

> Then they ordered all the women to get out of the train . . . the selection started. The young people were separated from the elderly and the children. Some thug asked me who the child standing next to me belongs to. My sister, who was standing close to me, wanted to save me, and said it was her daughter. When I called out that she's mine I received a blow for having lied. Then they took my child from me and my sister also went. And that was it.[7]

Israel Rosen, born in Dombrowa Gornicza, describes with frightening offhandedness the terrors of Auschwitz:

> We arrived in Auschwitz on 1.8.1943. When we arrived and got off the train, we heard shouts: "Put the packages on the side" . . . a group of prisoners arrived that was called the "Canada Commando," and they began to help in emptying the railway cars. They forcibly removed small, three to four months-old babies from their mothers' arms and from babies' prams and threw them into sacks which they loaded on vehicles that were prepared in advance for transporting.[8]

These early testimonies and books were almost uninfluenced by the way in which memory was shaped, or what would later become the accepted way of talking or telling about the Holocaust. Beyond chronological proximity to the events, we find a minimum of social influence arising from various opinions and reactions that appeared after the war, and to which givers of the testimonies or writers of memoirs were exposed in later periods. Thus, for example, we find that the people who appear in this corpus were less affected by the concept of "like sheep to the slaughter," by accusations regarding the use of feminine sexuality for the purpose of survival, and by other charges that were hurled at the survivors.

A prominent characteristic evident in this corpus is the terrible loneliness of the survivors. Anna Kovitzka discovered after the war that her baby daughter, whom she had left with a Polish woman, had been murdered as a result of a denunciation three weeks before the war ended. Her husband and the rest of her family had also been murdered: "And so I don't have the child . . . my people are no more. I am alone."[9] Jola (Yetta) Gross, from whose extensive family only her sister remained, described her return to Budapest in similar words: "Arriving in Budapest, I went to the Jewish Committee, and there I sat very despondent. I am alone."[10] And Jürgen Bassfrehnd, on being asked about the fate of his mother, responded: "Q: And where is your mother?/Here follows a long pause/A: My mother is apparently not alive any more . . ."[11]

Although my research makes a claim about the value of this corpus, I do not maintain that it is the only, or even the most accurate source for tracing the history of Auschwitz. In order to obtain a complete picture, we have to examine all the testimonies, autobiographies, Nazi documents, and so on. The freshness of the memory is also not the only consideration, for there are cases in which survivors needed to distance themselves from an incident in order to be able to speak or write about it. Primo Levi's words are relevant here: "For knowledge of the Lagers, the Lagers themselves were not always a good observation post: in the inhuman conditions to which they were subjected, the prisoners could barely acquire an overall vision of their universe."[12]

We have to ask ourselves, whose memories are we examining? What were their roles in the camp? Their sex? When did they arrive? Auschwitz, after all, was many places, and the experience of Auschwitz differed from person to person, from man to woman, from adult to adolescent. Likewise, survival in the camp was a complex patchwork of many factors. Age mattered, and family status was critical. So were nationality, the season, the daily "death quota," and the mood of the guards. And of course there was luck. Yet, despite all these, as Ruth Bondy, a survivor of Auschwitz states, it was difficult to assess an individual's chances of survival:

> Since then, the historians and the mental researchers repeatedly swoop down on us, the dinosaurs, before their final extinction, so that they can also know: How did a person survive the Holocaust? A distorted picture emerges from the testimony of the survivors: each one has a wonderful story about a talisman that protected him, about determination to survive in order to tell, about belief in Divine Providence, about a miracle that took place. If those millions who did not survive were able to give testimony, they too would mouth stories about a talisman, about the belief in the grace of God, about the determined decision to hold on, about the hope that strength gives—except that death overcame them, despite everything.[13]

In the rest of this chapter, I analyze three subjects that remain a focus of research on women and the Holocaust: the response to hunger, the establishment of "surrogate families," and the issue of sexual exploitation.

THE RESPONSE TO HUNGER, THE ESTABLISHMENT OF "SURROGATE FAMILIES," AND SEXUAL EXPLOITATION

> *And if the function of Auschwitz still exists, it is not in this place, but rather it is spread throughout the world, in splinters, in the memories of the survivors. There Auschwitz continues to live, day and night, to strike, and to strangle, to gnaw at and to consume, without escape.*[14]

One prominent feature of the testimonies and books written between 1945 and 1948 by women and men is the genuine engagement with the reality of life in the camp. One finds in this corpus a most sincere and painful confrontation with what the camp did to a person, to the "self." As opposed to later writers who offer many descriptions of mutual aid and support, the "shattering," as Charlotte Delbo referred to it, was the essence of life in the camp for Jewish women and men alike.[15] That essence consisted of unbearable experiences of dehumanization, fear, hunger, cold, terror, uncertainty, helplessness, and a general feeling of ceasing to exist, being "not quite alive, yet not quite dead," as Isabella Leitner described the extreme of this experience: transformation into a *musselman*.[16]

The camp crushed everything that the person believed about herself, her surroundings, and the values on which she had been raised. It was empty, nothing, chaos. It was the inverse of the Christian conversion: instead of discovering God, or by projection, the good in humanity and the world, it presented the opposite. Only if one left behind many of one's previous beliefs or values could one survive. And, wrote Margalit Nagel-Gross a few months after the liberation, "you could get used to anything, even to the fact that the crematoria burned day and night and devoured their victims. The motto: 'What is important—is that I won't get there.'"[17] Elsewhere she observed:

> Members of the Sonderkommando . . . in many cases these fellows carried the corpses of their parents and other family members. One morning they found a good friend of ours dead. He had hanged himself. The reason: in the previous night's transport his daughter-in-law arrived and he had to gas her to death. He couldn't take it. This was a rare instance, because usually everyone could take anything. Had I not experienced it personally, I would never have believed that people are capable of becoming non-human to such an extent, nor would I have believed how strong the will to survive and the life instinct are.[18]

In May 1945, during her recuperation in Sweden, Pola Schreiber Goldwasser wrote:

> Only to live from day to day like an animal, not to remind oneself of anything, not to think, otherwise you are liable to go insane. . . . From day to day, from week to week, my hatred of those around me grew, I ceased believing in human beings. I lived within a community of human beings who became animals, a community dominated by physical strength, one in which every step, every thing, was achieved by violence.[19]

Testimonies and writings from those years do not beautify or soften the life of the camp and the rupture it caused. Nor do they make allowances for survivors or their audience. Reading these sources raises the question of whether the oft-repeated claim regarding the survival of women in the camp, namely that they were helped by early feminine socialization and created different survival strategies from men, is valid.

Hunger

Even though women and men alike starved in Auschwitz, the research claims that hunger had a gendered component. Women and men, it is assumed, coped differently with hunger. It is claimed that the socialization to which women were exposed as cooks responsible for preparing meals for their families enabled them to set up communities that in turn were important in dealing with the inescapable hunger. Most men, on the other hand, did not have sufficient experience in the kitchen to create such communities. According to Myrna Goldenberg, women bore hunger well, or at least more tolerably than men:

> Women report talking about food, recollecting wonderful meals, and this often led to the next step: exchanging recipes and teaching another woman the art of cooking and baking. . . . These activities did not alleviate hunger. . . . But this kind of talk gave the women certain psychological and spiritual advantages that men didn't have. . . . In recalling their domestic roles of pre-Nazi days, women *created* communities that facilitated sharing recipes and food preparation experiences. As they described the food they once cooked to another prisoner, they shared a familiar experience and connected to another person, briefly breaking the isolation and despair brought on by prolonged hunger. Thus, in many women's memoirs, hunger created a social relationship. . . . Through this sharing and teaching, women resisted the dehumanization that was part of Nazi systematic debilitation.[20]

It has even been claimed that women had better strategies for sharing and making the most of the limited supply of food, and that techniques used by men and women to forget about hunger were different. Whereas starving men dreamed about meals they had been served, women exchanged recipes.[21]

The experience of hunger was universal and constituted one of the bitterest tortures and a major cause of death. Although it is possible to identify differences between women and men in descriptions of hunger and attitudes to it, the claim that women dealt with hunger better is too general, somewhat superficial, and overlooks the reality of daily life in Auschwitz. A claim of this kind by Sybil Milton, that previous patterns of behavior improved women's chances of survival, is possibly correct, but mainly with regard to other capabilities, such as the ability to sew on a button or match a garment to body size.[22] Regarding her claim that in many memoirs women described men (unlike women) as incapable of controlling hunger and unable to plan in advance and keep food, other sources present a contrary picture. Testimonies and autobiographies show that women spoke about hunger and thought about it incessantly. Like men, women fought over food like "animals" and trampled each other to obtain an extra crumb. In reality, the main gender difference regarding hunger is that women, more than men, sold their bodies for food.

Like many other women, Gisella Perl presents a complex picture of relationships between prisoners around the issue of hunger. In her first months in the camp, she encountered "animal-like" fights over food in the bitter struggle for survival:

> We counted each other's swallows, jealously, enviously, careful that none of us should get more than her share. . . . Quickly the strongest, most energetic among us jump down from their cages and run to the door, where they catch up with the prisoners carrying the empty pot. Screaming, pushing each other aside, fighting, they stick their arms into the pot to get another mouthful of turnips or potato, which stuck to the side of the pot. . . . Like wild animals they attack the carriers, unmindful of the blows and kicks showering down on them.[23]

After the meal, Perl, a doctor, would bandage the wounds sustained by the female prisoners. Perl determined that the Nazi method of dehumanization worked "wonderfully": "Only a very few, the strongest, the cleanest, the noblest were able to retain a semblance of human dignity; the rest were engulfed by the gurgling swamp of crime, mental deterioration and filth."[24]

Giuliana Tedeschi's book contains complex descriptions of relationships among female prisoners, relationships that ranged from mutual hate and loathing to deep friendship. But her account of the hunger and thirst are unequivocal regarding the terrible, infinite distress they evoked and the effect they had on the prisoners:

> Finally the water arrived and was poured from the buckets into red enamel bowls that were distributed to the prisoners: one bowl for each group, not more than two sips per person. With our hands hanging loosely in our laps, we couldn't detach our feverish gaze from the red bowl that passed from mouth to mouth, and we would watch our neighbor's throat rise with the two long swallows, as if we were seeing a few drops of water drip down through the transparent throat and get lost in the sand. If someone's lips would tarry too long on the rim of the bowl and her throat oscillate one more time, everyone would shout, feeling cheated.[25]

Elsewhere in the book, Tedeschi continues in this vein: "'Bread, bread!' We heard shouts. A large wagon whose shaft had bent had slid off the road and overturned. . . . The loaves of bread looked as if they had spilled out of a giant cornucopia. . . . The women pounced on the bread and each took as much as she could carry, fighting among themselves, sometimes savagely, face to face, over a loaf of bread."[26] Likewise, Pola Schreiber Goldwasser described the attitude of the prisoners to hunger and food:

> Or during the dishing out of lunch—a little, hot (not always), turbid soup to the terribly starved mass . . . the starved mass attacks the pot, often overturning it even though not a single drop of hot food remains. Anyone who has not seen how weak, sick, hungry, miserable people pounce on food has not seen anything terrible in his life. Without considering anything, not the butt of the guard's rifle, nor the warder's cane, the women would drop to the ground and lick the remains of the soup that had spilled.[27]

These depictions of a major battleground for survival in the camp—the struggle to obtain food—demonstrate that the daily reality of Auschwitz transcended lines of gender. Early writers of memoirs or givers of testimony express the despair to which hunger brought prisoners—women and men—and the vicious fights that broke out over food. In later writings, such as those of Ruth Elias, Eva Schloss, and Cila Liberman, descriptions are less blatant, and the bestial dimension is blurred.[28] This change was almost certainly a result of the internalization of conventions of dealing appropriately with hunger, conventions that extended to descriptions of Auschwitz itself.

Surrogate Families

In the conclusion of her 1984 article "The Unethical and the Unspeakable," Joan Ringelheim claimed that women's culture was different from men's. It is women's culture and not their biology, she said, that bestows different conditions on them regarding ethical decisions and significant behaviors in the course of their lives.[29]

Although many researchers conclude that women were more successful than men in developing surrogate families in the camp, my sources do not necessarily confirm this. The researchers' major claims are that, owing to the different material conditions women encountered, the relationships they experienced in the course of their lives, their socialization, and their traditional female capabilities, they were capable of creating or re-creating "families" and thereby creating a survival network. From women's narratives, we can see that they repeatedly attribute their survival to bonds with other women. Writers describe exceptional concern among women, in contrast to the way the men behaved by competing with each other. The claim is also made that in addition to a number of common characteristics of women's and men's support groups, the women's groups had unique features. One of these was the relatively large size of the female support group, a consequence of more intense feelings of helplessness among women, especially because of sexual abuse.

Many researchers echo Ringelheim's claims, although Ringelheim herself subsequently backed away from what she came to call the "cultural feminist" position.[30] The picture that is obtained, however, is one of research that quotes research that quotes previous research. Often it seems we are talking about Ringelheim's initial and general findings and not about comprehensive studies or additional examples. Despite Ringelheim's own reservations about the sweeping conclusions she reached, these are not considered in depth, and there has not until now been any research that significantly "corrects" the course her analysis took.

The concept of "surrogate families" describes small support groups that, according to female and male survivors, made survival a little more likely. The composition of such "families" changed according to the situation. Sometimes these were biological family members: mothers and daughters, fathers and sons, brothers and sisters, male and female cousins, brothers-in-law and sisters-in-law. In cases where all family members had been killed prior to transport to the camp, or were sent to their death in the course of the selection, or were not sent to the same camp, surrogate families comprised fellow prisoners. Often, such "families" were created against the background of a common denominator: nationality, religion, membership in the youth movement, underground activities, originating from the same city or town, common acquaintances, or meeting in the work kommando.

From my research, a more complex picture of Auschwitz emerges. Although it is possible to find "families" of this kind in all the testimonies and books I examined, this does not necessarily attest to the absence of similar practices among men. Indeed, such networks existed in all the books written by men that I analyzed.

It is possible to discern the influence of a number of variables in most of the testimonies and autobiographies that were published from the 1970s onward—such as what can be called the "zeitgeist" regarding friendships among women; a desire to create a more positive picture of what took place in the women's camp; and references to books by other women and ideas expressed by various historians, all of which led to emphasizing the friendship strategies adopted by women.

The picture in earlier testimonies and books, however, is different. For example, the books of Gisella Perl and Olga Lengyel and the testimonies of Margita Schwalb, Pola Schreiber Goldwasser, and Margalit Nagel-Gross describe bitter and desperate struggles between female prisoners. Relationships changed the longer these prisoners remained in Auschwitz-Birkenau, or if they found themselves in a work situation or a position that improved the conditions of their imprisonment, or if they became members of the camp underground. Friendships between women, like those between men, were more likely under better circumstances. Isabella Leitner, who was in the camp with three of her sisters, also shows how friendship and support sometimes created additional difficulties. Furthermore, even when we come across "surrogate families" or support groups among women, we can always find those who did not succeed in creating such networks. Some women had to struggle for survival alone.

In her account, Margita Schwalb provides an extreme description of the intolerable conditions, even for Auschwitz, that Slovakian women, the first to arrive at the camp, had to confront. They fought for survival with no empathy for other prisoners:

> The initial period in Birkenau camp was the cruelest. The number of prisoners grew as new transports arrived from all parts of conquered Europe. Communication between the prisoners was limited; we didn't know each other. . . . The mass murder continued with a vengeance. We ceased taking an interest in our friends and our relatives. In the morning you could still see them; by evening they were no longer alive, murdered or sent to the gas chambers.[31]

Pola Schreiber Goldwasser described the reduction of a person to the level of a bug, the lack of human value, and the all-encompassing brutalization:

> And you, battered human being, shoved from place to place, treated worse than an insect, you have no worth at all, no one will defend you against the injustice that has been done to you . . . the young girls, because of their weak character, surrender to this rotten, inhuman flow, and in their behavior they make the lives of their partners in fate more difficult.[32]

According to Margalit Nagel-Gross:

> Here there are no brothers, parents or friends, here there is only *me*. Furthermore, the bestiality reached such a level that in many cases a sister was pleased to have got rid of her sister. For anyone living a routine civilian life, this is difficult to understand. We had all become similar, only not to human beings. This is the only way to explain the fact that anyone who managed to hold on, survived.[33]

Gisella Perl's memoir describes the complex relationships among prisoners. The contacts she made became significant only after a few months in the camp, when she joined the hospital staff. Here, for the first time, she found friendship and a reason to continue living: helping other women. These descriptions reinforce the claim that in many cases, creation of a "surrogate family" or firm friendships was only possible after the prisoner had established herself in the camp, and especially after she obtained a place of work with relative privilege. The creation of social contact was facilitated by finding some "reason" to go on living; sometimes this was the friendship itself, and also the fact that in many cases contacts were consolidated on the basis of a shared professional/class, cultural, and sometimes national background.

The following is Perl's description of the friendship among the medical staff, which was highly significant in the context of the camp: "'Then we'll stick together and fight together,' she said. Solemnly we shook hands and from then on our friendship and common fight became our constant source of strength and endurance during all those infernal months in Auschwitz."[34] The close relationships among the medical staff led Perl to experience a small victory over the Nazis. According to her, the joy that enveloped the Nazis' faces when they succeeded in causing the women prisoners to descend to low moral standards dissipated when they observed the medical team in which she worked:

> Those evenings at the hospital are the only bearable memory of my Auschwitz days. We were nine friends, nine of the same cultural and social background, with the same interests, the same enthusiasms, the same ideals. We knew what we were living for and we helped one another in our common fight. When we were hungry, we consoled ourselves by talking literature. . . . When we were tired, when Mengele beat us—to break our spirit—we put our heads together and recited songs of freedom.[35]

Olga Lengyel describes a similar process. Lengyel began to create significant friendships in the wake of two developments: being accepted in the camp underground and joining the hospital staff. Before these took place, she describes the moral deterioration in the camp and the fact that even "decent" women deteriorated: "The washroom would have made a fine field for a moralist's observations. . . . Women who had been mothers of honest families, who formerly would not have taken a hairpin, became utterly hardened thieves and never suffered the slightest remorse."[36] Lengyel's supportive contacts only began to develop in the hospital, at a stage when the conditions of her life improved greatly relative to the rest of the camp:

> Imagine our joy when, one day, we were given "an apartment." . . . It was like a dream. . . . There we were at home. . . . Often we reminisced, speaking of the ones who were dear to us or simply discussing the tormenting problems of the day, such as should we not condemn the newborn to death in order to save the poor mother.[37]

One of the most complex accounts of human contacts in Auschwitz-Birkenau appears in Isabella Leitner's book. She spent all of her nine months in the camp in the company of her sisters. In their struggle for survival, they drew strength from each other and, in certain cases, they insisted on continuing to live for each others' sake. With great sensitivity and awareness, Leitner also describes the difficulties that arose from being part of a family under such circumstances. Being alone in the camp, she asserts, was a blessing: "If you are sisterless, you do not have the pressure, the absolute responsibility to end the day alive."[38] Leitner emphasizes that being sisters saved them and gave them hope. Even when they had no strength left, and the gas chambers seemed the only solution, there was a tremendous responsibility to live for the others. As a result, however, the duty to remain alive was painful and torturous, and the struggle to survive became guilt-ridden and tormenting. Sometimes Isabella longed to live alone.

Charlotte Delbo often mentions the need for a support system and the connection between such support and family constellations. Her book has generated much interest among researchers. Delbo was not Jewish, and thus the conditions of her imprisonment were better than those of Jewish prisoners. Delbo's status could explain the emphasis she places on connections between prisoners, which reinforces my claim that the better the conditions, the greater the number of friendships formed. In the following extract she describes the system of mutual support among French political prisoners. Here Delbo's friend Lulu, who played the role of her mother, helped her overcome a crisis:

> Lulu is worried. "What's the matter with you? Are you ill?" "No. I'm not ill, but I can't take it anymore . . ." "That's nothing. You'll get over it." "No, Lulu, I won't. I'm telling you I can't take it any more . . ." Lulu has a good look around us, and seeing there is no kapo in the vicinity, she takes hold of my wrist, and says, "Get behind me, so they can't see you. You'll be able to have a good cry . . ." Now I no longer know why I am crying, but Lulu suddenly tugs at me: "That's enough now! Back to work. Here she comes." She says it with such kindness that I am not ashamed of having cried. It is as though I had wept against my mother's breast.[39]

Claims about surrogate families often ignore those who did not succeed in creating networks of this kind. Of course, it is not possible to quantify how many families were created in the camp in general and within each barracks or work kommando in particular. We are dealing with representations and autobiographies, not with a representative sample. Despite the claim, partially correct, that survivors who gave testimony or published memoirs also described what happened around them, the picture is still limited. Thus some testimonies, especially earlier ones such as that of Raya Kagan, emphasize that not all the prisoners succeeded in creating support systems:

> When the SS guards went to eat at six in the evening, we would organize a meal. First—the dishing up. In the department Elza was in charge of this; she had acquired the reputation of an experienced and honest proprietress . . . she had a responsible and respected, yet unpleasant role. Our kommando, a random collection of exiles from all corners of Europe, began to bond together. The women and the girls started getting used to each other and communicating. Even the bad ones amongst us, who fortunately were few, were influenced by the general atmosphere and surrendered to the rule of the kommando. . . . The uniform character of our kommando was conspicuous, as opposed to the prevailing spirit in the political department: intrigues, jealousy, and hostility. In the political department, the prisoners would have been prepared to drown one another, sabotage each others' efforts, or inform on a colleague to the SS guards.[40]

Does comparable complexity emerge from books written by men? Like women, men describe an intricate set of relationships. And like women, particular variables played an important role for men: the date of arrival in the camp, the time the prisoner had spent there, his status, country of origin, religion, and political beliefs. When the configuration of variables enabled it, men, like women, created "surrogate families."

I will present a single example. Primo Levi writes both about the cruel and uncompromising struggles for survival and the mutual support group that he and his beloved friend Alberto created. On this subject, as in others, Levi permits himself no moral allowances, nor does he deal with the question of how these issues will be received by readers. In this respect his books are similar to early accounts by women. Thus, for example, he describes in a way that seems cruel to us the struggle for survival:

But in the Lager things are different: here the struggle to survive is without respite, because everyone is desperately and ferociously alone. If some Null Achtzehn vacillates, he will find no one to extend a helping hand; on the contrary, someone will knock him aside, because it is in no one's interest that there will be one more "musselman" dragging himself to work every day.[41]

Elsewhere, however, Levi describes how he and another Italian created a small support group: "Throughout the year of my imprisonment in Auschwitz I had Alberto D. as a fraternal friend: he was a robust, courageous young man, more clearsighted than the average."[42] Levi uses the term "us-ism" to describe their relationship:

How much water can a two-inch-wide pipe one or two meters high contain? A liter, perhaps not even that. I could have drunk all of it immediately; that would have been the safest way. Or save a bit for the next day. Or share half of it with Alberto. Or reveal the secret to the whole squad. I chose the third path, that of selfishness extended to the person closest to you, which in distant times a friend of mine appropriately called us-ism.[43]

Struggles for survival and the creation of "surrogate families" were common to women and men. In the context of the material on Auschwitz, the claim that women, more than men, tended toward solidarity appears essentialist and is possibly biased by the particular development of research on women in the Holocaust. Women may have tended to create larger "surrogate families" than men, but since we are not talking about a mass phenomenon—for there were also many women who created smaller support groups—this assertion should not be regarded as generally applicable. This case study provides an opening for further research that will concentrate more on comparisons and be "gender-oriented" in the full sense of the word.

Sexual Exploitation

Although Holocaust scholarship on women has addressed this subject, most researchers have limited their discussion to a narrow body of material.[44] Furthermore, the emphasis is on sexual abuse at the outbreak of the war and in the ghettos, acts perpetrated by the Einsatzgruppen, and sexual abuse in places of hiding. Researchers conclude that there is little evidence of harsh sexual abuse in the camps. But this scholarship does not adequately consider two major sets of documentation: testimonies and autobiographies written immediately after the war, including testimonies and autobiographies in Hebrew, and material related to Auschwitz.

What were the particular characteristics of sexual exploitation in the camps? Two major factors differentiate sexual exploitation in Auschwitz from other contexts: first, the racial definitions embodied in the Nazi worldview and, second, the gendered power relations within the camp.

The Nazi worldview explicitly prohibited sexual relations between the "superior" and the "inferior" races in order to prevent racial "contamination." In 1935 the third Nuremberg Law prohibited marriage and extramarital sexual relations between Jews and citizens with German blood or kindred blood:

> Firm in the knowledge that the purity of German blood is the basis for the survival of the German people and inspired by the unshakeable determination to safeguard the future of the German nation, the Reichstag has unanimously resolved upon the following law, which is promulgated herewith:
> 1. Marriages between Jews and citizens of German or kindred blood are forbidden.
> 2. Sexual relations outside marriage between Jews and citizens of German or kindred blood are forbidden.[45]

Transgressors would be punished by imprisonment, hard labor, or transfer to the front. In his analysis of the law, Saul Friedländer asserts that "the relation of the preamble to the text of the law reflected the extent of the racial peril represented by the Jew."[46]

Because of this law and other deeply entrenched conceptions of Nazi ideology, sexual relations, whether by consent or by force, were categorically prohibited between members of the "superior race" and inferior races, especially Jews. This prohibition was part of the notion of *Rassenschande:* racial shame, or crimes against the race. Although the prohibition did reduce the number of instances of rape in ghettos and camps, it did not completely prevent them. The stereotype of sexually impure Jewish women, a taste of which appears in *Mein Kampf,* made them vulnerable to sexual exploitation, including rape, and sometimes presented them with the choice of death or survival by means of prostitution.[47]

My research reveals that sexual abuse, especially of female inmates, in the camps in general and in Auschwitz-Birkenau in particular, was widespread, perpetrated both by SS men and by prisoners, generally non-Jewish prisoners with privileges. Here we have to add one important remark. Although a variety of sexually abusive practices took place in the camp, rape was the exception. Because of *Rassenschande*, Germans serving in the camp were forbidden to rape Jewish prisoners. In this regard, the Nazi German practice of sexual abuse may be unique in comparison with other "sexual war crimes": Red Army soldiers raped many women, German but also non-German. Later in the twentieth century, in Bosnia and Kosovo or in Rwanda, raping "enemy" women was an everyday practice. Because of their ideology the Nazis were not allowed to do it and, in most cases, did not.

Sex in Exchange for a Chance at Survival A second factor underlying sexual exploitation is bound up with the hierarchy of power in the camps, which, in most cases, was gender-based. Sexual exploitation is often a result of unequal power. In Auschwitz the contrast of absolute power and complete powerlessness led to a dual system of exploitation. At the top of the camp hierarchy were the Nazis, the undisputed lords, whose position allowed them to engage in abusive sexual acts. But there was a second power system consisting of male and female prisoners themselves. Prisoners who had survived for a comparatively long time and had become camp veterans could engage in exploitation because of the relative power they had accumulated. These prisoners managed to integrate better in the work kommandos, to find additional sources of food, link up with powerful forces in the camp, or organize themselves in various support groups. For reasons having to do with the camp's chronological development and its physical setup, prisoners in positions of power were usually male. Furthermore, only the women's camp had authority figures of both sexes, which increased opportunities to exploit female prisoners; in the men's camp, the SS and other authority figures were always men.

One reason the SS could control such a large number of prisoners with relatively few personnel is that the camp was actually run by privileged prisoners. The SS determined the policy, the arrangements, and the methods of punishment, but between the SS and the individual prisoner were the appointed prisoners who had charge of the direct running of the camp. These male or female prisoners enforced disciplinary rules, carried out—and sometimes delegated—punishments, were responsible for marching the prisoners out and placing them in position for roll calls, supervised the prisoners during work, and so on. Thus, in the initial years, the concentration camps were run by a staff of no more than 120 SS personnel for each camp. In the final phase of the camps, when prisoner populations had reached about seven hundred thousand, the overall number of SS personnel in all the Auschwitz camps together was about forty thousand, most of whom did guard duty and provided armed accompaniment for the work squads.[48]

Considerable power was concentrated in the hands of the privileged prisoners, which in many cases increased their chances of survival. In small camps the main privilege was the right to obtain additional food. In larger camps senior prisoner position-holders obtained many other benefits, including alcoholic drinks, clean, well-fitting clothes, a separate corner in the residential hut, and the satisfaction of their various cravings: singers and "entertainers" who helped them pass the time enjoyably, cooks who prepared delicacies for them, and women and boys who satisfied their sexual desires. More than in the other camps, these practices were prominent in Auschwitz. In Auschwitz, where extermination was carried out with industrial efficiency and where the Nazis' regime of terror reached its extreme, the relative abundance and property accumulated by privileged prisoners was particularly conspicuous. It was said of many of them that they attained a status and enjoyed a life of luxury they never experienced when they were free.

Some cases of sexual exploitation in the camp, and especially what I call "selling one's body for food," were characterized by the feeling, unrealistic in most cases, that a choice existed. In other words, a female prisoner in the camp could "choose not to" sell her body. Usually, no one "forced" her to do so. In reality, this was one of the last survival practices that women resorted to, one which, in many cases, was simply unavoidable. But the feeling of guilt and especially the associated feelings of helplessness were often intolerable.

Whereas many women, regardless of their age, suffered from sexually exploitative practices linked to the power structures in Auschwitz, such cases were relatively rare in the men's camps and were confined to a limited group of boys. Although this matter is not my focus, I will survey it briefly. We recall that most children under the age of sixteen

were sent directly to the gas chambers upon arrival. There were, however, exceptional cases of boys between the ages of twelve and sixteen
who managed to enter the camp as prisoners, usually because they
looked older than their age, or because they were advised by members
of the "Canada Kommando" to say during the selection that they were
older than they actually were.[49] Many of these boys worked in what
was known as "the school for builders" in Birkenau and were housed
in the "youth block" or one of the blocks in Auschwitz I. Others were
part of the general prisoner population.

The lives of these young boys were as difficult as those of other
prisoners in the camp, but in addition to "regular" horrors, they also
suffered from sexual exploitation. Veteran prisoners—usually non-
Jewish political or criminal prisoners—turned some into *pipels,* or "sex
slaves." O. Kraus and E. Kulka discuss the subject explicitly: "They
were exposed to a special danger from the German kapos who needed
boys to satisfy their sexual perversions, the intensity of which increased
during the years of their imprisonment."[50] Tomas Geva, a Berlin Jew
who arrived in Auschwitz as a thirteen-year-old boy, describes many
cases of sexual exploitation of boys:

> "I can no longer allow myself to help you without asking for some-
> thing in return. You know that not only are we longing for our
> women, we hardly remember their pleasures." He locked the door
> and began unbuttoning his trousers . . . I simply sat there without
> moving, without showing a single sign of agreement . . . "Never
> mind, I'll find many others."[51]

Scholars researching this phenomenon have determined that although sex in exchange for a chance of survival was sometimes part
of men's experiences, it does not feature prominently in their books.
They also suggest that when it did occur, it generally was voluntary
and involved homosexual relations between a younger and an older
person—a *pipel* and a kapo. Attention should be directed to the problematic nature of the assertion that such sexual relations were "voluntary." Given that we are talking about sexual relations in exchange for
an increased chance for survival, that is to say, as a survival practice,
it seems misguided to assume "consent." That such sexual relations
occurred between an adolescent boy and an adult kapo or veteran
prisoner with senior status reinforces the coercive aspect.

Many testimonies and memoirs published during the first wave include mention of "sex in exchange for food."⁵² In most cases, trading sex for food was a life or death decision: women inmates who did not manage to find another way to obtain the additional food essential for their survival were constrained to "sell" their bodies.⁵³ Gisella Perl describes such cases:

> These men were trusted old prisoners who knew everything there was to know about camp life, had connections in the crematories and were masters at "organizing." Their full pockets made them the Don Juans of Camp C. They chose their women among the youngest, the prettiest, the least emaciated prisoners and in a few seconds the deal was closed. Openly, shamelessly, the dirty, diseased bodies clung together . . . and the piece of bread, the comb, the little knife wandered from the pocket of the man into the greedy hands of the woman. . . . Our SS guards knew very well what was going on in the latrine. They even knew who was whose *kochana* (lover), and were much amused by it all.⁵⁴

In one case, a Polish inmate demanded Perl's body in return for a piece of string that she needed desperately: "I stopped beside him. . . . He looked me over from head to foot, carefully, then grabbed me by the shoulder and hissed in my ear: 'I don't want your bread . . . I want you . . . you. . . . Hurry up . . . hurry up . . .' he said hoarsely. His hand, filthy with the human filth he was working in, reached out for my womanhood, rudely, insistently."⁵⁵

Margalit Nagel-Gross laconically and in no uncertain terms describes being aware of this practice. According to her, it was widespread and accepted, an inherent part of the camp's organizational system:

> So, they "organized" . . . together with the "organizational" method, I should mention those who were called *Kochanita* (in Polish— lover). Nearly every girl had a Polish lover, or an Aryan lover. A Jewish lover did not enter into consideration, because he had nothing, for after all "love follows the stomach." Any fellow, as ugly, stupid, and anti-Semitic as he might be, was suitable to be a lover.⁵⁶

In a chapter titled "A Proposal in Auschwitz," Olga Lengyel, a Jewish doctor from Cluj, describes how a Polish prisoner offered her food and a shawl, for free. But after a few days the next scene took place: "He stood close to me. Then, as though talking to himself, he said: 'It's a strange thing, there is something very desirable about you.' I felt his arm around my waist. His other hand touched me and began to fondle my breast. My world fell to pieces."[57] And yet Lengyel understood that somehow, she had to obtain more food than the official ration in order to survive. So she went to the black market in the washroom, where she discovered the same thing: "The scene inside was demoralizing. . . . The place was crowded. Men and women huddled together in every corner of the room. Couples pressed against one another."[58] After that she "understood" that the first "proposal" she had received could be considered "generous." In her words, she "learned afterwards that his was the finest style of love-making in Auschwitz. The ordinary approach was much more crude and to the point."[59]

The non-Jewish Pole Tadeusz Borowski offers a male viewpoint on these practices:

> My comrades and I laid a roof over the shack of every block elder in the Persian Market. . . . We used "organized" tar-boards and melted "organized" tar, and for every roll of tar-board, every bucket of tar, an elder had to pay. She had to pay the kapo, the Kommando-führer, the kommando "bigwigs." She could pay in various ways: with gold, food, the women of her block, or with her own body. It depended. . . . A few women were usually wearing sheer stockings. Any one of them could be had for a piece of bright silk or a shiny trinket. Since time began, never has there been such an easy market for female flesh![60]

Although it was difficult, in fact impossible, to resist sexual abuse by Germans, sexual abuse by male prisoners generally took place with the women's "consent" and even on their "initiative." In my opinion, it was this element of "choice" that made the "internal" sexual abuse more difficult for female prisoners and aroused pangs of conscience and loss of self-esteem for many years afterward. Possibly this is one reason why the subject is rarely dealt with in testimonies and memoirs, except for the early ones.

Indeed, since about the mid-1960s, descriptions of sexual exploitation involving food are almost totally absent from testimonies and memoirs by women as well as men. Why? Existing scholarship has not addressed this question. As we know, even in non-wartime conditions, many women refrain from reporting sexual abuse. The sense of shame and feelings of guilt that victims characteristically experience are especially strong in cases of a sexual nature. The same was true for female survivors of the camps, although for them there was an additional factor: the guilt felt by so many survivors that they, and not others, survived. In addition, "accusations" came up, tacit or explicit, that attributed women's survival to their having sold their bodies. Here, for example, is what Ruth Bondy wrote:

> In Prague, upon my return from the camp, the Gentiles expressed only wonder mixed with displeasure: Jewish property had been entrusted to the care of many of them. The Jews had disappeared, the objects had remained—and, suddenly, there appear before us ghosts to remind us of the forgotten. However, here, in Israel, the Jews also wanted to know: How did you stay alive? What did you have to do in order to survive? And in their eyes, a glimmer of suspicion: Kapo? Prostitute?[61]

Bondy's words help explain why early testimonies and memoirs recount incidents of sexual abuse, whereas later publications do not. Survivors writing in the early years were less exposed to social judgments and accusations regarding the use of feminine sexuality for the purpose of survival.

Moreover, the women who wrote the early memoirs and testimonies cited above did not seem to suffer inhibitions about entering the "public sphere"[62] that later kept other survivors from sharing their stories.[63] As prisoners most of them had occupied relatively good positions in the camp and had, as a result, some influence on their fate and that of others. Their situation prevented them from becoming what Primo Levi called "the drowned." It afforded them a wider vantage point from which to observe the life of the camp, as well as the ability to preserve a certain "inner freedom," which enabled more "healthy" survival because they retained a feeling of relative agency.[64] These were women who had also been involved in the public sphere before the war.[65] All these factors contributed to diminishing the feelings of shame and guilt that overwhelmed most survivors, even to the extent that these women do not mention "reasons" for writing their memoirs.

Forms of Sexual Exploitation   Another feature of the earlier books is their accounts of types of sexual exploitation other than rape, including physical and verbal abuse. Most cases of physical sexual exploitation by the SS and prisoners in positions of authority took place when the prisoners entered the camp, during inspections and selections. There were also attempts to force sexual relations on female prisoners and threats of punishment for refusal to comply. These acts, like sexual exploitation involving food, were sometimes perpetrated by women as well as men. Furthermore, at the time of liberation and during subsequent months, survivors suffered sexual exploitation by Red Army soldiers, who raped and attacked Jewish as well as gentile women. Descriptions of some of these acts, mainly verbal sexual exploitation or attempts at exploitation by female guards, appear in later books. Whereas the earlier accounts detail blatant, invasive, and violent cases, however, in later books the descriptions are more refined or restrained. From the many references, I present a few examples.

Gisella Perl describes the process undergone by women who were chosen during the selection to enter the camp. Whereas most men depict this process in terms of dehumanization, Perl adds the dimension of sexual exploitation and abuse. Furthermore, the association that directs her thought is clearly gender-oriented. Perl writes how after liberation, when she was living in New York, she would be reminded of the "sauna" in Auschwitz—"the Auschwitz beauty parlor"—whenever she passed a beauty parlor. The aim of the Auschwitz site, of course, was the opposite of a regular beauty parlor: to remove any remnants of beauty the women had retained. The women who passed through it aroused morbid interest among the guards: "The first room into which we stepped was filled with young SS men. Their eyes shone with expectation, their ape-like movements betrayed an unhealthy, abnormal sexual excitement."[66]

Elsa (Frishman) Glieck, who arrived in Auschwitz in May 1942 with the first transports of women from Slovakia, talks about the humiliating physical examination she and the others underwent:

> After the roll call we, who arrived last, were led back to the *revir* where we stood in rows, and each time they ordered a certain number of women to go to the back of the *revir*. . . . The women who arrived first had already passed us with their heads shaved and wearing striped clothes. The expression on their faces was one of terror. They told us that they had been examined in intimate places with rods, and many said this had caused them to bleed. Later rumors reached us that the SS guards took statistics on how many of the Slovakian prisoners were still virgins.[67]

Rape, unlike other types of sexual abuse, was rare, but it did occur. Laura Varon, a Jewish woman from Rhodes, describes how she and her friends were raped by SS guards in Auschwitz. "And all of a sudden, the door opened and three Nazis came and they dragged us on the floor, they violated us, sexually violated us. They smelled like beer, you know. They raped us."[68] A blatant attempt at rape is described in Sophia Minc's diary:

> During the break I was called to the shift commander. I went into Richter's office. . . . He ordered me to sit in the armchair and began explaining to me what an honor it was for me to be found attractive by a German, an SS man, a member of the supreme race. The German grew angry at my long silence, and shouted: "Strip!" I was trembling, no, this I would not do, let him kill me! He jumped on me brutally and began tearing my clothes, I defended myself with all my might, I would not have submitted. Suddenly the door creaked. Richter jumped behind the desk and I moved in the direction of the exit. The woman in charge came in, looked at me with a strange gaze and ordered me to get back to work.[69]

More than other experiences, the sexual abuse suffered by female prisoners in the camp points to the fact that they were exposed to a "double risk," as Jews and as women. On the one hand, as Jewish prisoners in Auschwitz-Birkenau, they had to contend with all the difficulties that this entailed, while on the other, despite the annulment of their bodies—an annulment that centered on their physiological capacity to give birth—they remained "temporary" and available sexual entities whose lives and bodies were permitted both to the German staff and, in certain instances, also to the male prisoners, mainly the non-Jewish ones. To these men, the female Jewish prisoners ceased being "human women" and became a wide-open bodily site that possessed signs of sex but contained no humanity.

The corpus of testimonies and memoirs from 1945–48 unsettles some assumptions that have come to constitute the accepted story of Auschwitz. Reassuring notions about the nobility of suffering and the uniqueness of women's ways of surviving disappear before the unmitigated misery and profound loneliness of the Jews who survived the camp. "Who owns Auschwitz?" Imre Kertész asked amidst the controversy surrounding Roberto Benigni's 1997 film *Life Is Beautiful.* Kertész provides fragments of answers, but his somber words about the displacement of the survivors and how the survivors' memory is shaped, appropriated, and rejected capture what I have tried to convey in this essay:

> The survivor is taught how he has to think about what he has experienced, regardless of whether or to what extent this "thinking-about" is consistent with his real experiences. The authentic witness is or will soon be perceived as being in the way, and will have to be shoved aside like the obstacle he is. The words of [Jean] Améry prove their truth: "*We,* the victims, will appear as the truly incorrigible, irreconcilable ones, as the anti-historical reactionaries in the exact sense of the word, and in the end it will seem like a technical mishap that some of us still survived."[70]

NOTES

1. See Eleonora Lev, *Sug Mesuyam shel Yatmut: Edut al Masa* [*A Certain Kind of Orphanhood: Report of a Journey*] (Tel Aviv: N. B. Books, 1999), 254.

2. Primo Levi, *The Drowned and the Saved,* trans. Raymond Rosenthal (New York: Vintage International, 1989), 23–24.

3. Ibid., 17.

4. See, for example, Carol Ann Rittner and John K. Roth, eds., *Different Voices: Women and the Holocaust* (St. Paul, Minn.: Paragon House, 1993).

5. Shmuel Krakowski, "Memorial Projects and Memorial Institutions Initiated by She-erit Hapletah," in *Sheerit Hapletah 1944–1948: Rehabilitation and Political Struggle,* ed. Yisrael Gutman and Avital Saf, proceedings of the Sixth Yad Vashem International Historical Conference (Jerusalem: Yad Vashem, 1985), 351–52.

6. Archives of the Jewish Historical Institute (Zydowski Instytut Historyczny; hereafter referred to as JHI).

7. Batia Druckmancher testimony, Yad Vashem Archive (hereafter referred to as YVA), München Collection, M1/E/555, p. 3.

8. Israel Rosen testimony, April 24, 1945, JHI, M-49E/154, p. 3, in YVA.

9. Anna Kovitzka testimony, September 26, 1946, YVA, Boder Collection, O.36/2, p. 3.

10. Jola (Yetta) Gross testimony, August 3, 1946, YVA, Boder Collection, O.36/37, p. 29.

11. Jürgen Bassfrehnd testimony, September 20, 1946, YVA, Boder Collection, O.36/4, p. 20.

12. Levi, *Drowned and Saved,* 16–17.

13. Ruth Bondy, *Shevarim shelemim* [*Whole Fractures*] (Tel Aviv: Gevanim, 1997), 45.

14. Lev, *Sug Mesuyam*, 255.

15. Charlotte Delbo, *Auschwitz and After* (New Haven, Conn.: Yale University Press, 1965), 11–12.

16. Isabella Leitner, *Fragments of Isabella: A Memoir of Auschwitz* (Boston: Ty Crowell, 1978), 46.

17. Margalit Nagel-Gross, *Shalosh shanim be Auschwitz-Birkenau* [*Three Years in Auschwitz-Birkenau*], trans. Miriam Algazi (Israel: Ahuva Pondak-Grumer, 2003), 19 (originally written in Hungarian in Bratislava, 1945).

18. Ibid., 20.

19. Pola Schreiber Goldwasser, *Arba' mahbarot shehorot* [*Four Black Notebooks*] (Jerusalem: Yad Vashem, 2005), 67–78. *Arba' mahbarot shehorot* was originally written in Polish in 1945.

20. Myrna Goldenberg, "Food Talk: Gendered Responses to Hunger in the Concentration Camps," in *Experience and Expression: Women, the Nazis, and the Holocaust,* ed. Elizabeth R. Baer and Myrna Goldenberg (Detroit: Wayne State University Press, 2003), 172–74.

21. See, for example, Cara de Silva, *In Memory's Kitchen: A Legacy from the Women of Terezin* (Lanham, Md.: Jason Aronson, 1996).

22. Sybil Milton, "Women and the Holocaust: The Case of German and German-Jewish Women," in *When Biology Became Destiny: Women in Weimar and Nazi Germany,* ed. Renate Bridenthal, Atina Grossmann, and Marion Kaplan (New York: Monthly Review, 1984), 297–333, esp. 313: "Vignettes and diaries by women interned in Gurs, Ravensbrück, Auschwitz-Birkenau, and Bergen-Belsen revealed that women's traditionally domestic roles as wives, daughters, and mothers aided them under conditions of extreme duress."

23. Gisella Perl, *I Was a Doctor in Auschwitz* (Manchester, N.H.: Ayer, 1948), 40–41.

24. Ibid., 37–41.

25. Giuliana Tedeschi, *There Is a Place on Earth: A Woman in Birkenau,* trans. Tim Park (New York: Pantheon, 1992), 90.

26. Ibid., 163.

27. Schreiber Goldwasser, *Arba' mahbarot shehorot,* 53.

28. See Ruth Elias, *Triumph of Hope: From Theresienstadt and Auschwitz to Israel* (Canada: John Wiley, 1998); Eva Schloss, *Eva's Story* (New York: Castle-Kent, 1988); and Cila Liberman, *Tselinkah: yaldah she-śardah et Oshvits* [*Celinqa: A Child Survived Auschwitz*] (Jerusalem: Yad Vashem, 2002).

29. Joan Ringelheim, "The Unethical and the Unspeakable: Women and the Holocaust," *Simon Wiesenthal Center Annual* (1984): 87.

30. Joan Ringelheim, "Women and the Holocaust: A Reconsideration of Research," in *Different Voices,* ed. Rittner and Roth, 373–418.

31. Margita Schwalb, "Yehudiyot Slovakiot" ["Slovakian Jewish Women in Auschwitz Camp"], trans. Yehoshua R. Bücler, *Moreshet* 53 (November 1992): 93–101. Schwalb's article was originally published in Slovakian as a part of *Vyhasnutè oči* [*Lifeless Eyes*] (Bratislava: Requiem, 1948).

32. Schreiber Goldwasser, *Arba' mahbarot shehorot,* 51.

33. Nagel-Gross, *Shalosh shanim be Auschwitz-Birkenau,* 19 (emphasis in the original).

34. Perl, *Doctor in Auschwitz,* 88.

35. Ibid., 92–93.

36. Olga Lengyel, *Five Chimneys: The Story of Auschwitz* (Chicago: Academy Chicago, 1995), 56.

37. Ibid., 72.

38. Leitner, *Fragments of Isabella,* 45.

39. Delbo, *Auschwitz and After,* 104–5.

40. Raya Kagan, *Nashim be-lishkat ha-gehinom* [*Hell's Office Women*] (Palestine: Oświęcim Chronicle, 1947), 120.

41. Primo Levi, *Survival in Auschwitz,* trans. Stuart Wolf (New York: Touchstone, 1996), 88.

42. Levi, *Drowned and Saved,* 33. See also Levi, *Survival in Auschwitz,* 57, 145–50, 155.

43. Levi, *Drowned and Saved,* 88.

44. See Marlene Heinemann, *Gender and Destiny: Women Writers on the Holocaust* (New York: Greenwood, 1986), esp. 27–33; and Myrna Goldenberg, "Lessons Learned from Gentle Heroism: Women's Holocaust Narratives," *Annals of the American Academy of Political and Social Science* 548, no. 1 (1996): 78–93, esp. 81–86.

45. "Third Nuremberg Law, 1935," in *Nazism 1919–1945,* vol. 2, *State, Economy and Society 1933–1939: A Documentary Reader,* ed. Jeremy Noakes and Geoffrey Pridham (Exeter: University of Exeter Press, 2000).

46. Saul Friedländer, *Nazi Germany and the Jews,* vol. 1, *The Years of Persecution, 1933–1939* (New York: HarperCollins, 1997), 142.

47. Adolf Hitler, *Mein Kampf* (Mumbai: Jaico, 2006).

48. Israel Gutman, *Encyclopedia of the Holocaust* (New York: Macmillan, 1990).

49. The name "Canada" was coined by prisoners to describe the area where they were forced to sort the Jewish property. The official name was "Effektenlager Kommando." Their other "job" was to stand on the ramp during the selections.

50. Ota B. Kraus and Erich Kulka, *Bet-haroshet la-mavet: Aushvits* [*The Mills of Death: Auschwitz*] (Jerusalem: Yad Vashem, 1960), 105.

51. Thomas Geve, *Ne'urim bi-khevalim: Yeled nitsal min ha-Sho'ah* [*Guns and Barbed Wire: A Child Survives the Holocaust*] (Jerusalem: Yad Vashem, 2003), 85.

52. See, in this context, Jozefina Szepper-Mazowiecka testimony: January 9, 1946, YVA (taken from the Tenenbaum-Marzic Archives, Underground Archives in Białystok ghetto), M.11/180, no page mentioned (Polish-Hebrew); and review of the sexual aspects of life in the Blizin and Auschwitz camps, November 4, 1946, YVA (from the JHI collection), M.49.E-JHI/1456, no page mentioned (Yiddish). In her analysis of Auschwitz, the sociologist Anna Pawelczynska refers to the subject but without any references: "Paid prostitution existed in the camp and the choice of erotic partners was dictated by one's ability to pay—either in the form of help in gaining a better place in the camp structure or, at least in the form of food or better clothes." See Anna Pawelczynska, *Values and Violence in Auschwitz: A Sociological Analysis,* trans. Catherine S. Leach (Berkeley and Los Angeles: University of California Press, 1979), 99.

53. In Poland, both in ghettos and camps, sexuality was a way of "buying protection from the Jewish policemen and others who had means and power." See Ringelheim, "Unethical and Unspeakable," 69.

54. Perl, *Doctor in Auschwitz,* 78–79.

55. Ibid., 58.

56. Nagel-Gross, *Shalosh shanim be Auschwitz-Birkenau,* 28. By the phrase "an Aryan lover," Nagel-Gross is referring to a *Volksdeutscher,* not a member of the SS or Nazi Party.

57. Lengyel, *Five Chimneys,* 60.

58. Ibid., 61–62.

59. Ibid., 60–61.

60. Tadeusz Borowski, *This Way for the Gas, Ladies and Gentlemen,* trans. Barbara Vedder (New York: Penguin, 1967 [originally published in 1947]), 86–93.

61. Bondy, *Shevarim shelemim,* 44.

62. There were, of course, exceptions. Charlotte Delbo and Isabella Leitner finished writing their memoirs immediately after the war but did not publish them until the 1960s and 1970s. These writers expressed the fear that their books were not good enough to be published. See Lawrence L. Langer, "Introduction," in Delbo, *Auschwitz and After,* xvi.

63. See, for example, Heinemann, *Gender and Destiny,* 1–12.

64. Pawelczynska, *Values and Violence in Auschwitz,* 127.

65. For example, Gisella Perl was a medical doctor before her incarceration as well as during the period of her imprisonment, as was Olga Lengyel, who was also part of the camp underground. Raya Kagan worked in politics; Liana Milo-Milol-Millu was a journalist, teacher, and activist in the anti-

Fascist movement in Italy; and Lutiana Nisim was a medical doctor and a partisan.

66. Perl, *Doctor in Auschwitz*, 43.

67. Elsa Frishman Glieck, *Shalosh shanim be Auschwitz-Birkenau* [*Three Years in Auschwitz-Birkenau*] (Israel: self-published, 1995), 4.

68. Laura Varon testimony, September 1, 1996, YVA, O.3/10423.

69. Sophia Minc testimony, April 28, 1947, YVA, M49.E-JHI/2484, no page.

70. Imre Kertész, "Who Owns Auschwitz?" trans. John MacKay, *The Yale Journal of Criticism* 14, no. 1 (Spring 2001): 267–68.

Elizabeth R. Baer

Rereading Women's Holocaust Memoirs: Liana Millu's *Smoke Over Birkenau*

Rape has become a forgotten war crime.
—*Ruth Seifert*

THIS STUDY FOCUSES ON THE RELATIONSHIP BETWEEN THE GENER-ation of female Holocaust survivors who cast their experiences and memories into memoir or fictional form and the subsequent genera-tions of Holocaust scholars who have read and evaluated their writ-ings. Specifically, I explore the interaction between survivor-writers and scholar-readers by concentrating on the work of Italian survivor Liana Millu, whose collection of six narratives Primo Levi called "one of the most powerful European testimonies to come from the women's Lager at Auschwitz-Birkenau and by far the most affect-ing among Italian accounts."[1] Millu's *Smoke Over Birkenau* takes up gendered aspects of women's experiences in the *Lager:* pregnancy, childbirth, sexual violence, maternal love, forced prostitution, and the bartering of sexual favors for food. Because Liana Millu is rela-tively little known, as is her memoir, I open with some background on her biography and the publication history of the text. Then I focus on two themes in *Smoke Over Birkenau*—sexual violence and the consequences of women's bonding in the camp—and the ways in which Millu's depiction of these themes contradicts commonplaces of Holocaust scholarship.

Liana Millu was born into a Jewish family in Pisa; the year of her birth is listed variously as 1913, 1914, or 1920.[2] In her teens she had already conceived the desire to be a writer and, against expecta-tions for young women at the time, she approached a newspaper in

Milan and, having written and published a successful article for it, was invited to join the staff. Wishing to cut ties with her family and her religion, she changed her Sephardic birth name from Millul to Millu. After Mussolini's racial laws were established in 1938, she lost her position as a journalist and as a teacher in an elementary school. She worked variously as a seamstress, a clerk, and a nurse, using false identification papers; about this time she also allied herself with a group of freethinking and free-loving Marxists. In 1942 or 1943 she joined the Italian resistance as a member of the "Organizzazione Otto," which operated as a rescue team. In 1944 she was arrested with a group of partisans in Venice.[3] She was thirty years old, or perhaps twenty-four.

Sent initially to the Italian concentration camp of Fossoli, Millu then was deported to Auschwitz, arriving on May 23, 1944. She was selected for labor, tattooed with the number A-5384, and given a bloodstained jacket from a murdered prisoner that she still owned long after the war. After four months in Birkenau, Millu was transferred to Ravensbrück and then to labor in an arms factory in Malkow. Liberated in 1945 and returning almost immediately to Italy, Millu began drafting the stories that became *Smoke Over Birkenau*, finishing them that same year.

Here I would like to pause to acknowledge that I have gathered this biographical information from three sources: the single article on Millu I have been able to locate in English, entitled "Many Bridges to Cross: Sex and Sexuality in Liana Millu's Holocaust Fiction," by Risa Sodi of Yale University; a brief profile of the author written by American novelist Lynne Sharon Schwartz and included in her award-winning translation of the book; and an interview with Millu, available only in Italian, published in 1998.[4] That only one critical article has appeared on this memoir, which is both luminous in the telling and chilling in its effect, is, of course, an indication of the neglect of women's experiences in Holocaust studies until the last two decades of the twentieth century.[5] While it is the case that, unlike scholarly studies of gender, women's memoirs have been published steadily since 1945 (those of Millu and Nanda Herbermann being among the earliest), such memoirs were sometimes marketed for children and often lay unremarked, while memoirs by Elie Wiesel and Primo Levi were "canonized."[6]

Sadly, such neglect is also part of the publication history of *Smoke*

Over Birkenau. Millu published the first edition in Italy in 1947. It promptly went out of print until 1957 when, in the words of Lynne Sharon Schwartz, "it was reissued, half-heartedly, by the prominent Italian publisher, Mondadori, and went the usual way of unpublicized books."[7] Twenty years later, Millu decided something must be done. "I have no family. I am alone. I realized I couldn't neglect the future of my book," Millu stated in a letter.[8] With the help of a friend, she published subsequent editions with a small publishing house in Florence. It was finally the fifth edition, in 1986, that garnered attention and resulted in a sixth edition in 1991 and subsequent translations into German, French, and English.

The 1980s, of course, was the decade when some of the founding studies of gender, Nazism, and the Holocaust were published, such as those by Renate Bridenthal, Atina Grossmann, and Marion Kaplan; Marlene Heinemann; Claudia Koonz; Vera Laska; and Joan Ringelheim.[9] Undoubtedly, these studies, which called into question the master narrative of the Holocaust, created a wider audience for women's memoirs and provided the opportunity for more women's memoirs to be published. Scholarly studies, of course, relied on first-person accounts by women of their experiences in the Shoah; such studies, perforce, drew readers to these sources. In turn, more women survivors were encouraged to believe that an audience existed for their stories. An intriguing example in this regard is Lucille Eichengreen, whose first memoir, *From Ashes to Life: My Memories of the Holocaust,* recounts her journey from her home in Hamburg to the Łódź ghetto and then to Auschwitz. Not until that volume, which she wrote only after she had raised her family and retired from business in California, was well-received did Eichengreen sit down to write the "backstory" of her experiences in the Łódź ghetto, the story of her sexual abuse at the hands of Chaim Rumkowski.[10]

Smoke Over Birkenau first became available in English through a Jewish Publication Society edition in 1991 and then through the Jewish Lives series of Northwestern University Press in 1997. Some have called the book Holocaust fiction, but I have chosen to use the word *memoir* to describe the six interconnected accounts of women's experiences in the *Lager.*[11] I offer several reasons for this nomenclature. Millu situates herself as the first-person narrator/observer in each text, sometimes using her own name and sometimes assuming a pseudonym that, like her own given name, begins with *L*—Lianka,

Lianechka. Taking such an observer stance is the most important lesson she learned in Birkenau, according to Millu: "Never to put oneself
in sight, to always try to not attract attention, this was the wisdom that
one learned almost immediately. Because it was always dangerous to
attract attention from the Kapos."[12] Also, Millu was trained as a journalist and brings a journalist's eye for detail and a tone of objectivity
to recounting women's lives in Birkenau.

Significantly, Lynne Sharon Schwartz also considers the book to be
nonfiction: "Moreover, the book wasn't really fiction, or only fiction in
the loosest sense; it was a memoir, no doubt adorned and enhanced,
but the events really happened."[13] Evidence of the correlation between
Millu's own experiences and those of the characters in *Smoke Over
Birkenau* can be garnered by comparing Millu's account of her four
months in Auschwitz in her interview with Suzanne Branciforte to
the book itself. Among other things, she describes her desire to remain
beautiful as a form of resistance (compare "Lili Marlene"), her experience in the infirmary ("The Five Ruble Bill"), and Mia the kapo ("Lili
Marlene"); and she uses the names of real friends, Jeannette and Stella,
in several of the stories. Millu also declares that the book she wrote
next, *The Bridges of Schwerin,* is autobiographical, suggesting this is
an approach amenable to the training she had as a journalist.[14]

Many readers will be unfamiliar with *Smoke Over Birkenau.* The
following is an overview of the six stories that make up the book. They
vary from eighteen to forty-four pages in length.

"Lili Marlene" opens the book. The first-person narrator, identified
as Lianka, recalls the story of a seventeen-year-old, nicknamed after
one of the favorite songs of German soldiers, who has been socialized
to look pretty and attract attention. She does so with great effort in
Birkenau and draws the affection of her kapo's boyfriend. The jealous
kapo, Mia, severely beats her. Mia taunts Lili with sexual epithets:
"'So you don't want to work, do you? You just want to be a whore. . . .
You'll wind up in the crematorium . . . take my word for it. And it's
what you deserve.'" Mia is as good as her word. At the next selection,
she points Lili out to Mengele: "'This one, *Herr Doctor* . . . Always
kaputt. She can't do the work.'"[15] Lili is sent to her death.

"Under the Cover of Darkness" tells the story of Maria, who carefully hides her pregnancy in the *Lager* so that she can deliver her baby.
Her secret is given away by her bunkmate; she is abused, and put to
hard labor. The narrator muses on the question of why Maria would

want to carry a child to term in Birkenau: "Of course she wanted to give birth, it was an irresistible law of nature—but were the laws of nature still valid in a death camp?" an apt question for all the stories in Millu's text.[16] Maria does deliver the child but both mother and baby die; whether they are killed is left ambiguous. Like the first story, this one is narrated by an observer inmate who describes a sister prisoner who remains hopeful and determined to live. Yet both Lili and Maria perish because of the perfidy of another woman, demonstrating the danger of the will to live, of love, of being human in the *Lager*.

"High Tension" reveals the double entendre of its title: a mother, Bruna, manages to see her son Pinin daily as their kommandos pass each other. She often has a small treat to pass to him; the boy grows ill and is sent to the "rest" kommando. Bruna, a longtime inmate, knows that assignment to this kommando means the gas for her son, and she is desperate. Rather than comfort her, the other women in her barracks ignore her: "It wasn't for her sake that we'd left her alone, but because we couldn't bear to get too close to her anguish."[17] The following day, in a deliberate gesture, Bruna calls to Pinin and embraces him through the electrified wire. As a result, they both die. Once again, the reader encounters a situation where the natural order of things—maternal affection—has been perverted by the *Lager*. Here, the gesture of reaching out to another literally becomes a death sentence for both people.

"The Five Ruble Bill" is the fourth in the pattern of the narrator recounting a story of human affection where that affection leads to death. Zina lives for a reunion with her husband, Grigori, who is also in the camp. As the story opens, she is planning to leave the refuge of the infirmary despite her ongoing fever: "All that matters is that two days from now I'll see him!"[18] Instead, she learns that he has died. Humming a Russian folk song which tells the story of giving away one's last five rubles in an extravagant gesture, Zina takes risks delivering an "organized" jacket to her husband's friend. She is detected and dies as a result of a beating.

"Scheiss Egal" (translated by Lynne Sharon Schwartz as "I don't give a shit") recounts the lives of Dutch sisters, Lotti and Gustine, in Birkenau. When Gustine falls ill, Lotti determines to save her own life and obtain needed food for Gustine by "volunteering" for the *Puffkommando*, the brothel, in Auschwitz. Lotti justifies her decision to the narrator:

"I'm eighteen years old—I don't want to die. . . . I'm supposed to refuse life because it's offered on a dirty plate? I told Gustine all this but she didn't understand. . . . It had reached a point where we could hardly talk to each other anymore. It felt like words would destroy what was left of the bond between us. . . . Gustine and I are of the same blood . . . but now there is nothing left between us, because I was afraid to die and she believed God would save her."[19]

Although Lotti, unlike the other main characters in these stories, remains alive at the end of the story, her sister Gustine has declared her "dead," so disgusted is she with Lotti's new role. Gustine refuses to speak with her and, worse, to accept the life-giving food and medicines that Lotti obtains for her.

In the final story, "Hard Labor," Lise, a married woman whose husband Rudi has not been arrested and remains at home, is faced with a "choiceless choice" (in the apt phrase of Lawrence Langer): Should she refuse to barter sex for food in order to remain faithful to her husband but die of starvation?[20] Or should she succumb to such bartering, as she sees many women around her doing, and thus strengthen the chance of a reunion with Rudi? Again, the narrator recounts a situation in which the natural order of things is perverted. Lise tells her why she cannot consider obtaining life-giving food by trading sex: "'When we were married . . . I swore to be faithful in the eyes of the law.'" The narrator retorts: "'Well, but how could the law foresee that you'd end up in Birkenau?'"[21] In the last sentence of the story, the reader learns that Lise has decided to succumb to the advances of Sergio, which allows her to live, at least for the moment.

A careful reading of *Smoke Over Birkenau* reveals the ways in which these narratives contradict some of the scholarly pieties about gender and the Holocaust. Although the publication of Millu's book in Italian preceded the founding of the field of Holocaust studies, the neglect of the book meant that its contents were most likely not considered when certain generalizations were formulated. I would like to focus on two such pronouncements by scholars that are contradicted by *Smoke Over Birkenau.*

First, an assertion advanced by some historians has been that, because of the laws against *Rassenschande* (sexual relations between a so-called Aryan and a Jew), Germans did not rape Jewish women.[22] Yet as scholars read women's memoirs more extensively not only for what they say, but also for what is coded and for elisions and gaps, we have detected much more sexual violence than had been acknowledged. Similarly, scholarly work from the first decade of the twenty-first century on genocidal rape includes extensive accounts of German soldiers' sexual violence against Jewish and non-Jewish women.[23] In both "Scheiss Egal" and "Hard Labor," we read of women who faced a dilemma: would they trade sex for food, or accept starvation and inevitable death? While we might object to terming this "rape" on the grounds that the women "volunteered" for such an exchange, in the first instance to enter a brothel in Auschwitz for guards and privileged prisoners and in the second instance to barter with other inmates, Millu's stories make viscerally clear the ways in which such an exchange was a profound violation of these women, both physically and emotionally. In advance of their deciding to try to live, both women recognize that their subjectivities will be forever changed.

When the narrator encounters Lotti in the *Puffkommando* in Auschwitz, Lotti recounts the day she "volunteered," earning this sneer from the *blockowa*: "'Aha, so you want to go to the Puff? You want to have some fun and stuff your face, huh?'" Lotti begs the *blockowa* to keep her decision a secret, but instead the *blockowa* tells Lotti's sister, Gustine: "'She's going to become a whore.'" As Lotti describes this profound humiliation, she begins to sob convulsively. Suddenly a middle-aged soldier "with a coarse, menacing face" arrives at the door. Demanding to know what all the "whimpering" is about, he is told that Lotti's sister is sick. "'Her sister is sick? Scheiss egal! Who gives a shit?' the soldier thundered, unbuckling his belt." What will come next for Lotti is clear to the narrator who obeys the soldier's command to "beat it." As she exits the brothel, she gazes up at the smoke in the sky: "It was all nothing but smoke. Smoke drifting over the Lagers, the town, and the brothel; smoke drifting over evil and innocence, wisdom and folly, death and life. All of it 'Scheiss egal.'"[24] The smoke, which gives the book its title and is a pervasive symbol in all the chapters, blurs reality for the narrator, preventing her from making the distinctions that are the pieties of ordinary life. Lotti's identity, too, has been blurred and erased by the *blockowa*'s curses, by her sister's refusal to recognize her, and by the soldier's treatment of her as nothing more than a sexual convenience.

Scholars have begun to take a more nuanced approach to issues of sexual violence in the Holocaust. For example, in 2002 a special issue of the *Journal of the History of Sexuality* was devoted to the topic of "Sexuality and German Fascism." Elizabeth Heineman's ground-breaking contribution to that issue, entitled "Sexuality and Nazism: The Doubly Unspeakable," can be said to serve as a prolegomenon to future research on gender and sexuality in the Holocaust. Heine-man notes that the "history of sexuality in Nazi Germany unites two subjects vulnerable to sensationalist coverage: sex and Nazism."[25] She further states that the subject has been considered taboo in some circles and has suffered for lack of sources. Heineman goes on to pinpoint three reasons why this area of research began to open up in the preceding decade: first, a growing interest in the scientific basis of Nazism, specifically the science of eugenics; second, the emergence of women's history; and third, a lowering of taboos about studying sexuality. Heineman closes her article with suggestions for areas of future research, which include sexual violence in the Holocaust—a topic that has not only been understudied, but, indeed, studiously avoided. Heineman observes, "The relegation of . . . sexual violence against women to the subfield of women's history has led scholars in other areas, such as the history of the Holocaust, to overlook evidence regarding sexuality."[26]

An excellent example of what Heineman decries here—the lack of integration of women's studies and Holocaust studies—can be found by revisiting Susan Brownmiller's groundbreaking book *Against Our Will,* published almost thirty years ago. Some readers will recall that Brownmiller's key insight in this text, which profoundly changed both scholarly and social attitudes toward rape, was "that rape is not a crime of irrational, impulsive, uncontrollable lust, but is a deliberate, hostile, violent act of degradation and possession on the part of the would-be conqueror, designed to intimidate and inspire fear."[27]

Brownmiller included a thirty-page section on sexual violence during World War II, with extensive evidence of German disregard for the Nuremberg Laws against *Rassenchande.* In her assessment, "Fascism's very nature was an exaggeration of the values that normal society held to be masculine. . . . Therefore, it was not surprising that the ideology of rape burst into perfect flower as Hitler's armies goose-stepped over the face of Europe . . . [and] that rape would be employed by the German soldier as he strove to prove himself a worthy Superman."[28] She went on to cite instances of such "striving" imposed on Jewish women during the Kristallnacht pogrom in November 1938, on Soviet Jewish women by the Einsatzgruppen, and on a Polish Jewish woman by the Gestapo. Brownmiller also quoted *The Black Book of Polish Jewry* regarding the rape of Jewish girls in the Warsaw ghetto as well as the establishment of a brothel there, and she commented on the curious silence about such incidents in historical accounts of the Warsaw ghetto.[29] Finally, she quoted extensively from records of the Nuremberg War Crimes Tribunal that corroborated the routine use of rape as a weapon of terror. My point here is that Brownmiller, although not a scholar of the Holocaust, formulated insights on rape that might have been brought to bear on the understanding of sexual violence in the Holocaust.[30]

Given Brownmiller's assertion that rape is a crime of power, not lust, Holocaust scholars need to revisit the notion that the laws against *Rassenschande* precluded the rape of Jewish women by Nazi Germans. Those laws were focused on the Nazi obsession with blood and the interdiction against the mixing of "Aryan" and "Jewish" blood; they were laws meant to prevent procreation while serving the larger goal of marginalizing the Jewish people. For example, the second clause in the Nuremberg Law for the Protection of German Blood and German Honor, promulgated on September 15, 1935, states: "Extramarital intercourse between Jews and subjects of the state of German or related blood is forbidden." Clause number 5.2 clarifies: "A male who violates the prohibition [in clause] number two will be punished with a prison sentence with or without hard labor."[31] This language is far more suggestive of passion and sexual temptation that are prohibited than it is of a crime of aggression that expresses domination and power. It is important to emphasize that genocidal rape is not about procreation but rather about power and possession and is often followed by murder, so blood mixing does not become a reality.[32] When we think about the crime of rape in the mentality of a fascist soldier, we need to enlarge and refocus our definition; the prohibitions of the Nuremberg Laws may not have been a factor precisely because their emphasis was on lust, not power. Stories such as those of Liana Millu help this process of revision enormously.

The second assertion by Holocaust scholars that Millu's book contradicts is one advanced by the first generation of feminist scholarship. Some scholars have claimed that women bonded more closely than men in the camps and this bonding became an aid to higher rates of survival.[33] Although such an assertion can be substantiated in certain cases, this claim is problematic in two ways. First, it emerges from an essentialist approach to gender, that is, it claims that women, by nature, establish connections with each other more often and better than do men. Contemporary feminist theory rejects such essentialist claims, focusing instead on the construction of gender through socialization.[34]

Joan Ringelheim is an interesting case in this regard. Her early work asserted such a claim regarding the efficacy of women's bonding. A year later, in 1985, Ringelheim retracted such claims, ascribing them to misguided cultural feminism. Ringelheim, who has persistently and perceptively researched gendered approaches to the Holocaust for twenty-five years, recounts the stories of two Jewish women raped during the Shoah. She draws a conclusion about the continuing erasure of gender as a category of analysis:

> Some might argue that rape, abortion, sexual exploitation, and pregnancy are always potentially part of a woman's life and that the ubiquity of these experiences means that they can have no relationship to an event that has been described as unique. Others feel that discussions of sexuality desecrate the memory of the dead or the living or the Holocaust itself. While these positions are understandable, *the fact remains that the victimization of Jewish men during the Holocaust did not usually include their sexual exploitation.*[35]

The second problem with the claim that women bonded with one another more closely than men is that it establishes a hierarchy of gender—with women on top. Such a hierarchy invariably leads to comparative victimhood, a damaging approach that should be resisted by scholars, and one that would seem to be anathema particularly in the field of Holocaust studies.

Millu's stories function as a counter-example to the truism about women's bonding. Millu's narrative reveals that when women extended themselves with affectionate gestures—as lovers, wives, mothers, and sisters—they often died as a result. The cruel calculus of the camps meant that when women acted as they had been socialized to do, their reward was the opposite from what might be seen as "the natural order." It is Lotti's devotion to her sister, as well as her determination to survive herself, that drives her into the *Puffkommando*. Paradoxically, this action results in her sister refusing to acknowledge her existence or her help, and, though Lotti's fate is unknown at the close of the story, the survival rate for women in such brothels was abysmal.[36] In "Lili Marlene" the reader encounters an instance of female jealousy, rather than bonding, a jealousy that turns lethal when the kapo, to preserve the attentions of her boyfriend for herself, gets Mengele to select her rival for the gas. Similarly, the bonding between mother and child turns deadly in "High Tension," when a mother chooses joint suicide rather than have to live with the knowledge that her son died alone in the rest block or the gas chambers.

In each of the six stories in *Smoke Over Birkenau,* the first-person narrator keeps herself at a distance: she adopts an observer stance, not only in the telling, but also in the living. It is as if she has realized the risks of becoming involved, in acting as she had been socialized to do, in forming bonds, in making sacrifices for others. Primo Levi perhaps best describes the relationship Millu establishes between herself and the stories: "The author rarely appears in the foreground; she is rather a penetrating eye, a superbly vigilant consciousness recording and transcribing, in uniformly dignified and measured tones, events that were themselves beyond human measure."[37] Given that each story describes a woman who reaches out to bond with someone else and who dies as a result, the observer status to which the narrator relegates herself seems to help her survive. In contrast to the commonplace of early feminist scholarship that insists on women's bonding as an aid to survival, a careful reading of Millu's stories reveals that the opposite was often the consequence for women in the *Lager.*

Intriguingly, in the interview Millu gave to Suzanne Branciforte in Genoa in March 1997, she talked about gender differences within the camps in complex and even contradictory ways. On the one hand, early in the interview, she recounted an episode that occurred as she arrived at the selection platform in Auschwitz: "In front of me in the line there was a girl from Bologna whom I had known in the camp in Italy. And she said to me, 'Come in my line!' And I took three steps, exactly three steps, and I went into her line."[38] This turned out to be a life-saving gesture from her "camp sister," because all those in the other line were sent to the gas, an episode that appears to support claims for the value of women's bonding in the camps. On the other hand, Millu recalled a conversation that she had after liberation with a disbelieving woman, a conversation that revealed attitudes toward socialization:

Because on this one time, I almost quarreled with this one lady, who said "But how? You were in front of the crematoria, they burnt corpses, and you thought about how to make yourselves beautiful?" And I say "Yes, because this was the great test of resistance." Every week one received margarine, a spoon, here in the hand. I was in the group that licked the whole hand and left nothing. Instead my French friends with the last [remainders] who still looked at themselves, spread it under their eyes, like a wrinkle-preventing cream.[39]

This anecdote inspired the interviewer, Suzanne Branciforte, to ask Millu specifically about the perspective of women, as opposed to that of men. Millu responded: "It is different, completely different." She located this difference in what she termed "fantasy" and "pragmatism." To exemplify "fantasy," she explained that while men appreciated the beauty of flowers they might spy in the camp, women could imagine the blossoms that would appear on a prickly hawthorn bush come spring. "The man sufficiently admired the beauty of the flowers," Millu stated, whereas "for we women, the beauty of the flowers becomes a symbol. It becomes a reason for strength: our life will bloom again." And women were more pragmatic. Millu referred to Primo Levi's account of male speculation in the *Lager* of how they would be killed. By contrast, said Millu, "the women, we women, never would have made the speech 'How will they kill us?' No. We were projected toward life, simply without illusions. We had more strength, the women."[40]

Millu seemed to suggest that her real-life experience led her to accept both essentialist and social construction frameworks. And after all, this conclusion seems just right: that nature and nurture both influenced women's behavior, coping strategies, and survival in Birkenau. Eight years after giving the interview, Liana Millu died in Genoa on February 6, 2005.

In a 1998 essay Sara Horowitz, who has contributed so much to stimulating balanced and complex thinking about gender, notes that the few studies of women by historians have presented an either/or vision of gender in the Shoah. Either these studies have asserted the equality of men and women in all aspects of the Holocaust, thus "occluding experiences particular to women," or they have focused on pregnancy, menstruation, prostitution, and rape, thus "inadvertently reproducing the marginalization of women, by presenting their experiences almost exclusively in terms of sexuality." Instead, Horowitz calls for studies of what she calls "gender wounding," the ways in which the "Nazi genocide destabilized the boundaries of the self, unmaking the gendered self." Such studies would take into account the experiences of both men and women. In the same way, studying sexuality during the Shoah need not relegate women to the margins if such studies acknowledge the influence of both biology and socialization and contextualize the sexual violence perpetrated against women.[41]

Smoke Over Birkenau provides powerful evidence of sexual violence in the Holocaust, a topic that has been all too frequently ignored, self-censored, and silenced. As Rhonda Copelon notes in the book *Mass Rape:*

> With respect to women, the need is to acknowledge that gender has historically not been viewed as a relevant category of victimization. The frequency of mass rape and the absence of sanction are sufficient evidence. In the Holocaust, the gender persecutions— the rape and forced prostitution of women as well as the extermination of gay people—were obscured.[42]

A rereading of *Smoke Over Birkenau* should cause scholars to question and revise previously accepted concepts of rape within the context of the Holocaust. Similarly, revisiting Millu's text should serve as a warning to scholars against employing simplistic or single-minded approaches to understanding gender and the Shoah. Millu's own experiences encourage scholars to formulate more nuanced concepts of women's relationships and their experiences of sexual violence during the Holocaust.

NOTES

The chapter epigraph is from Ruth Seifert, "War and Rape: A Preliminary Analysis," in *Mass Rape: The War Against Women in Bosnia-Herzegovina,* ed. Alexandra Stiglmayer (Lincoln: University of Nebraska Press, 1994), 69.

1. See Primo Levi's brief foreword in *Smoke Over Birkenau,* by Liana Millu (Evanston, Ill.: Northwestern University Press, 1997), 7. All subsequent references to Millu's text will be to this edition.

2. The date of 1913 is cited by Suzanne Branciforte in the introduction to her interview with Millu entitled "Intervista con la storia: Una conversazione con Liana Millu," *Italianist* 18 (1998): 289–304. I am grateful to Emily Diamond-Falk for translating this interview. See the encyclopedia entry by Judith Kelly, "Liana Millu," in *An Encyclopedia of Writers and Their*

Work, ed. S. Lillian Kremer (New York: Routledge, 2002), 2:843–45, which also gives 1913 as the year of Millu's birth. Risa Sodi gives 1914 as the date in her article "Many Bridges to Cross: Sex and Sexuality in Liana Millu's Holocaust Fiction," *NEMLA Italian Studies* 21 (1997): 157–78; whereas Millu's birth year is given as 1920 in "About the Author," a brief biography provided by Lynne Sharon Schwartz in her translation of *Smoke Over Birkenau,* in the Jewish Publication Society edition of 1991.

3. Schwartz provides the date of 1943, and 1942 is cited by Sodi.

4. Schwartz's biographical profile of Millu can be found only in the Jewish Publication Society of America edition of *Smoke Over Birkenau* (New York: 1991).

5. The 1990s marked a crucial turning point in the acceptance of gendered analyses of the Holocaust. Five relevant books were published in English in 1993, the most influential of which is *Different Voices: Women and the Holocaust,* an anthology edited by Carol Rittner and John Roth (New York: Paragon House, 1993); and another five in 1998, including Dalia Ofer and Lenore Weitzman's anthology *Women in the Holocaust* (New Haven, Conn.: Yale University Press, 1998).

6. Nanda Herbermann's memoir has been published in English: *The Blessed Abyss: Inmate #6582 in Ravensbrück Concentration Camp for Women,* ed. Hester Baer and Elizabeth Baer (Detroit: Wayne State University Press, 2000). Examples of women's memoirs marketed for children include Johanna Reiss, *The Upstairs Room* (New York: Harper, 1972); Ruth Minsky Sender, *The Cage* (New York: Macmillan, 1986); and Aranka Siegal, *Upon the Head of a Goat: A Childhood in Hungary, 1939–1944* (New York: Signet, 1981); all three of these books have sequels.

7. See Lynne Sharon Schwartz's illuminating essay on the task of translating *Smoke Over Birkenau,* entitled "Found in Translation," in her book of essays *Face to Face: A Reader in the World* (Boston: Beacon, 2000), 49.

8. Schwartz, "Found in Translation," 49. Schwartz dates the letter to 1979.

9. For a thorough analysis of the historiography of gendered approaches to the Holocaust, see the introduction in *Experience and Expression: Women, the Nazis, and the Holocaust,* ed. Elizabeth R. Baer and Myrna Goldenberg (Detroit: Wayne State University Press, 2003), xiii–xxxiii, and the essay by Pascale Bos, "Women and the Holocaust: Analyzing Gender Difference," in the same text, 23–52. The early pioneers include Renate Bridenthal, Atina Grossmann, and Marion Kaplan, eds., *When Biology Became Destiny: Women in Weimar and Nazi Germany* (New York: Monthly Review, 1984); Marlene Heinemann, *Gender and Destiny: Women Writers and the Holocaust* (New York: Greenwood, 1986); Claudia Koonz, *Mothers in the Fatherland: Women, the Family, and Nazi Politics* (New York: St. Martin's, 1987); and

Vera Lasker, *Women in the Resistance and in the Holocaust: The Voices of Eye-witnesses* (Westport, Conn.: Greenwood, 1983). Deserving special mention is Joan Ringelheim, whose influential article "Women and the Holocaust: A Reconsideration of Research" appeared in *Signs* 10, no. 4 (1985): 741–61. In it, she courageously revoked her earlier published assertions on women and the Holocaust and proposed a new theoretical framework. Ringelheim published many other important articles and has been a continuing and influential presence at the United States Holocaust Memorial Museum since its opening in 1993.

10. Lucille Eichengreen, *From Ashes to Life: My Memories of the Holocaust* (San Francisco: Mercury House, 1994) and *Rumkowski and the Orphans of Lodz* (San Francisco: Mercury House, 2000). For an account of Eichengreen's initial reluctance to reveal her experiences in Łódź, see Elizabeth Baer, "Nachwort," in *Frauen und Holocaust: Erlebnisse, Erinnerungen und Erzähltes,* by Lucille Eichengreen (Bremen: Donat, 2004).

11. See Sodi, who in "Many Bridges to Cross" terms *Smoke Over Birkenau* a "series of interlinked short stories" (162) and "Italian Holocaust fiction" (177); and Suzanne Branciforte, who in "Intervista con la storia" calls the text "a collection of short stories" (289).

12. Branciforte, "Intervista con la storia," 292.

13. Schwartz, *Face to Face,* 65.

14. Liana Millu, *I ponti di Schwerin* [*The Bridges of Schwerin*] (Poggibonsi: A. Lalli, 1978).

15. Millu, *Smoke Over Birkenau,* 42, 47.

16. Ibid., 56.

17. Ibid., 113.

18. Ibid., 119.

19. Ibid., 171–73.

20. Langer first coined the phrase "choiceless choice" in an article entitled "The Dilemma of Choice in the Death Camps." The article was later expanded into a book. See Lawrence Langer, *Versions of Survival: The Holocaust and the Human Spirit* (Albany: State University of New York Press, 1982).

21. Millu, *Smoke Over Birkenau,* 191.

22. See, for example, Jack G. Morrison, *Ravensbrück: Everyday Life in a Women's Concentration Camp, 1939–45* (Princeton, N.J.: Markus Wiener, 2000), 177–78. Although Morrison acknowledges both the recruitment of women for camp brothels, which occasionally involved "trying out" a volunteer, and the fact that "consensual relations" between prisoners and SS guards cannot be regarded as consensual because of the "inequality inherent in these relationships," he concludes nonetheless that "camp regulations against fraternization between the SS and prisoners were overwhelmingly obeyed," failing to consider that few women survivors would have been

willing to testify about sexual violence they experienced. For an interesting perspective on the silence of rape victims, see Michael Nutkiewicz, "Shame, Guilt and Anguish in Holocaust Survivor Testimony," *Oral History Review* 30, no. 1 (2003): 1–22. Nutkiewicz recounts the story of a male survivor who gave testimony to Steven Spielberg's Shoah Foundation but failed to recount his rape in 1941 at the hands of SS men in the Riga ghetto, to which his family had been deported from Germany. When he later confided by telephone that he had been raped, he told the interviewer that he had omitted this from his testimony of his Holocaust experiences because "I heard many terrible stories but not like what had happened to me. Nobody spoke about it so I thought it just happened to me . . . it was my secret" (6–7). Nutkiewicz comments that this survivor's testimony "reveals that survivors sometimes filter their testimony, a mechanism very different from the repression that excludes painful memories from consciousness" (8). For a refutation of the common assumption about the Nuremberg Laws, see Omer Bartov, "Kitsch and Sadism in Ka-Tzetnik's Other Planet: Israeli Youth Imagine the Holocaust," *Jewish Social Studies* 3, no. 2 (1997): 42–76, although the refutation is achieved by virtue of his subject matter, rather than explicitly.

23. See Wendy Jo Gertjejanssen, "Victims, Heroes, Survivors: Sexual Violence on the Eastern Front During World War II" (Ph.D. diss., University of Minnesota, Minneapolis, 2004). A thoroughly researched and innovative account of its topic, this text has an invaluable bibliography. Gertjejanssen directly addresses the silence and denial around the topic of sexual violence by scholars (see especially pp. 12, 255, 303ff.); and she notes that violence against civilians, including sexual violence, was common on Germany's eastern front because of Nazi attitudes toward Slavs, Jews, and Romany and Sinti as "inferior." See also Doris L. Bergen, "Sexual Violence in the Holocaust: Unique and Typical?" in *Lessons and Legacies VII: The Holocaust in International Perspective,* ed. Dagmar Herzog (Evanston, Ill.: Northwestern University Press, 2006), 179–200. Bergen, too, confronts scholarly silence on this topic and provides a framework for further research and for teaching about sexual violence in the Holocaust. See also a very early essay by Sybil Milton, "Women and the Holocaust: The Case of German and German-Jewish Women," in *When Biology Became Destiny,* ed. Bridenthal, Grossmann, and Kaplan, 297–333. Milton acknowledges that Jewish women were raped as a form of harassment for marrying Christian men (300), during the Kristallnacht pogrom (301), and in concentration camps (304). For a more recent account, see the essay by survivor Felicja Karay, "Women in the Forced Labor Camps," in *Women in the Holocaust,* ed. Ofer and Weitzman, 285–309.

24. Millu, *Smoke Over Birkenau,* 174, 175, 175.

25. Elizabeth Heineman, "Sexuality and Nazism: The Doubly Unspeak-

able," *Journal of the History of Sexuality* 11, nos. 1/2 (January–April 2002): 22–66.

26. Ibid., 24.

27. Susan Brownmiller, *Against Our Will: Men, Women, and Rape* (New York: Bantam, 1976), 439.

28. Ibid., 43–44.

29. Ibid., 43–78.

30. An excellent example of bringing this notion of rape as an expression of power to bear on sexual violence during the Holocaust is found in Bergen, "Sexual Violence":

> In the Nazi system, sexual violence reinforced dominant hierarchies. The particular functions varied, depending on one's placement in the hierarchy at a given moment. For those cases where Germans had crossed the line from persecution to attempted total destruction, sexual violence served to dehumanize the victims and thereby maximize the distance between killers and their prey. Against people targeted for enslavement, sexual violence served to intimidate and demean in order to facilitate conquest and subjugation. (187)

31. Yitzhak Arad, Yisrael Gutman, and Abraham Margaliot, eds., *Documents of the Holocaust* (Jerusalem: Yad Vashem, 1981), 78–79.

32. It should be noted that this is also the case in the genocide occurring in Darfur, Sudan. Though the declarations of the Arab militia, the Janjaweed, suggest they wish to use rape to create a lighter-skinned race, their goal is ultimately the eradication of the black farming tribes so that they can capture their land. See Samantha Power, "It's Not Enough to Call It Genocide," in *Time,* October 4, 2004, 63. According to Article II of the United Nations Convention on the Prevention and Punishment of the Crime of Genocide, "genocide means any of the following acts committed with intent to destroy, in whole or in part, a national, ethnical, racial or religious group, such as . . . (d) Imposing measures intended to prevent births within the group; (e) Forcibly transferring children of the group to another group." See Carol Rittner, John K. Roth, and James M. Smith, *Will Genocide Ever End?* (St. Paul, Minn.: Paragon House, 2002), 209–10, for the full text. Thus, such an effort of the Janjaweed to "procreate" is viewed as an act of genocide, and the rape of women in Darfur is still an act of power and possession with the goal of the extinction of a people.

33. For example, see Judith Tydor Baumel, "Social Interaction among Jewish Women in Crisis During the Holocaust: A Case Study," in *Gender and History* 7 (April 1995): 64–84; Brana Gurewitsch, ed., *Mothers, Sisters, Resisters* (Tuscaloosa: University of Alabama Press, 1998); Myrna Goldenberg, "Memoirs of Auschwitz Survivors: The Burden of Gender," in *Women in the*

Holocaust, ed. Ofer and Weitzman, 327–39; and see also Bos's analysis of the implications of such a claim in "Women and the Holocaust," 23–50.

34. See Diana Fuss, *Essentially Speaking: Feminism, Nature and Difference* (New York: Routledge, 1989). For an example of the rejection of essentialist approaches, see Susannah Heschel, "Does Atrocity Have a Gender? Feminist Interpretations of Women in the SS," in *Lessons and Legacies VI: New Currents in Holocaust Research,* ed. Jeffry M. Diefendorf (Evanston, Ill.: Northwestern University Press, 2004), 300–321.

35. See Joan Ringelheim, "The Unethical and the Unspeakable: Women and the Holocaust," *Simon Wiesenthal Center Annual* 1 (1984): 69–87; Ringelheim, "Women and the Holocaust"; and Ringelheim, "The Split Between Gender and the Holocaust," in *Women in the Holocaust,* ed. Ofer and Weitzman, 340–50.

36. On the conditions and survival rates of women in the camp brothels, see Christa Schulz, "Weibliche Häftlinge aus Ravensbrück in Bordellen der Männerkonzentrationslager," in *Frauen in Konzentrationslagern Bergen-Belsen, Ravensbrück,* ed. Claus Füllberg-Stolberg et al. (Bremen: Edition Temmen, 1994); and Christa Paul, *Zwangsprostitution: Staatlich errichtete Bordelle im Nationalsozialismus* (Berlin: Edition Hentrich, 1994). For a first-person account, in English, of the recruitment of women in Ravensbrück to serve in the brothels in various camps, see Baer and Baer, *Blessed Abyss.*

37. Levi, in the foreword to *Smoke Over Birkenau,* 7.

38. Branciforte, "Intervista con la storia," 292.

39. Ibid., 293.

40. Ibid., 293–94.

41. Sara R. Horowitz, "Women in Holocaust Literature: Engendering Trauma Memory," in *Women in the Holocaust,* ed. Ofer and Weitzman, 364–77.

42. Rhonda Copelon, "Surfacing Gender: Reconceptualizing Crimes Against Women in Time of War," in *Mass Rape,* ed. Stiglmayer, 207.

Dori Laub

Breaking the Silence of the Muted Witnesses: Video Testimonies of Psychiatrically Hospitalized Holocaust Survivors in Israel

FOR GENERATIONS, CHRONICLERS OF GENOCIDE AND IN PARTICULAR of the Holocaust, recoiling from the enormity of the events, have attempted to restrict their source material to the primary, the documentary. Numbers, dates, locations—gleaned from documents, official correspondences, registries, and newspaper articles—were of paramount importance, but no attempt was made to obtain the personal eyewitness experiences (from multiple perspectives) that would tie them together. The work of political scientists and historians writing on the Holocaust in the early decades after World War II (for example, Raul Hilberg and Lucy Dawidowicz) illustrates this selective approach.[1] No assertion was considered substantiated unless documentation existed, even though questions were not always rigorously pursued regarding the slant, the distortion, or the motives of those who produced the documents. This documentary emphasis created a constricted field of knowledge composed of barren facts that did not merge into patterns or stimulate reflection and self-reflection or open questions of meaning. Testimony that could have given texture to the facts was treated as an unreliable source for the pursuit of truth. Omer Bartov's comments in his review of Christopher R. Browning's book *Nazi Policy, Jewish Workers, German Killers,* are quite informative regarding the difficulties, bordering on speechlessness, that historians experience when exposing "all the sordid and pitiful details" of genocide while trying to work with testimonial sources.[2]

The wars and genocides of the twentieth century put historians in the unprecedented situation of having to report and reflect on events of an unfamiliar, overpowering nature. The problems of postwar historiography were multiplied when it came to the mass killing of unarmed civilians in genocides—in particular, the Holocaust. Scholars found themselves confronting events that had no precedent and could not be articulated in the customary categories of traditional historiography. They were rendered speechless. I do not mean to say that they fell silent, which occasionally was the case. On the contrary, they increasingly assumed the role of chroniclers of and commentators on contemporaneous events. Yet in doing so, they also increasingly began to experience the constraints and the limits of their methodology.

Contemporary historiography indeed faced a crisis. It was confronted with past events that continued to repeat themselves in the present but did not yield to traditional historiographic approaches, like new computer files that cannot be read by outdated software. New tools had to be developed and employed in order to give form, structure, and intelligibility to the incomprehensible past that does not have an ending. Literary genres and formats had to be found or invented by which to tell the full truth. The long-established shaping of historical narratives around political processes and military campaigns simply did not suffice. The definition of "source" had to be reopened, in that official documents covered a mere fraction of what had happened. Neither did traditional historiographic approaches account for the continuation of the past into the present, of its impression on present and future events. Nor could the public echoes of such a past be properly heard and contribute to its comprehension, when traditional methodology was the only one that was employed.

Ultimately, in order to evade the crisis, an approach to comprehending present events emerged that literally breaks with the past, and more importantly, totally discounts its impact. Historian Carl E. Schorske put the matter quite succinctly:

> In the last one hundred years . . . "modern" has come to distinguish our perception of our lives and times from all that has gone before, from history as a whole, as such. Modern architecture, modern music, modern philosophy, modern science—all these define themselves not out of the past, indeed scarcely against the past, but in independence of the past. The modern mind has been growing indifferent to history because history, conceived as a continuous nourishing tradition, has become useless to it. This development is, of course, of serious concern to the historian, for the premises

of his professional existence are at stake in it. But an ur
ing of the death of history must also engage the attent
psychoanalyst.[3]

From the perspective of the historian, such a breach wit
alternatively, the admission of one's speechlessness in the face of trauma
or the acceptance of the limits of rational thought in attempting to
comprehend or explain events beyond one's grasp and imagination,
represents a surrender to mystification and sacralization. It is tanta-
mount to self-betrayal, or rather betrayal of the self-ideal, for scholars
and scientists with this mind-set.

There is an alternative, however, and that is to acknowledge the
presence of the irrational, the unconscious, and the roles they play
in the control of the rational mind, an alternative that calls for the
involvement with the psychoanalytic approach to the registration of
massive traumatic events. Once familiar with such an approach, one
can understand the phenomena of speechlessness and incomprehension "as countertransference," that is, the historians' own vicarious
traumatization through bearing witness to an instance of genocide.
Loss of coherent speech constitutes the ultimate step in an unconscious
empathic identification with the victim or the bystander, for whom
the perpetrated atrocities make no sense whatsoever and cannot even
be experienced as real. It is thus through their very speechlessness and
inability to comprehend that historians register and begin to know
and to transmit historical traumata in their utmost authenticity. The
historian thus gives voice to history as trauma. Yet historians are not
alone in testifying to "history as trauma." The very subjects of history,
those who experienced it, were rendered speechless too.

Walter Benjamin, in his essay "The Storyteller," describes the re-
sultant untransmissibility, the demise of both storytelling and sharing
of experience:

> With World War [I], a process began to become apparent, which
> has not halted since then. Was it not noticeable at the end of the war
> that men returned from the battlefield grown silent—not richer,
> but poorer in communicable experience: What ten years later was
> poured out in the flood of war books was anything but experience
> that goes from mouth to mouth. And there was nothing remark-
> able about that. For never has experience been contradicted more
> thoroughly than strategic experience by tactical warfare, economic

experience by inflation, bodily experience by mechanical warfare, moral experience by those in power. A generation that had gone to school on a horse-drawn streetcar now stood under the open sky in a countryside in which nothing remained unchanged but the clouds, and beneath these clouds, in a field of force of destructive torrents and explosions, was the tiny, fragile human body.[4]

This brings us to the issues of Holocaust survivors' testimony. Except for a brief period after World War II, survivors kept their silence for decades. This happened not only because they spent every ounce of energy in rebuilding their lives and not only because "no one wanted to listen and to hear." It happened because of their own inner speechlessness. They had no tellable story inside themselves. The traumatic event they had lived through persisted as a mere registration—a split-off, walled-off perception that lacked its concomitant cognitive and emotional conscious experience. The traumatic event became an "absent" experience because at the core of the executioner-victim interaction all human relatedness is undone. The external and the internal other, the "Thou" to whom one can address one's plea, tell one's story, no longer exists. Therefore the "story" is never known, told, or remembered. The frozen image, inscribed in a different part of the brain, is all that remains and is retained for life (like so many filmstrips taken by perpetrators and by liberators, which have no soundtrack). A perception of the traumatic event is inscribed that is not translated into symbolizing words; no narrative is formed. In a very important sense, the event has not yet been experienced. What the giving and receiving of testimony does is to set in motion a dyadic-dialogic process. The listener-companion, in his total presence, offers the possibility and the protected holding space, within which the external and the internal other or Thou can be reestablished, in facing the traumatic event. The story is told both to the listener and to oneself, and the process of narrativization can unfold.

To begin with, the survivor does not fully know what he knows. It is only as the testimony unfolds that he comes to know his full story and the impact it has had on his life. Even then, parts that are beyond the imaginable will remain left out or retained as frozen, encapsulated, and split-off foreign images. These are the parts of the story that are not to be told. Off-limits, hot, tumultuous, and dangerous as a bed of molten lava, they have no form. These parts of the survivor's story, and thus a piece of human history, are lost to silence. I have earlier searched for words for this muting or loss—calling it an erasure.

I began to ask myself a question: What is the ultimate in the absence of narrative? Where could we find it?

Through a series of newspaper articles that began to appear in the Israeli press in the 1990s, I learned that there were a large number of Holocaust survivors in various Israeli hospitals who have no recorded histories. The rumor was that there had been a ship with 1,500 passengers who were psychiatric patients—the last inmates in displaced persons camps in Germany that the German government wanted to close—that arrived in Israel about a decade after the war. Through a special agreement, the German government compensated Israel for their treatment. They were said to have been dispersed among various hospitals. When asked whether this story was true, Yehuda Bauer, a renowned historian and Holocaust scholar at Hebrew University, confirmed that such a ship had indeed arrived. I decided to take testimonies from these patient-survivors, asking myself if their psychological impairment, leading to long-term hospitalization, was related to the phenomenon of having no history—the erasure of narrative that I have described.[5]

In 1979 I cofounded the Holocaust Film Project at Yale University, which eventually became the Fortunoff Video Archive for Holocaust Testimonies.[6] It has since sprouted thirty-two affiliates all over the world, which have gathered more than four thousand testimonies. I was impressed by the power of the testimony to bring into relief the internal landscape of the survivors—their experience of themselves, of history, and of the world they lived in. I was also impressed by the possibilities that capturing the testimonies on videotape opened. These video testimonies, however, did not include psychotic survivors like those mentioned earlier. I proposed a project to find such Holocaust survivors and to interview them. I thought that there was something unique that they had to tell.

In 1996 the commissioner of mental health for Israel, Dr. Moti Mark, expressed strong support for this endeavor. He helped organize an international conference at Maaleh-Hachamisha for the purpose of planning a video testimony-based study of these survivors. It took six years to raise the funding, to find the institutions that housed these survivors, and to secure their agreement to participate in the project. The Institute for Social and Political Studies at Yale covered half the cost of the study, and the other half was covered by the Claims Conference. In October–November 2002, and again in April–May 2003, I was part of a team that recorded the testimony of these hospitalized survivors.

Each interview included myself, one other mental health professional, and a videographer. After the interviews were completed, the hospital staff began to work with the videotapes.

The sample for this study was drawn from a much larger population of chronically hospitalized Holocaust survivors. Among the approximately 5,000 long-term psychiatric inpatients in Israel in 1999, about 725 (a disproportionately high number) were identified as Holocaust survivors.[7] Review of these cases has shown that these patients had not been treated as a unique group, and that their trauma-related illnesses had been neglected in their decades-long treatment. Most of them had been diagnosed as having chronic schizophrenia, with no special attention given to the historical circumstances related to their psychiatric symptoms and disabilities. Their charts often included their date and place of birth (e.g., Poland, 1924) and the year of their immigration to Israel (1948), as if nothing had happened in between. Many of their treating psychiatrists insist today that they do not respond to traditional treatment such as antipsychotic medication.[8] We hypothesized that many of these patients could have avoided lengthy if not lifelong psychiatric hospitalizations had they been able, or been enabled by their caregivers and by society at large, to more openly share their severe persecution history. Instead, those gruesome and traumatic experiences remained encapsulated, split-off, causing the survivors to lead a double life. These patients may physically inhabit the world as geriatrics, but emotionally they have remained in adolescence.

The findings I write of here are the outcome of this video-testimony study of twenty-six chronically hospitalized Holocaust survivors in Israeli psychiatric institutions. About 30 percent of them have been hospitalized since World War II. They represent the "extreme" on the spectrum of speechlessness and silence. The clinical staff considered 20 percent of them as completely silent. They just did not speak to anyone. They walked around briskly, watched intently, smoking, and then unexpectedly walked away. Watching their facial expressions, one could see their ongoing struggle. They attempted to say something—but it came out as a barely audible scream or a moan. Once asked, these patients were nevertheless able and very willing to give testimony. Extensive psychological testing was carried out before and five months after the video testimony.

We were attempting to probe the limits of testimony in those who are believed to have given up on communicating with others and have withdrawn into their private psychotic world. In my opinion their psychotic silence is not schizophrenia, as most of them had been diagnosed, but an extreme case of the speechlessness of trauma that afflicts victims, witnesses, and those who attempt to be its chroniclers, like the historians I elaborated on earlier in this chapter.

I would like to describe an encounter with such a patient, one who did not participate in the study because the hospital he was in withdrew from it at an early stage. It was already dark when I entered the ward hoping to speak with a patient. The nurse in charge was extraordinarily helpful and directed me to somebody who was "clear-minded." I waited for a long time until he got dressed, only to find out that he had fled Warsaw when the bombing started and spent the war years in Siberia. I came back to her and asked for another person. She pointed out somebody who had been circling around me, a little man with stubby grey hair, who I had a feeling wanted to speak. I asked him if he would be willing to go to a separate room with me and he was ready to do so. The first thing he said to me was, "Could you help me? I'm alone in the world except for maybe a cousin who lives in Brooklyn by the name of Levine. This was her maiden name and she has probably married. Perhaps, though, she could be traced through the registers of the local synagogue. She may not be alive any longer, because she is my age, and I was born in 1926."

I asked him how come he was alone in the world, and he said because he was in Auschwitz with his parents and they did not come out. He himself somehow survived. He did not go into details, so I did not pursue it. When he arrived in Israel, he was already a mental patient, because while in the British detention camp in Cyprus, he had stopped eating. Upon reaching Israel, he was given insulin shock and electroshock treatments, which improved his clinical condition, so he was discharged from the hospital. He learned to do stone flooring and worked for a number of years and made some friends. But then a new war started, the conflict over the Suez Canal, and he became symptomatic again and stopped eating, so he was rehospitalized and received more shock treatment. There was another clinical improvement, and he was discharged and resumed his work. Only this time, he could not form any social attachments. When the next war erupted, the Six-Day War in 1967, he once again became symptomatic and was rehospitalized. This time however, treatment did not help. He did not leave the institution and has been in various hospitals since.

"Did you ever hallucinate, see things or hear things?" I asked him. He said "No." Did he have memories? "Yes," he said, "I do, but the medication I take slowly dulls them." "Do you feel pain?" I asked. He said, "I do, but also the medication takes the edge off, begins to dull it." When I asked, "Did anyone ever ask you about your life?" his response was "Never."

I felt quite spellbound with this man. Emotionally, he was able to make every connection with me and in no way resembled a chronic, deteriorating schizophrenic who had spent thirty-five years in a psychiatric facility. He made so much sense and had such a capacity for emotional bonding, yet clearly there had been no one to bond with. I told him I hoped that we would meet again when I returned and be able to talk some more.

When I reviewed the videotaped interviews I completed in Israel in October–November 2002 and in April–May 2003, I was impressed by certain features they have in common regarding the memory of the Holocaust experience. There is an underlying common thread to all of them, which is erasure. Strategies widely adopted by these survivors included claiming to have forgotten it all, doubting that it ever happened or what precisely happened, and claiming that their traumatic experiences were neither extraordinary nor unique and therefore did not matter and did not merit being spoken of. I am increasingly convinced that, indeed, the experience of trauma never took place consciously. As I mentioned before, it was registered and kept frozen in a different area of the mind.

The way in which testimonies of psychotic survivors differ from those who had not been hospitalized is captured by the nature of the phenomenon of testimony itself. Testimony in nonpsychotic, "normal" survivors, when appropriate conditions of listening are created, begins to have a life of its own. The survivor begins to remember, and memories, both cognitive and affective, exponentially increase. With survivors who have been chronically hospitalized for psychotic illness, this process does not take place. Testimony does not come to life in most instances. It is more like the work of dislodging something from stone. The interviewer has to be much more active and lead the way, through offering himself as an authentic new object—totally present and engaged for the moment in the mutual endeavor to come to know. In many instances survivors gave us not a coherent story but only fragments, often very affect-laden, and we, the interviewers, had to serve as a holding container that allowed such fragments to come together. We were the ones that constructed their narrative, or at least part of it, and told it back to them. They listened very attentively, vehemently agreed or disagreed with what we said, thus correcting it and participating in the construction of their narrative, as it was taking place.

With other survivors, we could see their horror without words, an affective state completely void of memory and of experience. Occasionally, the substitute of an experience, of a screen memory, of "having fled in time" deep into Russia and so having been saved, filled the void. In one survivor, who claimed never to have seen a German soldier because she spent all of World War II in Kazakhstan—thousands of kilometers from her home—the memory of one single day unexpectedly emerged, a Sunday, which, it turned out, was also the day the Germans entered the town and executed her bedridden father and many other Jews. Her mother and two brothers tried to flee and were apprehended and shot. When I asked whether that had happened the same day that the Germans entered the town and began carrying out the executions, she responded, "No, it was a few days later." She claimed that her Lithuanian neighbors had told her about that when she came back in 1953, after the war. The details that she did know, however, made me suspect that she might have been an eyewitness to the traumatic events, rather than only hearing of them long after the war from neighbors in a country notorious for having collaborated in the killing of Jews.

When the interviews started, we were stunned by the motivation, commitment, and persistence of these witnesses. For many it was an intense, difficult, perhaps even hazardous internal struggle to speak, yet most interviews lasted between one and a half and two and a half hours. What is noteworthy is that on psychological retesting five months after the interviews, the scores of trauma-induced symptoms (in particular withdrawal) had been reduced by close to 50 percent. A control group of survivors who had not given testimony showed no decrease of such posttraumatic symptoms after a five-month interval. After this group also gave testimony, we saw the same results.

It is yet to be determined whether the giving of testimony alone or shifts in the attitude and treatment approach of the staff who had viewed the testimonies, or a combination of both, brought about such symptom reduction. A clue to how to deal with this question emerges from the following vignette.

In December 2003 I returned to Israel to participate in an in-service training for the purpose of summarizing what we had learned from the project. I arrived at four o'clock in the morning of the meeting, my excitement protecting me from any experience of fatigue. The first person I met was the videographer. Our few moments together were precious. There was a sense of relief, not pressure, at the conference, a remarkable absence of tension. The comfort everyone experienced may well have been one of the accomplishments of the project—it was as if we all knew that we were part of something and had our place in it. Many of the staff members from both hospitals, Beer-Yaakov and Lev-Hasharon—close to one hundred people—were present. Most were, I think, members of the nursing staff.

After the commissioner of mental health for Israel opened the proceedings, the director of one of the hospitals spoke. His comments were simply stunning to me. He immediately began on a personal note. He was the third child in the family and the first one to be born in Israel after his survivor parents immigrated with their two older children. He was the child of their new life, and therefore it was decided not to involve him in the past, not to tell him anything. I knew of his history of having had a long and distinguished military career. He was known as a courageous officer. He was what his parents, I think, expected of him—the new Jew, without fear and without the shadow of Jewish persecution. He proceeded to say that it was only in 2002 that his daughter, who went on a trip to Poland to visit Auschwitz, called and asked him immediately to join her, and he did. Since then, everything had changed. Almost against his will, he was introduced to his family history by his daughter. Then he began to ask questions, insisting that his older siblings tell him everything. It is interesting to wonder whether he ever asked himself why he became the director of a hostel for Holocaust survivors. The bare and parsimonious story, in itself, sent a shock wave through the audience.

The person that followed him was the deputy director, who had been the most supportive person to the project throughout. He spoke about his parents, who never stopped telling stories of the Holocaust.

At breakfast every morning, his mother told him her Holocaust nightmares. He was simply bombarded by her stories, but even so, he chose to become a part of our work. Later in the evening, I overheard a staff member saying that she never knew that the director of the hospital, this authority figure, the army officer who was so self-disciplined, was part of the same world that she was. She had never met him on this level. This was a senior social worker, who had done a lot of work with survivors and actively interviewed with me on the project. Something had shifted in her view of who the people in charge were.

I think that this opening up, this quite self-disciplined form of self-revelation, is probably part of what the project set in motion. Without melodrama and without sentimentality, people became more profound, more deeply connected, and more human. Perhaps working with this highly traumatized survivor population had necessitated the establishment of overly rigid boundaries, or even attempts at trivialization. One did not give oneself permission to feel and to cry and often perhaps fled into lightness and superficiality. The project restored the authenticity and the dignity of what the work was all about. It was not about custodial care for hopeless invalids whose spirits you had to raise with vocational activities or light entertainment. It was a communal bearing of a destiny which affected some—the patients—far more harshly than it had affected the others, the treaters. Yet, as we discovered, everyone was affected, and the project provided a medium to express it, to experience it, and to begin to share it.

Throughout the day, I was impressed by the absence of competitive challenges. We all knew we were performing our task, part of a cooperative endeavor. We also knew that we were in the very beginning of a journey and that much more had to be accomplished.

I visited the hospital the next day and saw several of the patients, and it was like meeting old friends again, or at least acquaintances. None of them was psychotically absent. Those I spoke to immediately recognized me and were ready to pick up where we had left off. Though I now wish I had spent more time there and feel that my brief visit may have been insufficient, perhaps even a tease, what I realized was that the breaking of the silence, the lifting of muteness, that had begun with the arrival of a fully present and committed listener had, in fact, allowed memory, and with it narrative, to flow again.

What is needed for healing is the creation of a testimonial community. In this instance, the treatment staff—after having lifted their own inner obstacles to speaking about the Holocaust—allowed for a homecoming for the patients. They were now in a community that was no longer denying its shared history through ideological overcompensation—the creation of the new Jew—or through displacement of the horror of annihilation of the old war (World War II) to the newer ones of present-day Israel. Through the advent of testimony, all participants, treatment staff at all levels, patients, and researchers came to be part of a much larger historical narrative, which would be inaccurate and incomplete without the particular stories. So crucial are the tiniest details of each narrative that to miss even one—like the contradiction between the woman's claim to have been thousands of miles away on the day her parents and siblings were murdered and her ability to narrate other events of the same day so that you could "hear" the unspoken truth through her screen memory—means a significant loss. It may well be only through testimony that we can really write the history of such a cataclysm.

NOTES

An altered version of this essay has been published under a different title: Dori Laub, "From Speechlessness to Narrative: The Cases of Holocaust Historians and of Psychiatrically Hospitalized Survivors," *Literature and Medicine* 24, no. 2 (2005): 253–65. Copyright © The Johns Hopkins University Press. Reprinted with permission of The Johns Hopkins University Press.

1. For example, see Raul Hilberg, *The Destruction of the European Jews* (Chicago: Quadrangle Books, 1961); and Lucy Dawidowicz, *The War Against the Jews, 1933–1945* (New York: Holt, Rinehart and Winston, 1975).

2. See Omer Bartov's review of Browning's book: "Inside, Outside," *New Republic* 222 (April 10, 2000): 41. See also Christopher Browning, *Nazi Policy, Jewish Workers, German Killers* (Cambridge, Eng.: Cambridge University Press, 2000).

3. Carl E. Schorske, *Fin-de-Siècle Vienna: Politics and Culture* (New York: Random House, 1981), xvii.

4. Walter Benjamin, "The Storyteller: Reflections on the Works of Nikolai Leskov," in *Illuminations: Essays and Reflections,* ed. Hannah Arendt, trans. Harry Zohn (New York: Schocken, 1969), 84.

5. For a longer version of the study, see Rael Strous et al., "Video Testimony of Long-Term Hospitalized Psychiatrically Ill Holocaust Survivors," *American Journal of Psychiatry* 162 (December 1, 2005): 2287–94.

6. The Fortunoff Video Archive holds over 4,300 video testimonies

of survivors and witnesses of the Holocaust and is part of Yale University's Department of Manuscripts and Archives. For more information, see the Fortunoff Video Archive website at www.library.yale.edu/testimonies/.

7. Yaacov Bazak, "The Findings of the Public Committee of Inquiry into the Situation of the Psychiatrically Ill Patients Hospitalized in Israeli Psychiatric Facilities" (April 1999). This report was the outcome of a government investigation. In August 1998 the Israeli health and justice ministries had appointed members of a committee to investigate the living conditions of Holocaust survivors housed in psychiatric hospitals in Israel. The committee, led by retired district judge Yaacov Bazak, was composed of parliamentary members, government ministers, and experts in the field.

8. See Dianna Cahn, "Holocaust Survivors Mistreated," Associated Press, November 26, 1995; Matt Rees, "Surviving the Past," *Time,* January 8, 2002.

III. APPROACHES TO HISTORICAL STUDY OF THE HOLOCAUST

Christopher R. Browning

Spanning a Career: Three Editions of Raul Hilberg's *Destruction of the European Jews*

IN BEGINNING MY DISCUSSION OF THE THREE EDITIONS OF Raul Hilberg's *Destruction of the European Jews,* I would be remiss not to confess a total lack of any objective or dispassionate connection with this book on my part. As a young graduate student who had just completed an M.A. thesis on a less-than-scintillating topic in French diplomatic history—Edouard Herriot's diplomacy at the Geneva Disarmament Conference in 1932, to be precise—I, by a serendipitous sequence of events, had occasion to read the old Quadrangle paperback edition of Hilberg's book in the summer of 1969.[1] Insofar as I was conscious at that time of the Nazi genocidal assault on European Jewry from reading such books as Leon Uris's *Mila 18* or Jean-François Steiner's *Treblinka,* I still conceived of it as a sensational and aberrational episode.[2] It had received almost no mention in the undergraduate history course I had taken in modern German history, even though one entire lecture had been devoted to the "SS State." And the undergraduate seminar I had taken on European fascism, while broaching the topics of racism and antisemitism, had never explored its genocidal consequences. In short, I was a typical product of the academic world that Hilberg referred to when he wrote in the 1961 introduction that "the destruction of the European Jews has not yet been absorbed as a historical event."[3]

For me that situation changed abruptly with my reading of *The Destruction of the European Jews.* Indeed, I think the impact might best be described as an "academic conversion experience" that constituted a major turning point in my life, as I resolved to write my doctoral dissertation in the field that at that time had no name or academic standing but that we now call Holocaust studies. I share this not just to be open about my own connection to the book that I am discussing but also to remind us of the extraordinary void surrounding the topic when the book first appeared.

Let us look briefly at the publishing history of Hilberg's book.[4] Failing to find any university press that would accept it, the book was first published in 1961 by Quadrangle Books in Chicago with the help of a generous benefactor. Initially not reviewed in any major academic journal, it nonetheless became the center of heated controversy after Hannah Arendt—having recommended its rejection by Princeton University Press—subsequently both used and misused it in her controversial *Eichmann in Jerusalem*.[5] In the backlash against Arendt, Hilberg's book attracted considerable ire in its own right, perhaps none so extreme as Nathan Eck's characterization in the journal *Yad Vashem Studies* that it was "not a serious study" but rather a "slander on the Jews" possibly motivated by Hilberg's "hate of himself or the whole people."[6] Despite this rocky start, the greatness of the book was gradually accepted over time—it became available in paperback in 1967—even by its critics, who routinely referred to it as "magisterial," "monumental," and "a classic." Through a chain of corporate acquisitions, the publication of the book passed from Quadrangle to Franklin Watts to Harper. When Harper failed to keep the paperback in print, Hilberg was able to regain possession of the copyright.

Hilberg reached an agreement with Holmes and Meier for the publication of a revised and considerably expanded second edition, which appeared in a three-volume format in 1985. Hilberg made this agreement in no small part based on the publisher's assurance that it would never allow the book to go out of print. Holmes and Meier fulfilled this agreement, unfortunately, by blocking publication of a comprehensive paperback and keeping the price of the hardback so extravagantly high that unaffordable copies would remain in its warehouse in perpetuity. Finally, through the intervention of Hilberg's lifelong friend, Eric Marder, the rights to the book were pried loose from the stranglehold of Holmes and Meier and sold to Yale University Press, which published the third edition, again in a three-volume format, in 2003. This edition incorporated the numerous additions that Hilberg had incrementally inserted into an astonishing number of foreign translations in the nearly two decades since the second edition had appeared.

From the historian's vantage point of accessibility of sources, three editions mark three major phases in Holocaust documentation. The first edition in 1961 was primarily based on an exhaustive study of the captured German records that had been cataloged as "Nuremberg Documents," for both the initial International Military Tribunal and especially the subsequent American trials. The second edition from 1985 incorporated the documents and interrogations collected for the Eichmann trial as well as numerous German judicial investigations; archival records newly available in Germany, Israel, and elsewhere; and key Jewish sources, such as the Czerniaków diaries and Łódź ghetto chronicles. The third edition in 2003 incorporated the windfall of archival documentation that became accessible following the collapse of Communist control in Eastern Europe.

Each new edition contained new chapters or substantially revised chapters on topics that reflect the availability of these sources. Thus the second edition had important new sections on the Polish ghettos, the German railways, Eichmann's RSHA IV B 4 office, the camps of Operation Reinhard, "euthanasia," events in Croatia and Romania, and a twenty-page statistical appendix on how Hilberg had arrived at his contested figure of 5.1 million Jewish dead from the Holocaust. The new sections on Polish ghettos and German railways were the product of his own edition of the Czerniaków diaries and his monograph on the role of the German railways in the Final Solution that had been published in German but not in English.[7] In the third edition, new information relating to virtually every country in Europe is spliced into the text. More important, it contains a new section on "neighbors" alongside those on "perpetrators" and "victims," as well as much-expanded treatment on the Gypsies, Auschwitz, the death marches, the gas vans, East European auxiliaries, additional Polish ghettos such as Białystok and Tarnów, postwar trials and restitution in Austria, and the German aftermath since the 1980s.

In looking at all three editions together, what is more striking in some ways than the numerous and important additions is the startling encounter even in the first edition with so many topics that went totally unnoticed at the time but which years later became prominent subjects of debate. For instance, long before others were discussing bystander reactions and rescues, Hilberg's 1961 edition contained little-noted references to the Riegner telegram, the obstruction of the U.S. State Department, the Morgenthau Report, the Brand mission

t Becher negotiations, and the possibility of bomb-
s rail lines.[8]

dditions and revisions throughout the three edi-
and organization of the book have remained intact,
esis. The destruction of the European Jews is still
ministrative process carried out by bureaucrats in a
spanning a continent."[9] Hilberg divides the bureaucracy into nponents or hierarchies—party, civil service, industry, and military—but views their cooperation as "so complete that
we may truly speak of their fusion into a machinery of destruction."[10]
The German perpetrators who staffed this machinery of destruction
were "not a different kind of German" but rather "a remarkable cross-
section of the German population."[11] The administrative process was
so complex and wide-ranging that it required specialists of all kinds,
coming from every facet of life: "The machinery of destruction, then,
was structurally no different from organized German society as a
whole; the difference was only one of function. The machinery of
destruction *was* the organized community in one of its specialized
roles."[12] Hilberg asserts that this bureaucracy "had no master plan, no
fundamental blueprint, no clear-cut view of its actions."[13] Yet he writes
"that the German administration knew what it was doing. With an
unfailing sense of direction and with an uncanny path-finding ability,
the German bureaucracy found the shortest road to the final goal."[14]

How does Hilberg reconcile these seemingly conflicting views?
The answer is a kind of structural determinism. For Hilberg "a destruction process has an inherent pattern," and the "sequence of steps in a
destruction process is thus determined." If a bureaucracy is moved "to
inflict maximum damage upon a group of people," it is "inevitable,"
no matter how unplanned, that it subject its victims to the specific
stages of the destruction process. These are: definition, expropria-
tion, concentration, and annihilation.[15] All three editions are devoted
to analyzing in great detail how the four German hierarchies carried
out these four basic steps of the destruction sequence in all corners
of the German empire. As Hilberg argued from the beginning, "It
is not enough to know that the Jews have been destroyed; one must
also grasp how this deed was done. That is the story to be told in
this book."[16]

In the decades after the first edition appeared, two issues have
emerged as the most contested and debated aspects of perpetrator

history, namely the decision-making process that led to the Final Solution and the motivation of the perpetrators. I will concentrate on how Hilberg's book has shaped and contributed to these two debates. In the first edition, two factors drove the decision-making process. The first was a self-propelled bureaucracy that needed "no prodding" but merely a "signal from above." It "was so sensitive a mechanism that in the right climate it began to function by itself" and proceeded through the preliminary phases until it had to take "the step across the dividing line" that "inaugurated the killing process."[17] The second was Hitler's role as the key decision maker. Introducing for the first time the notion of a sequence of decisions for the Final Solution, Hilberg argued that "we are dealing with two of Hitler's decisions"— one in the spring of 1941 to murder the Jews on Soviet territory and a second "shortly thereafter" (namely the Göring mandate of July 31, 1941) that doomed the rest of European Jewry. "All measures during that phase were taken upon Hitler's orders to kill the European Jews," Hilberg concluded.[18]

The second edition appeared at the height of the intentionalist-functionalist controversy over what drove the Holocaust: Hitler's will or the dynamics on the ground. Although Hilberg did not address or even acknowledge that historiographical controversy explicitly, he was clearly affected by it. All references to Hitler decisions and orders for the Final Solution disappeared from the second edition with one exception.[19] Buried in a single footnote stood the solitary reference: "Chronology and circumstances point to a Hitler decision before the summer [of 1941] ended."[20] Jumping directly over the polarized interpretations of the intentionalist-functionalist controversy, Hilberg articulated in its place what I would call a "consensus model" that, in my opinion, has now become the dominant paradigm,[21] though he did not go into the interactive aspects of that model between center and periphery or above and below to the extent that others have done since.[22] In the second edition, decisions were not taken and orders were not given. Rather Hitler prophesied, commented, and wished; within the bureaucracy ideas crystallized, thinking converged, and atmosphere and expectation facilitated individual initiative. Influenced by the work of Uwe Dietrich Adam in particular, Hilberg described how the modus operandi of the Nazi regime changed.[23] A formal structure of public laws and written regulations dissolved into an increasingly opaque and formless network of secret directives, vague authorizations, oral communications, and "basic understandings of officials resulting in decisions not requiring orders or explanations."

In essence, then, there was an atrophy of laws and a corresponding multiplication of measures for which the sources of authority were more and more ethereal. Valves were being opened for a decision flow. The experienced functionary was coming into his own. A middle-ranking bureaucrat, no less than his highest superior, was aware of currents and possibilities. In small ways as well as large, he recognized what was ripe for the time. Most often it was he who initiated action. Hilberg concluded eloquently: "In the final analysis, the destruction of the Jews was not so much a product of laws and commands as it was a matter of spirit, of shared comprehension, of consonance and synchronization."[24]

In one regard, Hilberg followed rather than anticipated the trend of the historiographical debate on decision making. In the second edition, he noted that the veracity of SS Gruppenführer Otto Ohlendorf's testimony had been questioned by Alfred Streim, a leading prosecutor of Nazi war crimes in Germany, but Hilberg still relied on that and other testimony to the effect that the Einsatzgruppen commanders were aware of the impending genocide of the Soviet Jews before the invasion.[25] But in the third edition Hilberg allies himself with the Streit-Streim thesis. Before the invasion, he argues, the Einsatzgruppen commanders had been "left with impressions," but no "succinct set of orders for concrete action had been given." The series of directives issued in the first months of Barbarossa, both written and oral, still did not "reveal a preconceived plan" but only "an evolving policy with ever widening effect." Only when the killing began to encompass "Jews of both sexes and all ages" had the "objective" of the mission "crystallized."[26]

The second major historiographical debate over the perpetrators has focused on motivation. In the first edition, Hilberg took a two-pronged approach. On the one hand, he looked at "precedents." He declared himself less interested in "German race theory" than in the negative image of the Jews as "hostile, criminal, parasitical" that had become embedded in German culture long ago. Therefore, when Hitler came to power, this image was "already there"; "he could speak to Germans in a familiar language," and his fierce anti-Jewish tirades "awakened his Germans as if from slumber to a long-forgotten challenge."[27] This "precedent" faced another countervailing one, what

Hilberg called the "lingering effect of two thousand years of Western morality and ethics." Thus Hilberg was adamant that the major
obstacle facing the perpetrators was a moral one. Those who manned
the machinery of destruction were pervaded by "growing uneasiness"
due to "moral scruples." "To combat doubts and guilt feelings," the
perpetrator had to "clear his conscience." They did so not just by
finding justification for their actions as defensive measures against
the alleged Jewish threat of hostility, criminality, and parasitism, but
also through various psychological mechanisms of repression and
dissociation, thereby removing their actions from the "censuring gaze
of conscience." And they did so successfully. In contrast to Italian
officials, Hilberg noted, when German perpetrators "were put to the
test, there were very few lingerers and almost no deserters."[28]

In the years before the second edition, I heard Hilberg speak on
several occasions in which people in the audience posed two questions. The first was why did the Germans do it, and the second was
whether only Germans could have done it. His answer to the first
was "They wanted to," and the answer to the second was "I hope so."
Subsequently, in the second edition, Hilberg went beyond the psychological defenses that allowed the perpetrators to participate and
explored briefly what made them want to participate, to examine why
the German bureaucrats as perpetrators were "driven to accomplish-
ment" and unlike Italians, Hungarians, or Bulgarians "never contented
themselves with the minimum" but "always did the maximum."[29]
His answer was a combination of bureaucratic hubris and Faustian
temptation. For the perpetrators the Final Solution was not the by-
product of seeking "some ulterior goal." It was not a means of solving
some other problems, as has been suggested by those historians who
have emphasized such factors as logistical backups blocking deportation, overpopulation blocking modernization, and food or housing
shortages. Nor was it compensatory revenge for other failures. Rather
it was "an undertaking for its own sake, an event experienced as *Er-
lebnis.*" The Final Solution had "meaning to its perpetrators" as an
enormous, unprecedented historical undertaking. "Ordinary men"
performed "extraordinary tasks" in "reaching for the ultimate." They
experienced a kind of shared elation in going where no man had gone
before; they got high on making history in a way that no regime had
done before.[30]

There was a tension between Hilberg's emphasis on the inherent

and thus presumably universal structure of the bureaucratic destruction process on the one hand and his emphasis on the specifically
German characteristics on the other, namely the precedent of a cul-
turally embedded, negative Jewish image—Hilberg seldom uses the
word *antisemitism*—and a bureaucratic ethos of hubris and Faustian
ambition. These specifically German characteristics seemed to be the
basis for his "I hope so" answer to those who had asked whether only
Germans could have done the deed. Yet the first two editions also
contained an ominous warning: "The Nazis had built upon the experiences of the past. Now there are means that will allow still others to
seize upon the Nazi experience. . . . This is an unsettling thought."[31]

In my opinion, the most significant interpretative change contained in the third edition is found in the concluding chapter on
implications. No longer does Hilberg write about potential and future
dangers, and no longer does he "hope" that only the Germans might do
such a deed. Despite attempts on the part of many in the international
community "to make sure that the Jewish fate would not befall any
people anywhere at the hands of any power on earth," he acknowledges
that "the purest genocide was ignited in Rwanda." The final paragraph
of the final chapter of the third edition ends lugubriously: "The disaster
of the Tutsi took place in full view of the world. . . . The challenge was
posed and not met. . . . History has repeated itself."[32]

I have not dealt with several of the most controversial and disputed
aspects of *The Destruction of the European Jews,* namely its portrayal
of the "precedents" of Jewish history and the resulting incorporation
of Jews into the machinery of destruction on the one hand and the
absence of resistance as a Jewish response to the Holocaust on the other.
I will add just a few words concerning the issue of Jewish resistance.
Throughout the three editions, Hilberg has been consistent in defining resistance narrowly and specifically as armed resistance. And he
has been consistent in his analysis that such armed resistance occurred
rarely and had virtually no effect on the perpetrators' operations.

The response of Hilberg's critics was threefold. First, some tried
to refute Hilberg quantitatively by uncovering numerous cases of
hitherto unknown or underappreciated episodes of Jewish armed
resistance.[33] Ultimately, such efforts were doomed to failure, in my
opinion. Quite simply, the vast majority of Jewish victims did not
engage in armed resistance. As the vast majority never had arms, this
was in fact not an option, even if one did not accept Hilberg's causal

explanation of the enduring effects of centuries of diaspora-indu habits of accommodation and passivity. The second response has t to contextualize, compare, and conclude that European Jews faced greater obstacles than non-Jews in resorting to armed resistance and, given the unequal circumstances, did so at least as much if not more so than most of their less handicapped non-Jewish neighbors.[34] This response did not refute Hilberg's basic conclusions about the limited quantity and effect of Jewish resistance, but it did take the emotional sting out them, making the Jewish resistance that did occur a source of pride rather than of accusation or lament. The third response has been to reconceptualize the notion of resistance. In contrast to Hilberg's narrow concept of armed resistance, for instance, Yehuda Bauer has defined resistance as any concerted action intended to thwart German intentions.[35] Many activities that Bauer therefore defines as a form of Jewish resistance are included by Hilberg under his category of "alleviation." Once again, Bauer's broad definition may provide a salve to those who feel wounded by Hilberg's conclusions about the limited quantity and effect of Jewish resistance, but it does not meet those conclusions head-on.

My own sense is that Hilberg is correct concerning the minimal occurrence and impact of Jewish resistance but is unpersuasive in attributing the lack of Jewish resistance primarily to the crippling effects of diaspora culture. Like the comparativists mentioned above, I think much more weight has to be given to the extraordinarily difficult situation in which Jews found themselves under Nazi rule and, to borrow Lawrence Langer's essential concept, the "choiceless choices" that confronted them.[36] What is needed is a tragic rather than an accusatory framing of the issue. It is precisely such a tragic understanding that infused Hilberg's superb edition of Adam Czerniaków's Warsaw diaries and was reflected in small but significant changes in language concerning the Jewish councils, but did not find its way into a revised treatment of Jewish resistance in the subsequent editions of *The Destruction of the European Jews.*

Ultimately, the enduring impact of *The Destruction of the European Jews* is its insight and portrayal of the Final Solution as a massive bureaucratic/administrative process. Many aspects of the Holocaust, such as the blood-soaked executioners murdering their victims at point-blank range or the gratuitous cruelty of so many of the perpetrators—do not strike us as bureaucratic. But such behavior occurred, indeed was elicited and sanctioned, within a context organized by the machinery of destruction and would never have occurred without it. The context for cruelty and atrocity was in itself an administrative creation, for the Final Solution was not a giant pogrom.

When Hilberg began his work he was a lonely scholar, for there was no field of Holocaust studies. Such a conference as produced this volume would have still been impossible to implement two decades ago and totally unthinkable four decades ago. And no book has been more central in inaugurating this field of study, more long-lasting in its authoritativeness, more widely disseminated in numerous translations, than Raul Hilberg's *Destruction of the European Jews.*

NOTES

Portions of this chapter were first published in *Yad Vashem Studies* 35/2 (Fall 2007) and in an occasional paper of the United States Holocaust Memorial Museum. They are included here with the generous permission of Yad Vashem and the USHMM.

1. Raul Hilberg, *The Destruction of the European Jews,* 1st ed. (Chicago: Quadrangle Books, 1961; Quadrangle Paperback, 1967).

2. Leon Uris, *Mila 18* (Garden City, N.Y.: Doubleday, 1961); Jean-François Steiner, *Treblinka* (New York: Simon and Schuster, 1961).

3. Hilberg, *Destruction of European Jews,* 1st ed., v.

4. For more on the subject, see Hilberg's memoirs: *The Politics of Memory: The Journey of a Holocaust Historian* (Chicago: Ivan R. Dee, 1996).

5. Hilberg, *Politics of Memory,* 156.

6. Nathan Eck, review of *The Destruction of the European Jews,* by Raul Hilberg, *Yad Vashem Studies* 6 (1967): 430.

7. *The Warsaw Diary of Adam Czerniakow,* ed. Raul Hilberg, Stanislaw Staron, and Josef Kermisz (New York: Stein and Day, 1979); Raul Hilberg, *Sonderzüge nach Auschwitz* (Mainz: Dumjahn, 1981).

8. On the Riegner telegram, see Hilberg, *Destruction of European Jews,* 1st ed., 718–19. On the U.S. State Department, see ibid., 718–22. On the Morgenthau Report, see ibid., 672–73, 722. On the Brand mission, see ibid., 543–44. On Saly Mayer-Kurt Becher, see ibid., 532–33. On the bombing of Auschwitz, see ibid., 680–81.

9. Raul Hilberg, *The Destruction of the European Jews,* 3rd ed. (New Haven, Conn.: Yale University Press, 2003), xi.

10. Ibid., 58.

11. Ibid., 1084. In the earlier editions, Hilberg writes "not a special kind of German" rather than "different kind" (Hilberg, *Destruction of European*

Jews, 1st ed., 649; Raul Hilberg, *The Destruction of the European Jews,* 2nd ed. [Teaneck, N.J.: Holmes and Meier, 1985], 1011).

12. Hilberg, *Destruction of European Jews,* 3rd ed., 1061.

13. Ibid., 1064.

14. Ibid., 5–6.

15. Ibid., 1064–65.

16. Hilberg, *Destruction of European Jews,* 1st ed., v.

17. Ibid., 18–19.

18. Ibid., 177, 257–58, 261–62.

19. See the corresponding sections of Hilberg, *Destruction of European Jews,* 2nd ed., 273, 393–94, 399–402.

20. Ibid., 402.

21. To the best of my knowledge, Dieter Pohl, in *Von der "Judenpolitik" zum Judenmord: Der Distrikt Lublin des Generalgouvernements 1939–1944* ([Frankfurt am Main and New York: Peter Lang, 1993], 182), was the first to use the term *consensus* in this regard.

22. Peter Longerich, *Politik der Vernichtung: Eine Gesamtdarstellung der nationalsozialistischen Judenverfolgung* (Munich: Piper, 1998); Christopher R. Browning and Jürgen Matthäus, *The Origins of the Final Solution: The Evolution of Nazi Jewish Policy, September 1939–March 1942* (Lincoln: University of Nebraska Press, 2004).

23. Uwe Dietrich Adam, *Judenpolitik im Dritten Reich* (Düsseldorf: Droste, 1977).

24. Hilberg, *Destruction of European Jews,* 2nd ed., 54–55, 955–58.

25. Ibid., 290.

26. Hilberg, *Destruction of European Jews,* 3rd ed., 292–94.

27. Hilberg, *Destruction of European Jews,* 1st ed., 8–14.

28. Ibid., 12–13, 646–62.

29. Hilberg, *Destruction of European Jews,* 2nd ed., 1003–4.

30. Ibid., 993–94.

31. Ibid., 1187.

32. Hilberg, *Destruction of European Jews,* 3rd ed., 1293–96.

33. For example, see Reuben Ainsztein, *Jewish Resistance in Nazi-Occupied Eastern Europe: With a Historical Survey of the Jew as Fighter and Soldier in the Diaspora* (London: Elek, 1974); Yuri Suhl, *They Fought Back: The Story of the Jewish Resistance in Nazi Europe* (New York: Crown, 1967); and Lucien Steinberg, *Not as a Lamb: The Jews Against Hitler* (Farnborough, Eng.: Saxon House, 1974).

34. For example, see Nechama Tec, *Defiance: The Bielski Partisans* (New York: Oxford University Press, 1993); and Nechama Tec, *Resilience and Courage: Women, Men, and the Holocaust* (New Haven, Conn.: Yale University Press, 2003).

35. For example, see Yehuda Bauer, *They Chose Life: Jewish Resistance in the Holocaust* (New York: American Jewish Committee, 1973); Yehuda Bauer, "Jewish Leadership Reactions to Nazi Policies," in *The Holocaust as Historical Experience: Essays and a Discussion,* ed. Yehuda Bauer and Nathan Rotenstreich (New York: Holmes and Meier, 1981).

36. Lawrence Langer, *Versions of Survival: The Holocaust and the Human Spirit* (Albany: State University of New York Press, 1982).

Martin Dean

Holocaust Research and Generational Change: Regional and Local Studies Since the Cold War

THE MAIN THESIS OF THIS CHAPTER IS VERY SIMPLE: THAT SOME OF the major developments in the historiography of the Holocaust since the 1990s have been driven primarily by the availability of new sources. Among the key developments have been the trend toward regional studies and a greater sensitivity to the specific local context in which the events took place, including the role of local collaborators and bystanders, as well as the reexamination of the economic and political rationality, or at least rationale, behind Nazi genocidal policies. With regard to the sources, the most significant development was the fall of the Berlin Wall and the collapse of Communism, which opened up archives in Eastern Europe, not only of captured German documentation, but also of war crimes investigations. At the same time, the pursuit of some of the last remaining war criminals living in the West acted as a tool for levering open these archives. There is a subplot that I would like to interweave by asking the question whether perhaps, in some subtle ways, the history experienced while conducting this new research might also have informed both the questions asked and the answers that were found.[1]

Did the sudden and largely unexpected collapse of Communist dictatorships throughout most of Eastern Europe also have an impact on how historians have viewed past events? Was the "velvet revolution" of 1989–90 an example of history made from below, or the result of powerful economic forces that diverted attention away from the dictators as well? Was Hitler (or even Himmler) also removed from the pedestal and parked in the scrap heap of history alongside the busts of Lenin and Marx? These symbolic acts, especially the removal of the

Berlin Wall and the lifting of the "Iron Curtain," certainly opened up a vast new realm for historical research, representing a generational change or paradigm shift.

What has been the effect of the opening of Eastern European archives on Holocaust historiography since 1990? How has the emergence of a new generation of scholars conducting detailed case studies changed our understanding of how the Holocaust was implemented? What consequences do these sometimes weighty tomes have for our view of the Holocaust as a whole?

The devil lies in the details, and for this reason the full impact of this new research still remains hard to assess. We now know much more about how the Holocaust was carried out on a day-to-day basis throughout Eastern Europe; the focus has shifted away from the seemingly endless debates about a "Hitler order" and its precise timing and toward the motivations and worldview of the lower-level perpetrators, explaining how "functionalism" functioned.[2]

One important concept for understanding the thrust of much new research is that of "rationality." Rather than viewing the Holocaust as an "irrational" aberration that was only harmful to the German war effort, the new research has demonstrated that in many cases there was no contradiction for Nazi mid-level planners between the murder of the Jews and the achievement of the Nazis' other main ideological and practical goals. This realization has come particularly from examination of the Holocaust within the broader framework of Nazi racial, occupation, and war policies, including the reexamination of Nazi economic planning in wartime.[3]

Another key aspect has been to understand the implementation of the Holocaust within its specific local contexts. This shift has been accompanied by increased attention to the role of local collaboration in the Holocaust and the realization that models of Nazi genocide based on the bureaucratization and depersonalization of mass murder are not necessarily applicable to the shooting and starvation of more than two million of the Jewish victims in Eastern Europe. In this sense, the focus on Auschwitz and the smooth functioning of the death camps has been broadened to incorporate greater knowledge of the vast number of mass shootings and brutal ghetto clearances that required the participation of thousands of hands-on perpetrators, both German and non-German.

This chapter traces the development of research into German occupation policies and the implementation of the Holocaust in Eastern Europe by examining a select few of the many monographs, dissertations, and articles published since the mid-1990s which have contributed to our understanding both of the mechanics and the social context of the Holocaust. Several of the authors belong to the generation of German scholars trained in the late 1980s and early 1990s. In some instances, two scholars worked simultaneously on roughly the same topic. For example, Dieter Pohl[4] and Thomas Sandkühler[5] competed to be the first to publish the definitive account of the Holocaust in East Galicia. Meanwhile, the rivalry between Christian Gerlach[6] and Bernhard Chiari[7] over Belorussia[8] under German occupation resulted in two works from almost diametrically opposed perspectives—that of the occupiers versus that of the occupied. Several non-German contributions will also be examined, such as those by Shimon Redlich,[9] Sara Bender,[10] and Wendy Lower,[11] reflecting how the interest in regional studies has spread beyond Germany, driven not only by the unique archival opportunities but also by the "state of the field" in Holocaust research.

What was the state of the art in 1990 when the end of the Cold War opened up the Eastern European archives for historians of the Holocaust? At that time two major regional studies by Israeli historians of the survivor generation, Shmuel Spector and Shalom Cholawsky, had just reached completion.[12] With regard to the Jewish perspective, these monographs remain essential reading, laying out the main issues concerning the Jewish Councils, Jewish responses, and resistance efforts in Volhynia and western Belorussia. Both authors attempted to identify as many of the ghettos as possible in the regions they studied, and both examined Jewish responses on the basis of the Yizkor books (memorial books compiled by Jewish survivors to commemorate particular Jewish communities) and survivor testimonies. However, Spector and Cholawsky both lacked a clear analysis of the development of German policy and did not benefit from access to captured German documentation in former Soviet archives,[13] or even to the German postwar investigative materials at Ludwigsburg.[14]

The dominant analysis of German policy was that pieced together by Raul Hilberg and first published in 1961, with subsequent editions in 1985 and 2003.[15] Hilberg's masterpiece incorporated many specific local details available in Western archives but nevertheless constructed a largely top-down analysis of the mechanics of destruction, ll its recognition of the key role of individual bureaucrats within system. In 1992 Christopher Browning's monograph *Ordinary Men,* utilizing the thick description and motivational focus of German legal records, painted a complex and diffuse portrait of the foot soldiers of the Final Solution.[16] He argued that even quite arbitrarily chosen perpetrators were capable of becoming effective instruments of mass murder. These two key works remained very influential for the generation of scholars that burrowed into the newly opened archives in the 1990s.

In terms of synthesis, exploiting some of the materials from the newly opened archives, Götz Aly's powerful 1995 narrative *"Endlösung"* (*"Final Solution"*) focused on the key preparatory phase in 1939–41.[17] Aly demonstrated a number of economic and causal links between more general resettlement policies and the Final Solution, and he set the tone for future research. He influenced the work of others by reintegrating both economic rationality and contingency into the evolution of the Holocaust.[18]

The first, classic "regional case study" and in many respects the template that set the standard for those to follow was Dieter Pohl's 1996 study on East Galicia.[19] One major aim of his study was simply to document as thoroughly as possible the details of what happened in a key region that spanned both the General Government and the postwar Soviet Union, and from where more than five hundred thousand Jews were murdered. Pohl conducted extensive research in German legal and local Ukrainian archives. He asked and answered all the most salient questions. Pohl addressed the German administrative structure and its personnel and examined the main features of the development of the Holocaust and the chronology. He also covered briefly the role of collaborators, Jewish survival and resistance, and the judicial investigation of the perpetrators. This work benefited from his earlier experience writing a shorter M.A. thesis, an excellent regional study of the Holocaust in the Lublin District.[20]

Pohl not only covered every relevant aspect of German policy toward the Jews chronologically, but he also described the fate of each major Jewish community in East Galicia. He detected a broad antisemitic consensus in many of the occupation personnel, but did not see them as an undifferentiated mass. He stressed the role of activist elements, mainly among the six hundred men of the Security Police, who organized the killings. However, implementation still relied on a larger cadre of occupation personnel, including two thousand Order Police, four thousand Ukrainian auxiliary police (*Hilfspolizisten*), and the support of the civil administration.

Working in the same archives at the same time was Pohl's colleague Thomas Sandkühler.[21] Sandkühler combined a case study of the righteous gentile Berthold Beitz with a more compressed account of German policies. Beitz tried to exploit the economic rationality of German war production to save as many Jews as possible. Pohl's book was the more authoritative and detailed account of events in Galicia, but Sandkühler's imaginative use of sources, exploiting private papers and conducting oral histories, added a more personal dimension. On balance, Pohl's contribution was more striking. He brought neglected aspects, such as local collaboration, comparisons with Soviet crimes, and the evaluation of postwar judicial efforts, into the mainstream of historical research so that now whole monographs and dissertations are devoted to those matters.[22]

Christian Gerlach's ambitious 1999 study, whose title can be translated as *Calculated Murders: German Economic and Destruction Policy in Belorussia, 1941 to 1944* (the book itself has not been translated), documented in careful detail the deliberate mass murder of Soviet prisoners of war, Jews, and other civilians.[23] As the title suggests, Gerlach stressed the key role of economic considerations in the development and implementation of these policies. Gerlach's exposition included a full account of industrial, manpower, and agricultural policies, and the work demonstrated the thorough nature of German economic exploitation. The exhaustive footnotes and comprehensive analysis represented the consolidation of more than five years of intensive research.

For those who have the stamina to grapple with 1,232 pages of closely argued German text, there are many valuable insights. Gerlach's great strength lies in skillfully combining the examination of high-level decisions and their motivation with the practical frictions and initiatives from below that shaped their actual implementation. His analysis was based on an impressive mastery of the vast, available, German-language source material, including, perhaps surprisingly, many long-neglected collections of the German Federal Archives.

Genuinely innovative was Gerlach's analysis of how the implementation of economic policy influenced the transition to genocide against specific population groups. He viewed the so-called "hunger strategy," developed prior to the invasion of the Soviet Union, as leading directly to the deliberate starvation of prisoners of war and the shooting of Jews as "unnecessary mouths" during the transportation crisis in the autumn of 1941. His careful examination of the economic documentation of the military and civil authorities presented significant evidence in support of this thesis. He did not discount the ideological background of Nazi racism, but examined the implementation of these radical ideas in practical terms.

Gerlach's work reflected the interpretation of other German scholars, including Dieter Pohl, who stressed the general consensus of German occupation officials in support of genocidal policies.[24] Gerlach criticized earlier works that posited a "benign" role of "reformers" within the German administration. The responsibility for Nazi crimes was shared, he showed, by the Reich leaders who issued the instructions and by their subordinates who implemented them on the ground.[25]

Gerlach's reliance upon German source material and presentation of the big picture in facts and figures caused him to neglect some of the everyday nuances of the German occupation in Belorussia.[26] The parallel study of Bernhard Chiari,[27] by contrast, makes use of diverse, non-German sources, including some Soviet and Polish criminal investigations that present the local inhabitants much more as active participants in the unfolding cataclysm.[28] For Chiari, questions about collaboration and the responses of the local population were the main focus, and he paints a portrait of a Belorussian society torn apart by the stresses of war, economic collapse, and physical destruction.

I worked in the archives myself together with Chiari, and one of the most disturbing discoveries we made together was a photograph of young children from the orphanage in Domachevo, Belorussia, taken only months before they were brutally murdered. The children were dressed as angels and what appear to be dwarves or elves for a Christmas celebration. As detailed accounts in the Soviet Extraordinary Commission report make clear, the children in the orphanage suffered considerable privation from hunger before German police forces murdered them in September 1942, about the same time they killed the Jews from the ghetto in Domachevo. Among the orphans were initially fifteen Jewish children, but these were apparently transferred to the ghetto and shared the fate of the other inmates. The remaining children, who were not Jewish, were ntly murdered because the Germans needed the building for another purpose. Today, on the main road close to Domachevo, there is a memorial to the child victims of the German occupation.[29]

One of the major, synthetic works on the development of Nazi policy, Peter Longerich's *Politik der Vernichtung* (1998; *The Politics of Destruction*), attempted to reconcile the results of the regional studies with a more sustained focus on decisions taken at the center of Nazi power.[30] Longerich's work made a useful contribution to the ongoing scholarly debate in this area. On the one hand, some historians view decisions taken by the Nazi leaders in Berlin as the main arena for shifts in policy. On the other hand, some historians cite the regional differences in implementation as evidence for a considerable role being played by regional commanders. Longerich argued, for example, with regard to Einsatzgruppe B, which operated behind the central sector of the front in the Soviet Union, that the destructive results in the key period during the summer and fall of 1941 emerged from the interaction of ambiguous general instructions with the initiative of local unit commanders, but that in any case these initiatives were still corrected and subsequently steered from above (*korrigieren und nachsteuern*). Thus, Himmler's visits to the central sector of the Soviet front, to Minsk in mid-August 1941, for example, gave the opportunity for more specific and detailed instructions to be passed directly by word of mouth.[31] Wendy Lower made a similar point, citing a Himmler speech from his Hegewald compound near Zhytomyr, Ukraine, in the summer of 1942: "Himmler urged his subordinates to 'make decisions in the field,' claiming at the same time: 'I do not make decisions in Berlin, rather I drive to Lublin, Lemberg, Reval, etc., and at these places in the evening, then eight, ten, twelve major decisions are made on the spot.'"[32]

Longerich's directly instrumental use of regional studies stands in contrast to the grassroots focus of most recent contributions. Whereas Longerich repeatedly asked the question of what these regional studies and new findings tell us about decision making at the center, for most exponents of regional studies, their work has other important justifications, beyond what additional light might be shed on the now less-heated debates about decision making.[33]

Traveling to Eastern Europe to work in the archives, see the landscape, and talk to the local people certainly creates a personal link to the events. As Steve Zipperstein, the Stanford-based professor of Jewish culture and history, has noted, it was only after the end of the

Cold War, when he began to travel to the areas he had studied in the former Soviet Union, that he became more acutely aware of his previous neglect or avoidance of the Holocaust. He posed the rhetorical question: "Should we resist it when this new intimacy or, at least, knowledge of the terrain about which we write inspires an intense sense that these are the sites of east European Jewry's greatest horrors?"[34]

One side effect of Communist rule was to act as a time capsule and a reinforced container for some of the powerful nationalist sentiments that contributed to the Holocaust. In visiting the villages of Ukraine and Belarus in the 1990s, one seemed to travel back in time to small, local communities where people still have long memories, because very little has happened or changed since the war. At the same time, the artificial state constructs of the Soviet Union and Yugoslavia proved remarkably resilient in restraining pent-up nationalism; which also caused it to break out again with renewed ferocity, especially in Yugoslavia, when unleashed by the end of the Cold War. For those historians who witnessed the rapid collapse of these Communist empires in the early 1990s, it was almost instinctive to draw parallels to the ethnic conflicts that erupted and devastated large swaths of the contested Eastern European borderlands at the time of World War II.

The work of several historians has evoked the specter of "ethnic cleansing" in modern Yugoslavia as a familiar model to help understand the complex events of World War II. Foremost in this respect is the research of Tim Snyder, who described seven common features shared between the ethnic cleansing of Poles by Ukrainians in Volhynia in 1943 and the Yugoslav violence of the 1990s, noting that many of the Ukrainian nationalist partisans involved in Volhynia had been trained first by the Germans as members of the *Schutzmannschaft* (local police) employed directly in the liquidation of Jewish ghettos in late 1942.[35]

Omer Bartov has become a strong advocate of combining the study of genocide in the broader sense alongside detailed micro-studies of the Eastern European borderlands environment. Reacting partly against the perpetrator-centered studies of the new generation of German historians, his study of the town of Buczacz aims to understand how the genocide actually unfolded on the ground by analyzing closely the social fabric upon which these policies acted. This detailed local approach has clearly been influenced by Jan Gross's powerful study of events in Jedwabne, *Neighbors*. Gross's extended essay drew mainly

on postwar Polish criminal investigations to re-create the
in which, in his somewhat dramatized simplification, i
"one half of the town murdered the other."[36]

Gross's approach has already spawned a number of
works that analyze the events of the Holocaust and parallel
rivalries at the level of the town or village. An important example is
Shimon Redlich's study *Brzezany,* which made considerable efforts
to incorporate the perspectives of Jews, Poles, and Ukrainians, using
testimonies, oral histories, and some German trial materials. Redlich
pointed out that to some extent the histories created by each community remain mutually exclusive, "together and apart," but his model
remains a powerful one for attempting to reconstruct how these communities interacted and also failed to connect at a crucial time.[37]

An eloquent exposition of the micro-study concept can be found
in the project proposal of Curt Dunagan, concerning Polish-Jewish-
Ukrainian relations in the Galician town of Przemyśl between 1919
and 1944 (Przemyśl is now located just on the Polish side of the
border with Ukraine). In Dunagan's words: "In Przemyśl, as in other
towns and cities of this ethnically mixed region of Europe, tensions
were always present. During times of peace, mutual rapport generally
prevailed, while during periods of adversity and tragedy, conflicts,
violence, and even murder became the norm. This discord can only
be understood in light of the three-sided relationship of Poles, Ukrainians, and Jews."[38]

A similar trend toward more diversified regional and local studies
can be detected in the Israeli historiography of the 1990s and the first
years of the twenty-first century. Three significant exponents, who
have attempted to overcome the previous isolationism of many Israeli
works, while still focusing primarily on the internal debates within the
Jewish community during the Holocaust (or Shoah), are Sara Bender,
Tikva Fatal-Knaani, and Yehuda Bauer. All three incorporated German
and even some local Polish or Russian sources into their analyses. In
particular, they also made use of some of the rich vein of sources that
has become available since the end of the Cold War, much of which
is now accessible at Yad Vashem and the U.S. Holocaust Memorial
Museum on microfilm.[39]

Bender focused especially on reexamining the role of the Jewish
Councils. She argued, perhaps controversially on the basis of comparative studies, that in view of the incomplete knowledge of the Judenrat

leaders and the apparent need of the Germans for labor during the war, the strategy of Efrayim Barash in Białystok, for example, based on the principle of survival through work, was the only realistic option available, at least until November 1942. As Bender explained, "We see from the surviving reports of the Judenrat meetings, that this idea was the guiding principle behind its policies—as Barash put it, to make the ghetto so useful to the German administration that it would be detrimental for them to destroy it."[40]

Tikva Fatal-Knaani has also focused on portraying the Holocaust from the Jewish perspective in some of the major Jewish centers in eastern Poland. Her dissertation on the fate of the large Jewish community in Grodno exploited the wide variety of sources available to depict the responses of Jews to their ever-worsening predicament.[41] A subsequent article she published on the Jews of Pinsk under Soviet occupation and during the Holocaust drew on newly available documentation from Soviet archives to reconstruct in detail social conditions in the ghetto, again placing emphasis on the Jews as historical actors in their own right.[42] In recent years Yehuda Bauer has also taken it upon himself to document the Holocaust as experienced by Jews in several shtetls of eastern Poland, as a form of local history. In assessing the reactions of the Jews, Bauer stressed the need to understand their traditions and local cultural organizations, as well as the impact of the Soviet occupation, most of which was scarcely mentioned in the available Western historiography written mainly from the perspective of the perpetrators.[43]

The next logical development from the proliferation of microstudies was the preparation of more effective encyclopedias for Eastern Europe, integrating the new archival resources to fill in the still-large gaps in our knowledge. For many years the incomplete *Pinkas Hakehillot* series published by Yad Vashem, based almost exclusively on Jewish sources, served this function for those who read Hebrew.[44] However, this was recently updated by the *Encyclopedia of Jewish Life Before and During the Holocaust,* which incorporates at least some of the findings from other sources, although the absence of references leaves a scholarly reader with nowhere to go for further information.[45] A good companion to this for Ukraine is the encyclopedic volumes on the Holocaust prepared by Aleksandr Kruglov, which incorporate most of the findings from the Soviet Extraordinary Commission reports and the main German documentation, although here the Jewish side is completely absent.[46] My own current ambitious project of a comprehensive encyclopedia of German-administered ghettos (part of a larger "multi-volume encyclopedic history of detention, forced labor, and extermination sites" coordinated by Geoff Megargee at the Center for Advanced Holocaust Studies with the support of the Helen Bader Foundation) intends to fill this gap by integrating these diverse source bases in one volume, while also providing the reader with references and recommendations for further research.

One recent development that may have been influenced by post-colonial genocides, such as that in Rwanda in 1994, as well as by references to earlier colonial genocides, such as that committed against the Herero in German South-West Africa in 1904–7, or even the Australian aborigines, is a direct comparison of Nazi occupation and settlement policies with the traditions of Western imperialism. A prime example of this approach is Wendy Lower's study of the Holocaust in the Zhytomyr Region, which delved into the relationship between Hitler's notion of a colonial empire and Nazi practices in the East. In Lower's words: "Hitler, who fancied himself an emperor, expounded upon his imperialistic ambitions in the secret meetings at his Vinnytsia headquarters and elsewhere. However, the methods of colonial rule that he inspired and endorsed in Ukraine brought the Western tradition of imperialism and colonization to an unprecedented level of calculated mass murder."[47] A similar approach has been adopted fruitfully by David Furber, another historian from the United States, in analyzing the background, motivations, and behavior of German administrative personnel in occupied Poland.[48] However, the novel approach of these two authors has been informed more by traditional studies of Western colonialism and imperialism (as noted previously also by Hannah Arendt), and especially their links to Raphael Lemkin's concept of genocide, than by any explicit links to the modern practices of genocide in Rwanda or Sudan.[49]

Very closely related to the end of the Cold War has been the role of war crimes investigations, both in opening up new archival sources and developing into a field of research in its own right. Here it is worth mentioning that historians such as Dieter Pohl, Andrej Angrick, Jürgen Matthäus, and I all worked for war crimes investigations units in the West that could only function properly by gaining access to Soviet archives at the end of the Cold War.[50] The practice of using German war crimes investigations as a key historical source, pioneered especially by the group of German historians schooled by Wolfgang Scheffler, himself an expert "expert witness," was then transferred by Dieter Pohl, Bogdan Musial, and others to the war crimes records from Polish and Soviet archives.[51] The first studies of Soviet war crimes trials as a subject in their own right have now started to appear, for example, by Alexander Prusin, who is also currently working on a study of the Holocaust in the Kiev district.[52] In many respects the former KGB archives are the gift that keeps on giving, because after the trial files have been evaluated there remain further layers of captured German documentation, investigative files, and even search files for war criminals living abroad, to be extracted and evaluated.[53]

In some instances, the wealth of material to be found in the Soviet investigations can at least partially make up for the dearth of contemporary German documentation. For Ukraine, Tanja Penter's current study of the Donetsk region is based partly on a careful reading of Soviet postwar trials of local "collaborators," in the absence of significant collections of surviving wartime documentation. There are also references to a ghetto in Donetsk to be found in the statements from the Soviet trials, whereas no mention of a ghetto can be found in the sparse German records.[54] The extensive war crimes records already collected by the U.S. Holocaust Memorial Museum from KGB archives in Ukraine, Russia, Latvia, Lithuania, Estonia, Kazakhstan, and Uzbekistan, together with more in the pipeline, promise to fuel further research in this direction for some time to come.[55]

The significance of the new generation of researchers since 1989 has to be placed within the *longue durée* of Holocaust research. The question of where Holocaust research will go next can only be answered once findings from the new archives have been fully absorbed and the conclusions and implications incorporated into more widely read texts.

What have been the implications of breaking the Holocaust down into its different regional components and laying bare its complex layers as a societal process? For most historians this approach has led to a further distancing from monolithic and mechanistic interpretations, whereby orders were simply transmitted down and carried out. The ---~· of detailed local sources now available stress the contingent ed nature of this history and the active participation and ergy of many lower-level perpetrators. In particular, the history of the Holocaust cannot and should not be separated from the complex local histories of the places where it happened and of the people involved.

Of course, nearly all studies continue to reference Hitler and Himmler as the main fulcrum for Nazi policies of destruction and colonization. Indeed, new finds such as the missing parts of the Himmler appointment book have added fuel to the continuing research focused on the center.[56] However, even with regard to research on Nazi policies in Germany itself, the regional approaches of scholars such as Wolf Gruner and Frank Bajohr have upgraded the relative importance of local initiatives and structures that is the weight of the periphery against that of the center.[57]

It is arguable to what extent these developments have been driven by the availability of sources, the political and historical context of the work, or simply by the growth and diversification of the field of Holocaust studies itself. All three factors undoubtedly have played a part. Nevertheless, the impact of the end of the Cold War has certainly left a huge mark and will have a strong influence on what we study and how we study it for many years to come. If the outcome is for the Holocaust to be perceived much more through Eastern European rather than Western eyes, as an event that took place in its specific social context, stressing the agency of the perpetrators, viewing it much more as a human-made catastrophe than as an abstract process detached from society, then the detailed work of these scholars will not have been in vain.

NOTES

1. A simplified version of this proposition is what might be called the "Good-bye Lenin" syndrome. *Good-bye Lenin* was a film written and directed by Wolfgang Becker in 2003 that took a humorous look at the strange nostalgia some people had for the East German state. Set in 1990, the film portrays how a young man tries to protect his fragile mother from a fatal shock after a long coma by keeping her from learning that her beloved nation of East Germany has disappeared. In one scene a statue of Lenin is swung through the air as it is removed from its place of honor in the center of an East Berlin square. Here I am referring to the movie primarily as an icon for the dramatic regime change that took place in Eastern Europe, which

left some people behind, but opened up great opportunities, especially for historians prepared to rethink the past.

2. For a good summary of the "intentionalism-functionalism" debate, see Christopher Browning, "Beyond 'Intentionalism' and 'Functionalism': The Decision for the Final Solution Reconsidered," in *The Path to Genocide: Essays on Launching the Final Solution,* ed. Christopher Browning (Cambridge, Eng.: Cambridge University Press, 1992), 88–101.

3. See Götz Aly, *"Endlösung": Völkerverschiebung und der Mord an den europäischen Juden* (Frankfurt am Main: S. Fischer, 1995); for the English translation, see Götz Aly, *"Final Solution": Nazi Population Policy and the Murder of the European Jews,* trans. Belinda Cooper and Allison Brown (New York: Oxford University Press, 1999).

4. Dieter Pohl, *Nationalsozialistische Judenverfolgung in Ostgalizien 1941–1944: Organisation und Durchführung eines staatlichen Massenverbrechens* (Munich: Oldenbourg, 1996).

5. Thomas Sandkühler, *"Endlösung" in Galizien: Der Judenmord in Ostpolen und die Rettungsinitiativen von Berthold Beitz, 1941–1944* (Bonn: Dietz, 1996).

6. Christian Gerlach, *Kalkulierte Morde: Die deutsche Wirtschafts- und Vernichtungspolitik in Weissrussland 1941 bis 1944* (Hamburg: Hamburger Edition, 1999).

7. Bernhard Chiari, *Alltag hinter der Front: Besatzung, Kollaboration und Widerstand in Weissrussland 1941–1944* (Düsseldorf: Droste, 1998).

8. The country now known as Belarus. The 1937 spellings of place names will be used in this chapter in accordance with the usual practice of the United States Holocaust Memorial Museum.

9. Shimon Redlich, *Together and Apart in Brzezany: Poles, Jews, and Ukrainians, 1919–1945* (Bloomington: Indiana University Press, 2002).

10. Sara Bender, *Mul Mavet Orev: Yehude Byalistok be-Milhemet ha-'Olam ha-Shniya 1939–1945 [Against Lurking Death: The Jews of Białystok in the Second World War, 1939–1945]* (Tel Aviv: 'Am 'Oved, 1997).

11. Wendy Lower, *Nazi Empire-Building and the Holocaust in Ukraine* (Chapel Hill: University of North Carolina Press, 2005).

12. Shmuel Spector, *The Holocaust of Volhynian Jews, 1941–44* (Jerusalem: Achva, 1990); Shalom Cholawsky, *The Jews of Bielorussia During World War II* (Amsterdam: Harwood, 1998).

13. German documents captured by the Red Army are housed in the Russian State Military Archive in a collection entitled Special Archive (Osobyi Arkhiv) in Moscow.

14. Archival materials pertaining to West Germany's postwar investigations into the crimes of the Nazi era are housed in a branch office of the Federal Archives in Ludwigsburg.

15. Raul Hilberg, *The Destruction of the European Jews,* 3rd ed. (New Haven, Conn.: Yale University Press, 2003); earlier editions were published in 1961 and 1985.

16. Christopher Browning, *Ordinary Men: Reserve Police Battalion 101 and the Final Solution in Poland* (New York: HarperCollins, 1992).

17. Aly, *"Endlösung."*

18. See Gerlach, *Kalkulierte Mord,* 19.

19. Pohl, *Nationalsozialistische Judenverfolgung.*

20. Dieter Pohl, *Von der "Judenpolitik" zum Judenmord: Der Distrikt Lublin des Generalgouvernements, 1934–1944* (Frankfurt am Main and New York: Peter Lang, 1993). On the Lublin District, see also Bogdan Musial, *Deutsche Zivilverwaltung und Judenverfolgung im Generalgouvernement: Eine Fallstudie zum Distrikt Lublin 1939–1944* (Wiesbaden: Harrassowitz, 1999).

21. Sandkühler, *"Endlösung" in Galizien.*

22. For example, see Hilary Earl, "Accidental Justice: The Trial of Otto Ohlendorf and the Einsatzgruppen Leaders in the American Zone of Occupation, Germany, 1945–1958" (Ph.D. diss., University of Toronto, 2002); Martin Dean, *Collaboration in the Holocaust: Crimes of the Local Police in Belorussia and Ukraine, 1941–44* (New York: St. Martin's, 2000); and Bogdan Musial, *"Konterrevolutionäre Elemente sind zu erschiessen": Die Brutalisierung des deutsch-sowjetischen Krieges im Sommer 1941* (Berlin: Propyläen, 2000).

23. Gerlach, *Kalkulierte Morde.*

24. See Pohl, *Nationalsozialistische Judenverfolgung,* 300–311. Another study that has come to similar conclusions regarding areas under military administration in the Crimea, southern Ukraine, and the Caucasus is Andrej Angrick, *Besatzungspolitik und Massenmord: Die Einsatzgruppe D in der südlichen Sowjetunion 1941–1943* (Hamburg: Hamburger Edition, 2003).

25. See Gerlach, *Kalkulierte Morde,* 1149–58.

26. See Gerlach's own disclaimer in his introduction, ibid., 23–24.

27. Chiari, *Alltag hinter der Front.*

28. For a similar approach exploiting extensive local sources (although not Soviet war crimes trials) regarding the German occupation of Ukraine, see Karel C. Berkhoff, *Harvest of Despair: Life and Death in Ukraine Under Nazi Rule* (Cambridge, Mass.: Belknap, 2004).

29. Chiari, *Alltag hinter der Front,* 204–6. The fate of the children from the orphanage is described in detail by one of the women who cared for the children, in the Soviet Extraordinary Commission Report; see State Archives of the Brest Oblast', 514–1–195. This file also contains the original of the photograph.

30. Peter Longerich, *Politik der Vernichtung: Eine Gesamtdarstellung der*

nationalsozialistischen Judenverfolgung (Munich and Zurich: Piper, 1998). Other attempts to synthesize recent research on the evolution of Nazi policy include Christopher R. Browning and Jürgen Matthäus, *The Origins of the Final Solution: The Evolution of Nazi Jewish Policy, September 1939–March 1942* (London: Heinemann, 2004); and Florent Brayard, *La "solution finale de la question juive": La technique, le temps et les catégories de la decision* (Paris: Fayard, 2004).

31. Longerich, *Politik der Vernichtung,* 372–73.

32. Lower, *Nazi Empire-Building,* 8.

33. For a more recent summary of the decision-making debate, see Christopher Browning, *Initiating the Final Solution: The Fateful Months of September–October 1941* (Washington, D.C.: United States Holocaust Memorial Museum, Center for Advanced Holocaust Studies, 2003).

34. Steve Zipperstein, *Imagining Russian Jewry: Memory, History, Identity* (Seattle: University of Washington Press, 1999); Steve Zipperstein, *Past Revisited: Reflections on the Study of the Holocaust and Contemporary Antisemitism* (Washington, D.C.: United States Holocaust Memorial Museum, Center for Advanced Holocaust Studies, 2003), 6–7.

35. See Timothy Snyder, "The Causes of Ukrainian-Polish Ethnic Cleansing, 1943," *Past and Present* 179 (May 2003): 197–234. On the role of the Ukrainian local police in the clearing of the ghettos in Volhynia, see Dean, *Collaboration in the Holocaust,* 94–104.

36. Jan T. Gross, *Neighbors: The Destruction of the Jewish Community in Jedwabne, Poland* (Princeton, N.J.: Princeton University Press, 2001).

37. Redlich, *Together and Apart in Brzezany.* For another recent micro-study, see David Gaunt, Paul Levine, and Laura Palosuo, "Microcosm: Collaboration and Resistance During the Holocaust in the Mir Rayon of Belarus, 1941–44," in *Collaboration and Resistance During the Holocaust: Belarus, Estonia, Latvia, Lithuania,* ed. Gaunt, Levine, and Palosuo (New York: Peter Lang, 2004).

38. Curt Dunagan, "'Przemyśl, Pshemishl, Peremyshl': Polish-Jewish-Ukrainian Relations in Przemyśl, 1919–1944" (Ph.D. project description, supervised by Antony Polonsky at Brandeis University).

39. For an overview of the holdings of the U.S. Holocaust Memorial Museum Archives, see Brewster S. Chamberlin and Carl Modig, eds., *Archival Guide to the Collections of the United States Holocaust Memorial Museum* (Washington, D.C.: United States Holocaust Memorial Museum, Center for Advanced Holocaust Studies, 2003). This publication is updated periodically. For a listing of the record groups at Yad Vashem, see http://www1.yadvashem.org/about_yad/temp_about_yad/temp_index_about_yad_institute.html.

40. Bender, *Mul Mavet Orev,* 117–47; see also Tikva Fatal-Knaani, "The Jews of Pinsk, 1939–1943, Through the Prism of New Documentation," *Yad Vashem Studies* 29 (2001): 149–82; and Yehuda Bauer, "Jewish Baranowicze in the Holocaust," *Yad Vashem Studies* 31 (2003): 95–152.

41. Tikva Fatal-Knaani, *Zo lo otah Grodnoh: Kehilat Grodnoh u-sevivatah ba-milhamah uva-sho'ah, 1939–1943* [*Grodno Is Not the Same: The Jewish Community in Grodno and Its Vicinity During the Second World War and the Holocaust, 1939–1943*] (Jerusalem: Yad Vashem, 2003).

42. Fatal-Knaani, "Jews of Pinsk."

43. Yehuda Bauer, "Ostpolnische Shtetlach während der Shoah," in *NS-Gewaltherrschaft: Beiträge zur historischen Forschung und juristischen Aufarbeitung,* ed. Alfred Gottwaldt, Norbert Kampe, and Peter Klein (Berlin: Edition Hentrich, 2005), 290–306. See also Bauer, "Jewish Baranowicze in the Holocaust," 95–152; and Yehuda Bauer, "Kurzeniec, A Jewish Shtetl in the Holocaust," in *Yalkut Moreshet: Holocaust Documentation and Research* (Tel Aviv: Moreshet, 2003), 1:132–57.

44. For example, see *Pinkas hakehillot Polin: entsiklopedyah shel ha-yishuvim ha-Yehudiyim le-,min hivasdam ve-'ad le-ahar Sho'at Milhemet ha-'olam ha-sheniyah,* vol. 2, *Galicia Hamizrahit* [*Pinkas Hakehillot: Encyclopedia of Jewish Communities: Poland,* vol. 2, *Eastern Galicia*], ed. Danuta Dąbrowska, Abraham Wein, and Aharon Weiss (Jerusalem: Yad Vashem, 1980); and *Pinkas hakehillot Polin,* vol. 5, *Volhynia and Polesie,* ed. Shmuel Spector (Jerusalem: Yad Vashem, 1990).

45. Shmuel Spector and Geoffrey Wigoder, eds., *The Encyclopedia of Jewish Life Before and During the Holocaust* (New York: New York University Press, 2001).

46. For example, see Aleksandr I. Kruglov, *Katastrofa ukrainskogo evreistva 1941–1944 gg.: Entsiklopedicheskii spravochnik* (Kharkiv: "Karavella," 2001); Aleksandr I. Kruglov, *Entsiklopediia kholokosta: Evreiskaia entsiklopediia Ukrainy* (Kiev: Evreiskii Sovet Ukrainy, Fond "Pamiat' Zhertv Fashizma," 2000). A synthesis of these two works is now also available in English: Alexander Kruglov, *The Losses Suffered by Ukrainian Jews in 1941–1944* (Kharkiv: Tarbut Laam, 2005).

47. Wendy Lower, "Nazi Colonial Dreams: German Policies and Ukrainian Society in Zhytomyr, 1941–1944" (Ph.D. diss., American University, Washington, D.C., 1999), 452. See also the recent work of Jürgen Zimmerer, "Colonialism and the Holocaust: Towards an Archeology of Genocide," in *Genocide and Settler Society: Frontier Violence and the "Civilizing Process" in Australia,* ed. A. Dirk Moses (New York: Berghahn, 2002), which builds on earlier work regarding Nazi imperialism by Raphael Lemkin, Hannah Arendt, and Woodruff Smith.

48. See David Furber, "Going East: Colonialism and German Life in Nazi-Occupied Poland" (Ph.D. diss., State University of New York at Buffalo, 2003).

49. See Hannah Arendt, *The Origins of Totalitarianism* (New York: Harcourt Brace Jovanovich, 1951); and Raphael Lemkin, *Axis Rule in Occupied Europe: Laws of Occupation, Analysis of Government, Proposals for Redress* (Washington, D.C.: Carnegie Endowment for International Peace, Division of International Law, 1944).

50. Dieter Pohl worked for the Canadian Department of Justice; Jürgen Matthäus for the Australian War Crimes Prosecution Support Unit (previously the Australian Special Investigations Unit); Martin Dean for the British Home Office, the SIU, and the Metropolitan Police War Crimes Unit; and Andrej Angrick for the U.S. Office of Special Investigations. See Angrick, *Besatzungspolitik und Massenmord;* Jürgen Matthäus, *Ausbildungsziel Judenmord? "Weltanschauliche Erziehung" von SS, Polizei und Waffen-SS im Rahmen der "Endlösung"* (Frankfurt am Main: Fischer Taschenbuch, 2003).

51. See Pohl, *Nationalsozialistische Judenverfolgung,* 387–96; and Bogdan Musial, "NS-Kriegsverbrecher vor polnischen Gerichten," *Vierteljahrshefte für Zeitgeschichte* 47, no. 1 (1999): 25–56.

52. Alexander Prusin, "'Fascist Criminals to the Gallows!': The Holocaust and Soviet War Crimes Trials, December 1945–February 1946," *Holocaust and Genocide Studies* 17, no. 1 (Spring 2003): 1–30. In June 2005 the U.S. Holocaust Memorial Museum hosted a summer research workshop coordinated by Alex Prusin and Anton Weiss-Wendt and titled "Prosecuting the Perpetrators of the Holocaust: War-Crime Trials in the Soviet Union and Eastern Europe," and a volume of collected essays based on the papers presented at the workshop is in preparation.

53. See Martin Dean, "Soviet War Crimes Lists and Their Role in the Investigation of Nazi War Criminals in the West, 1987–2000," in *NS-Gewaltherrschaft,* ed. Gottwaldt, Kampe, and Klein, 456–70.

54. See Tanja Penter, "Die lokale Gesellschaft im Donbass unter deutscher Okkupation 1941–1943," in *Kooperation und Verbrechen: Formen der "Kollaboration" im östlichen Europa 1939–1945,* ed. Christoph Dieckmann et al. (Göttingen: Wallstein, 2003), 183–223.

55. See, for example, United States Holocaust Memorial Museum Archives, RG-06.025 (selected records from the FSB [former KGB], Moscow); RG-06.026 (selected Estonian KGB trial records); RG-06.027 (selected Latvian KGB trial records); RG-26.004M (war crimes investigation and trial records from the former Lithuanian KGB archives, 149 reels); and RG-31.018M (selected Ukrainian war crimes trials).

56. See Peter Witte et al., eds., *Der Dienstkalender Heinrich Himmlers 1941/42* (Hamburg: Christians, 1999).

57. Wolf Gruner, "The German Council of Municipalities (Deutscher Gemeindetag) and the Coordination of Anti-Jewish Local Politics in the Nazi State," in *Holocaust and Genocide Studies* 13, no. 2 (Fall 1999): 171–99; and Frank Bajohr, *"Aryanisation" in Hamburg: The Economic Exclusion of the Jews and the Confiscation of Their Property in Nazi Germany* (New York and Oxford: Berghahn, 2002).

Holly Case

Territorial Revision and the Holocaust: Hungary and Slovakia During World War II

V židovskej otázke už dávno sme videli (u nás) otázku maďarskú.

In the Jewish question, we had already for a long time seen (in our country) a Hungarian question.
—Alexander Mach, former head of the Hlinka Guard and interior minister of Slovakia (1939–45), February 1980

DURING THE TWENTIETH CENTURY, THE TERRITORY OF PRESENT-day Slovakia was part of several different states. Since it was the object of competing state and national interests—specifically those of the predominantly Czech leadership in post–World War I Czechoslovakia, Hitler and Nazi Germany, Hungary, and even Poland—the border shifts this region underwent were both frequent and tenuous. At the beginning of the century, the region was part of the Kingdom of Hungary within the Austro-Hungarian monarchy. In 1918, in the wake of World War I, it became part of the new state of Czecho-slovakia, which absorbed not only large sections of what had been Austria-Hungary but also many different national-ethnic groups of that collapsed state, including Czechs, Slovaks, Germans, Hungarians, Jews, Rusyns (Ruthenes), and Roma. Following the Munich Agree-ment in 1938, Hungary was given back part of southern Slovakia with the First Vienna Arbitration. The following spring when the Germans seized the western (mostly Czech) part of Czechoslovakia, they allowed the remainder of what is now Slovakia to declare its independence from Czechoslovakia on March 14, 1939. Hungary acquired still more territory from the dismantled Czechoslovak state in the weeks that followed, when Hungarian army forces entered Carpatho-Ukraine and other parts of eastern Slovakia.[1]

Throughout World War II this territory was divided between Hungary and the newly independent Slovakia. Neither state could conceal its dissatisfaction with this "half" solution, and both aspired to control more of the territory while protecting the territory they had. Nevertheless, the foreign policy of Nazi Germany made allies of both the two states. This meant that the state leaderships on both sides of the border had to employ indirect means to achieve maximum territorial gain. Their efforts invariably affected not only the Slovak and Hungarian populations in both states but also the Jews and other minorities living in the region.

This chapter seeks to determine the extent to which territorial concerns influenced policy vis-à-vis the Jews and other minorities in Slovakia and Hungary during the war. Like a study I have written on the territorial contest between Hungary and Romania for control of Transylvania, this work aims not only to enrich the overall picture of the region's World War II history but also to challenge some of the assumptions upon which our understanding of the Holocaust is based.[2] Specifically, instead of studying the Holocaust as it happened in discrete national contexts or as an outgrowth of Nazi policy, I argue that examining relationships between neighboring states can reveal much about why the fate of Jews varied widely between state contexts and over time.

The region that is the subject of this analysis is the territory, more or less, of present-day Slovakia and Carpatho-Ukraine.[3] As mentioned above, this territory was divided between Hungary and a newly independent Slovak state (often called a puppet state of Nazi Germany). Not surprisingly, an early and sustained preoccupation of the World War II Slovak leadership was to preserve the new state's boundaries and ultimately to win back what had been lost to Hungary. Similarly, Hungary's preoccupation was with restoring the territories of its thousand-year-old Hungarian kingdom, two-thirds of which it had lost to Romania, Czechoslovakia (the Slovak half), and Yugoslavia with the Treaty of Trianon following World War I. In both cases, these preoccupations affected the two countries' foreign policy, most notably their commitment to the Axis war effort, and generated vigilance regarding the actions and intentions of their revisionist neighbors. The conditions also influenced their domestic policies, including policies vis-à-vis the Jews and other minorities.

SECOND-GUESSING THE ALLY

The Vienna Arbitration (1938) gave to Hungary 10,390 square kilometers which, according to the 1930 Czechoslovak census, was inhabited by 854,218 people, of whom 503,980 were Magyars, around 272,145 were Slovaks (or Czechs), and about 26,151 declared themselves Jews by nationality, while probably around twice that number were Jews by religion.[4] This left Slovakia—still technically part of the Czechoslovak state at the time—with a population of just over 2.6 million, about 88 percent of which was Slovak (or Czech); 57,897 (about 2 percent) Hungarian by nationality; 128,347 (about 5 percent) German by nationality; 85,045 (about 3 percent) Jewish by religion; and 29,002 (approximately 1 percent) Jewish by nationality.[5]

The outcome of the arbitration incensed the Slovak leadership and public. Many Slovaks, including members of the Slovak political leadership, blamed the Jews for the loss of territory. On November 3, 1938, the day after the decision was announced, protracted demonstrations were held in Bratislava during which many homes and shops of Jews were targeted.[6] These demonstrations were in response to a "pro-Hungarian Jewish demonstration" that had taken place in the city on November 1. Police headquarters reported about flyers addressed to the Jews speaking against Slovak independence and for the territory's reannexation to Hungary. Purportedly, what started as a gathering of "500 Jewish-Hungarians" in front of the Carlton Hotel soon swelled to 2,500 to 3,000 singing the Hungarian national anthem and other Hungarian patriotic songs.[7]

One of the first initiatives of the Slovak leadership following the Vienna Arbitration was to "punish" the Jews for their pro-Hungarian attitude by deporting 7,500 Jews to the territory that was to be turned over to the Hungarians.[8] Hungarian authorities did not admit them, so many remained in a neutral zone between the two states for months.[9] Some in the Hungarian leadership also saw the Jews as somehow responsible for resistance to the territorial ambitions of revisionist Hungary. At the beginning of October 1938, the Hungarian ambassador in Prague had complained that "the uplands Jews are spreading pro-Czechoslovak propaganda."[10]

The Vienna Arbitration confirmed the regional suspicion that Nazi Germany was the only force both willing and able to move boundaries in East-Central Europe. As a result, both Hungary and the soon-to-be-independent Slovak Republic took the arbitration to mean that only Hitler and Nazi Germany could help them realize their territorial aspirations and secure present boundaries, and thus both countries made efforts to show their commitment to German interests. These gestures took the form of cooperation with the Reich in implementation of anti-Jewish legislation, troop commitment to the Axis war effort, and suggestions to German officials that the other country was behaving inappropriately or disloyally. It should be noted, however, that in the case of Hungary, Transylvania was of far greater importance than the lands reannexed from dissected Czechoslovakia in the north. Thus when Hungary played up to the Axis, it was not solely in the interest of gaining more territory from German-protected Slovakia but also to best Romania in the contest for the führer's favor in order to have a better chance of winning more territory back from its neighbor to the east.[11]

Still, Hungary had by no means relinquished its claim on Slovak territory, and its cooperation with the Axis constituted both a gesture of gratitude for territories regained as well as an investment in the future that it hoped would reap returns in the form of greater territorial compensation. Slovak historian Eduard Nižňanský goes so far as to argue that the implementation of anti-Jewish legislation in Hungary—namely the First, Second, and Third Jewish laws of 1938, 1939, and 1941—was timed to demonstrate Hungary's willingness to cooperate with Nazi Germany in return for territorial compensation.[12] Historian of Hungary C. A. Macartney also observed that "the first references to renewed antisemitic legislation [in Hungary] were made immediately after the arrival of the Felvidék [territory reannexed from Slovakia] Deputies. The pressure at least undoubtedly came from this quarter."[13]

The Slovak leadership's response to the Vienna Arbitration was to implement extensive anti-Jewish legislation designed to remove Jews from Slovak political, economic, and cultural life. It is worth noting that many of these actions ran parallel to policies designed to eliminate Czechs from the same positions of influence. For although Slovakia's primary revisionist preoccupation was with the territories it had lost to Hungary, both Hungary and Slovakia feared the resurrection of Czechoslovakia. The interwar Czechoslovak state had been the primary target of Hungary's revisionist aims, and Czechoslovakia's centralized governmental system was a thorn in the side of Slovak nationalist aspirations. During the interwar period the Slovak advocate of Czechoslovakism, the statesman Ivan Derer, argued that Slovak particularism was an invention of Hungarian nationalists to keep the Czechs and their Slav brethren to the east divided and maintain the "servile spirit" and childlike naiveté of the Slovaks.[14] Accordingly, in interwar Czechoslovakia, Czechs were often transplanted to Slovakia to serve in education, government, the cultural arena, and the legal system. Their presence underlined the assumption that Slovaks were either incapable or unready to fend for themselves and had to be "taught" statehood and made aware of their "true" national identity.[15]

Thus it was not merely the Hungarian revisionists against whom the new Slovak state was reacting but the Czechs as well. In fact, in the eyes of a number of state officials, the Czech question and the Jewish question were closely related. As late as October 1944, the new prime minister of the Slovak state, Štefan Tiso, declared that the Slovak nation "will be able to rid itself of every enemy of the state that has threatened the state and continues to threaten it politically, biologically, and morally. Therefore the government will begin to thoroughly solve the Jewish question, and similarly the Czech question will be solved in Slovakia."[16] Jews were regularly cast as loyal supporters of the Czechoslovak state and charged with "Czechoslovakism," a powerful slur in the new republic.[17] At the same time, Jews were aware of the extent to which the Czechoslovak polity protected them from antisemitic extremists. A. Frischer, president of the Jewish Party in Czechoslovakia, said in 1938 that "Czechoslovak Jewry must realize that it stands or falls together with the Czechoslovak republic."[18]

The Slovak leadership sought simultaneously to eliminate what it saw as Czech and Jewish power and influence over Slovak economic, political, and cultural life, often arguing that the one problem was inextricably tied to the other.[19] Antisemites also sought to explain persecution of the Jews in terms they believed the Slovak public would understand, namely as an extension of the Czech and Hungarian problem. To make clear to Slovaks the "correct" way to approach the Jewish question, an article in *Gardista* from April 1943 quoted Slovak interior minister Alexander Mach: "A Czech is a Czech, whether he is a Catholic, whether he leaves the church or returns to it. And I do not recall anyone in our country defending a Czech that had been deported from Slovakia with the argument that the Czech was no longer a Czech because he is a Christian."[20]

This explanation was offered to counter what many saw as the Slovak public's—and even the Slovak bureaucracy's—failure to understand the Jewish question in racial terms and its unwillingness to see Slovaks as a racially distinct "nation."[21] Although bureaucrats and state officials appear to have been confident in deciding who was Hungarian and Czech, they were far less consistent in assigning Jewish national identity to individuals of the Jewish faith.[22] Indeed, this hesitation seemed to represent a more or less serious challenge to the new leadership. A report on the "Jewish Question in Slovakia" prepared by the Security Service (Sicherheitsdienst, or SD) of the SS declared in August 1942 that "one fact is fundamental to the conceptualization of the Jewish question in Slovakia: it is not seen from the perspective of race." The report later commented on a speech by President Jozef Tiso in Holic, in which the Slovak president "himself advocated the deportation of the Jews. He explained that Slovakia must be rid of this troublesome element and would go about handling the Jewish problem just as categorically as it had proceeded in the fight against Prague and the Czechs."[23]

A further indicator that the Slovak leadership could not isolate the "Jewish question" from other nationality issues was the nature of the process of "Aryanization" of Jewish property and businesses in Slovakia. Shortly after it was initiated, the German ambassador to Slovakia, H. Bernard, complained that Aryanization was being undertaken as Slovakization, targeting all non-Slovak elements, not merely Jews.[24] And indeed, an article in *Gardista* on January 26, 1944, explained that "the autonomist program has taken as its goal the demand for the return of political power and national property, which has been in foreign hands, to Slovak hands." The article went on to say that "in order for Slovaks to be masters of their own home," they must remove Czechs from official positions, trade, and industry, and eliminate Jews' influence on the economy.[25] Similarly, the Slovak ambassador to Berlin, Matúš Černák, admitted to Germany's assistant secretary at the Foreign Office, Ernst Woermann, in November 1941 that recent "anti-Hungarian excesses," despite being provoked by the presence of Hungarian-speaking Jews, "beyond that had an anti-Hungarian character and thus the events cannot be viewed solely from the perspective of the Jewish question."[26] During that same month, Slovak foreign minister Vojtech Tuka told the foreign minister in Berlin that "the people in Slovakia were prejudiced against the Hungarians, and this fact could not simply be set aside with logical reasons."[27]

The Slovak Right's nervousness about the failure of many Slovaks to see the Jewish problem in racial terms was coupled with the sense that many Slovaks felt Hungarians were the main cause of everything bad that happened in Slovakia, including persecution of the Jews. When the Jews were being deported from Hungary through Slovakia in June 1944, a group of Slovak civilians witnessed a scene in which an SS man shot a Jew for throwing torn-up money out of the train. A newspaper saleswoman was said to have declared that the SS man was "no German, but a Hungarian. He may have been wearing a German uniform, but his heart was Hungarian."[28] A subversive publication circulated in Slovakia in early 1942 went so far as to suggest that the Slovaks were fighting the wrong enemy. Its authors, members of the "national guard" organized to resist German influence, argued that "our greatest enemies are our leaders, Germans and Hungarians who stole our freedom and our land!"[29] The guard called for all Slavs to unite against these common enemies. President Tiso had already sought to assure Hitler in July 1940 that "the leaflets circulated in Slovakia that advocated such a [pan-Slavic] policy . . . were machinations of Jews, Magyars, and Czechs designed to blacken Slovakia in the eyes of Germany."[30] Nevertheless, Hungarian regent Miklós Horthy did not miss the opportunity to interpret this kind of agitation to Hitler as evidence that the Slovaks held secret pan-Slavic sympathies and were hostile to German interests.[31]

This kind of condemnation of the other state's policies and practices as being incommensurate with or expressly damaging to Reich interests was a key part of the territorial contest. Both Hungarian and Slovak leaders sought to discredit the other country in Hitler's eyes, believing that Hitler's sympathy was the only way to achieve another shift in state boundaries. Their criticisms often took the form of charges of disloyalty to the Reich and delinquency in the implementation or enforcement of anti-Jewish measures. During a meeting with

Germany's secretary of the Foreign Office, Ernst von Weizsäcker, Slovak ambassador Matúš Černák complained that "there exist in Hungary noteworthy efforts against the policy of the Tripartite Pact."[32] The ambassador went on to express the suspicion that Hungary was making a less-than-substantial military commitment to the effort to fight Bolshevism, perhaps because it was holding back troops "in order to violently achieve its revisionist ambitions in the last hour." During a meeting with Hitler, when Regent Horthy rejected the idea that Hungary could take further measures against the Jews, the Hungarian leader was told that "Hungary could put the Jews in concentration camps just as the Slovaks had done."[33] Later in the conversation Horthy voiced the concern that "Hungary is no longer the 'favored child' of Germany," complaining that Hungarians "were subject to uninterrupted assaults from the Romanians and the Slovaks and had to stand by with their fists in their pockets without speaking out."[34]

Among such "assaults" were newspaper articles and radio broadcasts condemning Hungary for being pro-Jewish. One article from April 1939 spoke of the "Asiatic" Magyars and Jews who banded together to torture and humiliate Slovaks.[35] The same paper had published an article in January condemning Hungarian members of parliament for not wanting to vote for the anti-Jewish laws.[36] In December 1942, a Slovak diplomat reported that Reich officials were pleased that the "solution of the Jewish question" was proceeding in Slovakia, Croatia, and Romania but were angered by the fact that Hungary did not seem to recognize the need to act on the issue.[37]

Accusations and complaints of this type were regularly coupled with appeals to Hitler and other Nazi diplomats and officials for a revision of the boundaries and with expressions of paranoia that the Germans secretly favored the other side.[38] Despite Hitler's repeated admonitions that the revision of territorial settlements would have to wait until the end of the war, various members of the Slovak leadership made renewed appeals for territorial compensation.[39] The German stance aroused fear "that final decisions were being taken . . . regarding the frontiers in southeastern Europe . . . without Slovakia having an opportunity to state her wishes."[40] Hungarian leaders were also fearful that the Germans were helping Hungary's neighbors form an alliance—on the model of the Little Entente (of Czechoslovakia, Romania, and Yugoslavia)—to undermine Hungarian revisionist achievements and aspirations.[41]

The Hungarian state leadership's preoccupation with the retention and further acquisition of territory from Slovakia and Romania
in particular had a strong influence on the country's policy vis-à-vis
its Jewish population. Like Slovakia, Hungary also had difficulties
racializing Hungarian Jewish identity, because many in the Hungarian leadership understood how important the Hungarian-speaking
and -feeling Jews were to demonstrating the validity of Hungary's
claims on territory in neighboring states. In fact, for the 1941 Hungarian census, Jews did not have to declare themselves Jews by nationality, only Jews by religion. This option cleared the way for them to
declare themselves Hungarian by nationality—the most reasonable
choice for many, particularly since many of them spoke Hungarian and
identified with Hungarian culture—which helped the Hungarian state
to bolster its showing of Hungarians vis-à-vis other nationalities in the
newly annexed territories.[42] Furthermore, Hungary's regent, Miklós
Horthy, argued against the extreme solutions to the Jewish question
propounded by Hungarian right-wing radicals, saying that "we need
[the Jews] . . . they are tied to us by mutual interest."[43]

Efforts to racialize the Jewish question and initiate a radical solution were often accompanied by a combined policy of persecution
and national conversion of other minorities as well. Just as the Slovaks
targeted the Czechs and Hungarians, the Hungarian administration
targeted Slovaks, Romanians, and Serbs.[44] The commander in chief of
Hungary's armed forces went so far as to propose the forcible deportation of the country's entire Slovak, Romanian, and Serb population, a
proposal that would have meant the expulsion of around eight million
people.[45] Recently historians have begun to explore the links between
Hungary's Jewish policy and its resettlement plans for other national
minorities during World War II.[46] It is becoming increasingly clear
that it is impossible to consider the "Jewish question" in isolation
from the broader nationalities and territorial questions in states like
Hungary, Slovakia, and Romania.

Another area in which the contest for territory played an important role was in the deportation of Jews from the territory of Slovakia
and Hungary. Both countries were aware that their treatment of the
Jews and other minorities was being closely watched not only by the
Germans but also by the other state's leadership and even by the other
state's population, more generally speaking. It can be argued that the
expulsion of the Jews following the Vienna Arbitration was viewed

by some Slovaks as a means of exacting revenge for Jews' loyalty to Magyardom. Similarly, when domestic and German pressure to deport the Jews mounted in Slovakia in the spring of 1942, a law was drafted authorizing the government to go through with the deportations and confiscate the property of the deported Jews. Although the law was approved by the Slovak parliament on May 15, one of the individuals who refused to endorse it was János Eszterházy, the representative of the Hungarian minority in Slovakia and a member of the Slovak parliament. The press of the time took advantage of the opportunity to associate the Hungarian Eszterházy with Jewish interests, condemning both by association.[47]

Yet it was not only the decision to deport Jews that was understood by many in the Slovak leadership as a move against revisionist Hungary. The decision to stop the deportations from Slovakia—which came in October 1942—was also influenced by a shift in the domestic power hierarchy to favor the "moderates," a shift that had resulted from a propaganda campaign associating the radicals with Hungarian interests. By that time, some in the Slovak leadership were aware that "such a solution of the Jewish question cannot serve the Slovak nation in the world."[48] Furthermore, there was an intensifying power struggle between the Slovak "radicals," Vojtech Tuka and Alexander Mach, and the supposedly more "moderate" President Tiso. Hence, when an "old brother-in-arms of Tuka," Slovakia's military attaché to Rome, Lieutenant Colonel Viktor Snaczky, defected to Hungary in March 1942, "Tuka's opponents [used] the defection of Snaczky to the Hungarian camp in their campaign against Tuka." Woermann of the German Foreign Office observed that although "Tuka still managed to push through laws commensurate with the spirit of the times, such as the Jewish laws, for example, the Tiso-friendly majority in the cabinet nonetheless consistently manages—through skilled maneuvering—to upset Tuka's plans in practice."[49] In mid-April the German ambassador in Bratislava, Hans Elard Ludin, observed that Tiso "has—in a very skilled and Jesuit manner, used the fears [regarding Tuka's Hungarian sympathies] against Tuka."[50] While it is almost certain that the Snaczky affair was not the sole reason why the deportations were stopped, the political fallout of the affair highlights the ways in which Slovak politicians mobilized anti-Hungarian sentiment to justify their policy vis-à-vis the Jews, no matter what that policy was.[51]

Although the deportations of Jews from Hungary took place while the country was under German occupation in the spring and early summer of 1944, in the Hungarian case, too, territorial concerns had some bearing on the way in which the deportations were carried out and how they came to be halted at the outskirts of Budapest. First, it is worth noting that the Jews from the reannexed territories of Transylvania and the Felvidék were among the first to be deported.[52] Among members of the Hungarian leadership, including Horthy, there were many individuals who felt that the Jews of these areas had been disloyal to the cause of Magyardom by identifying themselves increasingly with the dominant national group and seeking to reap the benefits of state enfranchisement—however meager—that were afforded to them by the successor states.[53] Furthermore, just as the Jews were being ghettoized in these regions, Romania and Slovakia—the two countries with the largest stake in the future of Hungarian territory—not only had ceased much of the persecution of their Jewish populations but also had begun to take an interest in the fate of Jews living in Hungary. In the Romanian case, this was more or less overt politicking to protect Romanian interests at a future peace settlement, saving face with the soon-to-be-victorious Allies by "saving" Jews from Nazi death camps.

The Slovak case was somewhat more complicated. Slovak officials voiced concern for the fate of Jews with Slovak passports. This gave rise to suspicions among the Hungarian leadership that Slovakia, like Romania, was taking in Jewish refugees from Hungary by the thousands in order to sabotage the Hungarian action.[54] A report on the progress of the deportations in Hungary by SS Brigadier General Edmund Veesenmayer from early July 1944 reveals that it was this seeming change in the policy of Romania and Slovakia vis-à-vis the Jews that frightened Horthy and Hungary's then prime minister, Döme Sztójay, into halting the deportation of Jews from Hungary. Sztójay outlined the reasons why the Hungarian government had decided to stop the deportations. First, the Hungarian government had discovered that "in Romania no particular measures were being taken against the Jews there." The second, related reason was that Slovakia had also begun to protect its remaining Jewish population.[55] That the Hungarian government was following so closely the policies of these two countries in particular with regard to the Jewish question is a further indication of the inexorable links between territorial concerns and treatment of the Jews.[56]

At the end of the war, the Vatican complained to the Slovak administration about its treatment of the Jews. In response, Slovakia's ambassador to the Vatican, Karol Sidor, argued that Slovakia had been a haven for Jews compared to Hungary.[57]

POSTSCRIPT: THE BATTLE CONTINUES

When the Czechoslovak state was revived after the war, it included the territories Hungary had annexed during the war. The new Czechoslovak leadership blamed the Hungarians and the Germans for the destruction of Czechoslovakia and made plans to expel them from the country. In the end, several thousand people were expelled from the territories reacquired from Hungary, while others were resettled in the Czech lands in areas left vacant following the expulsion of the Sudeten Germans.[58]

When the Slovaks regained independence after the collapse of Communism and the dissolution of the Czechoslovak state in 1993, one of the first topics Slovak historians tackled was the examination of the last episode of Slovak independence during World War II. Some of the new Slovak historiography has taken as its mission the rehabilitation of figures like Slovak president Jozef Tiso and glorification of the Republic of Slovakia as a positive precedent for Slovak statehood. These historians note the renewed interest in Horthy and the Czech Protectorate's Emil Hacha and wonder why Slovaks are not allowed to glorify Tiso. In the words of one Slovak scholar:

> No one today faults the Hungarians that Hungary and its leader Miklós Horthy worked in close collaboration with the Nazi German Reich and turned 600,000 Jews over to the Germans to be sent to the gas chamber, among whom were 40,000 Jews from Slovakia, who inhabited the territory of Slovakia that Hungarians wrested from Slovakia in 1938 and annexed to Hungary. And Hungary has already rehabilitated Miklós Horthy and no one protested against it, not even the JEWS! And President Dr. Emil Hacha, who voluntarily signed onto Hitler's Protectorate of Bohemia and Moravia and turned 120,000 Jews over to the Germans, has also been rehabilitated as of 1 July 1995. After 50 years, Czechs

want to forget everything bad that their president did [and] have
forgiven him and put a memorial plaque up on the house where
he was born.[59]

There have been other efforts to compare Slovakia's wartime Jewish policy favorably with Hungary's. It is a common trope in such
works to implicate the Jews themselves as supporters of Hungary
who sealed their own fate by advocating Hungarian revisionism. In
an interview with "historian František Vnuk" printed in the Slovak
periodical *Koridor* in 1992, we read that

> from Hungary they deported Jews to the East already in the sum-
> mer of 1941, that is, before the promulgation of the Jewish Co-
> dex in our country and almost a year before deportations started
> from Slovakia. The first mass liquidation of Jews took place near
> the Ukrainian city of Kamenec Podolsk in the summer of 1941.
> Among the thousands of Jews massacred, the largest group was
> made up of Jews from Sub-Carpathian Ukraine and from the ter-
> ritory that Slovakia had to cede to Hungary with the Vienna Arbi-
> tration. . . . At a time when we [Slovaks] were afraid we would lose
> [Slovak areas to Hungary], the Jews of Bratislava sent a delegation
> to the Hungarian consulate requesting that Bratislava be annexed
> to Hungary. Should such actions inspire gratitude and friendship
> among Slovaks? Yet despite this, SLOVAKS protected Jews.[60]

This kind of finger-pointing, argues historian István Deák, has re-
sulted in the "conviction shared by the entire political center-right [in
Hungary], that Hungarian participation in and responsibility for the
Holocaust has been exaggerated by the country's hostile neighbors."[61]
In the words of Kalman Janics, "Hungary may have been, as charged,
Hitler's 'last satellite,' but fascist Slovakia under Jozef Tiso's presi-
dency was Hitler's first satellite. Slovakia joined in the war against Poland and preceded Hungary in participating in the Nazi 'final solution'
of the Jews. In general, Slovakia's record in repressing fundamental
freedoms certainly was worse than Hungary's." Janics goes on to say
that "Slovaks often made life miserable for the small community of
Hungarians left in Slovakia after the Vienna Arbitration of 1938,
denouncing them as enemies of National Socialism."[62]

Nor is Janics's analysis the only instance of Hungary's "hostile
neighbors," specifically Slovakia and Romania, being charged with
committing crimes against the Hungarian minority and of the link-

ing of such charges to discussions of the Holocaust in this region. In 1990 Hungarian commentator Rezső Döndő complained about the excess of "propaganda" surrounding Holocaust commemoration in Hungary:

> The Jewish Holocaust is an essential part—but only a part—of the Hungarian holocaust, of the Hungarian genocide. To us, who live in this country, the Holocaust of six to seven hundred thousand Jews is also painful, *but so is the planned genocide of three million Hungarians.* The fact is that the Jewish Holocaust has been repeatedly mentioned since the 1970s. But the fact that for decades there has been a constant elimination of Magyardom—not just fifty years ago, but today, as well!—has received not a word in the mass media.[63]

The "holocaust" to which Döndő refers in his article is the plight of the Hungarian minorities in Romania, (Czecho)Slovakia, and Serbia (Yugoslavia). Döndő goes on to express the hope that "the tragic Jewish holocaust of fifty years ago should not overshadow the problems of the Hungarian genocide that is still under way."

In 1999 Tamás Lang, president of the Jewish community of Érsekújvár/Nové Zamký (in the territory ceded to Hungary with the First Vienna Arbitration), delivered a speech at the dedication of the plaques commemorating the victims of the Holocaust and the labor battalions. He said that "the Jews of Slovakia and Hungary share a common and inseparable fate. They have common historical roots in a centuries-long cultural heritage. They are unseparated and inseparable in the realization of their shared fate."[64]

This statement was most likely an effort to forge a bond of solidarity between Hungarian and Slovak Jewry, but it is also indicative of the historical inextricability of the "Jewish questions" in Hungary and Slovakia. When considering in light of the Jewish question the case of the territorial contest between the Republic of Slovakia and Hungary on the one hand and the troubled relationship between Czechs and Slovaks on the other, we can see how both foreign and domestic policies in this region were tied to revisionist concerns. Thus, the implementation of policy initiatives affecting the Jews, Hungarians, Slovaks, and Czechs was viewed by the two states' leaderships as affecting foreign policy considerations, relations with the Axis, and chances for future territorial gain.

A related observation is that the fate of the Jews was tied up with the goals of the two state administrations and was, as a result, also to some extent determined by revisionist activism on the part of Slovakia and Hungary. Both states' leaderships lobbied Hitler and the Nazi administration for revision and took turns demonizing the other state in order to gain the favor of the powerful German leader. Furthermore, once the tide of war had shifted to favor the Allies, leaders in both Hungary and Slovakia expressed wariness about undertaking anti-Jewish measures and became especially watchful of how the other state was treating its Jews. Finally, this analysis demonstrates how policy and attitudes toward Jews in these two countries was influenced by policy and attitudes toward other minorities and vice versa. Together these observations gleaned from a more regional approach to study of the Holocaust give us a clearer and more complete picture of how states understood the "solution to the Jewish problem" and what other initiatives and aspirations sped along or slowed its implementation.

NOTES

The chapter epigraph is from Gabriel Hoffmann et al., *Zamlčaná Pravda o Slovensku: Prvá Slovenská republika, Prvý slovenský president Dr. Jozef Tiso, Tragédia slovenských židov podľa nových dokumentov* (Radošina: Garmond, 1996), 548. I would like to thank the library and archive staff of the United States Holocaust Memorial Museum, Cornell University's Institute for European Studies, and the Department of History at Cornell for their kindness and support, both morally and financially, and especially James Ward of Stanford University for his insightful comments and suggestions, and Martina Podsklanová for checking my translations from Slovak. All translations are the author's unless otherwise noted.

1. An agreement was reached on April 4, 1939, according to which Hungary obtained an additional 396 square kilometers of Slovak territory with a population of forty-one thousand. Dušan Škvarna et al., *Slovak History: Chronology and Lexicon* (Wauconda, Ill.: Bolchazy-Carducci, 2002), 140.

2. Holly Case, "The Holocaust and the Transylvanian Question in the 20th Century," in *The Holocaust in Hungary: Sixty Years Later,* ed. Randolph L. Braham and Brewster S. Chamberlin (New York: Columbia University Press, 2006).

3. On the region called here Carpatho-Ukraine, see Yeshayahu A. Jelinek, *Carpathian Diaspora: The Jews of Subcarpathian Rus' and Mukachevo* (New York: Columbia University Press, 2008).

4. See Gergely Sallai, *Az első bécsi döntés* (Budapest: Osiris Kiadó, 2002), 146n. See also Ladislav Lipscher, *Die Juden im Slowakischen Staat, 1939–1945* (Munich and Vienna: R. Oldenbourg, 1980), 17n. These figures do not include the so-called Kárpatálja (Carpatho-Ukraine), which was added later. There was conflict during the negotiations regarding which census should be used to determine the national feeling of the population: the Hungarians argued for the 1910 Hungarian census, while the Czechoslovak representatives used their own 1930 census figures. In Macartney, the numbers are given as follows: "540,000 indisputable Magyars, 120,000 indisputable Slovaks, 100,000 persons of disputable nationality (bilinguals, etc.), 52,000 Jews (most of them Magyar-speaking and feeling), 9,000 Germans and 27,000 others." See C. A. Macartney, *October Fifteenth: A History of Hungary, 1929–1945* (New York: Frederick A. Praeger, 1957), pt. 1, p. 302. The question of how many Jews declared themselves to be of a nationality other than "Jewish" can be answered for the whole of Slovakia according to the 1930 Czechoslovak census as follows: 136,737 declared themselves Jews by religion, and of those about 32 percent declared themselves Czech or Slovak by nationality, 7 percent as German, 7 percent as Hungarian, and 53 percent as Jewish (Lipscher, *Juden im Slowakischen Staat*, 13n).

5. Anton Štefánek, *Základy sociografie Slovenska* (Bratislava: Slovenská Vlastiveda, 1944), 179–80. It should be noted that this data, based primarily on the 1940 Slovak census, is unreliable in many respects because some of the numbers were pieced together using statistical information from earlier censuses. The figure given for Slovaks includes both Slovaks and Czechs (with Czechs comprising around 3 percent of that figure). Also, there were, of course, disincentives to declaring oneself Jewish by nationality, hence the relatively low figures for Jews by nationality as compared to those for Jews by religion.

6. Lipscher, *Juden im Slowakischen Staat*, 18.

7. "Hlásenie policajného prezidenta v Bratislave J. Juska o promaďarskej židovskej demonštrácii v Bratislave 1.11.1938," in *Holokaust na Slovensku, Obdobie autonómie, 6.10.1938–14.3.1939, Dokumenty*, ed. Eduard Nižňanský (Bratislava: Židovská náboženská obec Bratislava, 2001), doc. 108, pp. 226–27. Indeed, throughout the war Jews were accused by Slovak government officials and the press of being "instruments of Magyarization" or "spies" for Hungary. See, for example, two documents from 1944 in Slovenské Národné Múzeum, Múzeum Židovskej Kultúry, *Riešenie židovskej otázky na Slovensku, 1943–1945, Dokumenty*, part 3 (Bratislava: Edícia Judaica Slovaca, 1994), doc. 293, 299, pp. 88, 100.

8. Nižňanský, *Holokaust na Slovensku: Obdobie autonómie*, p. 328. See also Eduard Nižňanský, *Židovská komunita na Slovensku medzi československou*

parlamentnou demokraciou a slovenským štátom v stredoeurópskom kontexte (Prešov: Universum, 1999), 96–97, 100.

9. Eventually the Slovak leadership agreed to admit Jews who had residency on Slovak territory. Archives of the United States Holocaust Memorial Museum (hereafter referred to as USHMM), RG-48.003*01, Slovak State Archives records, 1938–1947, microfiche 1 of 14, 1938/3, no. 3.

10. In Lipscher, *Juden im Slowakischen Staat,* 17–18n.

11. Through Axis arbitration, the so-called Second Vienna Arbitration gave northern Transylvania back to Hungary on August 30, 1940. Southern Transylvania remained under Romanian state control. Throughout the war both Axis allies were dissatisfied with the half-and-half arrangement and lobbied the German leadership for a revision of the agreement.

12. Nižňanský, *Židovská komunita,* 219. Hungary gained territory from Czechoslovakia in 1938 (southern Slovakia) and 1939 (Carpatho-Ukraine); from Romania in 1940 (northern Transylvania); and from Yugoslavia in 1941 (Banat).

13. Macartney, *October Fifteenth,* pt. 1, 308n.

14. Ivan Derer, *The Unity of the Czechs and the Slovaks: Has the Pittsburgh Declaration Been Carried Out?* (Prague: "Orbis," 1938), 74–78. See also Ivan Derer, "The Autonomous Movement in Slovakia, 1938," Internet Modern History Sourcebook, at http://www.fordham.edu/halsall/mod/1838slovakia1.html (accessed September 12, 2005).

15. It is tempting to make a comparison with Croatia in the interwar Kingdom of Yugoslavia here, and indeed this comparison resonated with Croats and Slovaks of the time. In fact, Croat statesmen approached the Slovak leadership in Bratislava in the fall of 1943, saying that "the [Slovak] experience with the Czechs appealed to them, for their position in Yugoslavia was comparable to that of the Slovaks when Czechoslovakia existed." The Germans advised the Slovaks not to respond to these approaches. *Documents on German Foreign Policy, 1918–1945,* Series D (1937–1945), vol. 11, *The War Years, Sept. 1, 1940–January 31, 1941* (Washington, D.C.: Government Printing Office, 1949–), doc. 393, p. 694.

16. "4. októbra 1944, Bratislava. Z vystúpenia predsedu vlády dr. Štefana Tisu v sneme, časť týkajúca sa riešenia židovskej otázky," in Slovenské Národné Múzeum, *Riešenie židovskej otázky,* part 3, doc. 334, p. 154.

17. On March 3, 1940, an article appeared in *Slovák* regarding the implementation of legislation restricting Jewish business. The author offered a short synopsis of Jewish history in Slovakia with the goal of demonstrating how Jews had always left Slovaks in the lurch by serving "foreign" (specifically Hungarian and Czechoslovak) interests. The interwar state of Czechoslovakia was described as "an El Dorado for Jews." *Slovák* 52, March 3, 1940, in Slovenské Národné Múzeum, *Riešenie židovskej otázky,* part 4,

doc. 27, pp. 83–84. Indeed, more generally speaking, "Czechoslovakism" was more or less criminalized in independent Slovakia. A series of reports prepared by members of the Slovak military (1940–41) describe individuals with "Czechoslovak" sympathies as particularly treacherous. USHMM, RG-57.002M, selected records of the Slovak armed forces during World War II, 1914–1971, roll 2, Ministry of the Interior, 1939–1944, inventory no. 744–II/4, box 2, year 1940, pp. 25–26, 29–30, 67. See also roll 7, Veliteľstva Pozemného Vojska, inventory no. 18, box 3, year 1941.

18. Quoted in Nižňanský, *Židovská komunita*, 18.

19. See Viera Kováčová, "Analýza dobovej tlače v období procesu s Dr. Jozefom Tisom," in *Acta Judaica Slovaca* 4 (1998): 53–54.

20. "Úvodník *Gardistu* žiadajúci doriešiť židovskú otázku do dôsledkov," *Gardista* 86, April 13, 1943, in Slovenské Národné Múzeum, *Riešenie židovskej otázky,* part 3, doc. 261, p. 27.

21. The Slovak populist Štefan Polakovič argued that Slovaks were racially distinct from Czechs and Hungarians. See Pavol Mešťan, *Anti-Semitism in Slovak Politics, 2000–2002* ([Bratislava?]: SNM-Museum of Jewish Culture, 2004), 88. In 1943 Polakovič wrote, "The Slovak nation is not part of the Hungarian nation, nor a branch of some Czechoslovak nation, but exists of its own" (Štefan Polakovič, "Slovak Populism, 1943," at http://www2.tltc .ttu.edu/kelly/Archive/New/hsls.html).

22. See USHMM, RG-57.001, Slovak documents related to the Holocaust, 1939–1945, roll 285, Ministry of the Interior, box 20, files 78, 82, 86–88, 109–10, 113–14, 134; box 21, file 6. This collection includes background information on a number of individuals interned in camps (covering the period from 1941 to 1944). The forms include blanks for the official to enter "religion" and "nationality." Whereas some officials entered the nationality of individuals of the Jewish faith as "Jewish," others used "Slovak." In one instance different officials gave a different nationality for the same person; see the file for "Davidovič Juraj" in box 20, file 86–87.

23. In Eduard Nižňanský, ed., *Holokaust na Slovensku,* vol. 4, *Dokumenty nemeckej proveniencie, 1939–1945* (Bratislava: Židovská náboženská obec Bratislava, 2003), 158, 183–84.

24. Nižňanský, *Holokaust na Slovensku,* vol. 4, *Dokumenty nemeckej proveniencie,* 294. Also, from the Slovak perspective "Aryanization" was interpreted to mean clearing non-Slovaks out of business, trade, and industry. One author complained in *Gardista* in January 1941 that despite legislation, Jewish and Czech employers had not been replaced by Slovaks, which the author dubbed a failure of "Aryanization." *Gardista* 13, January 17, 1941, in Slovenské Národné Múzeum, *Riešenie židovskej otázky,* part 4, doc. 45, p. 136.

25. "26. januára 1944, Bratislava. Pripomienky Združenia štátnych a

verejných zamestnancov k vyhláške ÚHÚ o odpredaji bývalých židovských domov," *Gardista* 20, January 26, 1944, in Slovenské Národné Múzeum, *Riešenie židovskej otázky,* part 3, doc. 287, p. 62.

26. "Woermann 15.11.1941 Zahraničnému úradu o stretnutí so slovenským vyslancom M. Černákom, ktorý hovoril aj o promaďarskom správaní sa Židov na Slovensku," in Nižňanský, *Holokaust na Slovensku,* vol. 4, *Dokumenty nemeckej proveniencie,* doc. 24, p. 108.

27. "Memorandum by the Dirigent of the Political Department," in *Documents on German Foreign Policy, 1918–1945,* Series D (1937–1945), vol. 13, *The War Years, June 23–December 11, 1941* (Washington, D.C.: Government Printing Office, 1949–), doc. 500, p. 825.

28. "H. E. Ludin 23.6.1944 Zahraničnému úradu o transportoch Židov z Maďarska cez Slovensko," in Nižňanský, *Holokaust na Slovensku,* vol. 4, *Dokumenty nemeckej proveniencie,* doc. 91, p. 254.

29. In USHMM, RG-57.002M, selected records of the Slovak armed forces during World War II, 1914–1971, roll 7, inventory no. 19, box 3, year 1942.

30. "Conversation Between the Führer and Slovak President Tiso in the Presence of the Reich Foreign Minister, Slovak Minister President and Foreign Minister Tuka, Minister of the Interior Mach, and Minister v. Killinger, Berghof, July 28, 1940," in *Documents on German Foreign Policy, 1918–1945,* Series D (1937–1945), vol. 10, *The War Years, June 23–August 31, 1940* (Washington, D.C.: Government Printing Office, 1949–), doc. 248, p. 348.

31. See Horthy's letter to Hitler from January 15, 1942. "A large proportion of Slovakdom still seeks and hopes for its salvation from what can be called 'the ideology of Beneš.' In Slovakia, too, where the pan-Slavic movement was founded through the literary activity of Jan Kollar and from whence it spread, there are many who barely conceal their deep sympathy for Slavdom, which in our time is practically identical to Bolshevism." *Akten zur Deutschen Auswärtigen Politik, 1918–1945,* Series E: 1941–1945, vol. 1, *12. Dezember 1941 bis 28. Februar 1942* (Göttingen: Vandenhoeck and Ruprecht, 1969), doc. 130, pp. 236–37.

32. "Aufzeichnung des Staatssekretärs des Auswärtigen Amts Freiherr von Weizsäcker," in *Akten zur Deutschen Auswärtigen Politik, 1918–1945,* Series E: 1941–1945, vol. 3 (Göttingen: Vandenhoeck und Ruprecht, 1974), doc. 31, p. 55.

33. "Aufzeichnung des Gesandten I. Klasse Schmidt, 18. April 1943," in *Akten zur Deutschen Auswärtigen Politik, 1918–1945,* Series E: 1941–1945, vol. 5, *1. Januar bis 30. April 1943* (Göttingen: Vandenhoeck and Ruprecht, 1978), doc. 315, pp. 631–32.

34. Ibid., 636.

35. *Národnie Noviny,* April 19, 1939, in Magyar Országos Levéltár (Hungarian State Archives; hereafter referred to as MOL), K66, Külügyminisztérium (Ministry of Foreign Affairs), Sajtó és Kulturális Osztály (Press and Cultural Department), vol. 397, item I-5/a.-2., p. 85. This article was brought to the attention of the Germans when the Hungarian administration cited it as part of a complaint regarding the incendiary anti-Hungarian nature of the Slovak press.

36. *Národnie Noviny,* January 25, 1939, in MOL, K66, Külügyminisztérium, Sajtó és Kulturális Osztály, vol. 397, item I-5/a.-2., p. 75.

37. Slovenské Národné Múzeum, Múzeum Židovskej Kultúry, *Riešenie židovskej otázky na Slovensku (1939–1945), Dokumenty,* part 2 (Edícia Judaica Slovaca: Bratislava, 1994), doc. 252, pp. 175–76.

38. One example is an episode in which the Culture and Press Division of the Hungarian Foreign Ministry found out that German newspapers were publishing articles on the plight of the Slovaks in the territories reannexed by Hungary. The Hungarians discovered this from an article in the Slovak press boasting that the Slovak cause had been taken up in Germany. MOL, K66, Külügyminisztérium, Sajtó és Kulturális Osztály, vol. 397, item I-5/a.-2., pp. 117–24. In fact, the Hungarian Culture and Press Division regularly prepared reports in German describing Slovak breaches of the "press peace" that was supposed to exist between Hungary and Slovakia (ibid., 58–86).

39. In July 1940, Tiso spoke to Hitler about the "400,000 Slovaks living under Hungarian rule." See *Documents on German Foreign Policy, 1918–1945,* Series D (1937–1945), vol. 10, *The War Years, June 23–August 31, 1940,* doc. 248, p. 348. By April 1941, Tuka, Tiso, and Černák had all made appeals to the führer for revision of Slovakia's border with Hungary. See "The Foreign Minister to the Legation in Slovakia," in *Documents on German Foreign Policy, 1918–1945,* Series D (1937–1945), vol. 12, *The War Years, February 1–June 22, 1941* (Washington, D.C.: Government. Printing Office, 1949–), doc. 406, p. 640.

40. In April 1941, Tuka "pointed out" to the German special representative in charge of economic questions, Hermann Neubacher, that "the great territorial gains by the Hungarians made this a favorable moment for Slovak wishes which would have to be satisfied by Hungary. . . . With the aid of an ethnographic map, Tuka defended the justice of the Slovak demand for incorporation of Hungarian border areas settled by Slovaks." See "Memorandum by the Special Representative in Charge of Economic Questions," in *Documents on German Foreign Policy, 1918–1945,* Series D (1937–1945), vol. 12, *The War Years, February 1–June 22, 1941,* doc. 424, pp. 669–70.

41. See "Memorandum by the Dirigent of the Political Department," in *Documents on German Foreign Policy, 1918–1945,* Series D (1937–1945), vol. 13, *The War Years, June 23–December 11, 1941,* doc. 500, p. 825;

and "The Foreign Minister to the Legation in Slovakia," ibid., doc. 438, p. 723.

42. The Slovak right-wing press complained in March 1940 about "anti-Slovak" Jews: "Thanks to the fact that they were allowed into Slovak cities and villages, [the Jews] influenced nationality statistics in those places to the disadvantage of Slovak interests such that they helped numerous towns and communities to wind up on the other side of the border." *Slovák* 51, March 3, 1940, Slovenské Národné Múzeum, *Riešenie židovskej otázky,* part 4, doc. 29, p. 93.

43. From a letter to Hungary's minister president Pál Teleki, October 14, 1940. Miklós Nagybányai Horthy, *Horthy Miklós titkos iratai* (Budapest: Kossuth Könyvkiadó, 1972), 261. We should nonetheless be careful not to read such statements as expressions of true national-ethnic solidarity between Jews and Hungarians. The fact that Jews were allowed to declare themselves Hungarian by nationality on the census did not mean the Jews of the reannexed territories could escape persecution under the anti-Jewish laws. In fact, one could argue that, in a number of ways, these Jews were treated differently from—and arguably more harshly than—the Jews of Trianon Hungary. For one thing, they were considered traitors of the state who had "sold out" to the leaders and dominant nationalities of Hungary's successor states during the interwar period. (Horthy, *Horthy Miklós titkos iratai,* 221–22)

44. It is worth noting that the January 1942 massacre in Újvidék/Novi Sad (territory Hungary had recovered from Yugoslavia in 1941), carried out by Hungarian military personnel, targeted both Jews and Serbs. Furthermore, in some respects the treatment of national minorities in contested territories (like Transylvania, southern Slovakia, Bessarabia, Vojvodina, Volhynia, and Bukovina) often mirrored treatment of Jews. Although non-Jewish minorities' official legal status was different—and indeed much better—than that of the Jews, practically speaking, minorities often had similar difficulties obtaining or keeping jobs or property and receiving trade licenses or passports, and although in some places they were assigned to labor service battalions rather than serving in the regular army, they became the targets of violence, deportations, and even mass killings. (This was true to varying degrees of the Hungarians in Romania and Slovakia, the Romanians and Slovaks in Hungary, the Ukrainians in Romania, and the Serbs in Croatia.)

45. See Horthy, *Horthy Miklós titkos iratai,* 306.

46. Krisztián Ungváry argues that "there are many reasons why it makes sense to consider the Holocaust and population transfers in tandem." See Ungváry, "Kitelepítés, lakosságcsere és a holokauszt egyes összefüggései," in *A holokauszt Magyarországon európai perspektívában,* ed. Judit Molnár (Budapest: Balassi Kiadó, 2005), 85.

47. From a report on "Die Judenfrage in der Slowakei" from the Sicherheitsdienst, August 1942, in Nižňanský, *Holokaust na Slovensku*, vol. 4, *Dokumenty nemeckej proveniencie*, doc. 64, p. 177. A similarly telling incident from 1943 highlights the Slovak leadership's tendency to conflate Hungarian with Jewish interests. A German situation report from August of that year relates the politicking of the Slovak Abwehr officer Podhorsky, who tried to discredit a member of the German administration in Slovakia by reporting (falsely, as it turned out) that the individual in question had asked a singer in a bar to sing Hungarian songs and had friendly contacts with Jews and secret friendships with Hungarians who spread "revisionist propaganda." USHMM, RG-57.002M, selected records of the Slovak armed forces during World War II, 1914–1971, roll 7, Slovakia Collection, inventory no. 1091, box 27, years 1938–1945, pp. 9–12.

48. "Výpovede Ing. Andreje Steinera pred žalobcom Národného súdu o prenasledovaní Židov za slovenského štátu, 1. apríla 1946," in Slovenské Národné Múzeum, *Riešenie židovskej otázky*, part 3, doc. 349, p. 184.

49. "Aufzeichnung des Unterstaatssekretärs Woermann, Berlin, 25. März 1942," in *Akten zur Deutschen Auswärtigen Politik, 1918–1945*, Series E: 1941–1945, vol. 3, doc. 75, pp. 128–29.

50. "Die Gestandte in Preßburg (Bratislava) Ludin an das Auswärtige Amt, 19. April 1942," ibid., doc. 154, pp. 255–56.

51. Hungarian historian János Pelle argues that "the position [on the Jewish question] taken by the Hungarian government may also have influenced the Slovak government which, after the deportation of two-thirds of the Slovakian Jews, had also stopped the transports in the fall of 1942." János Pelle, *Sowing the Seeds of Hatred: Anti-Jewish Laws and Hungarian Public Opinion, 1938–1944* (New York: East European Monographs, 2004), 209.

52. From "Extracts from the Sworn Affidavit by Dieter Wisliceny, Former Member of the *Sonderkommando* in Hungary," in *The Destruction of Hungarian Jewry: A Documentary Account*, ed. Randolph L. Braham (New York: Pro Arte, 1963), vol. 2, doc. 440, p. 927.

53. The Jews in the reannexed territories of Slovakia, for instance, were suspected of having "Czechoslovak" sympathies (Nižňanský, *Židovská komunita*, 223). Similarly, Horthy complained to Hitler that "the Transylvanian Jews . . . were all satisfied with the Romanian regime, because they all figured out soon enough how much bribe money was needed, how much will be won in the course of a transaction, and whether it is worth it to make the trip to Bucharest. Our administration has always been incorruptible" (Horthy, *Horthy Miklós titkos iratai*, 221–22).

54. Slovenské Národné Múzeum, *Riešenie židovskej otázky*, part 3, doc. 313, pp. 120–21.

55. Towiah Friedmann, ed., *Vor 50 Jahren 1944–1994: Das SS-Sonderkommando Eichmann in Budapest und die Vernichtung der Juden Ungarns-Rumäniens* (Haifa: Institute of Documentation in Israel for the Investigation of Nazi War Crimes, 1994), doc. 677, pp. 1–2.

56. There is some evidence to suggest that such considerations came into play in the Czech case as well. In January 1939, for example, Hitler pressured the Czech foreign minister, František Chvalkovský, to take action against the Jews. The foreign minister replied that the Czech leadership would prefer to wait and see how the matter was settled in other Central European countries first, specifically Hungary, and expressed enthusiasm for the Romanian initiative, which called for an "international solution" (Lipscher, *Juden im Slowakischen Staat*, 23).

57. See Slovenské Národné Múzeum, *Riešenie židovskej otázky*, part 3, doc. 346, pp. 166–67.

58. For more on the expulsions, see Benjamin Frommer, *National Cleansing: Retribution Against Nazi Collaborators in Postwar Czechoslovakia* (Cambridge, Eng., and New York: Cambridge University Press, 2005). See also *Erzwungene Trennung: Vertreibungen und Aussiedlungen in und aus der Tschechoslowakei, 1938–1947; Im Vergleich mit Polen, Ungarn und Jugoslawien*, ed. Detlef Brandes, Edita Ivanicková, and Jirí Pesek (Essen: Klartext, 1999); and Imre Molnár, *Hazahúzott a szülőföld: Visszaemlékezések, dokumentumok a szlovákiai magyarság Csehországba deportálásáról, 1945–1953* (Budapest: Püski, 1992).

59. See Hoffmann et al., *Zamlčaná Pravda*, 3–4.

60. *Koridor*, April 22, 1992, p. 3, reprinted in Hoffmann et al., *Zamlčaná Pravda*, 528–32.

61. István Deák, "Anti-Semitism and the Treatment of the Holocaust in Hungary," in *Anti-Semitism and the Treatment of the Holocaust in Postcommunist Eastern Europe*, ed. Randolph L. Braham (New York: Columbia University Press, 1994), 119.

62. Kalman Janics, "The Hungarians of Slovakia: From Czechoslovak to Slovak Rule," in *The Hungarians: A Divided Nation*, ed. Stephen Borsody (New Haven, Conn.: Yale Center for International and Area Studies, 1988), 162. Also available at http://www.hungarian-history.hu/lib/bors/bors17.htm.

63. Rezső Döndő, "Holocaust és genocídium" ["Holocaust and Genocide"], *Magyar Nemzet*, October 15, 1990, 6.

64. Cited in Sándor Strba and Tamás Lang, *Az érsekújvári zsidóság története* (Pozsony: Kalligram, 2004), 273.

IV. P·O·S·T·W·A·R

L·E·G·A·C·I·E·S

Ronald Smelser

The Myth of the Clean Wehrmacht in Cold War America

IN 1945 THERE WAS LITTLE DOUBT AS TO THE COMPLICITY OF THE German Wehrmacht in the crimes of the Nazi regime. Even though Allied attorneys could not define a collective entity such as the "German High Command" for indictment, two German generals, Alfred Jodl and Wilhelm Keitel, were among the top twenty-two war criminals tried at Nuremberg, and both were executed.[1] The United States also tried a number of German generals in the successor trials.[2] By the late 1940s and early 1950s, however, the Cold War was in full swing and the United States found itself in the position of viewing former allies as enemies and former enemies as allies. As a result, the United States lost much of the impetus and interest in pursuing former German military officers for war crimes.[3]

This reluctance was heightened after the establishment of the West German army (Bundeswehr), the vast majority of whose officers consisted of former Wehrmacht officers.[4] The Cold War climate allowed the Americans, with the eager help of the former German officers, to forget their verdict of 1945 and develop a new image and interpretation of the Wehrmacht as having fought a "clean" war in Russia, while the real crimes were being committed by the SS and police. This impression was vastly enhanced by the so-called Halder project (1949–59), in which hundreds of former German officers, under the direction of former army chief of staff Franz Halder, wrote more than 2,500 manuscripts for the U.S. Army, in which they conveyed to the Americans their version of the war in the East.[5]

But an American readiness to believe this myth of the clean Wehrmacht preceded the Halder project by a number of years. In fact, there were several highly placed Americans in the army and intelligence communities who were quite open to a revisionist view even as the war was winding down, thanks in part to prewar involvement with the German military. Hence, the myth of the clean Wehrmacht in American eyes began even as the war was ending.[6]

The founding document of the postwar mythology about the clean Wehrmacht is the so-called "Denkschrift der Generale" ("Memorandum of the Generals") or "Das deutsche Heer von 1920 bis 1945" ("The German Army from 1920 to 1945").[7] Composed, signed, and submitted on November 19, 1945, by five former top Wehrmacht commanders, the memorandum, designed as a defense document for the upcoming Nuremberg Trials, is a tissue of lies, half-truths, and omissions. The authors—Walther von Brauchitsch, Erich von Manstein, Franz Halder, Walter Warlimont, and Siegfried Westphal—were themselves deeply complicit in the crimes of the regime, but no one would have guessed that from the contents.

The document is a brief history of the German army from 1920 to the end of the war. Its major purpose was to distance that army as far as possible from the Nazi regime and thus to restore its dignity and self-respect. It sought to establish that the army was always against the Nazi Party and the SS, that the army disapproved of nearly all the important decisions Hitler made, and that the army had fought against the commission of war crimes. One could conclude from the document that the army commanders were free of all guilt and responsibility. Any actions in violation of international law were either not mentioned, put into a sanitized form, or blamed on other organizations.

The lies begin already with the early 1930s, when, the generals maintained, they tried to protect their Jewish colleagues. In reality, the draft of the order to dismiss Jewish soldiers came from the Army Personnel Office. Many of the generals were outspoken antisemites, even those eventually associated with anti-Hitler attitudes, for example General Werner von Fritsch.[8]

The generals appear to have been ignorant of the institutions of the Nazi police state, including concentration camps. According to their version of events, they prized the order established by the regime but they do not mention the means by which it was obtained. Moreover, they claimed that the army tried from the outset to distance itself from the Nazi Party and National Socialist ideology. The opposite was, in fact, the case. Brauchitsch, one of the signatories, issued a decree in 1938 that called for binding the army and the regime even more closely together, claiming they shared the "same spiritual roots."[9]

The generals also claimed that their intent in rebuilding Germany's military strength during the 1930s was purely defensive. And when it seemed to take on an offensive capability, this was only to better counter the offensive strategies of potential enemies, as, for example, a putative French-Czech attack in 1938–39! Occasionally the generals portrayed themselves as unaware of Hitler's intentions. They supposedly did not think he was planning an aggressive war against Poland in 1939, for example, and only ordered an attack on Poland after the Poles mobilized on August 30! They also had no inkling that the Soviet Union would attack Poland from the east. They claim not to have desired a war against the Soviet Union and to have learned about the possibility of this from Hitler in December 1940. In any event, they insisted the war had been a defensive one, begun to thwart a looming Soviet threat to Germany. None of this was true. In fact, shortly after the victory over France in June 1940, the generals themselves were drafting plans for an aggressive war in the East, which they were as confident of winning in a few weeks as was Hitler himself.[10]

The generals claimed to have been outraged at Hitler's characterization of the coming war against the Soviet Union as one of racial annihilation and conquest and to have had nothing to do with the formulation of the "criminal orders" that laid the foundation for that war. In fact, not one of them protested at the notorious March 30, 1941, meeting where Hitler laid out his plans, and in fact, through their legal departments, they were actually responsible for drafting the orders in concrete form.[11]

In any case, the army, the generals claimed, did not carry out criminal orders, such as the "commissar order" that mandated the killing of all captured Communist commissars. In fact, the overwhelming evidence is that the Wehrmacht was deeply involved in predatory war-making in the Soviet Union.[12] As for the "hostage order," which in many cases called for the deaths of fifty to one hundred hostages for every German soldier killed by partisans, the generals, after pointing out parenthetically how cruel the partisans were, nevertheless claimed to have rejected the order out of hand and insisted on legal investigation of every case. They pleaded ignorance as to how often the "hostage order" had been implemented. They likewise pleaded ignorance as to the activities of the Nazi Security Service (SD), to whom they turned over many prisoners. The SD, they maintained, was not allowed to tell the soldiers about its "political tasks." As for the recruitment of civilian labor in the Soviet Union, they said, this lay outside the responsibility of the army, which, in any case, objected to the harsh methods used by the German civil administration. In reality, the army made widespread use of compulsory civilian labor.[13] As for the Jews, the very brief reference in this regard deserves to be quoted. "*Persecution of the Jews.* The measures taken against the Jews were conceived and carried out by the Reichsfuehrer-SS. They ensued outside the sphere of control of army units and without their knowledge."[14]

The Waffen-SS, which was much better armed and equipped than the regular army, was always an organization of brave fighters, the generals asserted. As for the final German defeat in the East, this was laid squarely at the feet of Adolf Hitler, who, the generals maintained, always insisted on the defense of every square foot of territory to the last man, something else that was not entirely true. One of Hitler's greatest crimes in the eyes of these men was to undermine the stature of the officer corps by taking control of operations and humiliating and firing many of them, incarcerating some of them in concentration camps, including, the authors did not fail to mention, Halder himself. In 1933, they maintained, the army was still unsullied. It embodied the best traditions of "strict discipline, chivalrous behavior vis-à-vis the enemy, hard work, and no politics." Now all that was ruined. According to this account, the army realized in 1945 what a catastrophe Hitler had caused. But by then it was too late, and a soldier had no choice but to defend the Fatherland to the end.

With respect to the main theme of this chapter, the etiology of the memorandum is interesting. The initiative came not from the German generals themselves but from, of all people, William Donovan, head of the American intelligence service, the Office of Strategic Services (OSS). Donovan had had prewar contacts with the German military through a friend, Paul Leverkuehn, who, like Donovan, was an attorney. During the 1930s, Leverkuehn had worked with Donovan in New York on several commissions. During the war, Leverkuehn had served as an Abwehr agent in Turkey. Now, at the end of the war, he was scheduled to serve as a defense attorney for the anticipated trial of the German High Command. That trial never ensued. Donovan, who apparently anticipated what would soon emerge as the Cold

War, was against trying German generals; they might be needed in the future. So, acting through Leverkuehn, he urged the prominent German generals to write up their brief.

One of the generals, Walter Warlimont, wrote to Donovan thanking him for the initiative:

> In consequence of the interrogation yesterday, I want to inform you that I am prepared to give testimony to open court as you suggested. After serious considerations, I feel that for me it is no more a matter of conscience, since I have established my standpoint long before. It however will be an [*sic*] unique opportunity to give evidence in favor of the German Army and its officer-corps. Therefore I feel obliged, General, to sincerely thank you for bringing forward this proposal.[15]

Donovan was assisting Supreme Court justice Robert Jackson, who would serve as the chief U.S. prosecutor at the Nuremberg Trials, but broke with him over the military trials. This was the kind of prominent American who was most susceptible to the tales and myths told by the German generals.[16]

Donovan was not alone. One can identify a number of Americans, highly placed in the military and intelligence communities, who harbored strong sympathies for the German military and would be the first conduits into American military culture of the myth of the clean Wehrmacht. They had much in common with the German military, including a strong affinity for German culture and Germans, especially soldiers; extensive prewar contact with Germans, especially army officers; sympathy for Germany in light of its post–World War I treatment; a mild antisemitism; an elite education, including West Point and Ivy League schools; a tendency before the war to be intensely anti-Roosevelt, anti–New Deal, and isolationist; and an intensively felt anti-Communism that led them to be prescient about the Soviet threat before most others were.

Besides Donovan, the most important of those who would cooperate with the former German generals in rescuing their tattered reputations were General Albert Wedemeyer, Colonel Truman Smith, Allen Dulles, and George Shuster. These men would buy into the version of war in the East propagated by the German officers. In many instances they became close friends with the Germans and were instrumental in rescuing a number of them from war crimes tribunals.

These well-placed Americans played an important role in helping several German generals achieve high positions in the future West German army, the Bundeswehr, and they corresponded with them at length well into the 1960s. I am indebted to Joseph Bendersky for his characterization of Wedemeyer and Truman Smith within the context of antisemitism in the U.S. Army, and I draw on Bendersky's research in the following sketches.

Albert Wedemeyer was a 1919 graduate of West Point. At the outbreak of World War II he was a lieutenant colonel and was asked to draw up what became known as the Victory Program, the overall plan for the defeat of the Germans in Europe. He was promoted rapidly and in 1943 was assigned to be chief of staff for Lord Mountbatten, commander of the Allies' Southeast Asia Command. Later he became commander of all U.S. forces in China/Asia. Wedemeyer wrote a report urging U.S. entry into the Chinese civil war, a report that he believed was suppressed by President Truman. His last posting was as commanding general of the Sixth Army in San Francisco. In 1951 he resigned from the army, and in 1958 he published his memoirs, *Wedemeyer Reports.* Ronald Reagan awarded him the Presidential Medal of Freedom.[17]

A formative experience for Wedemeyer was his two-year stay in Germany at the Kriegsakademie (War Academy) in Berlin from 1935 to 1937. Here he became acquainted with the emerging Wehrmacht military doctrine that would become known as "blitzkrieg." He later said in an interview: "The schedule was strenuous. The courses were well organized and well taught. The pedagogy, I thought, was better than that at Leavenworth. I was impressed with the practicality and thoroughness of the purely military work, as well as with the intellectual breadth of the curriculum."[18] He also made a number of friends among the German officers, some of whom, like Claus von Stauffenberg, Wessel Freitag von Loringhoven, and Ludwig Beck, would later be involved in the resistance against Hitler; and others, like Ferdinand Jodl, brother of Alfred Jodl—whom the United States would try at Nuremberg as a war criminal and execute—who would not. Wedemeyer later wrote: "Not that I approved of the Nazi regime or condoned its brutalities, but I had come to see Germany in a different light from most of my contemporaries."[19]

Wedemeyer's sympathies for the German military in part derived from his own background. His grandparents were German immigrants. Later he would relate to General Halder how humiliated he was to hear the atrocity propaganda about the Germans in World War I. "I recall during World War One, although I was only a cadet at West Point, the propaganda that was disseminated in my country. It was terrible. I have always been proud of my German ancestry and why shouldn't I be?"[20]

Wedemeyer was a product of a military education during and after World War I, at a time when racism and antisemitism of an often virulent sort were simply part of the curriculum and deeply imbedded in the mentality of the officer corps. Early on, Wedemeyer, like many of his generation, would see a close connection between Communism and the Jews, something that fit in exactly with the Nazi concept of "Jewish-Bolshevism." It was this perspective that also contributed to his fierce isolationism. He thought that the German quest for lebensraum in the East was quite legitimate and feared that the British, the Jews, and the Communists were attempting to provoke a war between the United States and Germany.[21]

Wedemeyer's antisemitism would continue in later years. In a letter to Franz von Papen, former German chancellor and Hitler's ambassador to Turkey who was himself put on trial after the war, Wedemeyer, who was seeking Papen's help in getting his memoirs distributed in Germany, noted that he insisted on approving the translation. "I do not want some individual—a pro-Nazi for example or a pro-Jew—to slant the ideas I have tried to convey." In the same letter, Wedemeyer pointed out that "there are many revisionists in America who feel as we do but they have been quite successfully repressed, rendered inarticulate by the so-called liberals, the internationalists, the Socialists and the avowed Communists." Wedemeyer could not resist pointing out to Papen that the editor of *U.S. News and World Report,* David Lawrence, "is a Jew whose name is really Lawrence David."[22]

In a letter to Gerhard Rossbach, a notorious Freikorps leader after World War I in whose apartment Wedemeyer had stayed in the 1930s, Wedemeyer attacked the new, soon to become classic study of Nazi Germany by William Shirer. "Obviously the book is slanted, emphasizing the faults of the Germans and deemphasizing or disregarding the good points. That is why it is particularly popular over in this country among a certain category of people who still spread hatred and suspicion, making exaggerated or false statements concerning the treatment that they or their relatives received from the Germans."[23]

Years later, in a letter to his close friend Truman Smith, Wedemeyer would blame the troubles of the world on Franklin Roosevelt:

> The world situation with powder kegs scattered hither and yon even in the most remote areas is a creature of our own making—a Frankenstein monster which was conceived in the jaded mind of FDR and his henchmen. . . . We Americans gave impetus to the grand design of interventionists, internationalists, and fuzzy-minded do-gooders.[24]

In early 1947 Wedemeyer, accompanied by his wife, toured Germany for the first time since before the war. His ostensible purpose was to comfort the widows of his friends who had died in the resistance to Hitler. But he was really visiting his own old friends with whom he had been at the Kriegsakademie, many of whom had been General Staff officers during the war.[25] It was they whom he had come to comfort. He was strongly opposed to denazification and said so bluntly. In a letter to former Field Marshal Albert Kesselring, the last German commander in Italy, Wedemeyer said:

> I visited your country several times after World War II and noted the great effort, spiritual and physical on the part of the German people to rehabilitate the war devastated areas. I also was aware of the unfortunate actions of certain American representatives some in uniform and some in civilian positions in carrying out the so-called de-Nazification and democratization of Germany. As an American I was humiliated and at times angry about this.[26]

He tried to intervene where he could, and "in a very modest way I did accomplish a little to curb abuses."[27] One concrete achievement was to track down the library of former General Ludwig Beck at the behest of his daughter, Gertrud Neubahr. Turning to Allen Dulles, Wedemeyer discovered that the collection had been "rescued" by the OSS at the end of the war and transported to West Point. Mrs. Neubahr received compensation for the library, which remained at the military academy.[28]

What these activities represent on the part of Wedemeyer—and others—was a high degree of sympathy for the German people and in particular for the former German officer corps and their esprit de corps. Wedemeyer made no secret of his admiration for the professionalism of the German military, for its willingness to act on orders, and for its stance "above politics." As he wrote to Halder later: "I have always had the greatest respect for the German officers, both as persons and for their professional abilities and their unquestioned loyalties to their country and to their God."[29] Some months later he elaborated for the same officer:

> I am completely in accord with the views you expressed concerning a soldier's service to his people and to his country. Actually military men do not get involved in politics and are not responsible for their leaders who direct the destinies of our nation. Some of those leaders happen to be men who abuse their authority and power, but they still are leaders of the nation and the military men must carry out the orders they receive. Sometimes civilians have difficulty in understanding this.[30]

These ideas, coming from an American general long after the war, but harbored and expressed in its immediate aftermath, could not have been a better expression of support for the "memorandum of the generals." They reflect a willingness—even eagerness—to accept the myth of the clean Wehrmacht.

The German generals were properly grateful. On numerous occasions they expressed their appreciation to Wedemeyer for his postwar understanding and support for their attempts to win back their honor—and establish their innocence. In the words of Franz Halder on the appearance of Wedemeyer's memoirs: "With this you testify anew to your friendly attitude toward Germany and its army, one which you demonstrated so impressively after the war to so many Germans, in particular soldiers. The German officer corps will never forget you for that."[31]

That Wedemeyer played a role in the literature which did such an effective job in disseminating the myth of the eastern front is attested to by his contribution to the promotion of German officers' memoirs and biographies. He wrote the foreword to the adulatory biography of Hasso von Manteuffel, a book dedicated to Heinz Guderian. At the end of the foreword Wedemeyer wrote:

> When General von Manteuffel knocks at St. Peter's gate, having fulfilled his mission on planet Earth, St. Peter's face will light up when he sets eyes on him and the good saint will leave the gate in charge of an assistant while he personally leads the soldier-statesman, von

Manteuffel, to the circle of German heroes—Frederick the Great, Scharnhorst, Gneisenau, Schlieffen, Clausewitz and Moltke.[32]

An influential soul mate and close friend of Wedemeyer was Truman Smith.[33] Smith came from the old New England elite; his family had lived there since the seventeenth century. One of his grand-fathers had been a senator from Connecticut. During World War I, after a short stint at Yale, Smith dropped out and joined the U.S. Army. He acquitted himself well in combat and was promoted from lieu-tenant to major. After the war he remained in Germany as a political liaison. He came to admire German culture deeply and steeped him-self in its literature and history. He also came to admire the infamous racial tract of Houston Stewart Chamberlain, *Foundations of the Nine-teenth Century,* the book that exerted so much influence on Adolf Hitler.[34] In 1920 Smith was reassigned as assistant military attaché in Berlin, where he got to know a number of German officers, some of whom, he later wrote, "were to continue as friends until 1964."[35] In 1922 he was also the first American to interview Hitler, whom he characterized as "a marvelous demagogue . . . Have rarely listened to such a logical and fanatical man."[36]

A product of the military education of his time, Smith betrayed antisemitic tendencies. He believed that the Nazis were respond-ing to the disproportionate influence that he saw the Jews exerting in Germany. That Germans were antisemitic was not surprising to Smith, for the Jews supposedly antagonized them by "display[ing] their wealth throughout Germany's years of misery (1921–1924) in any-thing but an unostentatious manner."[37] He also linked the Jews to Communism, as did many of his contemporaries. In his mind the Jewish threat also extended to America. He believed that Jews exerted undue influence in the United States, particularly in the circle around President Roosevelt, and that they were trying to get the United States into a war with Germany. Smith and his circle of friends harbored a strong antipathy toward the president and later took delight in Roosevelt's death. Like Wedemeyer, Smith was profoundly isolationist and felt that a war with Germany would destroy civilization. It was this position that undoubtedly prompted him, on his own initiative, to invite Charles Lindbergh to visit Germany in 1937.[38]

In 1935 Smith returned to Germany as military attaché, a post he held until his return to the United States in 1939. Again he met a number of German military men and cultivated friendships that would survive the war. Throughout this period Smith enjoyed a reputation for being particularly knowledgeable about Germany, and his reports were valued highly. After the war American authorities continued to value and use his expertise. In 1948 he served on the Military Advisory Committee of the National Security Organization.[39] In 1955 he was sent to Germany by Army Intelligence, G2, on a special mission involving the newly created West German army. Acknowledging his excellent contacts with former German officers who were now in the top ranks of the Bundeswehr, Smith's superiors asked him, among other things, to do the following: "Convince the leaders of the new German army that it is in their, our and the West's interest to play ball with us . . ."; establish a working relationship with German military intelligence; "assist [Ludwig] Cruwell, [Adolf] Heusinger, [Hans] Speidel and Company [the top generals in the Bundeswehr] to take such actions as will cement German-American relations"; and "confer at length with the U.S. Attaché Designate in Bonn, affording him some of your background and experience in dealing and getting along with the German military."[40] The officer who then organized Smith's visit confirmed that "his contacts are unbelievably good."[41]

Smith's contacts were indeed excellent, partly owing to the extensive nature of his prewar networks and friendships, and partly owing to his efforts on behalf of some of those same officers after the war, particularly those who would be involved in the new Bundeswehr. In fact, Smith became an unofficial liaison between Speidel and other German officers and General George P. Hayes, the U.S. deputy high commissioner in Germany, on matters of military planning.[42]

Donovan, Wedemeyer, and Smith were among many U.S. officers who had been isolationists before the war, perhaps in part because of their close contacts with the German military. They were known as the "Potsdam Club" after the city where the Kriegsakademie was located. Dean Rusk, the future U.S. secretary of state who served in G2 during the war, considered these men "so pessimistic as to be almost pro-German."[43]

It is some indication of the readiness of many U.S. officers to accept the myth of the clean Wehrmacht that even during the war admiration for the enemy was scarcely concealed. (This was prior to disclosures about Nazi mass murder.) A widely distributed volume from the War Department distributed to U.S. officers had the following to say about the Wehrmacht: "The German army of 1939 was a model of efficiency, the best product of the concentrated military genius of the most scientifically military of nations." It was also a tough army:

> The cause of this toughness, even in defeat, is not generally appreciated. It goes much deeper than the quality of weapons, the excellence of training and leadership, the soundness of tactical and strategic doctrine, or the efficiency of control at all echelons. It is to be found in the military tradition which is so deeply engrained in the whole character of the German nation and which alone makes possible the interplay of these various factors of strength to their full effectiveness.[44]

Secretary of War Henry Stimson complained about officers, like Smith in G2, who were too much influenced by German military proficiency.[45]

The high commissioner for Bavaria under John J. McCloy in the early 1950s was George N. Shuster. Shuster, a prominent lay Catholic and wartime president of Hunter College, came from German stock and was fluent in the language. He had traveled extensively in Germany before the war and developed a great appreciation for German culture.[46] He had previously written three books and a number of essays on Hitler's Germany, which some construed as being pro-Nazi, especially in light of several comments about German Jews, who, he alleged, had exhibited far too much ostentation in the twentieth century. "The besetting sin of the German Jew," he maintained, "has been vanity. Accustomed so long to a position of social inferiority, he could not and still can not resist the dangerous spell of limelight."[47] As for Nazi violence in the early years, Shuster noted: "No doubt too much has been written about 'atrocities' but there is a sense in which those who care for Germany cannot talk about them excessively. As individual crimes they are no more serious than many incidents which have occurred in the U.S. during times of war hysteria, Ku Klux Klan excitement, labor trouble or racketeering."[48] Clearly this was prewar and pre-Holocaust, and Shuster was no antisemite, as his work with the American Jewish Committee, his friendship with Zionist activist Rabbi Stephen Wise, and his membership in various

Christian-Jewish organizations would later demonstrate. But he was blind to the true nature of Nazism for too long for someone who had spent so much time in Germany and written so much, and his attachment to German culture made him very sensitive to what might happen to the Germans as World War II came to an end.

For one thing, Shuster was concerned about the Nuremberg Trials, particularly the justice that was meted out to military men. "We may as well admit," he said, "that probably not a single responsible American officer, from General Eisenhower on down, has failed to gulp at the sentences imposed. . . . When soldiers fail to do what they are told, there will be no more soldiers."[49] This attitude would leave him open to the Wehrmacht mythology already being devised by German generals at the end of the war. That exposure would come as a result of Shuster being named chairman of the War Department Historical Commission, which was set up at the end of the war to interrogate top Nazis who had fallen into American captivity. Between July and November 1945, Shuster and his colleagues would interview twenty-five former Nazi leaders, including Hermann Göring, Alfred Rosenberg, and Joachim von Ribbentrop, as well as military men like Albert Kesselring, Karl Dönitz, and Heinz Guderian.

The civilian Nazi leaders did not impress Shuster; he was contemptuous of Ribbentrop. But the military men did, especially Guderian.[50] Shuster's handwritten account of his interview with the panzer general on August 16, 1945, in Heidelberg began with these words:

> This interview began with no expectations other than to secure information about a minor matter. It proved, however, a most absorbing conversation and left upon the interrogator the definite impression that Guderian is the ablest general so far encountered and a fantastical source of historical information of the greatest value. Bringing him to the United States and sitting down with him for two weeks would help more in writing the history of the war than any other single factor within the scope of my imagination.[51]

The trip never materialized, but then it did not have to. The message was getting across. Reading the text of the interview, as well as the typescript of Shuster's official interrogation of Guderian on September 7, which focused on the Russian campaign, it becomes clear that

Guderian was already laying out the mythology of the eastern front and emphasizing how seriously the views of the High Command diverged from those of Hitler. Typical was the following statement, patently false: "The General Staff certainly had no plan to attack Russia. We were indeed all very happy about the pact with Russia and I had toasted my friends in champagne when the pact was concluded."[52]

Yet another prominent American had bought into the myth of the Wehrmacht here at the outset, and the experience cannot but have colored Shuster's approach to his job of high commissioner five years later. Indeed, after he had taken over as commissioner of Bavaria, it was felt by many that he did not pursue denazification as vigorously as he might have, because he believed that most diehard Nazis were already out of public service and those who remained had really only been nominal members of the party. Shuster's contacts with Guderian did not end with the interrogations. The two men conferred in early 1951, as Shuster took over his office as commissioner, on the issue of getting German officers who had been convicted of war crimes released from prison, a prerequisite for the formation of any future German military contingent. Guderian, in conclusion, hoped that Shuster would exercise his office "with the same humanity which I experienced so movingly in 1945."[53]

Finally we have Allen Dulles, the high OSS operative who, from Switzerland in 1945, negotiated the surrender of all German troops in Italy with Karl Wolff, Heinrich Himmler's personal chief of staff. Dulles was later to take over the CIA, while his brother John Foster was secretary of state under President Eisenhower. As prominent attorneys before the war at the firm of Sullivan and Cromwell, the Dulles brothers developed a strongly pro-German slant. Among their German clients was the Schroeder Bank in Cologne, whose owner was a member of Himmler's notorious "circle of friends" (*Freundeskreis*). The brothers kept many of their German clients right down to and even into the war. Eleanor Roosevelt complained about these contacts maintained in wartime.[54]

Nor was Allen Dulles entirely free from a touch of antisemitism. Shortly after World War I, he characterized a report on Poland as "a typical bit of Jewish propaganda." He also passed on to a friend as a remedy for "Jewish troubles" a "'hambone amulet' to keep off the evil eye of some of our hooknosed friends."[55] Allen Dulles always had his "good" Germans, even when sometimes they were not so good. The same Karl Wolff with whom he had negotiated in March and April 1945 (after Wolff had established his credibility with the American by obliging him in several requests) had arranged for the boxcars that transported three hundred thousand Jews from the Warsaw ghetto to Auschwitz between July and September 1942.[56]

Turning a blind eye to Wolff's activities prior to his ties with Dulles in 1945, Dulles intervened with the military governor of Germany, General Lucius Clay, on Wolff's behalf as he was being tried for war crimes. "It is a fact," Dulles wrote, "that in this situation General Wolff was one of those who acted where the great majority of Wehrmacht, SS generals and others sat meekly by and let the carnage go on. Wolff tried to stop it."[57] Dulles's top assistant Gero von Gaevernitz wrote a sworn affidavit for Wolff.[58] Wolff was later released with time served. He had apparently learned nothing from his experiences. Even in the presence of Allied soldiers he referred to Poles as "Slavonic mongrels."[59]

Another "good" German on whose behalf Dulles intervened was General Alexander von Falkenhausen, who was tried in Belgium because while in occupation there he had allegedly had numerous hostages murdered and ordered the deportation of twenty-five thousand Jews to killing centers. In 1950 Dulles tried to use the offices of U.S. High Commissioner John McCloy to get Falkenhausen off the hook. McCloy obligingly got the U.S. ambassador in Brussels, Robert Murphy, to intervene with the result that, although a Belgian court had sentenced Falkenhausen to twelve years, he was freed within three weeks.[60]

Finally, Dulles also used the good services of George V. Allen, U.S. ambassador in Belgrade, to secure the release of a German naval officer, Lothar Zechlin, whom the Yugoslavian government had sentenced to fifteen years for war crimes. Most of these interventions were prompted by letters to Dulles from friends or acquaintances who were related to those imprisoned. For example, in this case Zechlin's wife's cousin, Alexander von Puttkamer, a law professor at Chicago and classmate of Dulles, had taken the initiative.[61]

The question remains: why, then, even before the Cold War began, when the international community was ready to put people in the dock who had served various criminal Nazi institutions, when U.S. troops had liberated Dachau and Buchenwald, revealing the terrible things that had happened there, were these highly placed, intelligent Americans so ready to take up the cause of the Wehrmacht generals? In part their willingness lay in their own backgrounds, their experience with Germans, particularly the military, and their tendency to separate the German army from the regime it had served. They identified with men of similar class and caste. They had preconceived notions about the German army and Germans generally that could not be overturned despite a total war. In their eyes, the Nazis had taken over a people recognized as decent and even virtuous. It was easy, even at this early date, to slough off the Nazis, now defeated and no longer in charge, their leader safely dead, and to allow the normal relationship to reemerge, strengthened by renewed ties with men of shared background. The Americans were just as willing to distance "good" Germans from Nazis as the Germans were to do the same thing for themselves.

This tendency was not only true of these men; it also characterized Americans in general. Polls taken of Americans regarding their attitudes toward Germans over forty years—from the 1920s to the 1960s—show a remarkable consistency in positive views of Germans. There was a temporary shift toward the negative during World War II, but in an astonishingly short time after the war the pendulum swung back to prewar values. Even during the war, stereotypes of Germans as hardworking, methodical, and intelligent did not change.[62] One scholar explained this continuity by saying: "Consistency can largely be understood in terms of the strong tendency for people to see what they expect to see and to assimilate incoming information to preexisting images."[63]

The men discussed above were the pioneers in developing and propagating the myth of the clean Wehrmacht. That myth went on in the context of the Cold War to permeate much of American military culture and popular culture as well. At a time when the Holocaust was not yet a matter of discussion, the Wehrmacht myth had the stage to itself. In spite of widespread public awareness of the Holocaust since the 1980s, the myth of the "clean" Wehrmacht, indeed a romanticization of the German military in World War II, continues to exert a hold on the minds of many Americans in our popular culture three generations after Donovan and his contemporaries first embraced it.

NOTES

1. On the Nuremberg Trials, see Eugene Davidson, *The Trial of the Germans: Nuremberg 1945–1946* (New York: Macmillan, 1966); Bradley Smith, *Reaching Judgment at Nuremberg* (New York: New American Library, 1977); Robert Conot, *Justice at Nuremberg* (New York: Harper and Row, 1983); and Joseph E. Persico, *Nuremberg: Infamy on Trial* (New York: Penguin Books, 1994). On the pretrial period, see Richard Overy, *Interrogations: The Nazi Elite in Allied Hands, 1945* (New York: Penguin, 2001).

2. On trials before and after Nuremberg, see Gerd Überschärr, ed., *Der Nationalsozialismus vor Gericht: Die allierten Prozess gegen Kriegsverbrecher und Soldaten, 1943–1952* (Frankfurt: Fischer, 1999).

3. See Kai Bird, *The Chairman: John J. McCloy and the Making of the American Establishment* (New York: Simon and Schuster, 1992), 338–39. Bird points out how High Commissioner McCloy's increasing leniency toward German war criminals was a bellwether of changing times. Also, McCloy pointed out to President Truman in September 1950 that because of the emerging Cold War, "certain things we would like to see done in Germany will not be completed." See Thomas Schwartz, *America's Germany: John J. McCloy and the Federal Republic of Germany* (Cambridge, Mass.: Harvard University Press, 1991), 165.

4. See David Clay Large, *Germans to the Front: West German Rearmament in the Adenauer Era* (Chapel Hill: University of North Carolina Press, 1996).

5. Many of these manuscripts are located at the Center for Military History in Carlisle, Pennsylvania. For a good cross section of the larger group of reports, see Donald Detwiler et al., eds., *World War Two Military Studies: A Collection of 213 Special Reports on the Second World War Prepared by Former Officers of the Wehrmacht for the United States Army* (New York: Garland, 1979).

6. See Michaela Hoenicke-Moore, *Know Your Enemy: The American Response to Nazism, 1933–1945* (New York: Cambridge University Press, forthcoming).

7. Located in the Staatsarchiv Nuremberg, PS 3798. The best analysis of this document is that by Manfred Messerschmidt, "Vorwärtsverteidigung: Die 'Denkschrift der Generäle' für den Nürnberger Gerichtshof," in *Vernichtungskrieg: Verbrechen der Wehrmacht 1941–1944*, ed. Hannes Heer and Klaus Naumann (Hamburg: Hamburger Institut für Sozialgeschichte, 1995), 531–50. See also Georg Meyer, "Zur Situation der deutschen militärischen Führungsschicht im Vorfeld des westdeutschen Verteidigungsbeiträges 1945–1950/51," in *Anfänge westdeutscher Sicherheitspolitik 1945–1956*,

ed. Militärgeschichtliches Forschungsamt, vol. 1, *Von der Kapitulation bis zum Pleven-Plan,* ed. Roland Foerster et al. (Munich: Oldenbourg, 1982), 671–91.

8. On Fritsch's antisemitism, see Carl Dirks and Karl Heinze Janßen, *Der Krieg der Generäle: Hitler als Werkzeug der Wehrmacht* (Berlin: Propyläen, 1999), 184–85.

9. See Brian Bond, "Brauchitsch," in *Hitler's Generals,* ed. Correlli Barnett (New York: Grove Weidenfeld, 1989), 79.

10. On Halder's drafting of "Plan Otto," see Carl Dirks and Karl Heinze Janßen, "Plan 'Otto,'" in *Der Kreig der Generäle,* 127–45.

11. For a summary of the meeting without critique, see the entry for March 30, 1941, in the diaries of General Franz Halder: Arnold Lissance, ed., *The Halder Diaries: The Private War Journals of Colonel General Franz Halder* (Boulder, Colo.: Westview, 1976).

12. On the "criminal orders," see Helmuth Krausnick, "'Kommissarbefehl' und 'Kriegsgerichtsbarkeitserlass Barbarossa' in neuer Sicht," in *Vierteljahreshefte für Zeitgeschichte* 25 (1977): 682–738; and Ben Shepherd, *War in the Wild East: The German Army and Soviet Partisans* (Cambridge, Mass.: Harvard University Press, 2004). On the Polish campaign as a dress rehearsal by the Wehrmacht for the war against the Soviet Union, see Alexander Rossino, *Hitler Strikes Poland: Blitzkrieg, Ideology and Atrocity* (Lawrence: University of Kansas Press, 2003).

13. On the exploitation of civilian labor, see Christoph Rass, *"Menschenmaterial": Deutsche Soldaten an der Ostfront; Innenansicht einer Infanteriedivision 1939–1945* (Paderborn: Schöningh, 2003), 360–78.

14. On the Wehrmacht's role in the Holocaust, see Omer Bartov, *Hitler's Army: Soldiers, Nazis and War in the Third Reich* (New York: Oxford University Press, 1991); Omer Bartov, *The Eastern Front, 1941–1945: German Troops and the Barbarisation of Warfare* (New York: St. Martin's, 1986); and Hannes Heer and Klaus Naumann, eds., *War of Extermination: The German Military in World War Two, 1941–1944* (New York: Berghahn Books, 2000). For a good overview with bibliography, see Rolf-Dieter Müller and Gerd Überschärr, eds., *Hitler's War in the East, 1941–1945: A Critical Assessment* (Oxford: Berghahn Books, 1997).

15. See letter of October 17, 1945, in Donovan papers at the Cornell Law Library, vol. 5, part 2: 10:06. Jay V. Glebb of the Office of U.S. Chief of Council was not as taken in by the generals as Donovan. See his very critical reading of the generals' statement in a letter to Donovan of November 27, 1945, ibid., 10:04.

16. On Donovan's background with Leverkuehn, see Margaret Boveri, *Wir lügen alle: Eine Hauptstadtzeitung unter Hitler* (Olten: Walter, 1965), 169. On Donovan and the memorandum, see Meyer, "Zur Situation der

deutschen militärischen," 680–81. Donovan broke with Jackson and was fired, partly because of Donovan's long absences, and partly over the issue of using Hermann Göring as a prosecution witness, which Donovan wanted and Jackson thought ludicrous. See Telford Taylor, *The Anatomy of the Nuremberg Trials: A Personal Memoir* (Boston: Little Brown, 1992), 180–86. Donovan had also suggested that a distinction be made between German field commanders, who were "just doing their duty," and officers at Hitler's headquarters (Taylor, *Anatomy of the Nuremberg Trials,* 148). On Leverkuehn and the Abwehr, see Taylor, 182.

17. See Joseph W. Bendersky, *The "Jewish Threat": Anti-Semitic Politics of the U.S. Army* (New York: Basic Books, 2000). For an overview of Wedemeyer's career through his own eyes, see Albert C. Wedemeyer, *Wedemeyer Reports* (New York: Henry Holt, 1958). On Wedemeyer taking the side of German generals on World War II, see *Wedemeyer Reports,* esp. 415; on his experience at the Kriegsakademie, see 48–54; on his denial that Germans are by nature "aggressive," see 10–12; on his denial of German "war guilt" in World War I, see 2. On Wedemeyer's background, see William Stueck, *The Wedemeyer Mission: American Politics and Foreign Policy During the Cold War* (Athens: University of Georgia Press, 1984), 12–13, 20–21, 147n14.

18. Interviewed by a former aide-de-camp, Keith Eiler, in 1983; printed in *Hoover Digest* 4 (2001): 6. Background on Wedemeyer's career precedes the interview.

19. Quoted in Bendersky, *"Jewish Threat."* On Wedemeyer's denial of German aggressiveness, see Bendersky, 232.

20. See letter of December 17, 1963, Hoover Institution Archives (hereafter referred to as HIA), Wedemeyer Collection, box 40, folder 2: Halder.

21. See Bendersky, *"Jewish Threat,"* 274–75.

22. See letter of October 5, 1959, HIA, Wedemeyer Collection, box 55, folder 18.

23. See letter of January 3, 1962, HIA, Wedemeyer Collection, box 58, folder 34: Rossbach.

24. See letter of February 10, 1964, HIA, Truman Smith Collection, box 1, folder: Wedemeyer.

25. See Meyer, "Zur Situation der deutschen militärischen," 682.

26. See letter of March 9, 1953, HIA, Wedemeyer Collection, box 45, folder: Kesselring. Wedemeyer was particularly concerned that returning refugees (many of whom were Jews) working for the American military government did not represent the United States "creditably and effectively" and were self-aggrandizing (Bendersky, *The "Jewish Threat,"* 365).

27. See letter of March 9, 1953, HIA, Wedemeyer Collection, box 45, folder: Kesselring.

28. See correspondence in the Seeley G. Mudd Manuscript Library

(hereafter referred to as Mudd Library), Princeton University, Allen Dulles Papers, Series 1: Correspondence, box 57, folder 18: Wedemeyer.

29. See letter of July 10, 1962, HIA, Wedemeyer Collection, box 40, folder 2: Halder.

30. See letter of December 6, 1963, HIA, Wedemeyer Collection, box 40, folder 2: Halder.

31. See letter of January 30, 1959, HIA, Wedemeyer Collection, box 40, folder 2: Halder. All translations from German are by the author unless otherwise indicated.

32. See Donald Grey Brownlow, *Panzer Baron: The Military Exploits of General Hasso von Manteuffel* (North Quincy, Mass.: Christopher, 1975), 15. In 1943 and 1945 Manteuffel commanded several panzer divisions on the eastern front. In 1959 he was charged by a German court with manslaughter—for having one of his men shot for cowardice—and was sentenced to eighteen months in prison, of which he served four. See www .islandfarm.fsnet.co.uk.

33. On Smith, see Max Wallace, *The American Axis: Henry Ford, Charles Lindbergh, and the Rise of the Third Reich* (New York: St. Martin's, 2003), 104–19; and Bendersky, *"Jewish Threat,"* 230–31. Wedemeyer wrote an admiring foreword to Smith's memoirs: see Truman Smith, *Berlin Alert: The Memoirs and Reports of Truman Smith,* ed. Robert Hessen (Stanford, Calif.: Hoover Institution, 1988), vii–ix.

34. Houston Stewart Chamberlain, *Foundations of the Nineteenth Century* (London: Ballantyne, 1911).

35. Quoted in Wallace, *American Axis,* 107.

36. Ibid. On Smith's pro-German and antisemitic attitudes, see Bendersky, *"Jewish Threat,"* 236–42.

37. Quoted in Bendersky, *"Jewish Threat,"* 237.

38. Ibid., 274–75; Wallace, *American Axis,* 110–11. On the Lindbergh episode, see Wallace, *American Axis,* 112–19.

39. See the list of committee member names in the National Archives and Records Administration, CIA-RDP86B00269R000200010025–1.

40. See letter from Robert Schow, Office of the Assistant Chief of Staff, G2 Intelligence, to Smith, May 18, 1955, Herbert Hoover Presidential Library (hereafter referred to as HHPL), Truman Smith Papers, box 2: Germany-Army Development 1954–1956.

41. See letter from Major General Arthur Trudeau to Colonel Al Leonard, May 19, 1955, HHPL, Truman Smith Papers, box 2: Germany-Army Development 1954–1956.

42. See Donald Abenheim, *Reforging the Iron Cross: The Search for Tradition in the West German Armed Forces* (Princeton, N.J.: Princeton University Press, 1988), 84n43.

43. Quoted in Bird, *The Chairman,* 139; also refers to the "Potsdam Club."

44. See War Department, Military Intelligence Division TM-E, *Handbook on German Military Forces, March 1945,* I-1 and I-4; quoted in Uwe Heuer, *Reichswehr-Wehrmacht-Bundeswehr: Zum Image deutscher Streitkräfte in den Vereinigten Staaten von Amerika; Kontinuität und Wandel im Urteil amerikanischer Experten* (Frankfurt: Peter Lang, 1990), 200, 202.

45. See Bendersky, *"Jewish Threat,"* 284.

46. For background on Shuster, see Thomas E. Blantz, *George N. Shuster: On the Side of Truth* (Notre Dame, Ind.: University of Notre Dame Press, 1993).

47. Quoted ibid., 232.

48. Quoted ibid., 233.

49. Quoted ibid., 205.

50. On Shuster's own account of his experience with the commission, especially the interviews with military men, see George Shuster, *The Ground I Walked On: Reflections of a College President* (Notre Dame, Ind.: University of Notre Dame Press, 1961), 234–45.

51. See the George Shuster papers at the University of Notre Dame Archives, 1/06, for the handwritten account of the interview.

52. Ibid., for the typescript of the September 7 interrogation that Shuster carried out with Brigadier General R. C. Brock.

53. See letter of Guderian to Shuster, January 1, 1950, George Shuster papers at the University of Notre Dame Archives, 1/06.

54. See Burton Hersh, "The Last Gentleman Observer," in *The Old Boys: The American Elite and the Origins of the CIA* (New York: Scribner, 1992), 58–76. On the surrender of Italy, see Bradley F. Smith and Elena Agarossi, *Operation Sunrise: The Secret Surrender* (New York: Basic Books, 1979), 188–91. On Himmler's *Freundeskreis,* see Heinz Höhne, *The Order of the Death's Head: The Story of Hitler's SS* (New York: Ballantine, 1969), 158–60.

55. See Bendersky, *"Jewish Threat,"* 96, 99.

56. Hersh, *Old Boys,* 135.

57. See Dulles to Clay, November 20, 1947, Mudd Library, Princeton University, Allan Dulles Papers, Series 1, Correspondence, box 2, folder 22.

58. Ibid., box 27, folder 3.

59. See Smith and Agarossi, *Operation Sunrise,* 70.

60. See Dulles to McCloy, March 9, 1950, and McCloy to Dulles, March 16, 1950, Mudd Library, Princeton University, Allan Dulles Papers, Series 1, Correspondence, box 39, folder 8; and Hersh, *Old Boys,* 367.

61. Mudd Library, Princeton University, Allan Dulles Papers, Series 1, Correspondence, box 47, folder 8.

62. See Manfred Koch-Hillebrecht, *Das Deutschenbild: Gegenwart, Geschichte, Psychologie* (Munich: Beck, 1972), 213–14.

63. Robert Jarvis, *Perception and Misperception in International Politics* (Princeton, N.J.: Princeton University Press, 1976), 117, quoted in Heuer, *Reichswehr-Wehrmacht-Bundeswehr,* 98.

Ruth Kluger

Personal Reflections on Jewish Ghosts in Germany and the Memory of the Holocaust

NOT LONG AGO I WATCHED A SEGMENT OF TV'S NEVER-ENDING and ever-so-formulaic series *Law and Order*.[1] It was not a very good one, and once its premises were established, it ran on automatic pilot. But its premises and conclusions were of some relevance to our concerns in this volume. As most of you know, I am sure, the formula demands that there is a murder victim right at the beginning, then the detectives zero in, grab the suspect, and in the second half hour the prosecutors take over. The perpetrator is tried, and thoughtful attorneys meditate on the meaning of it all. In this case the corpse was a Holocaust survivor, a seventy-six-year-old woman who was scheduled to testify in the deportation proceedings of a former German concentration camp guard. The pursuit of her killer led to an American neo-Nazi organization and to Auschwitz deniers. The good guys, that is, the law enforcers, showed the appropriate righteous indignation, and the white supremacists were suitably brutish.

Now there is always a twist to these *Law and Order* cases, something that makes you think a bit about the nature of justice and morality. In the episode I have just described, the jury is so shocked by what the former Nazi did during the war that they convict him on that basis. However, he is on trial for the murder of the Jewish witness, the victim. And this is a crime that he did not commit. The American audience is left with the question of whether perhaps justice was served, though the law was not. Incidentally, that is the question posed in John Grisham's best seller *The Chamber* and also in Friedrich Schiller's classical drama *Maria Stuart*. The victims are executed for one crime though they have committed a different one.

Watching this television show, I asked myself: would this story, with its familiar details and clear conclusion, push different buttons in a German audience? If this had been a German film, I think the audience would have faced a different question. The focus of discussion would be on the "Jewish problem." It would be: Can the memory of the Holocaust subvert justice and the law? And is this the meaning of the program? If so, if it denigrates the concern with the genocide of the Jews, could one call the episode antisemitic? The discussion would be skewed in a different direction, which means that the whole film would look different in German eyes, because these are eyes that are still fixated, negatively or positively, on Jews, what happened to them, and what they are doing now. A Jew is the ultimate "other" in Germany, the quintessential minority member, even though there are so many other minorities in Germany by now.

How do Germans deal with the Holocaust, and how do their thinking and their emotions about Jews differ from that of Americans? Germans deal with it incessantly, even though you will often find an attitude that insists with considerable passion that it is all passé, ever so dated; what do we, the grandchildren, have to do with all this? But that dismissal, too, is part of the scene: people saying they do not want to hear anymore about what happened in the 1930s and 1940s, even though everyone is agreed that these were the most fascinating, if frightful, decades of the last century. The facts belie this pretended indifference: the bookstores are full of it, both fiction and nonfiction, TV is loaded with it, there are conferences and exhibits, and the pundits eagerly discuss the new European antisemitism. None of this would take place if people were not willing to give their time and their money and, presumably, some of their thought processes to this horrendous event. So the charge that the Jews, preferably foreign Jews, are engineering this interest does not hold water. The German public is anything but indifferent: Jews haunt them. To illustrate this, I propose to look at some German works of the imagination since the end of World War II that deal with Jews.

What Germans think and write about Jews is not always positive and rarely objective, whether they admire or berate us. That said, we have to distinguish between fact and fiction, between mind-set and policy. The Federal Republic of Germany has been a viable democracy for nearly sixty years and has treated the Jews within its borders exceptionally well. It is particularly generous toward Jewish immigrants, with the result that there is again a growing Jewish community in Germany. There used to be half a million Jews in prewar Germany, more if you count those who were assimilated and did not consider themselves Jewish; thus, about 1 percent of a population of about sixty million. Although it is true that few emigrants, that is, former German Jews, returned after the war, nevertheless there is a growing Jewish community in Germany now. Most of the postwar German Jews are from the former Soviet Union. After the war there were virtually no Jews in Germany; by 2004 there were again about one hundred thousand, a bit more than one-tenth of 1 percent in a population of eighty million.[2] Their children are integrated and contribute to the cultural and economic health of the country. The government supports and subsidizes Jewish community efforts in various ways. It is quite possible and quite comfortable for a Jew to live in Germany today, as long as one can cope with the past.

But at first, right after the war, there was wholesale denial, side by side with the discovery of what the Nazis had done. Remember, the term *Holocaust* for the Jewish catastrophe only came into use in the 1970s and was certainly not invented in Germany. Because language is so important to our way of thinking, the genocide of the Jews did not stand out from all the other misery that Hitler's Germany had inflicted on the world. And since it was not identified as a special problem, the Allies did not make it a special subject in the reeducation of the German people. Neither did the new German society itself deal with it. There was no attempt to remember or teach the history of European and German Jews, neither the history of their achievements nor of their persecution, and certainly no attempt to analyze the phenomenon of antisemitism.

If a society does not meet such cataclysmic events head-on— especially a country that had profited from and caused so much harm to its Jewish community, that is, a society that knows very well there used to be Jews and now there are none—the knowledge will become a curious, fetid, thoroughly unappetizing mishmash of memory, old resentments that are never explained, and self-justification. But West Germany did finally face up and started a process of reeducation.

Now take the case of East Germany, the former German Democratic Republic. Whatever its faults, it did not teach or preach anti-semitism or any form of racism (although it can be argued that it practiced some). While it did not teach racism, on the other hand, it also did not take part in restitution, arguing that it was not the good Germans but the bad Nazis who committed the crimes, and that they, the socialist good Germans, were not responsible. That was active denial. And because the issue of guilt was never properly addressed, and no one ever sorted out the difference between genocide and political reprisals—for example, the difference between incarcerating opponents of the regime and killing Jewish children—because of this lack of distinctions, the old subterranean anti-Jewish feeling simmered on, as the stew in a high-quality double boiler will remain hot for a long time after the heat has been turned off. The unreflected prejudice coming out of East Germany since unification is a lot like the mental scenery in West Germany for years after the defeat. In literature an interesting East German example was Bruno Apitz's best-selling novel *Naked Among Wolves* of 1958—also a popular film—set in the Buchenwald concentration camp.[3] It deals with the heroic Communist prisoners who hide a Jewish child and thus make his survival possible. The active adults whom the reader admires are political prisoners who at the end of the war liberate the camp. The Jews of Buchenwald are reduced to a passive child, their fate infantilized, as it were. The actual condition of the Jews in that camp was much harsher than that of non-Jews, who were mainly concerned with protecting their own.

During the early postwar period there was also little sense of responsibility toward the Jews who had been forcibly exiled by the Nazis. The postwar authorities acted as if the Jews had left voluntarily and forfeited their citizenship of their own accord. The poet Erich Fried is an example. He was a well-known and well-published Austrian poet who lived in London during the war and asked to have his Austrian citizenship restored after the war. Austria, which conveniently regarded itself as the first Nazi victim rather than a willing partner and part of the Third Reich, simply refused.[4] Another case is the Austrian Jewish writer Leo Perutz, who in the 1920s was a successful author of fantastic and supernatural tales, and also some science fiction. Nowadays all his books are in print again and many thoughtful critics regard them as serious literature.[5] (I am a bit addicted to them and have read them all; they are so much fun.) After the war he came back from Palestine with his best novel, *By Night Under the Stone Bridge,* a tale set in seventeenth-century Prague, about the dreamlike love affair of the Holy Roman emperor and a rabbi's wife. Perutz had worked on it for many years and knew that it was good, but he correctly feared that the Jewish aspects of the book would be a handicap in his attempt to find a publisher. And indeed, six years after the end of the war, in 1951, he got this note from his publisher: "Much as I love and esteem your work, I do believe that the attitude of present-day readers in Austria and Germany will prevent it from becoming a success."[6] It was to be long years before this book found its public. It is still in print and the Jewish angle, which was then the sticking point, is undoubtedly now an asset and a selling point.[7]

But let me interject some personal recollections of the early postwar years. I lived in Germany after the liberation in 1945 until October 1947. During that period I became friends with a young German veteran who planned to be a novelist and did become one of Germany's best-known and at times most controversial authors.[8] It is a career I have followed closely, because I stayed in touch with Martin Walser over the years. He lent me books that were important to him, Franz Kafka, for example—Walser was to write his Ph.D. thesis on Kafka—but that Kafka was a Jew seemed totally irrelevant to him, except to point out that he, Walser, could not possibly be anti-Jewish given his admiration for Kafka. My own experience in the camps from which I had just emerged was not a topic of conversation between us. Decades later Walser said he did not know that I had been in Auschwitz; he only knew about Theresienstadt, which (erroneously) was considered a ghetto where Jews lived a halfway decent life.[9] But I had an Auschwitz number on my arm that was pretty unmistakable. To be sure, neither one of us talked about our war experiences. The first Jewish character in one of his books occurs in a novel of the 1950s. She returns from South America and is so clueless that she is surprised to find any remnants of Nazism in Germany. She is a preposterous and unbelievable figure in her naiveté.[10] The naiveté is that of her denial, which, as we all know, is the first stage in dealing with a catastrophic psychological experience. But here it is projected by a German on a Jew, and Jews, if anything, were obsessively concerned with the remnants of past ideology in Germany. Walser had it upside down.

During this period of denial, even the words *Jude* or *jüdisch* were not in good taste and were left unspoken. German friends of mine who went to school in the 1950s have told me that direct references to Jews and Jewishness were somehow creepy and made them feel uncomfortable. And, of course, there were not any Jews around whom one could meet, except a few in the big cities. But there were books—quite a few of them—about good Germans who saved and hid Jews. In all cases the Jews themselves are passive, like the child in Apitz's novel.

There was even an enormously popular best seller of 1955 by one Hans Scholz about Berlin, called *On the Green Banks of the Spree*— Berlin's river.[11] The first part of this novel is in the form of a reliable narrator who keeps a diary while he serves as a German soldier in Poland. He witnesses Nazi brutalities and disapproves of the treatment of Jews. But the strange thing is that the Jews are more brutal than the Nazis. In one scene a little Jewish girl who is being beaten by what the author calls "members of her own race" runs to the narrator for protection. The scene is thoroughly absurd, given that German soldiers were known for their senseless and arbitrary shooting sprees on Polish streets, but it allows the reader to pity the child while despising the Jewish adults. A reader of the 1950s, who might feel guilty about the recent German past, would find this double gin-and-tonic of contempt and pity precisely the sort of drug he might crave. And there were many sentimental stories, about "Aryan" kids losing their Jewish childhood friends, and being sad about it, and about brave men helping Jews, and sometimes Gypsies, escape.

But lest we feel superior to such feel-good fantasies, consider a similar phenomenon in the treatment of African Americans in books and films, where the good white people save the unjustly accused blacks, thus restoring our sense of the intrinsic goodness of heart of the perpetrators of social injustice. There are some famous American examples that do this, books of excellent quality, for example Harper Lee's *To Kill a Mockingbird,* where the upright white Southern lawyer puts himself and his safety at risk, while his children are watching and learning.[12] A similar and earlier case in point is William Faulkner's *Intruder in the Dust,* where an innocent black man is saved by an old spinster and a child.[13] Both books were made into acclaimed movies as well.[14] In African American fiction the struggling blacks dominate the scene. Not that black writers rule out helpful whites in their fiction. In Toni Morrison's *Beloved* a white woman helps the heroine, an escaped slave, deliver her baby.[15]

In Holocaust fiction there are helpful non-Jews—most famously Oskar Schindler. You might object that the novel *Schindler's List* (or *Schindler's Ark*) is not by a Jew but by an Australian non-Jew, Thomas Keneally.[16] But the film is by Steven Spielberg, a Jew, so it seems fair to include it here as a Jewish vision of the Holocaust. Or take Louis Begley's fine novel, *Wartime Lies,* about Jewish survival in German-occupied Poland.[17] It features a helpful German. The main difference is that the minority people in these books and films by minority authors are not passive; they are the subjects, not the objects, of their stories. They struggle against the odds or die their own deaths. Put differently, these stories are their stories, not the stories of the perpetrators. And as a consequence, not merely the point of view but the events themselves change in the telling.

In Germany a new perspective gradually emerged in the decades after the war. What caused it is hard to say, maybe just that the truth will out and that Jews in other countries, notably in the United States, were busy researching and writing their history and gave a name to the Jewish genocide, calling it the Holocaust, later Shoah. But there are milestones in Germany itself. One of them occurred in the mid-1960s, with the Auschwitz trial that began in December 1963 in Frankfurt. The executioners and perpetrators of the most notorious Nazi camp were on trial in a German city, accused and judged by the German system of justice. That stirred up the nation as the Nuremberg Trials in the mid-1940s had not. The proceedings in Nuremberg had been considered the revenge of the victors on the defeated. But in 1964 and 1965 in Frankfurt, Germans were judging Germans.

The most memorable literary testimony inspired by the Auschwitz trial was the play *The Investigation* (*Die Ermittlung*) by Peter Weiss, himself a Jewish refugee in Sweden during the Nazi years.[18] *The Investigation* used the trial record, compressing the witnesses' testimony and the arguments of the defense into a manageable text. The play was performed throughout Germany and in translation in the United States, as well as in many other countries. Germans finally began to face up to what had been done by their neighbors, in their name, and ultimately by themselves. But we should also keep in mind that the chief prosecutor in the case, the person who instigated the investigation in the first place, was a returned Jewish refugee, Fritz Bauer.

My old friend Martin Walser, with whom I had remained in touch, wrote an essay that was to be widely quoted, entitled "Our Auschwitz," in which he voiced his horror and deep dismay at the revelations in the courtroom.[19] There is no reason to doubt his sincerity, but at the same time there is a curious distancing in this piece, a constant reminder of, "I am different, the people I know are different, this is not, was not us." What is more, there is also an emphasis on the gulf that separates the experience of the victims, which must forever remain foreign, incomprehensible to us, from the nation of the perpetrators. No bridge leads from the Jews to the Germans, it would seem, because their experience divides them, although this experience involved both Jews and non-Jewish Germans. I remember reading Walser's essay with dismay, and I began to understand why the subject of my own concentration camp experience had been more or less taboo between us. I accused him privately of climbing on a bandwagon. He was naturally indignant. I pointed out that all this time he had known a Jewish victim who had lost most of her family in the years prior to our first meeting. He seemed astonished. He had not thought of me in this way. The awe and respect he shows the victims in his essay is that of philosemitism, an attitude that makes most Jews cringe, and that we always suspect of lacking sincerity, though it is vastly preferable to its opposite.

Yet German intellectuals were stirred into a rethinking of what they had done to their Jewish fellow citizens, and this awareness increased in the following years. On May 8, 1985, memorializing the end of the war, German president Richard von Weizsäcker termed the defeat of Germany in World War II a liberation that should be celebrated. Looking back, he pronounced about the immediate postwar years:

> May 8, 1945, was a day of liberation for us, a day that freed all of us from the inhuman system of National Socialism. . . . There were many ways of not burdening one's conscience, of shunning responsibility, looking away, keeping mum. When the unspeakable truth of the Holocaust then became known at the end of the war, all too many of us claimed that they had not known anything about it or even suspected anything.[20]

The governing term had been *Niederlage* (defeat), not *Befreiung* (liberation). Only the prisoners in the camps had felt truly liberated. The genius of Weizsäcker's speech was that it pointed out a way to look at the past, a suggestion of reinterpreting the meaning and the benefits of the Allied victory. He went on to say, "Every day it becomes clearer . . . that the eighth of May was a day of liberation." And that view gradually took such a hold that many younger Germans do believe it and agree with it. In 1985 Weizsäcker said: "We surely have no reason to participate in any celebrations of victory, only a reason to recognize the eighth of May as the end of an aberration of German history and a day that held the hope of a better future."[21]

In 2004 Germany did participate in celebrations of Allied victory, when Chancellor Gerhard Schröder joined the Allied representatives in Normandy to remember D-Day. It was the ultimate confirmation of "German liberation," surely an unprecedented reversal in the history of warfare. As late as 1985, even President von Weizsäcker could not have imagined such a thing, but it was he who set it in motion.

After the Frankfurt trial of 1963–65, and with a new generation in control, it became not only possible to mention Jews, it was even fashionable to treat them with empathy. In Sweden the German Jewish refugee Nelly Sachs had been writing poetry about the Holocaust in German. Thanks to being championed by the German poet and essayist Hans Magnus Enzensberger, she became a celebrity in Germany and received the very prestigious annual Peace Prize of the German Book Trade in 1965.[22] The next year, 1966, she shared the Nobel Prize for Literature with the Israeli writer Shmuel Yosef Agnon. In 1967 Alfred Andersch, who had previously written some of the sentimental stories about Jews that I have mentioned, published the novel *Efraim* and won high praise for its first-person narrative, in which a returned Jew encounters his former compatriots.[23] It is a problematic book, for while it purports to come to terms with the Holocaust, its consistent message is that there is no explanation for the Holocaust, that it could happen to anybody anytime, and therefore why bother digging into possible causes?

The realization that Jews are people like you and me had a troubling flip side, the underbelly of philosemitism. If Jews are like you and me, they must have deep resentments against us (Germans) and will harm us where they can; they are therefore not trustworthy, like Shakespeare's Shylock wanting his pound of flesh because he had been disrespected by Antonio.

A similar attitude rears its ugly head in many films by Rainer Werner Fassbinder. Fassbinder, who grew up in Munich, did meet some Jews in his childhood and was told to treat them with special courtesy, because they were Jews. The result was his antipathy to Jews, a childish irritation, which in time morphed into full-blown antisemitism, though he would never admit it. Fassbinder's Jewish characters are sinister psychiatrists and criminal real estate magnates who feed like maggots on the corpse of a diseased society. Enthusiastic film critics all over the world chose to ignore this aspect of his work, because he was such a gifted filmmaker. But take the film *Lili Marleen* of 1981, a wish-fulfillment dream of a good German girl who profited from the Nazis but never liked them.[24] The film tells the story of a Nazi pop star whose song "Lili Marleen" was such a hit in World War II that the Allied soldiers sang it as well as the German army. In the film the protagonist is engaged to the rich Swiss Jew, Robert, whose family does not want her and succeeds in having her Swiss visa revoked, so that it is really the fault of the Jews if poor little Willie is sucked into Nazi stardom. Once she becomes a success, the Swiss Jews use her for antifascist activities, where she puts her life at risk. She willingly goes along, for she is still in love with Robert. But at the end of the movie, Robert has married a rich Jewess and lives in splendor in Switzerland, while his lover kills herself in the squalor and misery of postwar Germany. The message is clearly that Jews care only for themselves and their kind and are unscrupulous in their exploitation of Christians.

Somehow Fassbinder's admirers closed their eyes to this racist ugliness, perhaps because he was a champion of the rights of some minorities, like Turkish workers, and managed to link his Jews with the establishment and with exploitative capitalism. (Where have we heard that before?) It was only when he wrote a blatantly antisemitic play, *Garbage, Death, and the City,* that people finally took into account what he was doing. The performance scheduled for Frankfurt was so vehemently picketed that it could not be produced.[25] Fassbinder killed himself with an overdose of drugs in 1982.

Since the early 1980s, antisemitism in Europe has assumed a new face. We know the classical kind, Christian in origin, based on a reading or misreading of the New Testament, and how it later turned into a pseudoscientific biological superstition about inferior and superior races. (Science, not only religion, has its own burden of superstitions.) Add to this the anti-Judaism of radical Islam, something that came much later and is derived from Christian, from Western sources. Historically Islam has not been intolerant of Jews. Finally, and hardest to assess at this time, is a new politically reactive sort of antisemitism that orients itself around current events. Critics of the government of Israel are accused of being antisemitic; sometimes the charge is justified, sometimes it is not. The infamous idea of a Jewish world conspiracy has gained currency in the Arab world, where Jews are said to have engineered everything from false rumors about a holocaust that never really took place to the 9/11 plot to the invasion of Iraq. In Europe police have to guard Jewish synagogues and schools against terrorist attacks, and some Jewish cemeteries have been desecrated.

But the memory of the Holocaust lingers. In Germany the national memory is fragmented, in the sense that if you want to be proud of your country you have to check yourself in view of the twelve Nazi years. Where Americans call their fathers and grandfathers "the greatest generation," their coevals in Germany are the most despised generation, and their war memories are under a cloud and cannot be celebrated. It is obvious that this state of mind breeds ambiguities and ambivalences.

My old friend Martin Walser received the Peace Prize of the German Book Trade in 1995, thirty years after it was awarded to Nelly Sachs.[26] The recipient of the prize has to give a full-length speech. Walser called his half-humorously a Sunday sermon. By now he had come to the conclusion that too much was being made of German war guilt, to the detriment of the rest of German culture and history, and that it was time to stop clobbering the nation with its past misdeeds. This attitude is fairly widespread in Germany, and it often implies that the general interest in the Holocaust is part of something that an international Jewish conspiracy has imposed on the Germans. In fact, Jews naturally explore their own history, but if others are watching and learning from them, it is because they want to, for reasons of their own, not because they are forced to do so.

In his speech Walser talked of a moral cudgel (*Moralkeule*), a weapon, he said, used to make Germans feel bad about themselves. He did not say who was wielding the cudgel, but the implication was clearly that it was the Jews. The speech resonated. It hit a nerve. Many Germans felt relieved that a respectable public figure finally said what they had felt all along.[27] Many Jews felt that Walser was putting them down and implicitly accusing them of bad faith. In a heated public controversy between Walser and Ignaz Bubis, the head of the Jewish community in Germany, Walser deeply insulted this man. Referring back to his Auschwitz essay, he told Bubis, who was a survivor of the camps and had tried to bring together Christians and Jews in a new Germany, that he, Walser, had written about Auschwitz at a time when Bubis was merely minding his own business. It is worth noting that Bubis had been a model for Fassbinder's vicious Jew in his play. Bubis's business was, by implication, at worst shady and at best self-centered. I thought, what I had thought as long as I had known him, that Martin did not have a clue what it meant to be a survivor. Such controversies carry much more weight in Germany than they would in the United States. Bubis died shortly afterward with a feeling that his life's work had come to nothing. He asked that he be buried in Israel, where his grave would be safe from desecration. Throughout all this controversy, Walser insisted that there was not an antisemitic bone in his body and pointed to his many Jewish friends, of whom I was one.

On the German literary scene, Jews and Jewish characters had become popular, though in some strange ways. In 1995 the prestigious Suhrkamp house published a purported memoir by one Binjamin Wilkomirski.[28] Some of you will remember this case, since it spilled over to the United States.[29] Wilkomirski was a Swiss who claimed to have been smuggled into Switzerland from the East as a very young Jewish child who had lost his entire family in German concentration camps and killing centers, Majdanek and Auschwitz, to be precise. He tells how he survived and recounts horrendous scenes of suffering and evil, which he was not allowed to talk about in Switzerland, his new home. His Swiss foster parents strictly refused to listen to anything relating to his early years, and this caused him much anxiety and even paranoid reactions. For example, he would think that the story of William Tell, shooting the apple from his son's head, was the story of an SS man shooting Jewish children.

Wilkomirski grew up sheltered, in a well-to-do family, became a musician, and only in his fifties decided to write down these shards of recollections. The book has the title *Bruchstücke* (*Fragments*). *Fragments* is the title of the English version, with the subtitle *Memories of a Wartime Childhood*. The book received rave reviews and was translated into no less than twelve languages. Here is a quote from the *New York Times* review of January 12, 1997: "Wilkomirski recalls the Holocaust with the powerful immediacy of innocence, injecting well-documented events with fresh terror and poignancy. Constructed like flashes of memory, the book unfolds in bursts of association, the way children tell stories. . . . He writes with a poet's vision, a child's state of grace."[30]

Wilkomirski joined organizations of child Holocaust survivors and became a kind of spokesman for them. He appeared at psychiatrists' meetings and impressed everybody. The director of Berlin's Antisemitism Research Institute, a historian of high repute, went so far as to compare Wilkomirski's book favorably to Anne Frank's diaries and charged that readers are comforted by Anne Frank's account because it contains no horror; Wilkomirski, he argued, gives us the real thing and should therefore be considered the more important writer on children in the Holocaust.[31] Wilkomirski received the Holocaust Award of the French Jewish Federation in Paris, which was later rescinded. He made a TV film about his life and the loneliness and isolation that were the permanent symptoms of ineradicable memories. The film was moving and well received.

There had always been some doubts about Wilkomirski's veracity, but in 1998 a diligent Swiss journalist turned up evidence that the whole story was a fraud. Wilkomirski was not even a Jew. He was born in a village in French Switzerland to a non-Jewish woman and put up for adoption by his mother, because he was illegitimate. He then spent some time in an orphanage in Zurich—and that orphanage plays a part in his book—until he was adopted by a wealthy German Swiss couple. This hidden but genuine biography is complete, without gaps, and entirely Swiss. The story of his harrowing early years is a simple invention, whether based on intentional fraud or on paranoid delusions. His German publisher has admitted that while the book was in production, they were warned that there was something fishy about this autobiography. They stopped the presses and sent a scout to Israel to consult historians and psychiatrists. They got positive replies and asked the author to write a postscript about the authenticity of his work. Then they went ahead with production of the book. But the psychiatrists and historians whom the publisher consulted can only have told them whether these memoirs were plausible, not if the facts were based on lived experience.

In his preface, Wilkomirski virtually warned readers that they were not necessarily reading a fact-based book, but he did not call it fiction either. He was on the defensive, but there were enough people ready to receive his fantasies if they just had some accreditation. Here is a passage from the preface:

> Legally accredited truth is one thing—the truth of a life another. Years of research, many journeys back to the places where I remember things happened, and countless conversations with specialists and historians have helped me clarify many previously inexplicable shreds of memory, to identify places and people, to find them again and to make a possible, more or less logical chronology out of it.[32]

As you can see, there is a strange kind of prevarication in this: it is not the facts, it is the memories he insists on, and who are we to gainsay what is in his head?

But there had always been cases like Wilkomirski's, that is, fraudulent books about the camps. Right after the war there appeared badly printed and poorly written books and pamphlets with detailed accumulations of cruelties in Dachau, Buchenwald, and other camps. The camps, as it turns out, provide a vivid background for hard pornography. Such products were not taken seriously for the longest time; they were seen for what they were, a dubious type of entertainment. Wilkomirski's book attracted a better audience and more serious attention. Part of the reason has to do with the passing of time that has caused a mythologization of the victims and that makes improbable circumstances seem more likely. Instead of being unappetizing escapees, the living victims partake of martyrdom; that is, repulsion has been displaced by awe. When that happens, fictional beings, like ghosts, distort our sense of reality. And we are not averse to this effect. The essence of the Holocaust and of the camps was the total destruction of human beings, and that is not something that is easy to assimilate and to admit into our mental household. It is easier to cope with an improbable series of sadistic images.

If you think the case of Wilkomirski is strange in its appropriation of the Jewish experience by a gentile, let me tell you yet another variant on this theme. Jakob Littner was a Jewish philatelist with a store in prewar Munich. The Nazis deported him to Poland, where he barely survived in ghettos and hiding places. After the war he came back to Munich, where he actually wanted to resettle, though he later immigrated to America. But during the first year of his return he wrote a memoir, which he called "My Journey Through the Night" ("Mein Weg durch die Nacht").[33] He too had difficulties finding a publisher, because there was a widespread feeling that everyone already knew everything there was to be known about Nazi atrocities and that nobody needed to hear any more. Littner's manuscript was contemptuously rejected as not being literary enough. Nevertheless, he finally found a publisher, himself a newcomer, who insisted that an editor would have to go over the manuscript thoroughly before it could appear in print. Littner accepted the condition, albeit unhappily.

The editor was also unknown, a young, talented writer named Wolfgang Koeppen. Koeppen got the manuscript, met the author, and felt superior to Littner, for he saw himself as a budding literary genius and Littner as a small-minded petit bourgeois who did not even understand the higher or metaphysical implications of what had happened to him. Littner's book appeared in 1948. In that edition Koeppen, who had done the rewrite, was not mentioned. The title had been changed and made more sensational. It was now called *Notes from a Hole in the Ground* (*Aufzeichnungen aus einem Erdloch*). It got tepid reviews, the publisher went bankrupt shortly afterward, and Littner immigrated to America. He is said to have disliked the changes and deletions and was therefore disappointed with the finished product of his labors.

So far so good; just one of those bad-luck stories. But in the meantime the editor went on to write novels of his own and became one of Germany's foremost authors. The trouble was that after four highly acclaimed novels he developed a lasting writer's block and stopped writing. His publisher supported and subsidized him in the hope that some great works were still in the offing. And then Koeppen remembered that old memoir he had once edited, which had been out of print for many years. In the meantime it was 1992, and things Jewish were fashionable. He and his publisher decided that Littner's story had been Koeppen's book all along and that the changes he had made were so significant that he could, with a good conscience, pretend that he had really written it. In a preface to the new edition Koeppen denied that he had met the author personally. He pretended that he had worked from scattered notes which Littner had left with his publisher and that Littner had been looking for a writer to tell his story, whereas in reality Littner, having told his own story, had been merely looking for a publisher.

As an old novel of the famous Wolfgang Koeppen, the book was widely reviewed and treated with respect. Littner himself had died by then, but his relatives in America were understandably displeased. Nowhere in the new edition did it say that Koeppen had worked from a completed manuscript which was even longer than the book he had made of it. He had cut out some passages. Since the publisher was the prestigious Suhrkamp house, the case caused a bit of a scandal and a number of writers and scholars took sides. A not very good English translation became available, and finally, in 2002, the original Littner book came out in Germany. I did a careful comparison of the two versions for a review, and there is no doubt in my mind that virtually everything in Koeppen's so-called novel is plagiarized. There are some small stylistic changes that do not improve the text, in my opinion. But even if you prefer these poetic changes, they are not significant enough to stand up under scrutiny as an independent rewrite. In the paperback edition only Koeppen's photo appeared on the cover, whereas Littner, the true author, was reduced to a quasi-fictional character, the hero of the story. My sense of this affair was that someone whose peacetime life had been destroyed had been robbed of the last thing left to him, that is, his experience of deprivation and survival and the words he chose to tell about it. Moreover, it was the society that had robbed him in the first place that had done it again. Never mind that the man who appropriated his manuscript was a famous novelist; even if he had improved the text, which I do not think he did, he would still have committed yet another act of what used to be known as "Aryanization," the taking over of Jewish property by non-Jews.

The most recent case that has stirred a controversy with regard to a portrayal of a Jewish character is again a novel by Martin Walser, titled *Death of a Critic*, published in 2002.[34] Even before it appeared in print it was attacked and caused a literary-political controversy, which, incidentally, later helped to make it a best seller. Before publication, it was to appear in installments in a major newspaper, the *Frankfurter Allgemeine Zeitung*, which had previously serialized several of Walser's novels. This time the *Frankfurter Allgemeine Zeitung* rejected his manuscript, and the newspaper's literary editor wrote a long article attacking the book for its antisemitic slant. Copies for a select few were soon available by e-mail on the Internet, and everyone who had anything to do with literature in Germany weighed in, both before and after the novel's publication. The book is a satire, not a good one, on a Jewish critic who has great power to make or break a book but has crude tastes and no imagination, and who delights in destroying careers.

The problem is that this protagonist conforms to every Jewish stereotype. A heated controversy before and after publication took place in virtually every German newspaper and magazine, not to mention radio and TV, somewhat akin to what we experienced with regard to Mel Gibson's 2004 film *The Passion of the Christ*. I believe that Walser's book is unforgivably antisemitic, though its author cannot be simply called antisemitic. The case is complicated and adds up to the postwar confusion about Jews in the German mind. Walser has many defenders among German intellectuals and claims that what I call Jewish stereotyping is unknown to him. I think this claim by someone who was educated in the Hitler Youth is disingenuous. By the way, Elie Wiesel's work used to be published in German with an introduction by Martin Walser. Wiesel has asked to have Walser's piece deleted from future editions.

By this time you may well ask, "Is there no way out? Is there no writer who treats the Jewish experience as part of German or European history and manages to integrate the two?" Actually, there is one, whose books have also been successful in the United States. The most thoughtful, non-Jewish German writer about issues relating to Jews and the Holocaust was W. G. Sebald, who unfortunately died in 2001 of a heart attack while driving a car. There are two major works, a collection of stories called *The Emigrants* and his last novel, *Austerlitz*.[35] They deal with homelessness, Jewish or non-Jewish, and the decline of Europe into an indifference that erodes the environment as much as human lives; they deal with coldness and memory, and they are filled with a heart-wrenching though subdued sympathy with suffering. Sebald was not only a creative writer, he was also a teacher and scholar of German literature in an English college. Somehow Jewishness, being a Jew, was a preoccupation for him, presumably because it did not appear to him to be the exception but rather paradigmatic for modern man.

Even in his early scholarship, before he began to write his own creative works, Sebald often dealt with Jewish writers and felt a kinship with Jewish themes. For example, in an interpretation of Kafka's *Castle* he sees in this late novel a representation of the Jewish diaspora, calling it by the Hebrew word *galut,* and he interprets its hapless hero K as the expected Messiah.[36] Sebald wrote about the Jewish Austrian writers Hermann Broch, Arthur Schnitzler, and Elias Canetti, and about the ghetto authors at the edge of the Austro-Hungarian Empire, Joseph Roth and Karl Emil Franzos, and later about the Holocaust survivor Jean Améry, who has written memorably about the experience of torture.[37] These were not efforts at some kind of restitution. What attracted him to these men and their works was their lack of illusion, their pessimism, their melancholic outlook, and their outsiderdom, all qualities with which he could identify and that he later incorporated in his own stories and novels.

In Sebald's collection of stories *The Emigrants,* Jewish and non-Jewish characters are so intermingled that some careless readers have concluded they are all Jewish. The novel *Austerlitz*—his major work, I think—has for a hero a Czech Jewish boy who is sent to England to escape the Holocaust and grows up in a devout Christian family without knowing his background. Later in life he becomes a historian of architecture and retraces his own history together with Europe's. As you see, Jewish and non-Jewish concerns merge in these works.

There is no firm conclusion to the telltale signs of Germany's unease in confronting its past. However, West Germans have made valiant attempts since the 1960s to integrate those twelve infamous years into their consciousness and their view of themselves and their traditions. To see the difference, you only have to look at Austria, which has been much slower and more reluctant to do the same, and to East Germany under Communist rule. Nevertheless, there have been bumps in the road. Some of these, as they manifest themselves on the literary scene, I have tried to sketch. What remains a puzzle and a mystery to me is why the Jews, a tiny minority, still loom so large. Given this climate of consciousness, a TV drama, like the episode from *Law and Order* I described at the beginning, would dredge up associations that are different from the American ones because they touch on the question of collective guilt or the guilt of the fathers. It is as if the German imagination were a haunted house. And perhaps that is exactly what it is.

NOTES

1. *Law and Order,* "Evil Breeds," season 14, episode 18, March 24, 2004.

2. On this subject, see David Shyovitz, American-Israeli Cooperative Enterprise, "The Virtual Jewish History Tour: Germany," 2004, http://www.jewishvirtuallibrary.org/jsource/vjw/germany.html.

3. Bruno Apitz, *Nackt unter Wölfen: Roman* (Halle: Mitteldeutscher Verlag, 1958). The first English translation appeared in 1960; see Bruno Apitz, *Naked Among Wolves,* trans. Edith Anderson (Berlin: Seven Seas, 1960). The film *Nackt unter Wölfen* appeared in 1963 and was directed by East German Frank Beyer.

4. Chapters on Erich Fried can be found in James N. Hardin and Donald G. Daviau, *Austrian Fiction Writers After 1914* (Detroit: Gale Research, 1989); and Donald G. Daviau, *Major Figures of Contemporary Austrian Literature* (New York: Peter Lang, 1987). See also Gerhard Lampe, *Ich will*

mich erinnern an alles was man vergisst: Erich Fried, Biographie und Werk (Cologne: Bund, 1989); and Steven W. Laurie, *Erich Fried: A Writer Without a Country* (New York: Peter Lang, 1996).

5. Works written by Leo Perutz in the 1920s and later reprinted include *Master of the Day of Judgment* (New York: Arcade, 1994); *The Marquis of Bolibar* (New York: Arcade, 1989); *Turlupin* (London: Harvill, 1996); and *By Night Under the Stone Bridge* (London: Harvill, 1989).

6. See the afterword by Hans-Harald Müller in Leo Perutz, *Nachts unter der steinernen Brücke: Ein Roman aus dem alten Prag* (Vienna: P. Zsolnay, 1988).

7. For the most recent German-language edition, see Leo Perutz, *Nachts unter der steinernen Brücke* (Furth im Wald: Vitalis, 2003). For the most recent English-language edition, see Leo Perutz, *By Night under the Stone Bridge* (New York: Arcade, 1990).

8. On Walser, see *Frontline*, "October 1998: A National Controversy over Remembrance and Forgetting," May 31, 2005. See also PBS, "Frontline," http://www.pbs.org/wgbh/pages/frontline/shows/germans/germans/controversy.html.

9. See Ruth Kluger, *Still Alive: A Holocaust Girlhood Remembered* (New York: Feminist Press at City University of New York, 2001).

10. Martin Walser, *Ein Flugzeug über dem Haus, und andere Geschichten* (Frankfurt am Main: Suhrkamp, 1955).

11. Hans Scholz, *Am grünen Strand der Spree: So gut wie ein Roman* (Hamburg: Hoffman and Campe, 1955).

12. Harper Lee, *To Kill a Mockingbird* (New York: Harper Collins, 1955).

13. William Faulkner, *Intruder in the Dust* (New York: Random House, 1948).

14. Horton Foote (screenplay), *To Kill a Mockingbird,* 1962; Ben Maddow (screenplay), *Intruder in the Dust,* 1949.

15. Toni Morrison, *Beloved: A Novel* (New York: Knopf, 1987).

16. Thomas Keneally, *Schindler's List* (New York: Simon and Schuster, 1982).

17. Louis Begley, *Wartime Lies* (New York: Knopf, 1991).

18. Peter Weiss, *Die Ermittlung* [*The Investigation*], 1965.

19. Martin Walser, "Unser Auschwitz" ["Our Auschwitz"], *Kursbuch* 1 (1965): 189–200.

20. Richard von Weizsäcker, speech, May 8, 1985.

21. Ibid.

22. Nelly Sachs, Peace Prize of the German Book Trade, 1965.

23. Alfred Andersch, *Efraim* (Zurich: Diogenes, 1967).

24. Rainer Werner Fassbinder, *Lili Marleen,* 1981.

25. Rainer Werner Fassbinder, *Der Müll, die Stadt und der Tod* [*Garbage, the City, and Death*] (Frankfurt am Main: Verlag der Autoren, 1981).

26. Martin Walser, Peace Prize of the German Book Trade, 1995.

27. See *Frontline,* "October 1998"; and http://www.pbs.org/wgbh/pages/frontline/shows/germans/germans/controversy.html.

28. Binjamin Wilkomirski, *Bruchstücke: Aus einer Kindheit, 1939–1948* [*Fragments: Memories of a Wartime Childhood, 1939–1948*] (Frankfurt am Main: Suhrkamp, 1995).

29. For two early accounts of Wilkomirski's story, see Phillip Gourevitch, "The Memory Thief," *New Yorker,* June 14, 1999; and Elena Lappin, "The Man with Two Heads," *Granta* 66 (1999). The account by the Swiss journalist is Stefan Maechler, *Der Fall Wilkomirski* (Zurich: Pendo, 2000). It is available in English as *The Wilkomirski Affair: A Study in Biographical Truth,* trans. John E. Woods (New York: Schocken, 2001).

30. Julie Salamon, "Childhood's End," *New York Times,* January 12, 1997.

31. The reference is to Wolfgang Benz, director of Berlin's Antisemitism Research Institute.

32. Wilkomirski, *Bruchstücke.* There are some who believe that even if the book is a fraud, it still has power and is worth reading. On this subject, see Arthur Samuelson, publisher at Schocken, who stated that he might just "re-issue the book as fiction" because the book still had a kind of imagistic power; see the discussion in Susan Suleiman, *Crises in Memory and the Second World War* (Cambridge, Mass.: Harvard University Press, 2006); and Michael Bernard-Donals, "Beyond the Question of Authenticity: Witness and Testimony in the *Fragments* Controversy," *PMLA* 116, no. 3 (October 2001): 1302–15.

33. Jakob Littner, *Aufzeichnungen aus einem Erdloch* [*Notes from a Hole in the Ground*] (Munich: Helmut Kluger, 1948).

34. Martin Walser, *Tod eines Kritikers* [*Death of a Critic*] (Frankfurt am Main: Suhrkamp, 2002).

35. W. G. Sebald, *The Emigrants,* trans. Michael Hulse (New York: New Directions, 1996); W. G. Sebald, *Austerlitz,* trans. Anthea Bell (New York: Random House, 2001).

36. Franz Kafka, *The Castle* (New York: Dramatist's Play Service, 2003).

37. Sebald, *The Emigrants; Austerlitz; Vertigo,* trans. Michael Hulse (New York: New Directions, 2000); *The Rings of Saturn,* trans. Michael Hulse (New York: New Directions, 1998).

Geneviève Zubrzycki

"Poles-Catholics" and "Symbolic Jews": Religion and the Construction of Symbolic Boundaries in Poland

The logic of normal, correct, and healthy antisemitism is the following: "Adam Michnik is a Jew, therefore he is a hooligan, a thief, a traitor, a bandit, etc. . . . ." Magical antisemitism, however, works this way: "Adam Michnik is a thief, therefore he is most probably a Jew."

—*Adam Michnik*

I'm not an antisemite. That's how they are representing me everywhere. That's not true. I love Jews. I just don't want my homeland, Poland, to be ruled by Jews.

—*Kazimierz Świtoń*

IN THE SUMMER OF 1998, SELF-DEFINED "POLES-CATHOLICS" ERECTED hundreds of crosses just outside Auschwitz, in the backyard of what had been, from 1984 to 1993, the infamous Carmel Convent.[1] This action was spurred by rumors to the effect that an eight-meter-high cross known as the "papal cross" would be removed from the grounds.[2] (See figure 17.) Antoni Macierewicz, a well-known political figure, characterized the intended removal as "religious defamation and national humiliation," and Cardinal Józef Glemp's comments, whenever the papal cross and Auschwitz were brought up in interviews, were interwoven with antisemitic nuances. In mid-March 1998 some parishes had initiated special masses "for the respect and protection of the papal cross," alongside prayer vigils in the "defense" of crosses in Poland. At the annual, Jewish-sponsored March of the Living in

Figure 17. The eight-meter-high papal cross. Prior to its erection at Auschwitz, it was part of an altar located on the grounds of Birkenau. In 1979 Pope John Paul II conducted a mass there, hence the designation "papal cross." From the personal archives of Kazimierz Świtoń.

April that year, banners and posters proclaiming "Defend the Cross," "Keep Jesus at Auschwitz" (in English), and "Polish Holocaust by Jews, 1945–56" were displayed on the fence of the former convent yard—"the gravel pit," as it was still known, hearkening back to its function during the Auschwitz era.

In June, Kazimierz Świtoń, ex-Solidarity activist and former deputy of the Confederation of Independent Poland, initiated a hunger strike that lasted forty-two days.[3] Świtoń demanded a firm commitment from the Catholic Church that the papal cross would remain. This demand was not met, whereupon he appealed to his fellow Poles to plant 152 crosses on the grounds of the gravel pit, both to commemorate the execution of 152 ethnic Poles on that site in 1941 and to "protect and defend the papal cross." This appeal proved successful: during the summer and fall of 1998, the site was transformed into the epicenter of what became known as the "war of the crosses" as individuals, civic organizations, and religious groups from every corner of Poland (and from as far away as Canada, the United States, and Australia) answered the call. By August 21, there were 135 crosses on the site. A month later, 236 crosses were in place—96 of them measuring four meters or more in height. By the time the Polish army finally removed them in May 1999, there were a total of 322 crosses at the gravel pit.

The fourteen-month-long "war" was marked by debate, legal procedures, numerous declarations from public officials, and accusations and counter-accusations that embroiled the government and the opposition, Polish public intellectuals, Polish Jewish activists, groups from the extreme Right, the Catholic Church, and a schismatic brotherhood claiming to represent "true" Catholicism in defense of the Polish nation. Meanwhile, a group of U.S. congressional representatives and the Israeli government demanded the removal of all the crosses, while members of the Polish and Jewish diasporas added their own grains of salt to the boiling stew.

It took the concerned authorities several months to find a solution to the crisis. At first, the government stood on the sidelines, evoking the principle of separation of church and state as defined in the Concordat of 1997 in arguing that the papal cross was the property of the Catholic Church, which was responsible for the use of its religious symbols.[4] The church countered that the crosses stood on government property and that the Catholic Church had no monopoly over the symbol of the cross, which belonged to the entire Christian community of believers. Over time, however, as a growing number of crosses appeared at the gravel pit, the crisis became more acute. The government was subjected to pressure from the United States and from Israel precisely at a time when it was engaged in delicate negotiations regarding Poland's application for membership in NATO. The church was troubled both by the fact that many Catholics had disregarded the Polish episcopate's request (in mid-August) to stop planting crosses and by the persistent involvement of a schismatic group in the affair. In the end, concerted attempts were made to regain control of the gravel pit.[5] Following many legal battles and the passage of a law regarding "the protection of the grounds of former Nazi camps," on May 7, 1999, a one-hundred-meter zone was established around Auschwitz, giving the government the legal means to evict Świtoń from the gravel pit, where he had been encamped for nearly a year. The church arranged for the crosses to be relocated to a nearby sanctuary.

The papal cross, however, remained. Thus there was no resolution of the initial conflict concerning the presence of that specific cross. For this reason, Świtoń's "cross-planting" can be regarded (and is so regarded by him) as a success. By escalating the conflict and radicalizing their demands—from the retention of one cross to the retention of hundreds—the papal cross's defenders successfully altered the terms of any proposed compromise. In fact, by the end of the affair, removal of the papal cross was not even considered an option; at most, the removal of Świtoń and the three-hundred-odd crosses was the principal objective of those involved.

Fought on several fronts, the war of the crosses was structured along two main axes. The first, and more apparent, revolved around the contested meaning of Auschwitz and the problematic presence of a Christian symbol at that site and was played out between Poles and Jews.[6] The second concerned the contested meaning of the cross, and, more broadly, that of the nation in post-Communist Poland, which became a matter of serious debate among Poles. While the war of the crosses was without a doubt an interreligious and interethnic (and, as noted, even an international) conflict, it was also an *intra*national and *intra*religious crisis. It divided ethno-religious from civic-secular nationalists; it divided certain members of the clergy and of the episcopate from others; and it also drove a wedge between the institutional church and the self-defined Polish-Catholics who were responsible for planting the crosses. In short, it became the occasion for Poles to debate the relationship between Polish national identity and Catholicism.[7]

As I have shown elsewhere, the fall of Communism and the building of a legitimate state, a state of and for Poles, necessitated the specification of what Polishness "is" and brought about the examination of its association with Catholicism.[8] In this context, the post-Communist period has been shaped by a society-wide debate in which some call for the maintenance of a "Catholic Poland, united under the sign of the cross," while others demand the confessional neutrality of the state and advocate a civic-secular definition of national identity. Thus, the place of religion, religious symbols, and the role of the Catholic Church in public life have been fiercely debated since 1989. "Jews" occupy a privileged place in this debate, serving as a trope by which the relationship between Polishness and Catholicism is defined.[9] In this chapter, I address the ways in which various Catholic groups articulate, both in discourse and via their ritual use of symbols, the relationship between religion and national identity, and how Jewishness is constructed as a symbol through (and sometimes against) which Polishness is (re)defined.[10]

CATHOLICISM AND THE CHURCH AFTER COMMUNISM

According to most popular and some academic representations of the Catholic Church under Communism, the institution was solidly unified against the party-state, with the two monoliths confronting each other like sumo wrestlers in a stadium packed with the church's cheering fans. The church, so the story goes, was not merely indivisible; its historic symbiotic unity with "the nation" and with civil society (in the 1980s, under the banner of Solidarity) was unbreakable. Wyszyński, Wojtyła, and Wałęsa—the priest, the pope, and the prophet, the "Holy Trinity" of the fight against the Communist regime and its atheist state—symbolized the strength of the Catholic Church and its bond with civil society and the nation. There is, of course, some measure of truth in this picture, not to mention a genuine aesthetic appeal. The need for unity under adversity pushed aside differences of opinions, strategies, and styles, such that divisions within the church, as within Solidarity or society more broadly, were in fact kept to a minimum. Ironically, while the party-state's attempt to "divide and conquer" failed, the post-Communist process of building a sovereign and democratic state led to certain cleavages between church and civil society, as tensions that had been glossed over in the past were brought under scrutiny.[11] The decade following the fall of Communism witnessed an unprecedented drop in the popularity of the church, a rise in anticlericalism, and a crisis within the church: the monolith was breaking into a colorful, clashing mosaic, but the whole was less than the sum of its parts. At the same time, there was also a noticeable rise in antisemitism. As I will show, these two phenomena were related.

Several surveys conducted by the Centrum Badania Opinii Społecznej (Center for Public Opinion Research) indicate significant attitudinal changes toward the Catholic Church and its role. Positive appreciation of the church's activities fluctuated from a high of 90 percent in 1989 to an all-time low of 38 percent in 1993.[12] During the 1990s, almost three-quarters of Polish society felt that the political influence of the church was too great, regardless of which parties were represented in parliament.[13] This seismic shift in attitudes cannot be explained by the secularization thesis, since the change in attitude has not been accompanied by an increase of religious indifference or a drastic decrease in religious participation: according to 2001 data, 96 percent of Poles declare themselves to be "believers," and 58 percent go to church at least once a week.[14]

The drop in approval may instead be explained by the fact that many Poles have changed their expectations of the church since the fall of Communism, finding in the new political constellation a number of other, and sometimes competing, elements for the construction of their social identities. Polish national identity can now express itself through channels other than religion, and there exists a plurality of institutions through which Poles can make their voices heard. This new institutional pluralism has important implications, foremost among them the end of the moral and social monopoly of the Catholic Church. I have suggested elsewhere that the advent of a legitimate, democratic state provoked the rupture of the model of relations between the church and civil society.[15] The new dynamic was characterized by a growing critique of the church and by the church's attempt to compensate for the loss of its social influence both by trying to increase its institutional power and by intervening in the political sphere.[16]

The "recovery of independence" (*odzyskanie niepodległości*), as the transition from Communism is commonly termed, prompted tensions not only between civil society and the church but also within the church itself. Old cleavages resurfaced and new fissures were created. In consequence, a more expansive (though still restricted) "menu of Catholicisms" became available for clergy and the faithful. Over the last decade, four main orientations have evolved within the church and among Catholics: traditional-conservative, "purist," "open" or liberal, and "closed" or integrist Catholicism.[17] Key typological axes include the group's conceptualization of the relation between Polishness and Catholicism; the role of the church in the public sphere; church-state relations; "Europe" as threat or promise; and last, but not least, each group's relationship to Jews and antisemitism.

By far the most popular orientation is that of traditional-conservatives. Theirs is the Catholicism of "continuity," supported by Cardinal Glemp and the majority of clergy as well as by political figures such as Lech Wałęsa. It is characterized by its active engagement in the life of "the nation" (with the nation cast as a divine community and the church as its guardian), and by pressure for the public demonstration of faith. During the Communist era, this model of traditional religiosity and national activism on the part of the church was successful in resisting state-sponsored atheism; it also provided a mobilizing narrative of the nation as intrinsically and primordially Catholic. For traditionalists, the fall of Communism meant the return to "normalcy," which they understood as a pre–World War II model of church-state relations, with Catholicism holding the status of quasi-state religion.[18]

According to traditional-conservative Catholics, the specificity of the Polish way of life resides primarily in the tight relationship between religion and national identity. However, the *Polak-katolik* model is envisaged not as a reality that must be preserved at any cost, but rather as a summons and invitation: by being better Catholics, Poles become better, "truer" Poles.[19] Following this logic, which was codified in the writings of Roman Dmowski (the nationalist leader whose classic *Thought of the Modern Pole* was reedited in the 1990s with a preface added by Cardinal Glemp), non-Catholics are not "true" Poles, and Jews are irremediably "alien," that is, "strangers" among the Poles.

Traditional-conservatives did not oppose Poland's so-called return to Europe, but they argue that Europe would be stronger if it renewed its bonds to Catholicism. Accordingly, they see it as their mission to re-evangelize the continent, with Poland as the *Antemurale*

Christianitatis, the rampart of Christianity. No longer must Christians halt the advance of the (external) infidel; rather, Europe must be brought back to its forgotten values. A corollary to this is that Poland's integration into a "de-Christianized Europe" brings with it a threat to Polish and Christian values: in the wake of Communism's collapse, it is the West and its corrupted values that endanger this last European bastion of Christianity. Poland, then, must also remain Catholic in order to protect Europe from itself.

Contrary to the traditional-conservative model of Catholicism that accentuates the public dimension of faith and politicizes religion, "purists" focus on its private aspects: on the deepening of faith, on its active internalization. According to them, traditional Catholicism is overly associated with secular emotions and has become a political religion. They warn against the conflation of nation and religion: instead of emphasizing Polish Catholic exceptionalism, as do the traditionalists and integrists, the purists stress the universality of Catholicism. They also consistently promote the principles of Vatican II: namely, ecumenism and attempts to modernize the Polish church. Purists, therefore, should not be characterized as resistant to change; rather, the changes they endorse are those related to a universalist construction of faith-based Catholic renewal. Despite their multiple critiques of traditional Catholicism, they do not reject it altogether, but rather aim at modifying it so that it can better adapt to the new exigencies of the contemporary moment. The purist model has a strong base in the church hierarchy and is particularly popular among the younger generation.[20] As of the early years of the twenty-first century, it was also well positioned within the episcopate, represented by the orientations of Archbishops Damian Zimoń, Józef Życiński, Henryk Muszyński, and Tadeusz Pieronek.

"Open" Catholics are primarily those associated with "liberal" Catholic publications and groups: *Tygodnik Powszechny, Znak,* the Catholic Intelligentsia Club, and *Więź.* These loose formations actively embraced Vatican II even when the reigning Polish Catholic authority at the time, Cardinal Wyszyński, remained somewhat reluctant to implement its principles in the Communist context. "Open" Catholicism is much more elitist than the traditional and integrist orientations, both of which have strong populist accents. Its clerical supporters have included Józef Tischner (1931–2000), Stanisław Musiał (1938–2004), Stanisław Obirek, and Michał Czajkowski, and it is also embraced by lay intellectuals. Within the episcopate, however, it enjoys only a marginal appeal, and it is often attacked by traditional and integrist Catholics. The "open" Catholics' critique of traditional-conservative Catholicism is harsher than that of the purists. They are committed to creating a dialogue with the secular media, and they are frequent contributors to *Gazeta Wyborcza*.

Following Vatican II, "open" Catholics see dialogue with people of other faiths (or those without faith) as their duty and thus actively support pluralism. *Znak, Tygodnik Powszechny,* and *Więź* frequently publish articles on Judaism and advocate a rapprochement and recon-ciliation with their "older brothers in faith." Their contributors and publishers have also been at the forefront in denouncing antisemitism both within Polish society and within the church itself.[21] Father Musiał was certainly the church's most outspoken persona undertaking this mission: he was actively involved in the negotiations for the reloca-tion of the Carmelite nuns away from Auschwitz, and he openly criticized the church's "soft" stance on antisemitism. Aside from his vociferous condemnation of the war of the crosses and of the church for "putting its head in the sand," Musiał sharply criticized the church hierarchy for not taking more severe action against Father Henryk Jankowski, the renowned Solidarity chaplain who has since become notorious for both his stridently antisemitic sermons and his con-troversial Easter Sepulchers. Musiał's groundbreaking article, "Black Is Black," provoked a mini-scandal within the church, exposing and furthering tensions between the four main groups of Catholics.[22] The ensuing debate between Musiał and Father Waldemar Chrostowski (a traditional-conservative priest who defended the church's position vis-à-vis Jankowski) which filled the pages of the Catholic press was paradigmatic of this split.[23]

Finally, there is the group of Catholics at the opposite end of the continuum: integrists, or "closed" Catholics, personified by Jankowski and Father Tadeusz Rydzyk, the founder and director of the contro-versial Radio Maryja. Integrists represent a large though not dominant segment of Polish Catholicism. At the same time, they are probably its most vocal component, and they occupy the public space with immense semiotic force. Radio Maryja ("the Catholic voice in your home") and various print publications such as *Nasz Dziennik (Our Daily)* and *Nasza Polska (Our Poland)* exert a significant influence on the face of Catholicism in Poland by affixing the terms and relative positions that appear in public debate.[24] The voice of Radio Maryja in Polish homes is that of anti-Communism, antiliberalism, and anti-semitism, with Jews representing Communism and liberalism.[25] Like the traditionalists, but more strident in their message, integrists see the nation as a divine creation, not as the product of historical processes. As a result, the state, which is the guardian of the nation, must be confessional in order to preserve the divine order. As Dmowski put it, the equation between Polishness and Catholicism is God-given, and must be protected by the state.

The integrists are the group that compacts Polishness and Ca-tholicism most tightly. "Closed" Catholics see themselves as "true" Catholics and "true" Poles, whereas "open" Catholics are, in their eyes, "washed out" Catholics and "bad" Poles, or even crypto-Jews. Jerzy Turowicz (1912–99), for example, who for nearly half a century was editor-in-chief of the Catholic weekly *Tygodnik Powszechny,* was often suspected of being a Jew by "closed" Catholic circles, who in this way could understand his "selling out" to "Jews," a reference to Turowicz's contacts among left-leaning intellectuals and his promotion of Christian-Jewish dialogue in the pages of his weekly.

The language used by "closed" Catholics is one of exclusion, hence their label (which was given to them by "open" Catholics). Tellingly, the adjective they use when referring both to "open" Catholics and to the secular Center-Left is *Polish-speaking* (to denote a person) and *Polish-language* (to denote a publication). These adjectives pejora-tively distinguish such people, associations, and publications from "authentically" Polish ones. In addition, people who identify or are associated with Radio Maryja commonly refer to *Gazeta Wyborcza* as *Gazeta koszerna,* the "Kosher newspaper." This nickname refers to the Jewishness of Adam Michnik and of some of the newspaper's contribu-tors, but also, more broadly, to the paper's Center-Left position and to its position in support of Christian-Jewish dialogue, which "closed" Catholics see as "pro-Jewish" and "politically correct."

For integrists, the post-Communist period is seen as the con-tinuation of totalitarianism—totalitarianism with a new, liberal face, which "Europe" has come to symbolize. Even following Poland's entry into the European Union, Radio Maryja remains locked in its crusade against Poland's so-called return to Europe.[26] The European Union is perceived as a potential "new internationale" (referring to the Soviet Union's former aspirations), an unambiguous evil, one additional step toward a world order that will encircle and strangle Polishness. The position of the Far Right and the so-called national-Catholics (associated with "closed" Catholicism) is thus isolationist. Europe's *Antemurale Christianitatis* is redefined in peculiar fashion: now that the Iron Curtain has been lifted, Poland should seek to erect a different kind of barrier, not on its eastern border in order to protect Europe from the pagan East, but rather on its western edge, to protect itself from Europe and its degenerate Western values (consumerism and secularization) or the lack of values (ethical relativism).

THE BROKEN MONOLITH AND THE "WAR OF THE CROSSES"

These differences and divisions within Polish Catholic society were brought to light very clearly during the war of the crosses. During the crisis, the church hierarchy's position on the papal and the other crosses was neither unified nor consistent. The episcopate expressed various opinions, and Cardinal Glemp's declarations fluctuated from open approval to condemnation of the cross-planting.

Consider, to wit, Glemp's words about the papal cross at the beginning of the summer of 1998, when people were mobilizing for its defense but were not yet erecting additional crosses at the gravel pit:

> The Polish people [*lud*] have been put up on the cross. That is why they love this cross, [which is] a sign of love in suffering wherever it is: in the shipyards, in Warsaw or in Oświęcim. In Oświęcim the cross has been standing and will stand. . . . The Eiffel Tower did not and does not please everyone, but [that] is not a reason to remove it.[27]

The three Polish sites enumerated by Cardinal Glemp are closely associated with the nation, with Polish martyrdom and resilience. All three are symbols of the moral victory of Poles under occupation: Oświęcim and Warsaw during World War II, and the Gdańsk shipyards under Communism (where the dissident Solidarity movement had its genesis). The Polish nation is identified here with Christ, a continuation of Polish Romantic thought: its history and destiny are intimately linked to the cross. (See figure 18.) Most striking, however, is the analogy drawn by Glemp between the cross at Auschwitz and the Eiffel Tower in Paris, which shows the extent to which he misunderstood, downplayed, and belittled the Jewish objection. Both in his

Figure 18. The papal cross is surrounded by smaller crosses planted in the summer of 1998 on the invitation of Kazimierz Świtoń. In the background, behind the papal cross, is Auschwitz's Block 11, the so-called Block of Death. From the personal archives of Kazimierz Świtoń.

early allocutions and through his later prolonged silence on the matter, Cardinal Glemp implicitly and sometimes even explicitly justified the war of the crosses.

Once the war of the crosses was fully engaged, the harshest critique of the church's position came from Father Musiał:

> The shameful cross game at Auschwitz continues. What is going on here does not have anything to do with God or with the commemoration of the victims. For almost 45 years after the war this place did not interest either Catholics or patriots. . . . There is in this country an Authority [whose] mission and raison d'être require it to put an end to this battle of the crosses at Auschwitz. Everything, however, points to the fact that this Authority has buried its head in the sand, and what is worse, wants national and world public opinion to interpret this gesture of silence as a sign of virtue, discernment, and civic consideration. . . . It is high time

for the Church in Poland to awaken and raise its voice against the abuse of religious symbols for extra-religious goals. In truth, those against Christ's Cross are not the ones demanding that the crosses be removed from the gravel pit . . . but rather those who planted the crosses, and those who want them to remain. Christ's cross is not a tight fist. And that is what the crosses at the gravel pit in Auschwitz are.[28]

A few days later, in a message perceived by many, including Świtoń, as supporting the retention of the papal cross, Cardinal Glemp replied that the church had no monopoly over the symbol of the cross and therefore could not authoritatively intervene:[29] "The cross is not the property of the Catholic Church, but is linked with Christianity, and as a symbol it is understood and recognized in Western civilization as a sign of love and suffering. Conceived in that way, not only the episcopate, but all those who accept with faith . . . this cross have the right to its use and its defense."[30] Although Glemp stressed the right to defend the cross as a Christian symbol, he also indirectly justified its political instrumentalization by attributing responsibility for the crisis to the "Jewish side":

This is Polish land, and any imposition by others is taken as in-terference with sovereignty. . . . Mr. Świtoń and his group . . . are often singled out as the cause for the escalation of tensions. We have to say, in the name of truth, that this group did not arise out of nowhere, but rather in reaction to the constant and increasingly strident Jewish demands for the rapid removal of the cross.[31]

Cardinal Glemp also directly and contemptuously denounced Father Musiał's position:

Some are decidedly for the defense of the cross, others are sup-porters of the Jewish position, such as . . . Father Musiał, editor of *Tygodnik Powszechny.* The one-sided condemnation of the episco-pate [for not satisfying] the Jewish side—cannot bear fruit mostly because it is unfounded. . . . We have to ponder how the planting of new crosses can be used in the process of agreement and uni-fication. The affair must find a positive resolution on the condi-tion that people at the service of a one-sided solution, like Father Musiał for example, will not inflame [popular feelings] with their apodictic judgments.[32]

In his expressly personal rebuttal, Glemp accused Musiał of supporting the "Jewish option" instead of defending the cross, as a Catholic priest should. The same week, however, Archbishops Muszyński and Zimoń, purists according to the typology adopted here, characterized the cross-planting action as both a provocation and a harmful manipulation of the religious symbol for political purposes. "Those who are using the cross as an instrument in the fight against anyone," declared Muszyński in an appeal to stop planting crosses, "are actually acting as *enemies of Christ's cross*."[33] In response to this new twist, only four days after his declaration, Cardinal Glemp issued a new statement in which he charged that the cross-planting had been orchestrated by an "irresponsible group." Their action, he said, diminished the symbol of the cross: "The gravel pit, this way, loses its gravity." The primate appealed to those concerned to stop planting crosses at the gravel pit and he asked bishops to "try to control the rise of this un-Church-like action."[34] Similarly, Bishop Pieronek characterized the groups involved in the action as "anti-Church."[35]

Finally, at the end of August, the episcopate of Poland issued a long-awaited official declaration in which, echoing the position of purists within the hierarchy, it condemned the cross-planting:

> As shepherds of the Church, we address our words to the faithful, expressing our gratitude to those who have suffered for the cross during the unlawful Communist period. . . . At the same time, we categorically underline that it is forbidden for anyone to overuse the holy sign of the cross and turn it against the Church in Poland, by creating agitation and conflict. We declare that the action of planting crosses at the gravel pit has been undertaken without the permission of the relevant diocesan Bishop, and even against his will. . . . Planting crosses on one's own initiative at the gravel pit is provocative and is contrary to the dignity that such a place requires. . . . Organized in such a fashion, the action equally hurts the memory of the murdered victims and the well-being of the Church and the nation, in addition to inflicting pain on the different sensibility of our Jewish brothers. The cross, which for us Christians is the highest sign of love and sacrifice, can never serve as an instrument in the fight against anyone.[36]

Note here that the primary reasons for condemning the cross-planting were that it had negative repercussions on the church and had been undertaken without the hierarchy's permission and even against its expressed will. It is revealing that, in this statement, the Jewish perspective occupies the last position on the list of concerns. The action was said to hurt the memory of the victims, the church, and the nation, and only then was it observed to offend the "different sensibility of our Jewish brothers." Thus, events at the gravel pit were essentially placed in the framework of an internal affair: a conflict between the Catholic Church and disobedient Catholics that was harmful for the church and the fatherland.

In the wake of this declaration, it was decided that the papal cross would remain but the other crosses should be removed. Plans were undertaken by the church to find an appropriate site for the crosses' relocation, and it was suggested that any person or group who had brought a cross to the gravel pit could reclaim it. As noted, the crosses were finally removed only much later, in May 1999, when they were transferred to a Franciscan sanctuary in Harmęże, a small village about ten kilometers from Oświęcim. For Father Musiał, the declaration of August 1998, while welcome, came too late and did not go far enough.[37]

Although the framing of the war of the crosses as an "un-Church-like action" could be interpreted as a tactical device (Poles were certainly more likely to rally on behalf of the church than in support of Jews), it also reflected the episcopate's real concern regarding Catholic disobedience, especially as the conflict continued to escalate and as a schismatic group became involved in events at the gravel pit. I refer here to the Society of Saint Pius X, founded in 1970 by Archbishop Marcel Lefebvre, who refused to submit to the teachings of Vatican II and was subsequently excommunicated by John Paul II in 1988. The society participated in at least three rituals at the gravel pit over the course of the summer, celebrating Tridentine masses, erecting its own cross (the second highest, after the papal cross), and blessing all the newly delivered crosses.[38] Before the official declaration of the episcopate, Lefebvre's society had celebrated two masses at the site (on July 21 and on August 15, the Feast of the Assumption). This may have provided an additional incentive for the church finally to react to the war of the crosses, and it clearly had an impact on the framing of the events as an internal crisis.

The attitude of the church's hierarchy toward the war of the crosses also evolved through the summer from implicit approval to indifference, to apprehension, and finally to condemnation. These changes in perception and response went hand in hand with the drama's unfolding. The various reactions were also associated with specific types or groups of Catholics: an embrace of the cross-planting by "closed" Catholics; implicit approval or indifference by conservative-traditionalists; apprehension by purists; and strong condemnation by "open" Catholics such as Father Musiał. Whereas Cardinal Glemp supported the action at its beginning, its condemnation by Archbishops Muszyński and Zimoń forced him publicly to revise his position. Although traditional-conservative Catholicism is the most prominent orientation within the Polish Catholic Church, purists and to a certain extent even marginalized "open" Catholics such as Musiał were able to shape the church's official response to the controversial event.[39]

By the end of the summer, the church's hierarchy attempted to restrict the semantic orbit of the cross and regain the discursive and ritual control of the symbol. The bishops convened in order to emphatically promote a "correct theology of the cross," since it had become apparent that "a deeper reflection about the meaning of the cross [was] lacking."[40] Muszyński characterized this incorrect theology of the cross as "a great problem internal to the Church." According to him, "the cross is a sign of love, forgiveness, and unity, and not exclusively the symbol of a rather narrow conception of identity that can then be freely exploited in the fight with others." In his view, it had been easy to mobilize Poles around the symbol "because of their emotional attachment to the cross, attacked and destroyed by two totalitarian regimes"; traditionally, it was seen as "a beautiful patriotic-religious symbol, worshipped as such."[41] Father Andrzej Zuberbier, a respected theologian, noted that the war of the crosses revealed the problem of different understandings of the cross within the church itself with greater clarity than did the question of the different understandings of that cross by Christians and Jews.[42]

Archbishop Muszyński underlined both the Christian meaning of the cross and its special significance in Poland—a double signification, which he viewed as the root of an inevitable tension with Jews:

> For us Christians, the cross will always be the greatest holiness, the sign of salvation, and the symbol of the highest love freely accepted for saving the world. From the beginning of Polish history, the cross also became deeply inscribed in our forefathers' land so that there is no way to understand Poles and the Polish nation without the cross and resurrection, of which the cross is the symbol, the

condition, and sign. Conceptualized in this way, the cross deserves to be defended always and everywhere because it is the most complete symbol and sign of all of Christianity. One cannot forget, however, that our non-Christian Jewish brothers associate with the cross a completely different content. They expect the same respect for their convictions as we Christians do. The content of those cannot be reduced to a common denominator. The instrumental exploitation of the symbol of the cross and its Christian meaning in the fight with whomever is, however, the negation of Christianity and of the cross.[43]

While the Christian and Jewish views could not, in his opinion, be reconciled, he pointed out that the war of the cross actually constituted the "depravation of the cross," and he attempted to prevent the pope's words concerning the need to "defend the cross" from becoming a slogan (illegitimately) used by the Defenders of the Cross. As in the episcopate's declaration, the following statement shows the extent to which the controversy was framed as one detrimental to the church and the nation and only secondarily to the "Christian-Jewish dialogue":

> The reference to the words spoken in Zakopane by the Pope, "defend the cross," in order to justify the action of the crosses at the gravel pit constitutes an abuse, and is the evident deformation of the actual intentions of the Pope, just as it is the instrumentalization of the cross, which is made into a tool for one's own, unclear interests that affects the good of the Church, our Homeland, and the Christian-Jewish dialogue. . . . One must really be completely deprived of a sense of realism to think that the Holy Father desires that the defense of the cross be used in the fight against whomever.[44]

All these efforts were in vain. The episcopate's condemnation of the cross-planting, and its active promotion of a "correct" theology of the cross, had no real effect on those who continued to bring crosses to the gravel pit throughout the fall. In fact, two priests even consecrated the crosses as well as a small chapel built by Świtoń—an act that supplied the Defenders of the Cross with fresh ammunition. (See figure 19.) The group could now argue that not only the papal cross, but also all the other crosses, must not be removed.

According to Świtoń and the Defenders of the Cross, the church had no monopoly over the symbol—a position, it will be recalled,

Figure 19. A Catholic priest blesses crosses planted at the gravel pit during the summer of 1998 despite the official condemnation of the action by the episcopate in late August. From the personal archives of Kazimierz Świtoń.

that Cardinal Glemp himself had articulated in an early declaration. What was more, they argued: "We are the Church." In an interview conducted after the conflict's resolution, Świtoń explained this statement: "Our Church did not defend [the cross]. Because the Church is divided: there is the administration and there is the People of God. . . . But the real Church . . . is the People of God, just like Christ founded it, and not the administration, bureaucrats who are priests, bishops, or cardinals."[45] In this explanation, Świtoń distinguishes between the institutional church—the administration and its bureaucrats who did not come to the defense of the cross— and the People of God, a "truer" church, faithful to its mission of guarding the nation. Although the statement "We are the Church" is reminiscent of the democratic, post–Vatican II definition of the church as a "community of believers," Świtoń's comment more forcibly brings to mind the Weberian distinction between church and sect, between a routinized and institutionalized movement and a charismatic movement whose objectives have not been bent by the needs of the institution.[46]

What defines Świtoń's "People of God" is their "true" Polishness. According to Świtoń, "a Pole who does not defend the cross stops being a Pole." Moreover, by his logic, the hierarchy of the Catholic Church in Poland was no longer Catholic, since its members had stopped defending the cross as the symbol of Polishness.[47] The statement "We are the Church," therefore, places the no-longer "Catholic" Church (because not nationalist enough) in contrast to a truer church, the People of God—defined here as "true Poles," that is, those who defend the cross as a symbol of Polishness.

"By defending the cross," Świtoń told me, "I was defending Polish identity. Polish identity. Because Poland without the cross would not be Poland. Mickiewicz already said it a hundred-something years ago: 'Only under this cross/Only under this sign, Poland is Poland and a Pole is a Pole.'"[48] Indeed, many crosses at the gravel pit bore these verses as part of their inscriptions, which are commonly attributed to the Romantic national bard. One cross, however, in either a creative inversion or a Freudian slip, proclaimed instead: "Only under the Cross/Only under this sign, Poland is Poland, and a Catholic is a Pole." These formulations might be the best contemporary articulations of the fusion of Catholicism and Polishness within a single category, that of "Polak-katolik."[49]

For Świtoń, for the Defenders of the Cross, and for many other national-Catholic groups, Catholicism is so closely associated with the Polish nation that there is no perceived tension between the universalist reach of the religion and its nationalist interpretation. The supra-national dimension of Catholicism is simply absent from the logic of this discourse, and although the cross defenders borrow freely from some of the rhetoric of Vatican II, their interpretation is far removed from post-Council teachings. In fact, the National Council of Lay Catholics came to the defense of the church and denounced the usurpation of the language of Vatican II for what they perceived to be political ends:

> The fanatic agitators from the Oświęcim gravel pit declared that they are the Church. We categorically protest against such a caricatured vision of Catholicism. The teachings of the Second Vatican Council about the Church as the People of God are very dear to

us. That is why we do not agree with its perversion, when in the
name of a private conception of Christianity, the slogan "we are the
Church" is used in the fight against the ecclesial hierarchy. The National Council of Lay Catholics expresses solidarity with the pas-
tors of our Church, and deplores the actions of those persons who
insult the Bishops, disrespecting their mission in the Church. We
appeal to all Catholics—lay and religious—for whom the words
"we are the Church" are not the call for fighting anyone but the
expression of the deepest identity: Let us give . . . the testimony of
our position and of the word that "to be in the Church" means to
live according to the commandment of love.[50]

Note that it is the illegitimate use and claim to ownership of Catholic
rhetoric that prompted the reaction of this lay Catholic group, not the
nationalist and antisemitic sentiments and actions that such rhetoric
suggests and invites. Once again, the discourse of the Defenders of
the Cross is perceived and interpreted as a direct attack on the church
and as such is denounced.

The meaning of the war of the crosses changed as the crisis persisted and deepened. It was at first interpreted by diverse communities
of discourse as a conflict over the meaning of Auschwitz/Oświęcim and
narrated as a "war" waged by Poles to keep the memory of "Oświęcim"
alive. The normative evaluations of the event diverged greatly—while
some denounced the takeover of the gravel pit as a despicable antisemitic gesture, others saw in the event the just and legitimate fight
of Poles for their nation and its symbols. Once the schismatic Society
of Saint Pius X became involved, however, the event's interpretation and narration were altered. Reconfigured as primarily a crisis of
Catholicism and more specifically an attack on the church and on
the good name of the nation, different communities of discourse,
previously split in their normative evaluation of the event, converged
unanimously to condemn the action. By the fall of 1998, voices such
as that of Father Musiał had been muted: the war of the crosses was
progressively reframed as a problem not originating from within Polish
society or even within the church, as the Jesuit priest had suggested,
but rather outside of it and developing without, in spite of, and even
against it. The culprits for the war of the crosses were forces external
to the church—Jews and disobedient Catholics—who caused internal
damage to the Polish Catholic body.

JEWISHNESS AS SOCIAL CLOSURE

The empirical analysis of a single event, the war of the crosses, high-lights divisions within the church and the different ways in which Catholics of different groupings articulate the relationship between national identity and religion, as well as their relationship to Jews and antisemitism. In this last section, I discuss the role of "Jews" in shaping the discourse of what Polishness is and is not.

The war of the crosses shattered the myth of Polish society's homogeneity: Poland's population is 97 percent ethnically Polish and 95 percent Catholic, but the question of what Polishness and Catholic identity "are" is polysemous and contested. Contrary to the myth of Poland's intrinsic Catholicism, and of the church's monolithic moral authority in that country, the lines of division run deep within Polish society and within the church itself. The Pole-Catholic association is produced only by determined cultural work on specific symbols, events, and their meanings. This cultural "work," moreover, is carried out by specific social groups and performed through various media and on a variety of staging grounds to create communities of discourse. Their formulations are in turn disseminated—though not necessarily assimilated—throughout the population at large.

It should already be clear to the reader that Świtoń and his followers were not mainstream figures. Although the drama's main characters, they remained marginal in the social and political landscape. Their views are close to those expressed in the national Catholic daily *Nasz Dziennik,* tied to Radio Maryja, and to those of *Nasza Polska,* a Far Right weekly.[51] They are part of a subculture feeding on elaborate conspiracy theories, according to which international Jewry and Freemasonry are out to destroy Poland from within and from without in order to facilitate the Jews' return to Poland, the Promised Land. Nevertheless, the war of the crosses did mobilize support and the issues it raised were not themselves marginal, but rather became a lightning rod for mainstream commentary and discussion of Polishness, its traditional association with Catholicism, antisemitism, and the state of Catholicism in post-Communist Poland.

Debates about the cross within Poland not only concerned whether religious symbols should or should not be present at Auschwitz or its immediate proximity—an issue that is at the core of theological arguments between Christians and Jews—but what the cross in Poland means. In other words, the debate about the cross(es) at Auschwitz was about the appropriateness and legitimacy of the fusion of national and religious categories of identifications in the post-Communist context. The discussion rarely directly involved Poles and Jews in direct dialogue, although Jews remained the implicit (and often explicit) external and internal "other" in exchanges between Poles. As noted, Jews and Jewishness served as a key trope in the discussion of Polishness, as well as of the role of Catholicism in defining and shaping the latter. This trope also appeared clearly in the discourses surrounding the writing of the Polish constitution's preamble and especially during the document's ratification process.[52]

Significantly, under Communism, Catholicism and the cross marked the group's boundaries: "us," the nation, against "them," the alien atheistic Communist regime. Catholicism managed to coalesce different social groups against the party-state, including atheists and Jews. In post-Communist Poland, however, the cross is used by ultra-nationalist Catholics within civil society to define the boundaries between "true" Poles and "non-Poles": in addition to Jews (Poland's traditional internal "other"), "bad Catholics," "cosmopolitan secularists," and Freemasons have also become categories of symbolic exclusion from the nation. Often, the last two are also code words for "Jews." Religion is used by these groups to define the symbolic boundaries of the "Polish nation," where the determination of who truly belongs depends to a great extent on one's commitment to a very specific—and narrow—vision of Polishness; that of the *Polak-katolik.* These ideological criteria do not determine legal membership in the Polish community (formal citizenship), but are central in defining social membership.[53]

Through a complex chain of associations, a "Jew" is anyone who does not adhere to a strictly exclusive ethno-Catholic vision of Poland. Even certain bishops are accused of being "crypto-Jews," and the civic nation, according to the editor of *Nasza Polska,* is an invention of Jews.[54] Among "closed" Catholics, the European Union is similarly held to be the product of Jewish machinations aimed at the institutional and structural annihilation of nation-states. From this perspective, Poland is ruled by "Jews," that is, by symbolic Jews. Any opponent to the ethno-Catholic vision of the nation is accused, through a series of associations and double entendres, of being a "Jew." Jewishness, in this context, itself becomes a symbol, standing for a civic-secular Poland. As seen in the epigraph to this essay, Adam Michnik defines this peculiar phenomenon as "magical antisemitism."

Thus Polishness as a category is understood not only in ethnic terms, following the German, Romantic model of nationhood, but also in an ideological-political sense.[55] Certain Poles, because of their political allegiances and ideological positions (mostly with the liberal Left), are deemed "un-Polish," "anti-Polish," or else are dismissed as "fake Poles" or "Jews" by the conservative Far Right.

As the war of the crosses and several other events demonstrate, Catholicism in post-Communist Poland is no longer a uniting and inclusive force aimed at building an open society but rather is often understood as excluding those who are not considered worthy of full membership. Whereas such symbolic exclusion is typical of places where the nation is understood in civic terms, and where, therefore, one's national identity—at least ideally—is determined by his or her adhesion to the principles of the social contract, it seems unlikely and ill-befits a place where the nation is primarily understood in ethnic terms.[56] In Poland, national identity is perceived as being primordial, transmitted through birth, flowing through one's veins. In line with this conception, national identity can neither be chosen nor escaped; it is constitutive of the self. How is it possible, given this understanding of national identity, to encounter ideological forms of exclusion from the ethnic nation? How is the tension between these two modes of social closure, one based on blood and culture, the other based on ideological orientations and political bonds, reconciled?

In the Polish case, ideological difference is "ethnicized," such that an "un-Polish" or "Polish-speaking" (that is, "non-Polish") liberal intellectual advocating a civic-secular Poland becomes a "Jew." "Magical antisemitism" is activated against a specific set of values, whether capitalism or Communism, since each of these threatens a traditional, conservative way of life and religious values. Both Communism and Western-style capitalism are associated with cosmopolitanism and both are associated with Jewishness. "Jewishness" becomes an ethno-religious category opposed to the *Polak-katolik* and serves to exclude "unwanted ideological elements." Hence, we witness the strange phenomenon of antisemitism in a country virtually without Jews.[57]

Under Communism, the notions of a *żydokomuna* (Jewish "cabal") and, later, of a Zionist plot were used to purge Polish society of "undesirable social elements." The antisemitic campaign of 1968 purged the old Communist guard but also rid the country of a significant contingent of young students, a reservoir of proto-opposition. Whereas most of those targeted in 1968 were actually Jewish, the purges and repression also included several "Jews." This logic of exclusion was not used by the Communist elite alone; it also pervaded the opposition. In a familiar logic, Communists could not be "Poles" but were rather believed to be disproportionately "Jewish": the *żydokomuna* phantom haunting Poland. Thus, in spite of the party-state's success in establishing and securing a homogeneous nation-state for the first time in Polish history, the Polish People's Republic was not considered to be "Poland." Hence, Solidarity's mission, which followed the motto taken from a popular song, "So that Poland be Poland . . ."

The "Defenders of the Cross" at Auschwitz were actively engaged in what Pierre Bourdieu, David Kertzer, and others have described under the rubric of "symbolic violence."[58] Neither direct coercion nor direct persuasion, symbolic violence instead entails the establishment of categories and divisions that inform social reproduction. The cross, in this light, is the key symbol in the making of Polish-Catholic hegemony: it establishes the categories that promote social divisions. Even those who reject the cross at Auschwitz articulate their mutiny in terms of that very symbol. Everyone speaks in its shadow, whether raising their lips in reverent praise, or pursing them to spit in disgust.

Yet even within these structuring categories, there is the radical malleability both of the symbol of the cross and of its moral valuation. Under Communism, it was regarded by a great number of Polish citizens as "good" because it marked the line dividing atheist colonizers from "authentic Poles" and marked an area of (relative) freedom from the state. Engaging in religious practices or articulating religious discourse in the public sphere were activities that, de facto, created a "plural" society in place of the totalizing society the Communist party-state endeavored to impose. In the post-1989 context, that signification is no longer persuasive. The cross is a multivocal symbol, and far from creating social cohesion, it serves both to sharpen existing divisions within Polish society and exacerbate social conflicts. The cross is now used within civil society to define the boundaries between "true" Poles and "non-Poles": "bad Catholics," Jews, secular-cosmopolitans, and

Freemasons. As we have seen, "Jewishness" itself becomes a symbol that stands for a civic-secular Poland oriented toward Europe and it serves as a potent mode of social closure.

Though the most reactionary groups in Poland attempt to sustain the symbolic potency of the cross, "planting" it before a new "Other"—the civic-secular-internationalist West (aka "Jews")—the majority of Poles reject this effort.[59] Indeed, for many Poles, the cross has come to stand not for a free and independent Poland but for right-wing oppression within the nation. In this way, the cross's symbolic vector is reversed from national "freedom" to national "constraint," from being "progressive" to being anachronistic and reactionary.

NOTES

This chapter has been previously published as Zubrzycki, G., "Poles-Catholics and 'Symbolic Jews,'" pp. 65–87 from *Studies in Contemporary Jewry* vol. 21, ed. Lederhendler, E. (OUP, 2005); reprinted by permission of Oxford University Press, Inc. The first chapter epigraph is taken from Adam Michnik, "Wystąpienie," in *Rachunek Sumienia: Kościół polski wobec antysemityzmu, 1989–1999,* ed. Bohdan Oppenheim (Kraków: Wydawnictwo WAM, 1999), 73; and the second is from an interview with Kazimierz Świtoń, April 25, 2001. All translations in this chapter, unless otherwise noted, are those of the author.

1. In 1984 Carmelite nuns established a convent in a building that, while being outside Auschwitz per se, overlooks the former camp and was used to store Zyklon B during the war. After protests from (non-Polish) Jewish groups objecting to the presence of the nuns at that site, an agreement was reached and ratified in Geneva in 1987 between representatives of the Catholic Church and European Jewish leaders. The accord stipulated that, by 1989, the convent would be moved from the proximity of Auschwitz. For various reasons, the nuns failed to move by that date and tensions escalated as a group of Jews from New York, under the leadership of Rabbi Avraham Weiss, occupied the grounds of the convent in July of that year and were forcibly ousted from its premises. Protests and resistance followed in Poland, many times in the form of declarations by the head of the Polish Catholic Church, Cardinal Józef Glemp, which were often unashamedly antisemitic in content and tone. The Carmelite nuns finally relocated in 1993, when John Paul II personally intervened in the conflict by asking them to leave. For detailed accounts of the Carmelite dispute, see Władysław Bartoszewski, *The Convent at Auschwitz* (London: Bowerdean, 1990); Marek Głównia and Stefan Wilkanowicz, eds., *Auschwitz: Konflikty i dialog* (Kraków: Znak, 1998);

and Carol Rittner and John K. Roth, eds., *Memory Offended: The Auschwitz Convent Controversy* (New York: Praeger, 1991). For a conservative, pro-Polish view, see Peter Raina, *Spór o klasztor sióstr karmelitanek bosych w Oświęcimiu* (Olsztyn: Warminski Wydawnictwo Diecezjalne, 1991).

2. The cross was originally part of an altar located three kilometers away, on the grounds of Birkenau, the camp adjacent to Auschwitz. In 1979 Pope John Paul II conducted a mass there, hence its popular designation as the "papal cross." After being stored in a local church's basement for a decade, the cross was brought one night, without fanfare, to the site of the convent. A local priest and a group of former (Polish Catholic) Auschwitz prisoners were responsible; although religious considerations may have played a role, it is clear that the act was also, and perhaps mainly, politically motivated and clearly related to the Carmelite controversy.

3. Born in 1931, Świtoń organized the first Committee of Free Professional Unions (Komitet Wolnych Związków Zawodowych) in Poland in 1978. He was a member of Solidarity between 1980 and 1989 and a deputy in the Sejm from 1991 to 1993. During the late 1970s and throughout the 1980s, he participated in a number of hunger strikes.

4. A concordat is an agreement negotiated by the Vatican with a given state, which regulates the relations between the secular power and the Catholic Church in that state. In Poland, an agreement of this kind was reached in July 1993 and was ratified four years later. Some saw in the official reestablishment of diplomatic relations with the Vatican (broken unilaterally by the Communist regime in September 1945) a return to the "normalcy" that Communism had interrupted. Others viewed it as an outdated project that threatened the separation of church and state. The concordat reached in 1993 was the focus of vigorous debate in the 1990s. In addition to controversial issues related to it, such as the question of religious instruction in public schools and the recognition by the state of church marriages, the actual validity of the concordat was questioned, since it had been negotiated before one of the two parties involved—the Republic of Poland—had acquired its legal foundations. Debate on this question was structured along two familiar poles: pro-church, conservative, Center-Right Catholics versus liberal, Center-Left secularists.

5. The war of the crosses was complicated by a number of complex legal issues originating in the fact that, in the course of negotiating with the Carmelite convent in 1993, the government had purchased the building and its grounds. Before the sale took effect, however, the nuns had rented out the property for a thirty-year period to the Association for the Victims of the War (Stowarzeszenie Ofiar Wojny). This contract could not be easily annulled. The leader of the association, Mieczysław Janosz, allowed Świtoń and the pilgrims free access to the grounds.

6. On the various meanings of Auschwitz (Oświęcim), see Emanuel Tanay, "Auschwitz and Oświęcim: One Location, Two Symbols," in *Memory Offended*, ed. Rittner and Roth, 99–112; Tomasz Golban-Klas, "Pamięć podzielona, pamięć urażona: Oświęcim i Auschwitz w polskiej i żydowskiej pamięci zbiorowej," in *Europa po Auschwitz*, ed. Zdzislaw Mach (Kraków: Universitas, 1995), 71–91; Peter Novick, *The Holocaust in American Life* (Boston: Houghton Mifflin, 2000); Jeffrey C. Alexander, "On the Social Construction of Moral Universals: The 'Holocaust' from War Crime to Trauma Drama," *European Journal of Social Theory* 5, no.1 (2002): 5–86; Antoni Sułek, "Wokół Oświęcimia: Spór o krzyże na tle wyobrażeń Polaków o sobie i Żydach," *Więź* (November 1998): 61–70; Marek Kucia, "KL Auschwitz in the Social Consciousness of Poles, A.D. 2000," in *Remembering for the Future: The Holocaust in an Age of Genocide*, ed. John Roth and Elisabeth Maxwell (New York: Palgrave, 2001); Geneviève Zubrzycki, "'We the Polish Nation': Ethnic and Civic Visions of Nationhood in Post-Communist Constitutional Debates," *Theory and Society* 30, no. 5 (2001): 629–69; and Jonathan Huener, *Auschwitz, Poland and the Politics of Commemoration, 1945–1979* (Athens: Ohio University Press, 2004). For an excellent analysis of the meaning of Auschwitz and its mythologization by Israeli and diaspora Jews, Soviet Russians, and Poles, as well as for the multiple and often contradictory philosophical preoccupations raised by Auschwitz, see Jonathan Webber, "The Future of Auschwitz: Some Personal Reflections" (First Frank Green Lecture, Oxford Centre for Postgraduate Hebrew Studies, 1992). On Holocaust memorial sites in Communist and post-Communist Poland, see James E. Young, *The Texture of Memory: Holocaust Memorials and Meaning* (New Haven, Conn.: Yale University Press, 1993).

7. My focus here is exclusively on the lines of conflict within the Catholic Church and among Catholics. For an analysis of the Polish Christian-Jewish axis of the controversy, see Geneviève Zubrzycki, *The Crosses of Auschwitz: Nationalism and Religion in Post-Communist Poland* (Chicago: University of Chicago Press, 2006).

8. Ibid. See also Zubrzycki, "'We the Polish Nation'"; Rogers Brubaker, *Nationalism Reframed: Nationhood and the National Question in the New Europe* (Cambridge, Eng.: Cambridge University Press, 1996).

9. The quotation marks indicate the symbolic and discursive nature of the category. It is the image of Jews and representations of Jewishness that are used to define Polishness, not real, existing Jews—even when actual Jewish persons are referred to or are verbally and symbolically abused, as was a frequent occurrence during the war of the crosses.

10. The evidence for this examination includes official church documents, sermons and homilies, pastoral letters, editorials, and letters to the editor that were written during the war of the crosses. I reviewed newspapers

(dailies, weeklies, biweeklies, and monthlies) representing diverse ideological and political orientations: *Nie, Polityka, Gazeta Wyborcza, Wprost, Tygodnik Powszechny, Nasz Dziennik,* and *Nasza Polska,* in addition to two Jewish publications, *Midrasz* and *Słowo Żydowskie.* I consulted the reports published in *Rzeczpospolita,* which is Poland's most ideologically neutral newspaper, in order to reconstruct the events that took place, and I analyzed reports appearing in *Katolicka Agencja Informacyjna* (hereafter referred to as *KAI*), which publishes official declarations of the episcopate and commentary from individual priests, bishops, and other members of the clergy. I have also conducted field interviews with priests and with Catholic intellectuals, as well as with Kazimierz Świtoń, who initiated the cross-planting action. Participant observation among members of the Covenant in Defense of the Papal Cross at Auschwitz (i.e., the Defenders of the Cross) also yielded significant data. This group has been meeting by the fenced area surrounding the papal cross (just outside of the Auschwitz-Birkenau Museum) every day since 1993. Among other things, its members pray on behalf of the papal cross and for the prompt return of the Carmelite nuns to the site.

11. Communist strategies to divide the church from within and thereby diminish its social support included the internment of Cardinal Wyszyński (1953–56), the establishment of the "Priests-Patriots" organization to collaborate with the Communist Party (1949–55), and the creation, in 1945, of Pax, an association that, until 1989, recognized the regime and the leading role of the Communist Party.

12. Approval of the church's activities stabilized toward the end of the 1990s in the mid-50s percentile range, and has gone up by a few percentage points since the beginning of the new century. (See the surveys conducted by the Centrum Badania Opinii Społecznej [hereafter referred to as CBOS]: "Kościół w III Rzeczypospolitej" [Warsaw, 1999] and "Stabilizacja opinii o wpływie Kościoła na życie w kraju" [Warsaw, 2004].) The period from 1989 to 1993 was marked by important ideological debates and controversies concerning, among other things, the character of the state, the return of mandatory religious instruction in public schools, and abortion. At the beginning of 1993, a new debate entered the public sphere with regard to a proposed law concerning respect for Christian values in the media, which was passed in March of that year. This law was interpreted by many as the return of censorship. In popular culture, references to the church and to the clergy as the "black mafia" or the "black totalitarian regime" (replacing the "red" regime of the Communists) became common at that time.

13. Jarosław Gowin, *Kościół w czasach wolności 1989–1999* (Kraków: Znak, 1999), 35.

14. CBOS, "Religijność Polaków na przełomie wieków" (Warsaw, 2001). Approximately 50 percent of the population participates in religious services

once a week, and 8 percent participates several times a week. Another 15 percent goes to church once or twice a month. In 2001, therefore, about 73 percent of Poles were involved in religious practices at least once a month.

15. Geneviève Zubrzycki, "De la nation ethnique à la nation civique: Enjeux pour l'église catholique polonaise," *Social Compass* 44, no. 1 (1997): 37–51.

16. Political intervention on the part of the church was particularly pronounced from roughly 1989 to 1993, after which the church became subtler in its interventions and its social approval, as we have seen, once again increased. In the initial post-Communist period, church officials publicly endorsed various political candidates and parties, posting lists of the "right" candidates for whom "good Catholics" should vote, as well as lobbying strongly for issues dear to the church. Although the church's involvement in political life was perceived as necessary under Communism, this was not the case in a fully sovereign and democratic Poland. Over time the church, which had been used to playing a significant role in oppositional politics, was forced to modify its intervention. See CBOS (1999) for statistical data on social approval of the church as this corresponded to specific debates in the public sphere; and Gowin, *Kościół w czasach wolności 1989–1999,* for an analysis of the evolution of the church in the 1990s.

17. This typology was initially inspired by that of Gowin; see *Kościół w czasach wolności 1989–1999;* and Jarosław Gowin, *Kościół po komunizmie* (Kraków: Społeczny Instytut Wydawniczy Znak, 1995).

18. The constitutions of 1921 and 1935 guaranteed that "the Roman Catholic faith, being the religion of the overwhelming majority of the nation, holds in the state a primary position among the religions equal under the law." See Gowin, *Kościół w czasach wolności 1989–1999,* 16.

19. Gowin, *Kościół po komunizmie,* 235.

20. Gowin, *Kościół w czasach wolności 1989–1999,* 350–56.

21. See, for example, *Więź,* "Pod Wspólnym Niebem," special issue, 1998; Oppenheim, *Kościół polski wobec antysemityzmu;* and the numerous articles appearing in the pages of *Tygodnik Powszechny. Tygodnik's* publishing house, Znak, is also very involved in this dialogue, both through its publications and via a special Web page, "Forum: Jews-Poles-Christians," that is explicitly devoted to the Polish-Jewish and Christian-Jewish dialogue. Among other things, this site features reviews of the Polish press, personal testimonies, editorial comments and responses, book promotions, and a calendar of events organized by various associations and cultural centers. The site appears (in Polish) at www.forum-znak.org.pl; in English, at www.forum-znak.org.pl/index-en.php.

22. "Czarne jest czarne," *Tygodnik Powszechny,* November 16, 1997; a translation appears in *Polin: Studies in Polish Jewry* 13 (2000): 303–9. See

also the essay by Joanna Michlic and Antony Polonsky that appears in this symposium issue of *Polin*, "Catholicism and Jews in the Post-Communist Poland."

23. A few weeks after the publication of Father Musiał's article, Father Waldemar Chrostowski published a critique titled "A Rainbow Painted in Black" ("Tęcza na czarno," *Tygodnik Powszechny,* November 1, 1998). Musiał's response, "The Sin of Antisemitism," was published on the same page, along with a short endorsement of Musiał's position by Stanisław Krajewski, the co-chairperson—together with Chrostowski—of the Commission of the Christian-Jewish Dialogue. Shortly thereafter, Chrostowski resigned from the commission; he was later replaced by Father Michał Czajkowski, an "open" Catholic. Since then, Chrostowski, a traditional-conservative Catholic close to Cardinal Glemp, has been active in denouncing "Jewish excesses" and "Jewish anti-Polonism," ranging from the Judaization of Auschwitz to the (American) Jewish attempt to prevent Mel Gibson's film *The Passion of the Christ* from being adequately promoted. He refused to be interviewed by me in 2001 because he does not trust "American milieus." An account and discussion of the "Black Is Black" debate can be found in Oppenheim, *Kościół polski wobec antysemityzmu.*

24. Note here the emphasis on "our," as opposed to an implied "their." The Catholic Far Right attempts to re-create the distinction between "us, the nation," and "them, atheist Communists"—a foreign power imposed from outside and above. This dichotomous frame, however, is expanded in the post-Communist era: it is now "us, true Poles," versus "them, fake Poles and Jews." In the post-Communist context, "them" becomes anyone who does not share or advocate an ethno-Catholic vision of Poland: bad Catholics, Jews, secularists, and Freemasons.

25. For a theorization of antisemitism's "double-sidedness," see Moishe Postone, "Anti-Semitism and National Socialism," in *Germans and Jews Since the Holocaust: The Changing Situation in West Germany,* ed. Anson Rabinbach and Jack Zipes (New York: Holmes and Meier, 1986), 301–14.

26. In May 2004, after Poland had already officially joined the European Union, Radio Maryja began rebroadcasting interviews with "experts" who predicted the end of national independence (and various other ills) should Poland ever join the EU.

27. Cardinal Glemp's remarks can be found in *KAI,* March 24, 1998, 1.

28. Quoted in *Tygodnik Powszechny,* August 9, 1998.

29. Interview with Świtoń, April 25, 2001.

30. *KAI,* August 11, 1998, 1.

31. Ibid.

32. Ibid.

33. Ibid., 3 (emphasis in original text).

34. Quoted in *Rzeczpospolita*, August 11, 1998.

35. Quoted in *Wprost*, August 23, 1998, 19–20.

36. The declaration, titled "Oświadczenie Rady Stałej Konferencji Episkopatu Polski w sprawie krzyży w Oświęcimiu," was issued on August 26, 1998, following the conferences of the episcopate; it was published a week later. See *Tygodnik Powszechny*, September 6, 1998, 11.

37. Interview with Father Stanisław Musiał, May 10, 2001. Other prominent "open" Catholics, however, were satisfied by the episcopate's resolution. Stefan Wilkanowicz, the editor in chief of the monthly *Znak* and co-chairperson of the International Commission of the Auschwitz-Birkenau Museum, reiterated in an interview conducted in April 2001 that, for Christians, the site could not be left without the cross; the absolute proscription of religious symbols (as demanded by the Jewish side) was simply untenable for Christians. That said, Wilkanowicz stressed that it need not be the papal cross, eight meters high and visible from inside the former camp. Rather, Wilkanowicz would deem appropriate a small monument (including the cross) to commemorate those Christians who died at Auschwitz.

38. A Tridentine mass is a mass celebrated in Latin, with a strict ritualistic code. The Second Vatican Council replaced the Tridentine mass with the "new mass," which is celebrated in vernacular languages. Although the public celebration of Tridentine masses is not banned, it is restricted by most bishops.

39. The final text of the declaration is ambiguous, which may result from the fact that such documents are written through a more or less democratic and consensual process. A small group of bishops usually drafts a first version, which is then discussed, rewritten, and resubmitted until it is deemed "acceptable" by all members. The final product, in consequence, is nearly always a compromise.

40. *KAI*, September 1, 1998, 4.

41. Ibid.

42. Quoted in *Tygodnik Powszechny*, August 2, 1998, 1.

43. *KAI*, August 11, 1998.

44. Ibid.

45. Interview with Świtoń, April 25, 2001.

46. Max Weber, *Economy and Society: An Outline of Interpretive Sociology*, 2 vols. (Berkeley: University of California Press, 1978).

47. Świtoń also explained to me that the hierarchy was not defending the cross because many of its members were not, "in truth," Poles. He told me a story that I have heard many times in my conversations and interviews with ultranationalist Catholics: namely, that Jewish children during World War II were rescued and hidden by—and therefore survived thanks to—Catholic nuns who raised them as "good Polish children." These children

grew up to become Catholic, and some even entered the priesthood. However, they never really ceased to be Jewish; their allegiance remains to their "true" Jewish identity and nature, with their superficial Catholicism and "insider" status allowing them to attack the church from within.

48. Interview with Świtoń, April 25, 2001.

49. For a classic ethnography of the *Polak-katolik* stereotype, see Stefan Czarnowski, "La culture religieuse des paysans polonais," *Archives des Sciences Sociales des Religions* 65, no.1 (1988): 7–23. For an analysis of the Catholicization of the national tie, a process that was accentuated and generalized only under socialism, see Paul Zawadzki, "Le nationalisme contre la citoyenneté," *L'Année Sociologique* 46, no.1 (1996): 169–85. For an analysis of the contemporary significance of the *Polak-katolik* stereotype in processes of inclusion and exclusion, see Ewa Nowicka, "Polak-katolik: O związkach polskości z katolizmem w społecznej świadomości Polaków," *Nomos* (1991): 117–38.

50. Document issued on August 22, 1998, and printed in *KAI,* August 25, 1998, 28–29.

51. According to research conducted by Ośrodek Badań Opinii Publicznej (OBOP) in February 1999, *Nasz Dziennik* has a circulation of 300,000 and an average issue readership (AIR) of 170,000—that is, approximately 0.6 percent of Poles above the age of fifteen read the newspaper. See OBOP, "Index Polska—Badania czytelnictwa prasy," at www.obop .com.pl.index_polska9902.htm; see also Ośrodek Badań Prasoznawczych, *Katalog Mediow polskich 1999/2000* (Kraków, 2000). In comparison, *Gazeta Wyborcza,* Adam Michnik's Center-Left daily, has a circulation of 570,000 (720,000 on Saturdays) and an AIR of two million—that is, it is read by 7.2 percent of Poles above the age of fifteen. Since the fall of Communism in Poland, it has consistently been the most popular and influential nationwide daily (its circulation is actually higher than any other paper in Eastern Europe). See Grzegorz Ekiert and Jan Kubik, *Rebellious Civil Society: Popular Protest and Democratic Consolidation in Poland, 1989–1993* (Ann Arbor: University of Michigan Press, 1999), 15.

52. Zubrzycki, "'We the Polish Nation.'"

53. Edward A. Shils, "Primordial, Personal, Sacred and Civil Ties," in his *Center and Periphery: Essays in Macrosociology* (Chicago: University of Chicago Press, 1975), 111–26; Morris Janowitz, "Observations on the Sociology of Citizenship," *Social Forces* 59 (1980): 1–24.

54. During the debate regarding the naming of the constituent entity in the constitution's preamble ("We, the Polish nation," or "We, Polish citizens"), Stanisław Krajski declared that the civic nation was an invention of Jews: "Not everyone knows that one of the inventors of this new 'meaning' of the word 'nation' is Tomasz Wołek, editor in chief of the daily *Życie.*

Who is Tomasz Wołek, and what is *Życie*? To this question, we can answer indirectly by noting that the assistant editor in chief is a certain Bronisław Wildstein" (quoted in *Nasza Polska*, April 23, 1997). See also Zubrzycki, "'We the Polish Nation.'"

55. Of course, even though its ideologues insist on its primordial character, the ethnic nation, like any other form of nation, is a social construction. Whereas the civic nation is conceived as a construct, the ethnic nation is conceived of as a given. This is not, however, what I am underlining here. Rather, I am pointing out the ideological criteria used by the Right in determining one's Polishness (or lack thereof) and the tension such criteria entails for the (ideally) ethnically defined nation. For a discussion of ethnic and civic nationalism, see Rogers Brubaker, *Citizenship and Nationhood in France and Germany* (Cambridge, Mass.: Harvard University Press, 1992); Dominique Schnapper, *La communauté des citoyens: Sur l'idée moderne de la nation* (Paris: Gallimard, 1994); Bernard Yack, "The Myth of the Civic Nation," *Critical Review* 10, no. 2 (1996): 193–211, reprinted in *Theorizing Nationalism*, ed. Ronald Beiner (Albany: State University of New York Press, 1999), 103–18; Kai Nielsen, "Cultural Nationalism, Neither Ethnic nor Civic," *Philosophical Forum* 28, nos. 1/2 (1999), reprinted in Beiner, *Theorizing Nationalism*, 119–30; Zubrzycki, "'We the Polish Nation'"; and Geneviève Zubrzycki, "The Classical Opposition Between Civic and Ethnic Models of Nationhood: Ideology, Empirical Reality and Social Scientific Analysis," *Polish Sociological Review* 3 (2002): 275–95.

56. The American case is the paradigmatic example of ideologically defined national identity, where "being" American means supporting a specific set of values and practices, and where, therefore, it is possible to be "un-American" by, say, supporting Communism during the McCarthy era or criticizing the Bush administration after the events of September 11, 2001. See Seymour Martin Lipset, *Continental Divide: The Values and Institutions of the United States and Canada* (Washington, D.C.: Canadian-American Committee, 1989), for an analysis of this mechanism.

57. It is very difficult to establish the exact number of Jews in Poland. Estimates vary greatly, ranging from 1,055 individuals (2002 Polish census) to 40,000 (*American Jewish Year Book*, 2003). The wide variation in these data is the outcome of different measures of "Jewishness": self-declaration in the census versus ancestry or formal membership in Jewish organizations. The numbers have also steadily grown in the last decade, as better sources for estimating them have become available, and as the Jewish community has witnessed a cultural, religious, and institutional renaissance. In 1989 and 1990 the *American Jewish Year Book* estimated the total Jewish population of Poland to be 5,000, of whom nearly 2,000 persons were "registered"— that is, were formally affiliated with one or more religious or secular Jewish

organizations. This figure was widely cited in Polish publications throughout the 1990s. During that decade, however, the total number of Polish Jews was reestimated to be closer to 10,000 (*American Jewish Year Book,* 1992, 1995). By the beginning of the new millennium, the number of Polish Jews affiliated with religious or secular Jewish organizations totaled 7,000 to 8,000. Moreover, between 10,000 and 15,000 people showed interest in rediscovering their Jewish ancestry, and as many as 40,000 Polish citizens are now thought to have "some" Jewish ancestry (*American Jewish Year Book,* 2002, 2003). The numbers cited by Piotr Kadlčik, the president of the Jewish community in Warsaw and president of the Union of Jewish Communities in Poland, are slightly more conservative: according to him, there are now 4,000 to 6,000 "registered" Jews and approximately 20,000 to 25,000 Polish citizens of Jewish descent who do not maintain a formal connection to any Jewish institution (radio interview, available at http://fzp.jewish.org .pl/english/engind.html). For Polish census data, see http://www.mswia.gov .pl/mn_narod_zydzi.html; for other Polish estimates, see Sławomir Łodziński, "Dyskryminacja czy nierówność: Problemy dyskryminacji osób należacych do mniejszości narodowych i etnicznych w Polsce po 1989 roku," in *Integracja czy dyskryminacja? Polskie wyzwania i dylematy u progu wielokulturowości,* ed. Krystyna Iglicka (Warsaw: Instytut Spraw Publicznych, 2003), 30.

58. Pierre Bourdieu, *Pascalian Meditations,* trans. Richard Nice (Cambridge, Eng.: Polity, 2000); David I. Kertzer, *Rituals, Politics and Power* (New Haven, Conn.: Yale University Press, 1988).

59. Zubrzycki, *The Crosses of Auschwitz.*

Notes on Contributors

ELIZABETH R. BAER is a professor of English and genocide studies at Gustavus Adolphus College in St. Peter, Minnesota, where she previously held the Florence and Raymond Sponberg Chair of Ethics. She is the coeditor (with Myrna Goldenberg) of *Experience and Expression: Women, the Nazis, and the Holocaust*, an anthology of essays on gender and the Holocaust, and (with Hester Baer) of *The Blessed Abyss: Inmate #6582 in Ravensbrück Concentration Camp for Women*, a memoir by Nanda Herbermann.

OMER BARTOV is the John P. Birkelund Distinguished Professor of European History at Brown University. His recent books include *Erased: Vanishing Traces of Jewish Galicia in Present-Day Ukraine*, *The "Jew" in Cinema*, *Germany's War and the Holocaust*, *Mirrors of Destruction*, and *Murder in Our Midst*.

ANNETTE BECKER is a professor of modern history at the University of Paris-X. She has written extensively on the two world wars and is associate editor of the *Encyclopedia of Europe, 1914–2004*. She is the editor of a forthcoming book on French doctors who survived Auschwitz and a special issue of the *Revue d'Histoire de la Shoah* on war, violence, and genocide before 1939. Together with survivors, she is preparing a mobile video guide to the camp of Auschwitz-Birkenau.

DORIS L. BERGEN is the Chancellor Rose and Ray Wolfe Professor of Holocaust Studies at the University of Toronto. She is the author of *Twisted Cross: The German Christian Movement in the Third Reich* and *War and Genocide: A Concise History of the Holocaust* and is the editor of *The Sword of the Lord: Military Chaplains from the First to the Twenty-First Century.*

KATE BROWN is an associate professor of history at the University of Maryland, Baltimore County. She is the author of *A Biography of No Place: From Ethnic Borderland to Soviet Heartland,* which won the American Historical Association's George Louis Beer Prize for the Best Book in International European History, among other awards.

CHRISTOPHER R. BROWNING is the Frank Porter Graham Professor of History at the University of North Carolina, Chapel Hill. His books include *The Origins of the Final Solution* (with contributions from Jürgen Matthäus), *Collected Memories,* and *Ordinary Men: Reserve Police Battalion 101 and the Final Solution in Poland.* He is the coeditor (with Richard S. Hollander and Nechama Tec) of *Every Day Lasts a Year: A Jewish Family's Correspondence from Poland.*

HOLLY CASE is an assistant professor of history at Cornell University. She earned her Ph.D. from Stanford University in 2004. Her book *Between States: The Transylvanian Question and the European Idea During World War II* will be published in 2009. She is the coeditor (with Norman M. Naimark) of *Yugoslavia and Its Historians: Understanding the Balkan Wars of the 1990s.*

MARTIN DEAN is an applied research scholar at the United States Holocaust Memorial Museum's Center for Advanced Holocaust Studies in Washington, D.C. He is the author of *Robbing the Jews: The Confiscation of Jewish Property in the Holocaust, 1933–1945* and of *Collaboration in the Holocaust: Crimes of the Local Police in Belorussia and Ukraine, 1941–44,* and is a coeditor (with Constantin Goschler and Philipp Ther) of *Robbery and Restitution: The Conflict over Jewish Property in Europe.*

RUTH KLUGER is the author of *Still Alive,* a Holocaust memoir that has been translated into nine languages and has received numerous awards. She was born in Austria in 1939, emigrated to the United States in 1947, and studied English and German literature at Hunter College and the University of California, Berkeley. She is a retired professor of German at the University of California, Irvine.

Dori Laub was born in Cernauti, Romania, in 1937. Currently a practicing psychoanalyst in New Haven, Connecticut, he works primarily with victims of massive psychic trauma and their children. He is a clinical professor of psychiatry at the Yale University School of Medicine and a cofounder of the Fortunoff Video Archive for Holocaust Testimonies. In 2000 and 2003 he was acting director of the Genocide Studies Program at Yale. Since 2001, he has also been deputy director for Trauma Studies there.

Na'ama Shik is the director of the Internet Department at the International School for Holocaust Studies of Yad Vashem, the Holocaust Martyrs' and Heroes' Remembrance Authority in Jerusalem. She is completing her Ph.D. at Tel Aviv University under the guidance of Shulamit Volkov, with a dissertation on "Jewish Women in Auschwitz-Birkenau, 1942–43."

Ronald Smelser is a professor of history at the University of Utah. He is the author of *The Sudeten Problem, 1933–1938: Volkstumspolitik and the Formulation of Nazi Foreign Policy* and *Robert Ley: Hitler's Labor Front Leader;* the coauthor (with Edward Davies) of *The Myth of the Eastern Front: The Nazi-Soviet War in American Popular Culture;* and a coeditor (with Rainer Zitelmann and Enrico Syring) of *The Nazi Elite.* He is a past president of the German Studies Association and the American Historical Association's Conference Group for Central European History.

Christina von Braun is a professor of cultural studies at Humboldt University in Berlin and the author of numerous books and films on cultural history, gender, and the history of antisemitism. Most recently she coedited (with Eva-Maria Ziege) *Das "bewegliche Vorurteil": Aspekte des internationalen Antisemitismus.*

Jürgen Zimmerer is a lecturer in international history at the University of Sheffield. He is editor of the *Journal of Genocide Research,* president of the International Network of Genocide Scholars, and founding director of the Sheffield Centre for the Study of Genocide and Mass Violence. His publications include *Deutsche Herrschaft über Afrikaner: Staatlicher Machtanspruch und Wirklichkeit im kolonialen Namibia* and *Von Windhuk nach Auschwitz: Beiträge zum Verhältnis von Kolonialismus und Holocaust* (2007). He is the coeditor (with Dominik J. Schaller) of *Raphael Lemkin "On Genocides": The "Founder of the Genocide Convention" as a Historian of Mass Violence.*

GENEVIÈVE ZUBRZYCKI is an assistant professor of sociology at the University of Michigan in Ann Arbor. Her book *The Crosses of Auschwitz: Nationalism and Religion in Post-Communist Poland* examines the relationship between Polish nationalism and Catholicism, with specific attention to memory wars and the use of religious symbols by ultranationalist Poles at Auschwitz. In 2007 it received the Distinguished Book Award in the Sociology of Religion from the American Sociological Association and the Orbis Books Prize from the American Association for the Advancement of Slavic Studies.